Globalizing Europe

Globalizing Europe explores modern Europe's myriad entanglements with the wider world, considering the continent not only as an engine but also as a product of global transformations. It looks at the ways in which the global movements of peoples and ideas, goods and raw materials, flora and fauna have impacted life on the continent over the centuries. Bringing together a group of leading historians, the book shows how the history of Europe can be integrated into global history. Taken together, its chapters will help reshape our understanding of the boundaries of Europe – and the field of modern European history.

DAVID MOTADEL is Associate Professor of International History at the London School of Economics and Political Science. He is the author of *Islam and Nazi Germany's War* (2014), which was awarded the Ernst Fraenkel Prize, and the editor of *Islam and the European Empires* (2014). In 2018, he received the Philip Leverhulme Prize for History.

Globalizing Europe

A History

Edited by

David Motadel
London School of Economics and Political Science

CAMBRIDGE
UNIVERSITY PRESS

Shaftesbury Road, Cambridge CB2 8EA, United Kingdom

One Liberty Plaza, 20th Floor, New York, NY 10006, USA

477 Williamstown Road, Port Melbourne, VIC 3207, Australia

314–321, 3rd Floor, Plot 3, Splendor Forum, Jasola District Centre,
New Delhi – 110025, India

103 Penang Road, #05–06/07, Visioncrest Commercial, Singapore 238467

Cambridge University Press is part of Cambridge University Press & Assessment,
a department of the University of Cambridge.

We share the University's mission to contribute to society through the pursuit of
education, learning and research at the highest international levels of excellence.

www.cambridge.org
Information on this title: www.cambridge.org/9781009262897

DOI: 10.1017/9781009262873

When citing this work, please include a reference to the DOI 10.1017/
9781009262873

First published 2025

A catalogue record for this publication is available from the British Library

*A Cataloging-in-Publication data record for this book is available from the Library
of Congress*

ISBN 978-1-009-26289-7 Hardback
ISBN 978-1-009-26288-0 Paperback

Contents

Figures

Contributors

Sven Beckert is Laird Bell Professor of History at Harvard University. He is the author of *Empire of Cotton: A Global History* (2014) and the forthcoming *Capitalism: A Global History* (2025).

Maxine Berg is Professor of History Emeritus at the University of Warwick and Honorary Professor at the European University Institute. Her recent books include *Slavery, Capitalism and the Industrial Revolution* (2023), co-authored with Pat Hudson, *Luxury and Pleasure in Eighteenth-Century Britain* (2005), and the edited volume *Writing the History of the Global: Challenges for the 21st Century* (2013).

Elizabeth Buettner is Professor of Modern History at the University of Amsterdam. Her publications include *Empire Families: Britons and Late Imperial India* (2004), *Europe after Empire: Decolonization, Society, and Culture* (2016), and the co-edited volume, with Britta Timm Knudsen, John Oldfield, and Elvan Zabunyan, *Decolonizing Colonial Heritage: New Agendas, Actors and Practices in and beyond Europe* (2022).

Sebastian Conrad is Professor of Global History at Freie Universität Berlin. His publications include *Die Königin: Nofretetes globale Karriere* (2024), *What Is Global History?* (2016), and *German Colonialism: A Short History* (2012).

Lucy Delap is Professor of Modern British and Gender History at Cambridge University and a Fellow of Murray Edwards College. Her publications include *The Feminist Avant-Garde: Transatlantic Encounters of the Early Twentieth Century* (2007), *Knowing Their Place: Domestic Service in Twentieth Century Britain* (2011), and *Feminisms: A Global History* (2020).

Richard Drayton is Professor of Imperial and Global History at King's College London. His latest publications are essays on Walter Rodney in *African Economic History* (2022) and *Small Axe* (2023).

Richard J. Evans is Regius Professor Emeritus of History at the University of Cambridge. His many publications include *The Pursuit of Power: Europe 1815–1914* (2016).

Anne Gerritsen is Professor of History at the University of Warwick and the Chair of Asian Art at Leiden University. Her latest book is *The City of Blue and White: Chinese Porcelain and the Early Modern World* (2020).

Abigail Green is Professor of Modern European History at the University of Oxford and a Tutorial Fellow of Brasenose College. Among her publications are *Fatherlands: State-Building and Nationhood in 19th Century Germany* (2001), *Moses Montefiore: Jewish Liberator, Imperial Hero* (2010), and the co-edited volumes *Religious Internationals in the Modern World: Globalization and Faith Communities since 1750* (2012), with Vincent Viaene, *Jews, Liberalism, Antisemitism: A Global History* (2020), with Simon Levis-Sullam, and *Jewish Country Houses* (2024), with Juliet Carey.

J. R. McNeill is Professor of History and University Professor at Georgetown University. He is the author of *Something New under the Sun: An Environmental History of the Twentieth-Century World* (2000), *Mosquito Empires: Ecology and War in the Greater Caribbean, 1640–1914* (2010), *The Great Acceleration: An Environmental History of the Anthropocene since 1945* (2016), and *The Webs of Humankind* (2021).

David Motadel is Associate Professor of International History at the London School of Economics and Political Science. He is the author of *Islam and Nazi Germany's War* (2014) and the editor of *Islam and the European Empires* (2014). He is also the editor of *The Global Bourgeoisie: The Rise of the Middle Classes in the Age of Empire* (2019), with Christof Dejung and Jürgen Osterhammel, and the editor of *Revolutionary World: Global Upheaval in the Modern Age* (2021).

Michelle Moyd is Associate Professor of History and Red Cedar Distinguished Professor at Michigan State University. She is the author of *Violent Intermediaries: African Soldiers, Conquest, and Everyday Colonialism in German East Africa* (2014) and the co-author of *Linguistic Disobedience: Restoring Power to Civic Language* (2019), with David C. Gramling and Yuliya Komska.

Samuel Moyn is Kent Professor of Law and History at Yale University. His most recent book is *Liberalism against Itself: Cold War Intellectuals and the Making of Our Times* (2023).

Priya Satia is Raymond A. Spruance Professor of International History and Professor of History at Stanford University. She is the author of *Spies in*

Arabia: The Great War and the Cultural Foundations of Britain's Covert Empire in the Middle East (2008), *Empire of Guns: The Violent Making of the Industrial Revolution* (2018), and *Time's Monster: History, Conscience and Britain's Empire* (2020).

Stephen W. Sawyer is the Ballantine-Leavitt Professor of History at the American University of Paris. His publications include *Adolphe Theirs, la contingence et le pouvoir* (2018), *Demos Assembled: Democracy and the International Origins of the Modern State, 1840–1880* (2018), and his forthcoming *Demos Rising: Democracy and the Popular Construction of Public Power in France, 1800–1850* (2025).

Kira Thurman is Associate Professor of History, German Studies, and Musicology at the University of Michigan. She is the author of *Singing like Germans: Black Musicians in the Land of Bach, Beethoven, and Brahms* (2021).

Caroline van Eck is Professor of Art History at University of Cambridge and a Fellow of King's College. Her most recent publications include *Piranesi's Candelabra and the Revival of the Past: Excessive Objects and the Emergence of Style in the Age of Neoclassicism* (2023) and "From Nineveh to Pergamon and Back: Animal Hybrids in German Historiography of the Nineteenth Century," *Res: Anthropology and Aesthetics* 81–82 (2024).

Acknowledgments

The idea behind this book emerged in 2015–16, the year I moved from Cambridge to the LSE. I noted that some historians of modern Europe at the time, particularly at Cambridge, expressed some skepticism about global history, which was becoming increasingly influential in historical studies. My own work on European history, though, exploring Europe's entanglements with the wider world, benefited greatly from the growing body of scholarship in global history. There were, in fact, more and more historians interested in understanding modern Europe as part of a globalizing world.

The chapters of this volume bring together a group of scholars to discuss the impact of the "global turn" on different fields of European history. Some of them (1–6, 10, 16, Afterword) were first published in the *Annales* 76, 4 (2021). I am grateful to the editors of the journal for allowing them to be reproduced – slightly extended in some cases – in this volume.

I owe a great debt of thanks to Iona Tait for her thorough copy-editing of the final manuscript. James Swarbrick, with much attention to detail, prepared the index. I would also like to express my gratitude to the anonymous readers at Cambridge University Press, who, in their reports, made insightful suggestions which helped to improve the chapters. Our brilliant editor, Liz Friend-Smith, believed in the book from the outset, and it was an immense pleasure to work with her. I would also like to thank Michael Watson at Cambridge University Press, who supported the project throughout. Cambridge University Press's copy-editor, Dan Harding, and publication manager, Dhivyabharathi Elavazhagan, ensured the smooth production of the volume.

Finally, it has been a real privilege to work with a group of distinguished historians, whose chapters have created a panorama which will, I hope, help us reshape our understanding of the history of Europe in the Global Age.

1   Global Europe

David Motadel

In 2010, the historian Denis Crouzet discovered a remarkable unpublished manuscript inside a dusty suitcase in the storeroom of a sixth-floor *fin-de-siècle* Paris apartment. Written in 1950, under the impression of the horrors of the Second World War, by two of France's greatest historians of the twentieth century, Lucien Febvre, patron of the Annales school and professor at the Collège de France, and his junior colleague François Crouzet, a scholar of economic history at the Sorbonne (and Denis Crouzet's father), it challenged the established narratives of national (and European) history. Entitled *Origines internationales d'une civilisation: Éléments d'une histoire de France*, the book offered a breathtaking survey of centuries of global influences on the Hexagon.[1]

First, its authors looked at the country's inhabitants. Dismissing the idea of a "pure race," they argued that the French had always been a mixture of peoples, including Turks, Arabs, and Africans. The same was true for France's flora and fauna. The trees considered to be the most French, they explained, came from Asia: The plane tree was imported in the sixteenth century, the chestnut arrived in the early seventeenth, the cedar had not put down roots in the country before the end of the eighteenth, and so on. Next, they turned to cuisine, reminding their readers that some of the most classic French foods originated abroad: oranges, mandarins, and lemons from the Far East; tomatoes and potatoes from America; coffee from Africa. Not even the tobacco in Gauloises was French. In a sweeping tour de force, they demonstrated that the history of France was one of constant "borrowings" from all parts of the world, with these adoptions, adaptations, and appropriations making the French the "heirs" of diverse pasts.[2]

---

[1] Lucien Febvre and François Crouzet, *Nous sommes des sang-mêlés: Manuel d'histoire de la civilisation française*, ed. Denis Crouzet and Élisabeth Crouzet (Paris: Albin Michel, 2012); for the context and information on the book's background, see the "Avant-propos" and "Postface" by Denis Crouzet and Élisabeth Crouzet-Pavan, respectively, pp. 7–15 and 295–392.

[2] Ibid., 289.

The book had been commissioned by the newly created, Paris-based United Nations Educational, Scientific, and Cultural Organization (UNESCO) to overcome the narrow narratives of national and European history. By providing an example of a more open history, showing how much every country and continent owed to the outside world, some functionaries in the organization wished to encourage "international understanding."[3] Their hope that this example would prompt historians of other countries to engage in similar work remained unfulfilled. The publication was blocked by those in the organization who considered it an assault on the idea of the nation and Europe's global supremacy. Rejected by UNESCO, the manuscript was abandoned by its authors.[4] It was only published sixty years later, in 2012, following its rediscovery in Crouzet's suitcase.

Times have changed. But even today, as they continue to write local-, nation-, and continent-centered histories, some scholars of the European past still feel uneasy about attempts to open up the continent's history. This became most evident in 2017, when a group of historians around Patrick Boucheron, following in the footsteps of Febvre and Crouzet, produced an 800-page *Histoire mondiale de la France*, seeking to understand French history as a dimension of global history.[5] In the ensuing controversy, Pierre Nora rejected the work as "the end of common truth," while Alain Finkielkraut declared its authors the "gravediggers of the great French heritage."[6] Denouncing it as an attempt to destroy France's "national narrative" (*roman national*), the country's conservative enfant terrible Éric Zemmour went as far as to speak of "the war of history."[7] A bestseller was born. "After several decades of somnolence,

---

[3] Crouzet and Crouzet-Pavan, "Postface," 335. On the UNESCO project, see Paul Betts, "Humanity's New Heritage: Unesco and the Rewriting of World History," *Past & Present*, no. 228 (2015): 249–85; and Gabriela Goldin Marcovich and Rahul Markovits, "Editing the First Journal of World History: Global History from Inside the Kitchen," *Journal of Global History* 14, no. 2 (2019): 157–78.

[4] An abridged version was published in German in 1953, see Lucien Febvre and François Crouzet, "Der internationale Ursprung einer Kultur: Grundegedanken zu einer Geschichte Frankreichs," *Internationales Jahrbuch für Geschichtsunterricht* 2 (1953): 5–31. Unpublished thirty-two-page French and English copies of this abridged version are stored in the UNESCO archives, see Lucien Febvre and François Crouzet, "Origines internationales d'une civilisation: Éléments d'une histoire de France," 18 December 1951, and "International Origins of a National Culture: Experimental Materials for a History of France," 28 December 1951, UNESCO Archives, UNESCO/ED/TB/10; WS/031.101 REV.

[5] Patrick Boucheron, ed., *Histoire mondiale de la France* (Paris: Éd. du Seuil, 2017). A more recent and equally important book on the subject is the more focused volume by Quentin Deluermoz, ed., *D'ici et d'ailleurs: Histoires globales de la France contemporaine (XVIIIᵉ–XXᵉ siècle)* (Paris: La Découverte, 2021).

[6] Pierre Nora, "Histoire mondiale de la France," *L'Obs* 2734, 28 March 2017; and Alain Finkielkraut, "La charge d'Alain Finkielkraut contre 'les fossoyeurs du grand héritage français'," *Le Figaro*, 25 January 2017.

[7] Éric Zemmour, "Dissoudre la France en 800 pages," *Le Figaro*, 19 January 2017. More serious conceptual criticism was voiced by Sanjay Subrahmanyam in an interview with Gilles Wullus

academic history is a hit," commented Robert Darnton in the *New York Review of Books*.[8] A similar volume, *Storia mondiale dell'Italia*, was published shortly after in Italy.[9] Dutch, Spanish, Sicilian, Flemish, and Catalan equivalents followed within a year, German, Portuguese, and Hungarian versions a bit later.[10] And yet such works are still the exception.[11]

Although European history is one of the vastest fields of historical scholarship, encompassing research on local, national, regional, and continental spaces, the continent's global entanglements have long remained marginalized.[12] This is particularly true for national history, so closely connected with

and Pouria Amirshahi, "Sanjay Subrahmanyam: 'L'histoire nationale tyrannise les historiens'," *Politis*, 25 July 2018; and in another interview with Charles Jaigu, "Colère d'un historien contre Mme Taubira," *Le Figaro*, 19 September 2019.

[8] Robert Darnton, "A Buffet of French History: 'Histoire mondiale de la France' edited by Patrick Boucheron," *New York Review of Books* 64, no. 8, 11 May 2017.

[9] Andrea Giardina, ed., *Storia mondiale dell'Italia* (Bari: Laterza, 2017), which patriotically celebrates a global Italy.

[10] Lex Heerma van Voss et al., eds., *Wereldgeschiedenis van Nederland* (Amsterdam: Ambo/Anthos uitgevers, 2018), which was followed by Lex Heerma van Voss et al., eds., *Nog meer wereldgeschiedenis van Nederland* (Amsterdam: Ambo/Anthos uitgevers, 2022); Xosé M. Núñez Seixas, ed., *Historia Mundial de España* (Madrid: Ediciones Destino, 2018); Giuseppe Barone, ed., *Storia mondiale della Sicilia* (Bari: Laterza, 2018); Marnix Beyen et al., eds., *Wereldgeschiedenis van Vlaanderen* (Kalmthout: Polis, 2018), which was also published in French translation as Marnix Beyen et al., eds., *Histoire mondiale de la Flandre* (Waterloo: Ranaissance du livre, 2020); Borja de Riquer, ed., *Història mundial de Catalunya* (Barcelona: Edicions 62, 2018); Andreas Fahrmeir, ed., *Deutschland: Globalgeschichte einer Nation* (Munich: C. H. Beck, 2020); Carlos Fiolhais, José Eduardo Franco, and José Pedro Paiva, eds., *História Global de Portugal* (Lisbon: Temas e Debates, 2020), which was also published in English translation as Carlos Fiolhais, José Eduardo Franco, and José Pedro Paiva, eds., *The Global History of Portugal: From Prehistory to the Modern World* (Liverpool: Liverpool University Press, 2022); and Laczó Ferenc and Varga Bálint, eds., *Magyarország globális története, 1869–2022* (Budapest: Corvina, 2022). Nathalie Büsser, Thomas David, Pierre Eichenberger, Lea Haller, Tobias Straumann, and Christa Wirth, eds., *Transnationale Geschichte der Schweiz/Histoire transnationale de la Suisse* (Zurich: Chronos, 2020), is a slightly different but noteworthy publication. A pioneering project that should also be mentioned here is Sebastian Conrad and Jürgen Osterhammel, eds., *Das Kaiserreich Transnational: Deutschland in der Welt, 1871–1914* (Göttingen: Vandenhoeck and Ruprech, 2004); it was more recently followed by H. Glenn Penny, *German History Unbound: From 1750 to the Present* (Cambridge: Cambridge University Press, 2022).

[11] Similar attempts have not been made for other countries, notably Great Britain, Austria, Russia, and Poland, though noteworthy works in this respect are Martin Aust, ed., *Globalisierung Imperial und Sozialistisch: Russland und die Sowjetunion in der Globalgeschichte, 1851–1991* (Frankfurt: Campus Verlag, 2013); and Niall Whelehan, ed., *Transnational Perspectives on Modern Irish History* (New York: Routledge, 2015). Tehila Sasson et al., "Britain and the World: A New Field?," *Journal of British Studies* 57, no. 4 (2018): 677–708, offers thoughts on the global history of Great Britain.

[12] Dominic Sachsenmaier, "Recent Trends in European History: The World beyond Europe and Alternative Historical Spaces," *Journal of Modern European History* 7, no. 1 (2009): 5–25, was one of the first to discuss this problem. Other important interventions are Sebastian Conrad and Shalini Randeria, "Geteilte Geschichten: Europa in einer postkolonialen Welt," in *Jenseits des Eurozentrismus. Postkoloniale Perspektiven in den Geschichts- und Kulturwissenschaften*, ed. Sebastian Conrad, Shalini Randeria, and Regina Römhild (Frankfurt: Campus Verlag, 2002),

the birth of history as an academic discipline, which remains the dominant approach to European history. The classic surveys in the field, from Hans-Ulrich Wehler's history of Germany to Christophe Charle's history of France, present their nations as almost hermetically closed spaces.[13] Popular national histories, such as Robert Tombs's *The English and Their History* (2014), which consciously aim to uphold the notion of historically closed national communities in the public imagination, continue to top our bestseller lists.[14]

European continental history, which as a genre of historical writing originated in the early modern period, has traditionally been no more open.[15] Classical histories of Europe often presented self-asserting grand narratives of Western civilization reaching back to antiquity.[16] In the twentieth century, particularly in the aftermath of the world wars, scholars eager to overcome nationalism made copious efforts to create European histories that would reconcile Europeans.[17] Toward the end of the century, as European integration

9–49; Andreas Eckert, "Europäische Zeitgeschichte und der Rest der Welt," *Zeithistorische Forschungen* 1, no. 3 (2004): 416–21; and Christof Dejung and Martin Lenwiler's introduction to *Ränder der Moderne: Neue Perspektiven auf die Europäische Geschichte (1800–1930)*, vol 1, ed. Christof Dejung and Martin Lenwiler (Cologne: Böhlau Verlag, 2016), 7–35. The essays in Catala Michel, Jeannesson Stanislas, and Éric Schnakenbourg, eds., *Les Européens et la mondialisation du XVe siècle à nos jours* (Rennes: Presses universitaires de Rennes, 2023), are practical attempts to write a global European history.

[13] Hans-Ulrich Wehler, *Deutsche Gesellschaftsgeschichte*, 5 vols. (Munich: C. H. Beck, 1987–2008); and Christophe Charle, *Histoire sociale de la France au xixe siècle* (Paris: Éd. du Seuil, 1991).

[14] Robert Tombs, *The English and Their History* (London: Allen Lane, 2014), which is reminiscent of Germany's far-right leader Alexander Gauland, *Die Deutschen und ihre Geschichte: Eine nationale Erzählung* (Berlin: WJS Verlag, 2009); and Pierre Nora, *Présent, nation, mémoire* (Paris: Gallimard, 2011), which follows in the footsteps of Fernand Braudel's notorious *L'identité de la France*, vol. 3, *Les hommes et les choses, deuxième partie* (Paris: Arthaud/ Flammarion, 1986) and its promotion of the idea of *la France profonde*.

[15] Richard J. Evans, "What Is European History? Reflections of a Cosmopolitan Islander," *European History Quarterly* 40, no. 4 (2010): 593–605, provides an excellent brief overview of European history writing about Europe. William Robertson, *The History of the Reign of the Emperor Charles V*, 3 vols. (Dublin: W. and W. Strahan, 1769) was arguably the first European history, surpassing patchier earlier works, such as Pier Francesco Giambullari, *Historia dell'Europa* (Venice: F. Senese, 1566).

[16] Leopold von Ranke, *Geschichten der romanischen und germanischen Völker von 1494 bis 1514* (Leipzig: Duncker und Humblot, 1824); Gabriel Monod and Charles Bémont, *Histoire de l'Europe et en particulier de la France de 395 à 1270* (Paris: F. Alcan, 1891); and John Emerich Edward Dalberg-Acton, First Baron Acton, *Lectures on Modern History* (London: Macmillan, 1906), are examples of European histories which are more reflective. At the turn of the century, Lord Acton, a cosmopolitan who distrusted nationalism, made a powerful call for a common European history in his outline of the *Cambridge Modern History*, published in thirteen volumes between 1902 and 1912, see Roland Hill, *Lord Acton* (New Haven: Yale University Press, 2000), 394.

[17] Henri Pirenne, *Histoire de l'Europe: Des invasions au xvie siècle* (Paris: F. Alcan, 1936), written in 1917–18; G. P. Gooch, *History of Modern Europe, 1878–1919* (London: Cassel and Company, 1923); A. J. Grant and H. W. V. Temperley, *Europe in the Nineteenth Century* (London: Longmans, Green and Co., 1927); and Arnold Toynbee, *A Study of History*, 12 vols.

accelerated, an unprecedented number of books (and new journals) appeared which aimed to Europeanize the continent's national histories.[18] These new histories highlighted similarities and differences using comparative approaches, as well as transnational connections.[19] And yet, despite these

(London: Oxford University Press, 1934–1961), were written under the impression of the First World War. Volumes that appeared following the Second World War included Lucien Febvre, *L'Europe, genèse d'une civilisation: Cours professé au Collège de France en 1944–1945* (Paris: Perrin, 1999); John Bowle, *The Unity of European History: A Political and Cultural Survey* (London: Jonathan Cape, 1948); Oscar Halecki, *The Limits and Divisions of European History* (London: Sheed and Ward, 1950); Albert Mirgeler, *Geschichte Europas* (Freiburg: Herder, 1953); Christopher Dawson, *Understanding Europe* (London: Sheed and Ward, 1952); Denys Hay, *Europe: The Emergence of an Idea* (Edinburgh: Edinburgh University Press, 1957); Carlo Curcio, *Europa: Storia di un'Idea* (Florence: Vallecchi Editore, 1958); and Geoffrey Barraclough, *European Unity in Thought and Practice* (Oxford: Basil Blackwell, 1963).

[18] Norman Davies, *Europe: A History* (Oxford: Oxford University Press, 1996); John Merriman, *A History of Modern Europe from the Renaissance to the Present* (New York: W. W. Norton, 1996); Asa Briggs and Patricia M. Clavin, *Modern Europe, 1789–1989* (London: Longman, 1997); Hagen Schulze, *Phoenix Europa: Die Moderne, von 1740 bis heute* (Berlin: Siedler, 1998); Mark Mazower, *Dark Continent: Europe's Twentieth Century* (London: Allen Lane, 1998); Wolfgang Schmale, *Geschichte Europas* (Stuttgart: Utb Für Wissenschaft, 2001); Richard Vinen, *A History in Fragments: Europe in the Twentieth Century* (London: Little, Brown, and Company, 2000); Harold James, *Europe Reborn: A History, 1914–2000* (New York: Longman, 2003); Tony Judt, *Postwar: A History of Europe since 1945* (London: W. Heinemann, 2005); Konrad Jarausch, *Out of the Ashes: A New History of Europe in the Twentieth Century* (Princeton: Princeton University Press, 2015); Pío Moa Rodriguez, *Europa: Una introducción a su historia* (Madrid: La Esfera de los Libros, 2016); Johannes Paulmann, *Globale Vorherrschaft und Fortschrittsglaube: Europa, 1850–1914* (Munich: C. H. Beck, 2019); and Paul Betts, *Ruin and Renewal: Civilising Europe after the Second World War* (London: Profile Books, 2020), which is exceptional in that it takes global entanglements seriously, are among the most important accounts of modern European history produced since the 1990s. Other important examples of this wave were Jacques Le Goff's series "The Making of Europe" (published simultaneously in five languages by publishers in Great Britain, France, Germany, Italy, and Spain), which includes volumes by Le Goff, Peter Burke, Umberto Eco, Jack Goody, and Charles Tilly, and David Cannadine's "Penguin History of Europe" series, which includes volumes by Chris Wickham, William Chester Jordan, Tim Blanning, Richard J. Evans, and Ian Kershaw. The most important European history journals created under this momentum were the *European History Quarterly* (1984), *Contemporary European History* (1990), the *European Review of History – Revue européenne d'histoire* (1994), *Jahrbuch für Europäische Geschichte* (2000), and the *Journal of Modern European History* (2003).

[19] Michael Geyer, "Historical Fictions of Autonomy and the Europeanization of National History," *Central European History* 22, nos. 3/4 (1989): 316–42, provides a brilliant overview of the Europeanization of European history. Johannes Paulmann, "Internationaler Vergleich und inter-kultureller Transfer: Zwei Forschungsansätze zur europäischen Geschichte des 18. bis 20. Jahrhunderts," *Historische Zeitschrift* 267, no. 3 (1998): 649–85 also discusses some practical implications. The contributions to Deborah Cohen and Maura O'Connor, eds., *Comparison and History: Europe in Cross-National Perspective* (New York: Routledge, 2004); Konrad H. Jarausch and Thomas Lindenberger, eds., *Conflicted Memories: Europeanizing Contemporary Histories* (New York: Berghahn Books, 2007); Martin Conway and Kiran Klaus Patel, eds., *Europeanization in the Twentieth Century: Historical Approaches* (New York: Macmillan, 2010), provide more detailed discussions of the Europeanization of the continent's history. For a programmatic article advocating this historiographical shift from the perspective of German

efforts, European history writing remained fixated on the nation-state. Equally problematic, some European histories have overcome the national only to revive, consciously or unconsciously, older civilizational narratives of the "West," the "Occident," or even "Christendom." Most strikingly, general works of European history are often remarkably inward-looking.

None of the major surveys of modern European continental history on our course reading lists – including the magna opera by Mark Mazower, Tony Judt, and Ian Kershaw – consider global entanglements seriously.[20] Most of these works tend to treat the continent as a closed historical space, almost completely ignoring exchanges of goods, people, and ideas with the outside world. Even Eric Hobsbawm's classic history of the modern age concentrates on Europe and America while showing little interest in these regions' (nonimperial) global connections.[21] If these works consider the world at all, they focus on Europe's global impact rather than global influences on Europe itself.

The rise of global history over recent years has affected almost every field of historical study. Historians of Europe, however, have seldom played a central role in these debates. The major works in the field have been written by historians of the non-European world – Jürgen Osterhammel, a scholar of modern China, Christopher Bayly, a scholar of modern India, and so on.[22] Some see global history by definition as non-European history. Indeed, certain advocates of the global turn, determined to decenter world history from Europe, have been quite critical of the intellectual dominance of the field of European history. At the same time, some Europeanists have reacted defensively to the global turn. Anxious about the marginalization of their field both intellectually and professionally (e.g., in departmental battles over new faculty hires), they consider calls to provincialize Europe a threat.

-

history, see Ute Frevert, "Europeanizing German History," *Bulletin of the German Historical Institute* 36 (2005): 9–24; and David Blackbourn, "Europeanizing German History: Comment," *Bulletin of the German Historical Institute* 36 (2005): 25–31.

[20] Mazower, *Dark Continent*; Judt, *Postwar*; Ian Kershaw, *To Hell and Back: Europe, 1914–1949* (London: Allen Lane, 2015); and Kershaw, *Roller-Coaster: Europe, 1950–2017* (London: Allen Lane, 2018). The same holds true for most of the great surveys listed in note 18.

[21] Eric J. Hobsbawm, *The Age of Revolution: Europe, 1789–1848* (London: Weidenfeld and Nicolson, 1962); Hobsbawm, *The Age of Capital: 1848–1875* (London: Weidenfeld and Nicolson, 1975); Hobsbawm, *The Age of Empire: 1875–1914* (London: Weidenfeld and Nicolson, 1987); and Hobsbawm, *The Age of Extremes: The Short Twentieth Century, 1914–1991* (London: M. Joseph, 1994).

[22] C. A. Bayly, *The Birth of the Modern World, 1780–1914: Global Connections and Comparisons* (Malden: Blackwell, 2004); and Jürgen Osterhammel, *Die Verwandlung der Welt: Eine Geschichte des 19. Jahrhunderts* (Munich: C. H. Beck, 2009), which was published in English as Jürgen Osterhammel, *The Transformation of the World: A Global History of the Nineteenth Century* (Princeton: Princeton University Press, 2009).

Yet European and global history do not, of course, contradict each other. Global history should not only be defined by the geographical location of its subject. Its aim should not be to examine far-flung regions, as distant from Europe as possible. Instead, global history provides a conceptual approach, namely the study of global interrelations as well as parallel and divergent developments and transformations in different parts of the world. For us Europeanists, the global turn is not only a challenge but also a huge opportunity – an opportunity to open up modern European history, to look at the history of modern Europe as part of the history of a globalizing world, to globalize modern European history. Indeed, one of the most significant developments in our field at the moment is the attempt to interweave European and world history. This will ultimately help us to look at European history from entirely new angles – and to redefine the field.

In concrete terms, global history opens various new avenues of research for scholars of European (urban, local, national, regional, and continental) history. First, it allows us to see similarities and differences (as well as convergences and divergences over time) through comparison between historical phenomena in different parts of the world, and to contextualize developments in Europe globally.[23] This also means that we need to rethink assumptions about European uniqueness.[24] Where, in the past, historians of Europe have tended to use global comparisons selectively to underline the continent's alleged historical singularity (and indeed superiority), we now need to pay attention to both differences *and* similarities.[25] Second, global history allows us to explore

---

[23] Comparative history as a method is discussed in Patrick O'Brien, "Historiographical Traditions and Modern Imperatives for the Restoration of Global History," *Journal of Global History* 1, no. 1 (2006): 3–39; and in the contributions to Heinz-Gerhard Haupt and Jürgen Kocka, eds., *Geschichte und Vergleich: Ansätze und Ergebnisse international vergleichender Geschichtsschreibung* (Frankfurt M.: Campus, 1996); and Heinz-Gerhard Haupt and Jürgen Kocka, eds., *Comparative and Transnational History: Central European Approaches and New Perspectives* (New York: Berghahn, 2009). Michel Espagne, "Sur les limites du comparatisme en histoire culturelle," *Genèses: Sciences Sociales et Histoire* 17 (1994): 112–21, provides a critical reflection.

[24] Some pioneering historians have compared, for example, labor service in Germany and America, postwar memory cultures in Japan and Germany, or revolutionary activism in Russia and China, see Sebastian Conrad, *Auf der Suche nach der verlorenen Nation: Geschichtsschreibung in Westdeutschland und Japan, 1945–1960* (Göttingen: Vandenhoeck and Ruprecht, 1999), which was published in English as Sebastian Conrad, *The Quest for the Lost Nation: Writing History in Germany and Japan in the American Century* (Berkeley: University of California Press, 2010); Kiran Klaus Patel, *Soldiers of Labor: Labor Service in Nazi Germany and New Deal America, 1933–1945* (Cambridge: Cambridge University Press, 2005); and S. A. Smith, *Revolution and the People in Russia and China: A Comparative History* (Cambridge: Cambridge University Press, 2008).

[25] Jack Goody, *The East in the West* (Cambridge: Cambridge University Press, 1996); Goody, *The Theft of History* (Cambridge: Cambridge University Press, 2006); and Goody, *Renaissances: The One or the Many?* (Cambridge: Cambridge University Press, 2010), offer an insightful critique of Eurocentric exceptionalism. Stuart Hall, "The West and the Rest: Discourse and

Europe's direct and indirect connections with the wider world.[26] This also means that we need to question traditional historical narratives, which have almost exclusively focused on a one-way diffusion from a European center to a non-European periphery (Europeanization, Westernization, and, more universally, modernization), an approach which all too often assumes European superiority and reduces the non-European regions of the world to mere imitators.[27] The continent has always been not only an engine but also a product of global transformations.

The contributions to this book discuss how European history can be integrated into global history. This introductory chapter examines the ways in

Power," in *Formations of Modernity*, ed. Stuart Hall and Bram Gieben (Cambridge: Polity, 1992), 275–332, offers some thoughts on the discourse that created a dualism between the "West" and the "rest" of the world to affirm Western uniqueness. The exceptionalist literature, depicting, based on selective comparison, the uniqueness of European historical developments, is vast, and includes Eric L. Jones, *The European Miracle: Environments, Economies and Geopolitics in the History of Europe and Asia* (Cambridge: Cambridge University Press, 1981); Henri Mendras, *L'Europe des Européens. Sociologie de l'Europe occidentale* (Paris: Gallimard, 1997), which focuses on western Europe; Michael Mitterauer, *Warum Europa? Mittelalterliche Grundlagen eines Sonderwegs* (Munich: C. H. Beck, 2004); and, most recently, Niall Ferguson, *Civilization: The West and the Rest* (London: Penguin, 2011). Eurocentric exceptionalism, based on selective comparisons, is also widespread in the social sciences, going back to their founders; classical examples are, culturally, the "Protestant ethic" of Max Weber, "Die protestantische Ethik und der Geist des Kapitalismus," *Archiv für Sozialwissenschaft und Sozialpolitik* 20, no. 1 (1904): 1–54 and 21, no. 1 (1905): 1–110; economically, the "Asiatic mode of production" of Karl Marx, *Zur Kritik der politischen Ökonomie* (Berlin: Verlag von Franz Duncker, 1859), vi, and his later works, including *Das Kapital*; and, politically, following on from Montesquieu and Marx, the "Oriental despotism" of Karl A. Wittfogel, *Oriental Despotism: A Comparative Study of Total Power* (New Haven: Yale University Press, 1957).

[26] Connective history as a method is discussed in Sanjay Subrahmanyam, "Connected Histories: Notes towards a Reconfiguration of Early Modern Eurasia," *Modern Asian Studies* 31, no. 3 (1997): 735–62; and, identically, Subrahmanyam, "Connected Histories: Toward a Reconfiguration of Early Modern Eurasia," in *Beyond Binary Histories: Reimagining Eurasia to c. 1830*, ed. Victor B. Lieberman (Ann Arbor: University of Michigan Press, 1997), 289–316; Michael Werner and Bénédicte Zimmermann, "Vergleich, Transfer, Verflechtung: Der Ansatz der Histoire croisée und die Herausforderung des Transnationalen," *Geschichte und Gesellschaft* 28, no. 4 (2002): 607–36; Michael Werner and Bénédicte Zimmermann, "Beyond Comparison: Histoire Croisée and the Challenge of Reflexivity," *History and Theory* 45, no. 1 (2006): 30–50; and Caroline Douki and Philippe Minard, "Histoire globale, histoires connectées: un changement d'échelle historiographique?," *Revue d'histoire moderne et contemporaine* 54-4bis, no. 5 (2007): 7–21.

[27] James M. Blaut, *The Colonizer's Model of the World: Geographical Diffusionism and Eurocentric History* (New York: Guilford Press, 1993), 1–49, offers a compelling critique of Eurocentric diffusionism. The diffusionist literature, depicting a triumphant Europeanization (Westernization) of the world, is also vast and includes Frank C. Darling, *The Westernization of Asia: A Comparative Political Analysis* (Boston: G. K. Hall, 1979); Theodore H. von Laue, *The World Revolution of Westernization: The Twentieth Century in Global Perspective* (New York: Oxford University Press, 1987); and, to some extent, Benjamin R. Barber, *Jihad vs. McWorld: How the Planet Is Both Falling Apart and Coming Together – and What This Means for Democracy* (New York: Crown, 1995); and John M. Headley, *The Europeanization of the World: On the Origins of Human Rights and Democracy* (Princeton, NJ: Princeton University Press, 2007); a good discussion of the last book is offered by Jerry Bentley, "Europeanization of the World or Globalization of Europe?," *Religions* 3, no. 2 (2012), 441–54.

which historians of Europe have responded to the "global turn," providing a broad historiographical overview. It also demonstrates that individual scholars have shown an increasing interest in Europe's entanglements with the wider world. Although their studies remain often disconnected (and have not yet fully entered the historiographical canon), taken together they may reshape our understanding of European history.

-

In terms of physical borders, it is practically impossible to draw clear lines between Europe and the outside world. The continent's natural boundaries are indistinct and in all cases highly permeable. As early as 1949, Fernand Braudel described the Mediterranean as a space of exchange, not a strict continental barrier, noting that "from the Black Sea to the Straits of Gibraltar, the Mediterranean's northern waters wash the shores of Europe. Here again, if he wants to establish boundaries, the historian will have more hesitation than the geographer."[28] Scholars of Atlantic history and, to a lesser extent, historians of Europe's northern shores have explored similar connections.[29] Their studies have shown that these oceans can hardly be seen as boundaries but instead constitute spaces in which all seaboards form integral parts. Even scholars of Europe's eastern and southeastern borderlands have pointed to the close-knit routes of exchange across borders.[30] In terms of climate history, too, as Sam White has shown, it is virtually impossible to divide the Balkans from Asia Minor.[31] Indeed, the division between Europe and Asia seems

---

[28] Fernand Braudel, *The Mediterranean and the Mediterranean World in the Age of Philip II*, 2 vols. (1972–3; Berkeley: University of California Press, 1995–6), 1:188, which was first published in French in 1949. David Abulafia, *The Great Sea: A Human History of the Mediterranean* (London: Allen Lane, 2011), is an excellent more recent study of the Mediterranean as a space of exchange. David Abulafia, "Mediterranean History as Global History," *History and Theory* 50, no. 2 (2011): 220–8, offers some conceptual reflections.

[29] Marcus Rediker and Peter Linebaugh, *The Many-Headed Hydra: Sailors, Slaves, Commoners, and the Hidden History of the Revolutionary Atlantic* (Boston: Beacon Press, 2000); Bernard Bailyn, *Atlantic History: Concept and Contours* (Cambridge, MA: Harvard University Press, 2005); David Bell, *Men on Horseback: The Power of Charisma in the Age of Revolution* (New York: Farrar, Straus and Giroux, 2020); and the classic C. L. R. James, *The Black Jacobins: Toussaint L'Ouverture and the San Domingo Revolution* (New York: Dial Press, 1938), are key works on Atlantic history. On Europe's northern oceanic history, see Jørgen Ole Bærenholdt, *Coping with Distances: Producing Nordic Atlantic Societies* (Oxford: Berghahn Books, 2007); John McCannon, *A History of the Arctic: Nature, Exploration and Exploitation* (London: Reaktion Books, 2012); and the contributions to Michael Bravo and Sverker Sörlin, eds., *A Cultural History of Nordic Scientific Practices* (Canton: Science History Publications, 2002).

[30] Alfred J. Rieber, *The Struggle for the Eurasian Borderlands: From the Rise of Early Modern Empires to the End of the First World War* (Cambridge: Cambridge University Press, 2014).

[31] Sam White, *The Climate of Rebellion in the Early Modern Ottoman Empire* (Cambridge: Cambridge University Press, 2011); and, more generally, Geoffrey Parker, *Global*

particularly arbitrary; topographically, Europe is "a western peninsula of Asia," as Alexander von Humboldt once observed.[32]

The physical geographic concept of Europe has therefore, unsurprisingly, changed throughout history. There have been age-old controversies over whether Russia is part of the continent or not; most now consider the Ural Mountains as the border between Asia and Europe, following the eighteenth-century Swedish cartographer Philipp Johann von Strahlenberg.[33] Still, Leopold von Ranke famously claimed that "New York and Lima" were closer to "us" than "Kiev and Smolensk."[34] The nineteenth-century Prussian geographer August Rühle von Lilienstern suggested including North Africa and the lands to the Indus, Amu, Tobol, and Ob in Europe.[35] The German historian Karl Krüger in the 1950s argued that North Africa and the Middle East were part of a "greater Europe," united by the Mediterranean as a Hellenistic-European cultural space.[36] The British scholar Oscar Halecki, in contrast, claimed that the Ottoman Empire was not part of Europe because of its Islamic-majority population, whereas Russia, with its Christian majority, had been part of Europe up until the Bolshevik Revolution.[37]

Too difficult to demarcate physically, Europe was often defined abstractly, as a sociocultural space.[38] "Europe," Peter Burke observed, "is not so much a

---

Crisis: War, Climate Change and Catastrophe in the Seventeenth Century (New Haven: Yale University Press, 2013).

[32] Alexander von Humboldt, Kosmos: Entwurf einer physischen Weltbeschreibung, vol. 2 (Stuttgart: J. G. Gotta, 1847), 150, translated as Cosmos: A Sketch of a Physical Description of the Universe, vol. 2 (London, 1948), 115.

[33] Philipp Johann von Strahlenberg, Das nord-und ostliche Theil von Europa und Asia, in so weit solches das gantze Russische Reich mit Siberien und der grossen Tatarey in sich begreiffet, in einer historisch-geographischen Beischreibung . . . (Stockholm: Verlegung des Autoris, 1730). Mark Bassin, "Russia between Europe and Asia: The Ideological Construction of Geographical Space," Slavic Review 50, no. 1 (1991): 1–17, looks at the history of the broader debate on this subject.

[34] Leopold von Ranke, Geschichte der Romanischen und Germanischen Völker von 1494 bis 1535 (Leipzig: G. Reimer, 1824), xxxix.

[35] August Rühle v. Lilienstern, Der Wechsel der politischen Gränzen und Verhältnisse von Europa während der zwei letzten Jahrzehnte (Leipzig, 1811).

[36] Karl Krüger, Weltpolitische Länderkunde: Die Länder und Staaten der Erde (Berlin: Safari-Verlag, 1953), 119–21.

[37] Halecki, The Limits and Divisions of European History.

[38] On (physical and sociocultural) concepts of Europe, see the contributions to Kevin Wilson and Jan van der Dussen, eds., The History of the Idea of Europe (London: Routledge, 1995); James Carrier, ed., Occidentalism: Images of the West (Oxford: Oxford University Press, 1995); Bo Stråth, ed., Europe and the Other and Europe as the Other (New York: Peter Lang, 2000); Anthony Pagden, ed., The Idea of Europe: From Antiquity to the European Union (Cambridge: Cambridge University Press, 2002); and Hans-Åke Persson and Bo Stråth, eds., Reflections on Europe: Defining a Political Order in Time and Space (New York: Peter Lang, 2007). Hartmut Kaelble, Europäer über Europa: Die Entstehung des europäischen Selbstverständnisses im 19. und 20. Jahrhundert (Frankfurt: Campus Verlag, 2001), traces the emergence of continental identities in modern Europe. Susan Rößner, Die Geschichte Europas schreiben: Europäische

place as an idea."[39] Europe, as Jürgen Kocka has argued, is a construct of our minds.[40] This is not the place to discuss the different traits that have been ascribed to this space, though it is noteworthy that Europe has routinely been defined in relation to an exterior Other, often the "Orient," usually portrayed as inferior.[41] "The battle of Marathon, even as an event in English history, is more important than the battle of Hastings," John Stuart Mill once remarked.[42] "If the issue of that day had been different, the Britons and the Saxons might still have been wandering in the woods." "Marathon was the birth cry of Europe," commented a certain General Fuller a hundred years later.[43] Outside Europe, particularly in the colonial and postcolonial world, images of Europe could be quite different, of course. (It is worth noting here that, even though non-European conceptions of Europe also varied, across many parts of the world, similar terms emerged to designate the continent – *Frenk* in the Ottoman Empire, *farangi* in Iran and Afghanistan, *färänji* in Ethiopia, *farang* in Thailand, and *barang* in Cambodia – as a geographical space and, and more importantly, as an idea.) In the end, sociocultural notions of Europe have been just as contested as physical ones. "Numerous attempts to define the cultural or

Historiker und ihr Europabild im 20. Jahrhundert (Frankfurt: Campus Verlag, 2009), discusses ideas of Europe among European historians. Derek Heater, *The Idea of European Unity* (New York, 1992), discusses ideas of European integration. Concise overviews are Jan Nederveen Pieterse, "Fictions of Europe," *Race and Class* 32, no. 3 (1991): 1–10; Gerald Stourzh, "Europa, aber wo liegt es?" in *Annäherungen an eine europäische Geschichtsschreibung*, ed. Gerald Stourzh (Vienna: Österreichische Akademie der Wissenschaften, 2002), ix–xx; Hans-Dietrich Schultz, "Europa: (K)ein Kontinent? Das Europa deutscher Geographen," in *Welt-Räume: Geschichte, Geographie und Globalisierung seit 1900*, ed. Iris Schröder and Sabine Höhler (Frankfurt: Campus Verlag, 2005), 204–31; and Paul Stock, "Towards a Language of 'Europe': History, Rhetoric, Community," *European Legacy* 22, no. 6 (2017): 647–66. The chapters in Kumkum Chatterjee and Clement Hawes, eds., *Europe Observed: Multiple Gazes in Early Modern Encounters* (Lewisburg, PA: Bucknell University Press, 2008) and parts 1 and 3 of Michael Wintle, ed., *Imagining Europe: Europe and European Civilisation as Seen from Its Margins and by the Rest of the World, in the Nineteenth and Twentieth Centuries* (Brussels: Peter Lang, 2008), provide views from the outside.
[39]   Peter Burke, "Did Europe Exist before 1700?" *History of European Ideas* 1, no. 1 (1980): 21–9, here p. 21.
[40]   Jürgen Kocka, "Europa und die Anderen: Historische Perspektiven," in *Geschichte als Experiment: Studien zu Politik, Kultur und Alltag im 19. Und 20. Jahrhundert*, ed. Daniela Münkel and Jutta Schwarzkopf (Frankfurt M.: Campus, 2004), 259–65.
[41]   Edward W. Said, *Orientalism* (London: Routledge, 1978); and, tracing this image back to antiquity, Hans-Joachim Gehrke, "Gegenbild und Selbstbild: Das europäische Iran-Bild zwischen Griechen und Mullahs," in *Gegenwelten zu den Kulturen Griechenlands und Roms in der Antike*, ed. Tonio Hölscher (Munich: K. G. Saur, 2000), 85–109. Another example is anti-Americanism: Dan Diner, *Feindbild Amerika: Über die Beständigkeit eines Ressentiments* (Munich: Propyläen, 2002); and Phillipe Roger, *The American Enemy: The History of French Anti-Americanism* (Chicago: University of Chicago Press, 2005). Hall, "The West and the Rest," looks at the discursive dualism between "Europe" and "non-Europe" more generally.
[42]   John Stuart Mill, "A Review of the First two volumes of Grote's History of Greece," *Edinburgh Review* 11 (1846): 271–305, here p. 271.
[43]   J. F. C. Fuller, *A Military History of the Western World*, vol. 1 (New York, 1954), 25.

social peculiarities of Europe suffer from the juxtaposition of such phantoms and from the untested claim that salient European virtues are absent in other parts of the world," Osterhammel observed.[44] "In the worst case," he added, "the clichés about Europe itself are no less crude than those about Indian or Chinese society." *Homo europeaeus* never existed.[45] And in any case, however we define Europe, there are always links transcending its borders, influencing its local, national, regional, and continental spaces. Acknowledging the changing conceptions of the continent's borders, Norman Davies spoke about a "tidal Europe."[46] A. J. P. Taylor concluded that "European history is whatever the historian wants it to be."[47]

From the perspective of environmental history, flora and fauna from far-flung continents have always impacted Europe's natural life. These influences could also be directly connected to Europe's imperial enterprise.[48] This became most obvious in places such as London's Kew Gardens, a global microcosm of nature and empire, examined in Richard Drayton's *Nature's Government* (2000).[49] Germs, too, have never known borders.[50] The Asiatic cholera came to Europe from Bengal along trade routes after the British conquest of North India. Later outbreaks, studied in Richard J. Evans's work on the Hamburg cholera epidemic, spread from India via Persia and Russia to western Europe.[51] "Gentlemen, I forget that I am in Europe," Robert Koch remarked to his colleagues at the time, expressing not only a sentiment of European civilizational superiority but also a sense of global interconnectedness.[52] The same is true for Europe's ecological crises, as, for example, experienced in 1816, the "year without a summer," after an eruption of the Mount Tambora volcano near Java in 1815 blocked solar energy and cooled

[44] Osterhammel, *Die Verwandlung der Welt*, 1058.
[45] Kiran Klaus Patel, "The Making of *Homo Europaeus*: Problems, Approaches and Perspectives," *Comparativ* 25 (2015): 15–31; and the contributions to Lorraine Bluche, Veronika Lipphardt, and Kiran Klaus Patel, eds., *Der Europäer, ein Konstrukt: Wissensbestände Diskurse, Praktiken* (Göttingen: Wallstein Verlag, 2009).
[46] Davies, *Europe*, 9.
[47] A. J. P. Taylor, contribution to the forum "What Is European History? Historians Grapple with a Difficult Subject," *History Today* 36, no. 1 (1986): 46–50, here p. 46.
[48] Alfred W. Crosby, *The Columbian Exchange: Biological and Cultural Consequences of 1492* (Westport: Greenwood, 1973); and, conversely, Crosby, *Ecological Imperialism: The Biological Expansion of Europe 900–1900* (Cambridge: Cambridge University Press, 1986), are classics.
[49] Richard Drayton, *Nature's Government: Science, Imperial Britain and the "Improvement" of the World* (New Haven: Yale University Press, 2000).
[50] William H. McNeill, *Plagues and Peoples* (New York: Anchor Books, 1977).
[51] Richard J. Evans, *Death in Hamburg: Society and Politics in the Cholera Years, 1830–1910* (Oxford: Clarendon Press, 1987).
[52] Cited in ibid., 312–13.

the climate globally, leading to crop failures and Europe's last subsistence crisis.[53]

Human mobility, too, has changed Europe's population over the centuries. A fast-growing literature on migrations and minorities in European history traces these movements, ranging from African settlers in the Renaissance to twentieth-century postcolonial and labor migrants from Asia, Africa, and the Americas.[54] There is now a substantial body of studies on the history of Afropeans, for example.[55] Giants of European literature such as Alexander Pushkin and Alexandre Dumas had part-African ancestry. Black musicians, as we know from the work of Kira Thurman, performed in the greatest concert halls of German-speaking central Europe throughout the twentieth century, complicating their audiences' understanding of Austro-German classical musical culture.[56] As global mobility accelerated, the continent's population became more diverse. Empire, of course, is an important part of this history. At the same time, Europeans, too, spread across the globe, building vast settler

[53] Gillen D'Arcy Wood, *Tambora: The Eruption that Changed the World* (Princeton: Princeton University Press, 2014).

[54] Jan Lucassen and Leo Lucassen, "The Mobility Transition Revisited, 1500–1900: What the Case of Europe can offer to Global History," *Journal of Global History* 4, no. 3 (2009): 347–77, provides an overview. P. C. Emmer and M. Mörner, eds., *European Expansion and Migration: Essays on the Intercontinental Migration from Africa, Asia, and Europe* (New York: Berg, 1992); and Stephen Castles and Mark J. Miller, *The Age of Migration: International Population Movements in the Modern World* (London: Macmillan, 1993), are more detailed accounts. Coll Thrush, *Indigenous London: Native Travelers at the Heart of Empire* (New Haven: Yale University Press, 2016); and Caroline Dodds Pennock, *On Savage Shores: How Indigenous Americans Discovered Europe* (London: Weidenfeld and Nicolson, 2023), are fascinating case studies.

[55] Peter Fryer, *Staying Power: The History of Black People in Britain* (London: Pluto Press, 1984); Marc Matera, *Black London: The Imperial Metropolis and Decolonization in the Twentieth Century* (Berkeley: University of California Press, 2015); David Olusoga, *Black and British: A Forgotten History* (London: Macmillan, 2016); Miranda Kaufmann, *Black Tudors: The Untold Story* (London: Oneworld, 2017); Tiffany N. Florvil, *Mobilizing Black Germany: Afro-German Women and the Making of a Transnational Movement* (Urbana: University of Illinois Press, 2020); Olivette Otele, *African European: An Untold History* (London: Hurst and Company, 2020); Johny Pitts, *Afropean: Notes from Black Europe* (London: Allen Lane, 2020); Hakim Adi, *African and Caribbean People in Britain: A History* (London: Allen Lane, 2022); and John Woolf and Keshia N. Abraham, *Black Victorians: Hidden in History* (London: Ducksworth, 2022), as well as the contributions in Marianne Bechhaus-Gerst and Reinhard Klein-Arendt, eds., *AfrikanerInnen in Deutschland und schwarze Deutsche, Geschichte und Gegenwart* (Münster: Lit, 2004); and Ulrich van der Heyden, ed., *Unbekannte Biographien: Afrikaner im deutschsprachigen Europa vom 18. Jahrhundert bis zum Ende des Zweiten Weltkrieges* (Berlin: Homilius, 2008). Hans Werner Debrunner, *Presence and Prestige: Africans in Europe: A History of Africans in Europe before 1918* (Basel: Basler Afrika Bibliographien, 1979), offers some fascinating biographical sketches.

[56] Kira Thurman, *Singing like Germans: Black Musicians in the Land of Bach, Beethoven, and Brahms* (Ithaca, NY: Cornell University Press, 2021).

communities.[57] Their stories show, as demonstrated in David Blackbourn's magnificent *Germany in the World*, that the histories of European peoples cannot just be told as if they solely took place within their countries' European geographic boundaries.[58] Global family and community networks connected these European migrants to their home countries in Europe, just as non-European migrant groups in Europe maintained links beyond the continent's borders. Heightened mobility was accompanied by the creation of new mechanisms to bureaucratically control movement across borders, whether national or, more recently, European, with passports, identity cards, and visas. Ultimately, encounters with "foreigners" both overseas and at home would shape the ways in which Europeans saw themselves and mapped the world's populations. Some non-Europeans were put on display (and studied) in Imperial Europe's human zoos.[59] A large body of research now stresses the importance of colonial environments in the history of modern racist theories, theories which, in turn, directly influenced human interactions in Europe and the wider world.[60] To claim, as one historian has done, that racism did not shape thought in an imperial hub such as mid-Victorian Britain is odd.[61]

---

[57] James Belich, *Replenishing the Earth: The Settler Revolution and the Rise of the Anglo-World, 1783–1939* (Oxford: Oxford University Press, 2009); and the contributions in Dirk Hoerder and Leslie Page Moch, eds., *European Migrants: Global and Local Perspectives* (Boston: Northeastern University Press, 1996), provide insights from different perspectives.

[58] David Blackbourn, *Germany in the World: A Global History, 1500–2000* (New York: Liveright, 2023).

[59] Sadiah Qureshi, *People's on Parade: Exhibitions, Empire, and Anthropology in Nineteenth-Century Britain* (Chicago: University of Chicago Press, 2011), looks at the connection between human zoos and anthropology. Other important works on the subject are Hilke Thode-Arora, *Für fünfzig Pfennig um die Welt: Die Hagenbeckschen Völkerschauen* (Frankfurt M: Campus, 1989); Rea Brändle, *Wildfremd, hautnah: Völkerschauen und ihre Schauplätze in Zürich 1880–1960* (Zurich: Rotpunktverlag, 1995); Gabi Eißenberger, *Entführt, verspottet und gestorben: Lateinamerikanische Völkerschauen in deutschen Zoos* (Frankfurt: IKO-Verlag, 1996); Werner Michael Schwarz, *Anthropologische Spektakel: Zur Schaustellung "exotischer" Menschen, Wien 1870–1910* (Vienna: Turia und Kant, 2001); Olivier Razac, *L'Écran et le zoo: Spectacle et domestication des expositions coloniales à Loft Story* (Paris: Denoël, 2002); Anne Dreesbach, *Gezähmte Wilde: Die Zurschaustellung "exotischer" Menschen in Deutschland 1870–1940* (Frankfurt: Campus, 2005); and, more generally, Andrew Zimmerman, *Anthropology and Antihumanism in Imperial Germany* (Chicago: University of Chicago Press, 2001). Nicolas Bancel, Pascal Blanchard, Gilles Boetsch, Éric Deroo, and Sandrine Lemaire, eds., *Zoos humains: De la Vénus hottentote aux reality shows* (Paris: La Découverte, 2004), provides a broad overview.

[60] George M. Fredrickson, *Racism: A Short History* (Princeton: Princeton University Press, 2002); Francisco Bethencourt, *Racisms: From the Crusades to the Twentieth Century* (Princeton: Princeton University Press, 2014), which provide concise overviews; and George L. Mosse, *Toward the Final Solution: A History of European Racism* (New York: H. Fertig, 1978), which remains one of the best intellectual histories of racism.

[61] Peter Mandler, "Race and Nation in Mid-Victorian Thought," in *History, Religion, and Culture: British Intellectual History 1750–1950*, ed. Stefan Collini, Richard Whatmore, and Brian Young (Cambridge: Cambridge University Press, 2000), 224–44, makes this strange claim.

As global mobility accelerated, Europeans increasingly tried to segregate humans inside and outside Europe according to their racial categorizations.

Historians have also long pointed out that modern Europe's economy can only be fully understood in its global context. One of the most prominent examples is the Industrial Revolution, which, as Hobsbawm argued in *Industry and Empire* as early as 1968, was directly connected to European imperialism.[62] Similarly, Europe's major economic crises, from the crash of tulipmania to the Great Depression, originated beyond its borders.[63] Modern Europe has always been integrated into the global economy, shaped by the movement of raw materials, goods, and labor – albeit unevenly and to different degrees at different times. Today, many decades after the publication of Eric Williams's pioneering *Capitalism and Slavery* (1944), historians are still debating the connection between the global slave trade and the rise of European capitalism.[64] The global commodity trade, from cotton, silver, and gold to sugar, salt, and oil, had a dramatic impact on Europe, as shown by a rapidly growing body of literature.[65] Global trade, Maxine Berg has demonstrated, transformed Europe's market for luxury goods.[66] Fashions, from *turquerie* to *chinoiserie* to *japonaiserie*, were globally inspired. A particularly fascinating study on the subject is Sarah Stein's work on African ostrich feathers, which decorated the hats of Europe's bourgeois ladies in the nineteenth and early twentieth centuries.[67] Cacao, as William Clarence-Smith, Marcy Norton, and others have shown, had been shipped since the seventeenth century from the

[62] Eric J. Hobsbawm, *Industry and Empire: From 1750 to the Present Day* (London: Weidenfeld and Nicholson, 1968); and, for a (European and global) comparative perspective, Robert C. Allen, *The British Industrial Revolution in Global Perspective* (Cambridge: Cambridge University Press, 2009). Paul Bairoch, *Economics and World History: Myths and Paradoxes* (Chicago: University of Chicago Press, 1993), part 2, argues that imperialism was not crucial for European industrialization.

[63] Anne Goldgar, *Tulipmania: Money, Honor, and Knowledge in the Dutch Golden Age* (Chicago: University of Chicago Press, 2007); and Charles P. Kindleberger, *The World in Depression, 1929–1939* (Berkeley: University of California Press, 1973).

[64] Eric Williams, *Capitalism and Slavery* (Chapel Hill: University of North Carolina Press, 1944). Alexander Anievas and Kerem Nişancıoğlu, *How the West Came to Rule: The Geopolitical Origins of Capitalism* (London: Pluto Press, 2015), is a more general non-Eurocentric history of the rise of capitalism. Patrick Karl O'Brien, "The Deconstruction of Myths and Reconstruction of Metanarratives in Global Histories of Material Progress," in *Writing World History, 1800–2000*, ed. Benedikt Stuchtey and Eckhardt Fuchs (Oxford: Oxford University Press, 2003), 67–90, provides a critical assessment. Maxine Berg and Pat Hudson, *Slavery, Capitalism and the Industrial Revolution* (London: Polity, 2023), offers a nuanced view on the question.

[65] Sven Beckert, *Empire of Cotton: A Global History* (New York: Knopf, 2014), is an outstanding example.

[66] Maxine Berg, *Luxury and Pleasure in Eighteenth-Century Britain* (Oxford: Oxford University Press, 2005).

[67] Sarah Abrevaya Stein, *Plumes: Ostrich Feathers, Jews, and a Lost World of Global Commerce* (New Haven: Yale University Press, 2008).

Americas to Europe, where consumers quickly developed a taste for it.[68] The same holds true for tobacco, coffee, and tea, all of which transformed European consumption cultures.[69] Worldwide commodity trade shaped fashion, interior design, and culinary taste even in the remotest corners of the continent.

Modern Europe's global political relations have been comparatively well studied, although most of the literature on the subject deals with imperialism. Older generations of historians were often quick to explain Europe's global imperial hegemony as a result of the continent's inherent qualities, a "European miracle," as Eric L. Jones put it.[70] The story may not be so simple. Some scholars have pointed out that it was non-European political crises and subsequent colonial exploitation that enabled Europe's rise and imperial expansion.[71] And imperialism was, of course, never a one-way exchange but impacted Europe almost as much as the colonial world, if in very different ways. Some, most notably Ann Laura Stoler and Frederick Cooper, have even suggested that Europe's imperial powers and their overseas possessions should be considered a contiguous space without a clear center.[72]

---

[68] William Gervase Clarence-Smith, *Cocoa and Chocolate, 1765–1914* (London: Routledge, 2000); and Marcy Norton, *Sacred Gifts, Profane Pleasures: A History of Tobacco and Chocolate in the Atlantic World* (Ithaca, NY: Cornell University Press, 2008); for a good popular history, see Sophie D. Coe and Michael D. Coe, *The True History of Chocolate* (London: Thames and Hudson, 1996).

[69] Julia Laura Rischbieter, *Mikro-Ökonomie der Globalisierung: Kaffee, Kaufleute und Konsumenten im Kaiserreich 1870–1914* (Cologne: Vandenhoeck & Ruprecht, 2011), is a good example.

[70] Jones, *The European Miracle*, and the other literature on European exceptionalism referred to in note 25. More balanced accounts, also considering the role of global interconnections and non-European crises in enabling Europe's imperial expansion, are William H. McNeill, *The Rise of the West: A History of the Human Community* (Chicago: University of Chicago Press, 1963); Kenneth Pomeranz, *The Great Divergence: China, Europe, and the Making of the Modern World Economy* (Princeton: Princeton University Press, 2000); Ian Morris, *Why the West Rules – For Now: The Patterns of History and What they Reveal about the Future* (London: Profile Books, 2010); Prasannan Parthasarathi, *Why Europe Grew Rich and Asia Did Not: Global Economic Divergence, 1600–1850* (Cambridge: Cambridge University Press, 2011); and, to a lesser extent, Philip T. Hoffman, *Why Did Europe Conquer the World?* (Princeton: Princeton University Press, 2015). Patrick Karl O'Brien, "The Deconstruction of Myths and Reconstruction of Metanarratives in Global Histories of Material Progress," in *Writing World History, 1800–2000*, ed. Benedikt Stuchtey and Eckhardt Fuchs (Oxford, 2003), 67–90, provides a short critical assessment.

[71] Janet L. Abu-Lughod, *Before European Hegemony: The World System A.D. 1250–1350* (Oxford: Oxford University Press, 1989); K. N. Chaudhuri, *Asia before Europe: Economy and Civilisation of the Indian Ocean from the Rise of Islam to 1750* (Cambridge: Cambridge University Press, 1990); Blaut, *The Colonizer's Model of the World*, 50–213; and John M. Hobson, *The Eastern Origins of Western Civilisation* (Cambridge: Cambridge University Press, 2004), elaborate further on these observations.

[72] Ann Laura Stoler and Frederick Cooper, "Between Metropole and Colony: Rethinking a Research Agenda," in *Tensions of Empire: Colonial Cultures in a Bourgeois World*, ed. Ann Laura Stoler and Frederick Cooper (Berkeley: University of California Press, 1997), 1–56.

Works on anti-colonial radicals in European metropolises, such as Michael Goebel's *Anti-Imperial Metropolis* (2015), have shown that struggles between colonizers and colonized could take place at the very heart of Europe.[73]

And imperialism was not the only form of modern Europe's global power relations. In the heyday of empire, European governments had multifaceted relations with independent states of the non-European world – China, Ethiopia, Japan, the Ottoman Empire, Persia, and Siam. Europe's nobility was part of a global aristocratic caste, most spectacularly displayed during visits of Persian, Siamese, and Ottoman royalty to European capitals.[74] After decolonization, twentieth-century Europe's political entanglements with the wider world became even more multifaceted. Today, the European Union includes territories as far away as Martinique in the Caribbean and Mayotte in the Indian Ocean.[75]

Yet internal European politics was also continuously shaped by the world. The history of the emergence of Europe's liberal and democratic movements cannot be written without taking into account the Atlantic world, as has been explored by scholars since R. R. Palmer and Jacques Godechot.[76] Nationalism, too, was often deeply influenced by global encounters, a process described to great effect in Sebastian Conrad's *Globalisierung und Nation im Deutschen Kaiserreich* (2006).[77] The movements in western Europe that culminated in the events of 1968 drew on the ideas of distant revolutionary thinkers such as Mao Zedong, Ho Chi Minh, and Che Guevara.[78] Modern ideologies (even if

---

[73] Michael Goebel, *Anti-Imperial Metropolis: Interwar Paris and the Seeds of Third World Nationalism* (Cambridge: Cambridge University Press, 2015).

[74] David Motadel, "Qajar Shahs in Imperial Germany," *Past & Present*, no. 213 (2010): 191–235.

[75] Megan Brown, *The Seventh Member State: Algeria, France, and the European Community* (Cambridge, MA: Harvard University Press, 2022); and, with a focus on agricultural markets, Muriam Haleh Davis, "North Africa and the Common Agricultural Policy: From Colonial Pact to European Integration", in *North Africa and the Making of Europe: Governance, Institutions and Culture*, ed. Muriam Haleh Davis and Thomas Serres (London, 2018), 43-65, look at the early entanglements between the European Community and the colonial world. Anne-Isabelle Richard, "A Global Perspective on European Cooperation and Integration since 1918," in *The Cambridge History of the European Union*, ed. Mathieu Segers and Steven Van Hecke (Cambridge: Cambridge University Press, 2023), 459–480, offers a truly global view on European integration.

[76] R. R. Palmer, *The Age of the Democratic Revolution: A Political History of Europe and America, 1760–1800*, 2 vols. (Princeton: Princeton University Press, 1959–1964); and Jacques Godechot, *Les Révolutions, 1770–1799* (Paris: Presses universitaires de France, 1963), published in English as *France and the Atlantic Revolution of the Eighteenth Century, 1770–1799* (New York: Free Press, 1965).

[77] Sebastian Conrad, *Globalisierung und Nation im Deutschen Kaiserreich* (Munich: C. H. Beck, 2006), translated as *Globalisation and the Nation in Imperial Germany* (Cambridge: Cambridge University Press, 2010).

[78] Christoph Kalter, *Die Entdeckung der Dritten Welt: Dekolonisierung und neue radikale Linke in Frankreich* (Frankfurt: Campus Verlag, 2011), translated as *The Discovery of the Third World: Decolonization and the Rise of the New Left in France, c. 1950–1976* (Cambridge: Cambridge University Press, 2016); Quinn Slobodian, *Third World Politics in Sixties West Germany*

predominantly studied within national and at times European frameworks) spanned the globe.[79] The dualist distinction between pure European ideologies – liberalism, communism, fascism, and so on – and their unpure variants outside Europe, where there are no more than a "derivative discourse," ignores the global environment in which they emerged and evolved.[80] Moreover, global comparative history has also put political developments in Europe into perspective. Europe's great revolutions, for example, were almost all part of global revolutionary moments – 1789, 1848, 1917, 1989, and so on.[81]

Finally, transcontinental entanglements were equally important in shaping social and cultural life in many parts of Europe. This is most evident in the history of the emergence of modern class structures. The rise of Europe's middle classes and bourgeois cultures was profoundly shaped by global transformations, as discussed in *The Global Bourgeoisie* (2019).[82] The same can be said for other social groups, from the working classes to the aristocracy. European cultures, like all cultures, developed through complex processes of appropriation, adaptation, and hybridization. Western, northern, eastern, and southern Europe's cultural landscapes were profoundly shaped by the colonial world, as Catherine Hall, Andrew Thompson, David Ciarlo, and others have shown.[83] Similarly, the history of Europe in the second half of the twentieth

(Durham, NC: Duke University Press, 2012); and Timothy Scott Brown, *West Germany and the Global Sixties: The Antiauthoritarian Revolt, 1962–1978* (Cambridge: Cambridge University Press, 2013).

[79] Karl Dietrich Bracher, *Zeit der Ideologien: Eine Geschichte politischen Denkens im 20. Jahrhundert* (Stuttgart: Deutsche Verlags-Anstalt, 1982); Mazower, *Dark Continent*; and Jan-Werner Müller, *Contesting Democracy: Political Ideas in Twentieth-Century Europe* (New Haven: Yale University Press, 2003).

[80] Partha Chatterjee, *Nationalist Thought and the Colonial World: A Derivative Discourse* (London: Zed Books, 1986).

[81] Palmer, *The Age of the Democratic Revolution*; Jacques Godechot, *Les institutions de la France sous la Révolution et l'Empire* (Paris: Presses universitaires de France, 1951); David Armitage and Sanjay Subrahmanyam, eds., *The Age of Revolutions in Global Context, c. 1760–1840* (New York: Macmillan, 2010); Suzanne Desan, Lynn Hunt, and William Max Nelson, eds., *The French Revolution in Global Perspective* (Ithaca, NY: Cornell University Press, 2013), on the Atlantic Revolutions. Miles Taylor, "The 1848 Revolutions and the British Empire," *Past & Present*, no. 166 (2000): 146–80; and Kurt Weyland, "The Diffusion of Revolution: '1848' in Europe and Latin America," *International Organization* 63, no. 3 (2009): 391–423, on the impact of 1848 beyond Europe. Silvio Pons, *The Global Revolution: A History of International Communism, 1917–1991* (Oxford: Oxford University Press, 2014), 7–42, which was first published in 2012, on 1917 beyond Europe. A general global history of revolutionary waves is provided by the essays in David Motadel, ed., *Revolutionary World: Global Upheaval in the Modern Age* (Cambridge: Cambridge University Press, 2021).

[82] Christof Dejung, David Motadel, and Jürgen Osterhammel, eds., *The Global Bourgeoisie: The Rise of the Middle Classes in the Age of Empire* (Princeton: Princeton University Press, 2019), provides chapters on this entangled history.

[83] Catherine Hall, *Civilising Subjects: Metropole and Colony in the English Imagination, 1830–1867* (Chicago: University of Chicago Press, 2002); and the essays in Catherine Hall, ed., *Cultures of Empire: Colonizers in Britain and the Empire in the 19th and 20th*

century, as explored in Elizabeth Buettner's *Europe after Empire* (2016), is impossible to write without taking into account postcolonial cultural influences.[84] Even the history of gender relations and sexuality in Europe, as traced by Todd Shepard, is inextricably connected to their postcolonial environments.[85] To be sure, global influences on Europe's social and cultural life went beyond empire. The continent's high culture in particular has always been shaped from the outside. Jack Goody famously argued that Europe's Renaissance owed much to the Arab, Indian, and Chinese renaissances.[86] Similarly, any history of Europe's Enlightenment will be incomplete without

Centuries: A Reader (New York: Routledge, 2000); and Catherine Hall and Sonya O. Rose, eds., *At Home with the Empire: Metropolitan Culture and the Imperial World* (Cambridge: Cambridge University Press, 2006); as well as the chapters in John M. MacKenzie, ed., *Imperialism and Popular Culture* (Manchester, 1986); Julie F. Codell and Dianne Sachko Macleod, eds., *Orientalism Transposed: Impact of the Colonies on British Culture* (London: Routledge, 1998); Kathleen E. Wilson, ed., *A New Imperial History: Culture, Identity, and Modernity in Britain and the Empire, 1660–1840* (Cambridge: Cambridge University Press, 2004); and Andrew Thompson, *The Empire Strikes Back? The Impact of Imperialism on Britain from the Mid-nineteenth Century* (London: Routledge, 2005), on Great Britain. On France, see Pascal Blanchard and Sandrine Lemaire, eds., *Culture coloniale 1871–1931: La France conquise par son Empire* (Paris: Autrement, 2003). On the Netherlands, see Susan Legêne, *Spiegelreflex: Culturele sporen van de koloniale ervaring* (Amsterdam: Bert Bakker, 2010). On Belgium, see Guy Vanthemsche, *La Belgique et le Congo: L'impact de la colonie sur la métropole* (Brussels: Éditions Complexe, 2007), translated as *Belgium and the Congo, 1885–1980* (Cambridge: Cambridge University Press, 2012); and the contributions to Vincent Viaene, David Van Reybrouck, and Bambi Ceuppens, eds., *Congo in België: Koloniale Cultuur in de Metropool* (Leuven: Leuven University Press, 2009). On Germany, see Markus Seemann, *Kolonialismus in der Heimat: Kolonialbewegung, Kolonialpolitik und Kolonialkultur in Bayern 1882–1943* (Berlin: Ch. Links, 2011); and David Ciarlo, *Advertising Empire: Race and Visual Culture in Imperial Germany* (Cambridge, MA: Harvard University Press, 2011). On Italy, see the contributions in Patrizia Palumbo, ed., *A Place in the Sun: Africa in Italian Colonial Culture from Post-unification to the Present* (Berkeley: University of California Press, 2003). On Portugal, see the essays in Margarida Calafate Ribeiro and Ana Paula Ferreira, eds., *Fantasmas e fantasias imperiais no imaginário português contemporâneo* (Porto: Campo das letras, 2003). The chapters in John M. MacKenzie, ed., *European Empires and the People: Popular Responses to Imperialism in France, Britain, the Netherlands, Belgium, Germany and Italy* (Manchester: Manchester University Press, 2011), provide a comparative perspective.

[84] Elizabeth Buettner, *Europe after Empire: Decolonization, Society, and Culture* (Cambridge: Cambridge University Press, 2016). On individual countries, see Todd Shepard, *The Invention of Decolonization: The Algerian War and the Remaking of France* (Ithaca, NY: Cornell University Press, 2006); Gert Oostindie, *Postkoloniaal Nederland: Vijfenzestig jaar vergeten, herdenken, verdringen* (Amsterdam: Bert Bakker, 2010), translated as *Postcolonial Netherlands: Sixty-Five Years of Forgetting, Commemorating, Silencing* (Amsterdam: Amsterdam University Press, 2014); the contributions in Elleke Boehmer and Sarah De Mul, eds., *The Postcolonial Low Countries: Literature, Colonialism, and Multiculturalism* (Lanham: Lexington Books, 2012); Jordanna Bailkin, *The Afterlife of Empire* (Berkeley: University of California Press, 2012); and Britta Schilling, *Postcolonial Germany: Memories of Empire in a Decolonized Nation* (Oxford: Oxford University Press, 2014); as well as the literature cited in note 83.

[85] Todd Shepard, *Sex, France, and Arab Men, 1962–1979* (Chicago: University of Chicago Press, 2017).

[86] Goody, *Renaissances*.

consideration of the global context in which it evolved.[87] European scholars were increasingly part of a global republic of letters stretching from Harvard to Kolkata and beyond.[88] Some of the continent's greatest twentieth-century thinkers had biographies that linked them to lands beyond Europe – Thomas Mann to his Brazilian ancestry, George Orwell to his birthplace in India, and so on. Fernand Braudel's history, Albert Camus's philosophy, Pierre Bourdieu's anthropology, Jacques Derrida's linguistics, and Yves Saint Laurent's haute couture all were influenced by their creators' ties to Algeria.[89] Even more marked was the world's impact on Europe's popular cultures. The most important twentieth-century example is cultural Americanization, from jazz in the interwar years to postwar Hollywood, so forcefully described in Victoria de Grazia's *Irresistible Empire* (2005).[90] Europe's body cultures were shaped by outside influences; just consider the twentieth-century history of the rise of Europe's Brazilian waxing salons.[91] Historians have also shown an increasing interest in the global influences on European culinary culture, from Indian curries to Turkish kebabs.[92] Likewise, Europe's religious landscapes have for centuries been influenced by global exchange. In western Europe, Muslim communities became institutionalized in the early twentieth century.[93] Buddhist, Sikh, and other groups followed. Spiritualism, as brilliantly shown in Ruth Harris's work, was a global

---

[87] Sebastian Conrad, "Enlightenment in Global History: A Historiographical Critique," *American Historical Review* 117, no. 4 (2012): 999–1027.

[88] Kapil Raj, *Relocating Modern Science: Circulation and the Construction of Knowledge in South Asia and Europe, 1650–1900* (Basingstoke: Macmillan, 2007); and more generally, the contributions in Kapil Raj et al., eds., *The Brokered World: Go-Betweens and Global Intelligence, 1770–1820* (Sagamore Beach: Science History Publications, 2009); as well as Kris Manjapra, *Age of Entanglement: German and Indian Intellectuals across Empire* (Cambridge, MA: Harvard University Press, 2014).

[89] Sandra Ponzanesi and Adriano José Habed, eds., *Postcolonial Intellectuals in Europe: Critics, Artists, Movements, and Their Publics* (London: Rowman and Littlefield International, 2018), provides an overview. Manuel Borutta, "Braudel in Algier: Die kolonialen Wurzeln der 'Méditerranée' und der 'spatial turn'," *Historische Zeitschrift* 303, no. 1 (2016): 1–38, offers a case study for the field of History. George Steinmetz, *The Colonial Origins of Modern Social Thought: French Sociology and the Overseas Empire* (Princeton: Princeton University Press, 2023), looks at social science.

[90] Victoria de Grazia, *Irresistible Empire: America's Advance through Twentieth-Century Europe* (Cambridge, MA: Harvard University Press, 2005); see also Nicholas Hewitt, "Black Montmartre: American Jazz and Music Hall in Paris in the Interwar Years," *Journal of Romance Studies* 5, no. 3 (2005): 25–31.

[91] Maria Lidola, "Negotiating Integration in Berlin's Waxing Studios: Brazilian Migrants' Gendered Appropriation of Urban Consumer Spaces and 'Ethnic' Entrepreneurship," *Journal of Contemporary History* 49, no. 1 (2014): 228–51.

[92] Panikos Panayi, *Spicing up Britain: The Multicultural History of British Food* (London: Reaktion Books, 2008).

[93] David Motadel, "The Making of Muslim Communities in Western Europe, 1914–1939," in *Transnational Islam in Interwar Europe: Muslim Activists and Thinkers*, ed. Götz Nordbruch and Umar Ryad (London: Macmillan, 2014), 13–43.

phenomenon.[94] Most importantly perhaps, modern Europe's public sphere, which emerged in the eighteenth century and soon reached even the smallest village, became global.[95]

Taken together, this growing literature, although still fragmented, compellingly demonstrates that Europe has always been an arena of transcontinental interactions, as much a recipient of outside influences as a force transforming the world. To be sure, its interconnections with the world were never static but changed over time. Their impact was uneven, affecting some parts of the continent, such as port cities, university towns, and capitals, more (and in different ways) than others.

–

Apart from allowing us to see Europe's deep entanglements with the wider world, global history forces us to rethink our epistemological parameters when studying the continent's history. It prompts us to question some of the major concepts of modern European history, such as class, nation, revolution, public and private, industrialization, urbanization, and secularization. And it enables us to critically reflect on some of our field's fundamental paradigms – most prominently, perhaps, modernity – and periodizations. It forces us to question the universality of our analytic weights and measures. Noting that the categories of European history are neither objective nor universal, Dipesh Chakrabarty and his disciples have compellingly warned against imposing them on the history of the non-European world.[96] No doubt, such categories offer lenses that can distort as much as they allow us to see. What is more, they impose European standards on the world, making non-European history appear to be deficient. Some have even questioned whether societies around the world share the most basic cognitive ground, an assumption made by those who use European concepts to study the world.

Yet radical relativism cannot be the answer, as Chakrabarty himself has acknowledged. There is a tension between the need to sufficiently consider the

---

[94] Ruth Harris, "Rolland, Gandhi and Madeleine Slade: Spiritual Politics, France and the Wider World," *French History* 27, no. 4 (2013): 579–99.

[95] Valeska Huber and Jürgen Osterhammel, eds., *Global Publics: Their Power and Their Limits, 1870–1990* (Oxford: Oxford University Press, 2020) provides some contributions about this phenomenon. Heidi J. S. Tworek, *News from Germany: The Competition to Control World Communications, 1900–1945* (Cambridge, MA: Harvard University Press, 2019), is an insightful case study. Jürgen Habermas, *The Structural Translation of the Public Sphere: An Inquiry into a Category of Bourgeois Society* (Cambridge: Polity Press, 1989), which was first published in 1962, offers the more general European context.

[96] Dipesh Chakrabarty, *Provincializing Europe: Postcolonial Thought and Historical Difference* (Princeton: Princeton University Press, 2000). Hajime Nakamura, *Parallel Developments: A Comparative History of Ideas*, ed. Ronald Burr (New York: Kodansha, 1975), argues that some concepts are similar across the world.

uniqueness of every smaller geographic space we study and the need to have some basic (ecumenical) consensus on major historical concepts when writing world history.[97] Besides, it is not unproblematic to brand all concepts of modernity, from urbanization to secularization, as European (or Western), as to do so assumes that these phenomena are essentially European when in fact they often were not: They were neither embraced universally in all parts of Europe (which we should be careful not to essentialize), nor completely absent in other parts of the world, and were themselves shaped by global entanglements. These debates can help historians of modern Europe be more critical when using allegedly universal concepts, paradigms, and periodizations. At the same time, when studying European history, and particularly the history of Europe's global connections, we may find it useful to adopt concepts developed in the field of world history that stress hybridity, syncretism, and interconnectedness.

-

Overall, the growing body of literature on the global history of the continent may come to critically reshape our notion of Europe (and European history) and its boundaries. Although Europe is, as we have seen, almost impossible to define either as a physical concept or a sociocultural idea, historians all too often treat it as a monolithic entity, ignoring its inherent diversity and permeability.[98] A truly global history of Europe, which takes into account not only the continent's internal heterogeneity but also its connections to the outside world, would counter essentialist notions of Europe.

These reflections on Europe also shed light on broader questions about continents as ontological categories.[99] The concept of continents (from *terra*

---

[97] Dominic Sachsenmaier, "World History as Ecumenical History?" *Journal of World History* 18, no. 4 (2007): 465–89, convincingly stresses this need for consensus.

[98] Celia Applegate, "A Europe of Regions: Reflections on the Historiography of sub-National Places in Modern Times," *American Historical Review* 104, no. 4 (1999): 1157–82, on diversity within Europe and within European nation-states.

[99] Important reflections on the relationship between continental and global history have also been provided by historians of Africa, see Frederick Cooper, "What Is the Concept of Globalization Good for? An African Historian's Perspective," *African Affairs* 100 (2001): 189–213; Leslie Witz, "Africa (Not) in World History: A Review from the South (Part 1)," *Journal of World History* 27, no. 1 (2016): 103–20; and Witz, "Surveying Africa in World History: A View from the South (Part 2)," *Journal of World History* 27, no. 4 (2016): 669–85. Moreover, over the last years, historians from various other regions of the world, such as Latin America, North America, or the Middle East, have begun to systematically reflect about the global history of their regional spaces, see Matthew Brown, "The Global History of Latin America," *Journal of Global History* 10, no. 3 (2015): 365–86; the chapters in Liat Kozma, Cyrus Schayegh, and Avner Wishnitzer, eds., *A Global Middle East: Mobility, Materiality and Culture in the Modern Age, 1880–1940* (London: Bloomsbury, 2016); David Thelen, "The Nation and beyond: Transnational Perspectives on United States History," *Journal of American History* 86, no. 3 (1999): 965–75; and Thomas Bender, *Rethinking American History in a Global Age* (Berkeley: University of

continens), commonly defined as large, continuous landmasses usually separated from one another by water, has been used to map the world since antiquity, when the threefold continental scheme of Europe, Asia, and Africa was invented. Although historians are generally cautious about the use of generalizing geographies, references to continents are, curiously, seldom questioned. Yet the division of the world into continents is hardly indisputable. In their 1997 book *The Myth of Continents*, Martin Lewis and Kären Wigen issued a powerful warning about the continental taxonomy: "Otherwise sophisticated and self-critical works habitually essentialize continents, adopting their boundaries as frameworks for analyzing and classifying phenomena to which they simply do not apply."[100] "Dividing the world into a handful of fundamental units in this way may be convenient," they noted, "but it does injustice to the complexities of global geography, and it leads to faulty comparisons." Their critique in a way echoed the words of the German geographer Alfred Hettner, who as early as 1893 mocked those who felt enchanted "when looking from Gibraltar to Africa or from Constantinople to Asia or crossing the Urals from Europe to Asia" and who believed that "the words European, Asian, African, American, Australian" alluded to "a distinctive characteristic of land and people" in specific parts of the world.[101] This does not mean that the epistemological distinctions between continents – or, indeed, "European history" as a disciplinary category – are useless in historical research. It does mean, however, that we need to be conscious of different spatial layers that allow us to consider internal diversity and external relations.[102]

California Press, 2002). Matthias Middell and Katja Naumann, "Global History and the Spatial Turn: From the Impact of Area Studies to the Study of Critical Junctures of Globalization," *Journal of Global History* 5, no. 1 (2010): 149–70; and, more broadly, the essays in Birgit Schäbler, ed., *Area Studies und die Welt: Weltregionen und neue Globalgeschichte* (Vienna: Mandelbaum Verlag, 2007), offer more general insights into the relationship between regional and global history.

[100] Martin W. Lewis and Kären E. Wigen, *The Myth of Continents: A Critique of Metageography* (Berkeley: University of California Press, 1997), here p. 1, is a path-breaking work, although I do not share the authors' enthusiasm for area studies and the history of world regions, which also includes "Europe" as a category. On the construction of (subcontinental) "regions" as categories of study, see the contributions in Diana Mishkova and Balázs Trencsényi, eds., *European Regions and Boundaries: A Conceptual History* (New York: Berghahn Books, 2017).

[101] Alfred Hettner, "Über den Begriff der Erdteile und seine geographische Bedeutung," in *Verhandlungen des Zehnten Deutschen Geographentages zu Stuttgart am 5., 6. und 7. April 1893*, ed. Georg Kollm (Berlin: Geographische Verlagshandlung Dietrich Reimer, 1893), 188–98, here p. 189. Alfred Hettner, "Die geographische Einteilung der Erdoberfläche," *Geographische Zeitschrift* 14 (1908): 1–13, offers further reflections.

[102] Jacques Revel, *Jeux d'échelles: La micro-analyse à l'expérience* (Paris: Gallimard/Éd. du Seuil, 1996).

Spatial categories will remain important units of analysis in historical studies.[103] We constantly, consciously or unconsciously, map the world using local and urban, national and imperial, regional and continental, and other spatial taxonomies, and at times make even simpler distinctions, be they civilizational or cultural (East and West), economic (North and South), or political (First, Second, and Third World); indeed, such broad essentialist geographies can be found at the heart of works by intellectuals as diverse as Oswald Spengler, Samuel Huntington, Niall Ferguson, Dipesh Chakrabarty, and Edward Said.[104]

Yet the use of spatial categories in general is not unproblematic. It is not just that they can obscure the internal heterogeneity of a discrete space and its connections to (and similarities with) the outside world. Spatial divisions all too often also conflate physical and sociocultural criteria. The spatial units we use, from the local to the continental, are usually understood to be not only coherent physical entities (physical geography) but also coherent human (cultural, social, economic, and political) entities (human geography). In reality, however, there is no necessary congruence between physical and human spaces. Human life cannot always be meaningfully divided according to physical geographies or maps. The use of spatial categories may thus mislead us into making false generalizations about the inhabitants of a particular territory. Indeed, ascribing distinctive social, cultural, political, or economic features (and histories) to the peoples living in a specific physical territory is a form of environmental determinism. Physical maps cannot simply be superimposed onto sociocultural human maps. Moreover, physical spaces are usually difficult to define along clear lines in terms of natural

---

[103] Henri Lefebvre, *The Production of Space* (London: Blackwell, 1991), which was first published in 1974, remains one of the most thoughtful reflections on physical, social, and mental spaces. The chapters in Phil Hubbard, Rob Kitchin, and Gill Valentine, eds., *Key Thinkers on Space and Place* (London: Sage, 2004), provide a good overview of the works of major intellectuals on space. On more general reflections about space in historical studies, following the spatial turn, see Jürgen Osterhammel, "Die Wiederkehr des Raumes: Geopolitik, Geohistorie und historische Geographie," *Neue Polititsche Literatur* 43 (1998): 374–97; Reinhart Koselleck, *Zeitschichten: Studien zur Historik* (Frankfurt: Suhrkamp, 2000), 78–96; Iris Schröder and Sabine Höhler, "Welt-Räume: Annährungen an eine Geschichte der Globalität im 20. Jahrhundert," in *Welt-Räume: Geschichte, Geographie und Globalisierung seit 1900*, ed. Iris Schröder and Sabine Höhler (Frankfurt: Campus Verlag, 2005), 9–47; and, more generally, Sebouh David Aslanian et al., "AHR Conversation: How Size Matters: The Question of Scale in History," *American Historical Review* 118, no. 5 (2013): 1431–72.

[104] Oswald Spengler, *Der Untergang des Abendlandes: Umrisse einer Morphologie der Weltgeschichte*, 2 vols. (Munich: C. H. Beck, 1918–22); translated as *The Decline of the West*, 2 vols. (New York: Knopf, 1926–8); Samuel P. Huntington, *The Clash of Civilizations and the Remaking of World Order* (New York: Simon and Schuster, 1996); Ferguson, *Civilization*; Chakrabarty, *Provincializing Europe*; and Said, *Orientalism*.

topography, tectonic plates, climate, or flora and fauna. Likewise, human spaces are fragile constructs created through human interaction (and imagination), which are constantly evolving and are not naturally determined. They are not given but socially created, forged through social, cultural, economic, and political practices and discourses. In any case, any geographical space we might use in our studies is no more than an abstract construct based on a mental map.[105] And finally, we must also be aware that the spatial division of the world can (and often does) imply hierarchies of and value statements about spatial units.

In short, we need to bear in mind that spatial units are imprecise categories of analysis. We also need to be mindful that physical space and human (sociocultural, economic, or political-legal) space do not necessarily correspond. Moreover, to take into account internal heterogeneity and external connections (and similarities), we must consider multiple scales when studying the past, interweaving different spaces in our analysis.[106] There is no contradiction between local, national, regional, continental, and global history, as humans almost always act in multiple spaces simultaneously. Although different spaces have varying degrees of importance depending on the topic, any serious work of historical scholarship will be multilayered, considering different spatial levels. Ultimately, spatial categories are important units of analysis, which – along with thematic and temporal concepts – will in all likelihood remain, not least for pragmatic, heuristic reasons, crucial in organizing historical knowledge (and structuring our discipline).

It seems almost impossible to write a modern world history without Europe, which has shaped global interactions over the last centuries more than any other continent. Conversely, a history of modern Europe that ignores the wider world will inevitably remain incomplete. Global history is not the tombstone of European history. It is a necessary impulse that will enrich the field and prompt us to question its most fundamental assumptions. This will mean rethinking the continent's political, social, cultural, and economic histories from a global angle, taking into account sources in languages and archives not previously considered and transgressing history's geographical sub-disciplines. This will ultimately help reshape our understanding of the boundaries of modern Europe – and the field of modern European history.

---

[105] Elspeth Graham, "What Is a Mental Map?," *Area* 8, no. 4 (1976): 259–62.
[106] Richard Drayton and David Motadel, "The Futures of Global History," *Journal of Global History* 13, no. 1 (2018): 1–21.

In the end, the idea of Europe as a closed entity has always been an illusion. Europe and the world are not as far apart as some of us might like to believe. Europa herself, after all, as any student of her mythological past will confirm, was non-European, a Phoenician beauty abducted from the shores of Asia. Europe *per se* was constituted from the outside. In short, it is time to deprovincialize Europe.

2   Global Conjunctures and the Remaking of European Political History

Sebastian Conrad

Writing the history of Europe is never neutral and hardly a mere scholarly exercise. When the European past is invoked, politics are at stake. A recent instantiation is the vogue of European histories that has appeared since the turn of the millennium. In response to the manifold predicaments of the "West," symbolized by 11 September 2001, and the financial crisis of 2008 (and manifest in the nostalgic populisms that have since swept across Europe and elsewhere), historians and other pundits have come to the rescue of what they see as an embattled civilization. To the perceived threats posed by massive cross-border migration, political Islamism, and the economic rise of East Asia, they have reacted with a renewed emphasis on Europe's uniqueness: a Europe made by science, secularism, the Enlightenment, and human rights. Much of this reads like plain, old-fashioned Eurocentrism – but it is not quite the same thing. Even though frequently written in a triumphalist tone, many works in this camp nonetheless betray the sense of a castle under siege and the fear that "what we are living through now is the end of 500 years of Western predomin- ance."[1] On the surface, it is still the same old story, but the new Eurocentrism is no longer the unquestioned bedrock of European hegemony; it is now defensive in nature.[2]

While this particular manifestation is thus only a decade old, the pattern looks highly familiar. For many years, the history of most European societies, and of Europe as a whole, was largely narrated as a set of self-contained stories, decoupled from the rest of the world. Historians presented European history as self-generated, autonomous, sui generis – and thus ignored, if not

---

[1] Niall Ferguson, *Civilisation: The West and the Rest* (London: Allen Lane, 2011), 322.

[2] Examples include John M. Headley, *The Europeanization of the World: On the Origins of Human Rights and Democracy* (Princeton: Princeton University Press, 2008); Anthony Pagden, *Worlds at War: The 2,500-Year Struggle between East and West* (Oxford: Oxford University Press, 2008); Heinrich August Winkler, *Geschichte des Westens: Von den Anfängen in der Antike bis zum 20. Jahrhundert* (Munich: C. H. Beck, 2009); Toby E. Huff, *Intellectual Curiosity and the Scientific Revolution: A Global Perspective* (Cambridge: Cambridge University Press, 2010); Ricardo Duchesne, *The Uniqueness of Western Civilization* (Leiden: Brill, 2011).

28   Sebastian Conrad

effaced, the global conditions in which this history unfolded. Has this changed as a result of the global turn, and in what ways?

There are indeed signs that things have begun to shift. Over the past decades, the writing of European history – in both its incarnations, as the history *of* Europe and as the histories of nations *in* Europe – has seen fundamental transformations. Many historians across the continent have begun to move beyond writing isolated histories of individual countries and have abandoned container-thinking when analyzing the national past. This was, to be sure, not entirely a new beginning: Themes such as migration, trade, and imperialism had always been a regular feature of national narratives. In addition, the comparative projects initiated in the 1980s and 1990s have emphasized parallels and pointed out general patterns, and thus collectively undermined the sense that nations were out there all on their own.[3] More recently, scholars have sought to go beyond comparisons, with history becoming connected, trans-regional, and *croisée*.[4] Postcolonial approaches were instrumental in challenging the idea of Europe as the autonomous entity it had long been taken to be. Imperialist forays not only left their traces in the colonial world but also fundamentally transformed European societies, which increasingly felt "at home with the empire."[5] Beyond the strictly colonial

---

[3] These studies were, however, still firmly focused on Europe. See Heinz-Gerhard Haupt and Jürgen Kocka, eds., *Comparative and Transnational History: Central European Approaches and New Perspectives* (New York: Berghahn Books, 2009); Deborah A. Cohen and Maura O'Connor, eds., *Comparison and History: Europe in Cross-National Perspective* (New York: Routledge, 2004); Heinz-Gerhard Haupt and Jürgen Kocka, eds., *Geschichte und Vergleich: Ansätze und Ergebnisse international vergleichender Geschichtsschreibung* (Frankfurt am Main: Campus, 1996).

[4] Michael Werner and Bénédicte Zimmermann, "Penser l'histoire croisée: entre empirie et réflexivité," *Annales HSS* 58, no. 1 (2003): 7–36; Michel Espagne, "Sur les limites du comparatisme en histoire culturelle," in "Les objets et les choses," ed. Francine Soubiran-Paillet, special issue, *Genèses: Sciences Sociales et Histoire* 17 (1994): 112–21; Sanjay Subrahmanyam, "Connected Histories: Notes towards a Reconfiguration of Early Modern Eurasia," in *Beyond Binary Histories: Re-imagining Eurasia to c. 1830*, ed. Victor B. Lieberman (Ann Arbor: University of Michigan Press, 1997), 289–315.

[5] To reference the title of Catherine Hall and Sonya O. Rose, eds., *At Home with the Empire: Metropolitan Culture and the Imperial World* (Cambridge: Cambridge University Press, 2006). See also Kathleen E. Wilson, ed., *A New Imperial History: Culture, Identity, and Modernity in Britain and the Empire, 1660–1840* (Cambridge: Cambridge University Press, 2004); Wendy Webster, *Englishness and Empire, 1939–1965* (Oxford: Oxford University Press, 2005); Andrew Thompson, *The Empire Strikes Back? The Impact of Imperialism on Britain from the Mid-nineteenth Century* (Harlow: Pearson, 2005); Nicolas Bancel et al., eds., *Ruptures post-coloniales: Les nouveaux visages de la société française* (Paris: La Découverte, 2010); Margarida Calafate Ribeiro and Ana Paula Ferreira, eds., *Fantasmas e fantasias imperiais no imaginário português contemporâneo* (Porto: Campo das Letras, 2003); Nicola Labanca, "Imperi immaginati: Recenti cultural studies sul colonialismo italiano," *Studi piacentini* 28 (2000): 145–68; Patrizia Palumbo, ed., *A Place in the Sun: Africa in Italian Colonial Culture from Post-unification to the Present* (Berkeley: University of California Press, 2003); Ruth Ben-Ghiat and Mia Fuller, eds., *Italian Colonialism* (New York: Palgrave Macmillan, 2005);

sphere, transnational history allowed historians to see that European nations were part of a globalizing world and, at the same time, that the world reached deep into European societies themselves.[6]

Since the early 2010s, however, the vocabulary that evokes a cutting-edge appeal has shifted to the "global." Is this yet another turn, or rather a fancy label for more of the same? What is the purchase of the new designation, and is it able to do analytical work that the earlier approaches could not? Maybe it is still too early to tell – not least because the rhetoric of the "global" has become so pervasive that the term itself remains rather fuzzy. Should it be equated with a focus on connections, with the inclusion of non-Western societies, or with planetary coverage? There are now many competing approaches claiming that label, frequently in rather impressionistic ways. In some cases, the terminology of "world" and "global" is used freely whenever cross-border movements are touched upon. As soon as we move from theoretical debates to historiographical practice, it is not always easy (nor even helpful) to erect rigid boundaries between approaches that are not hermetically sealed off from one another.[7]

If the concept of the "global" nevertheless comes with a certain appeal, it is because it promises to move scholars beyond two impasses into which previous approaches regularly ran. First, global perspectives help to break out of what may be called the bilateral framework of connected and transnational histories. In histories of reception, of colonizer and colonized, of migrants from A to B, "transnational" is all too frequently a shorthand for simply connecting two locations. While it does mean that historians are no longer confined to just one place, ultimately such a bilateral framework remains problematic as it still tends to disregard the larger, potentially global, context within which the two histories in question unfolded.

Second, transnational approaches only go so far in integrating broader contexts into their narratives. Especially when dressed up as transnational

---

Hubrecht Willem van den Doel, *Afscheid van Indië: De val van het Nederlandse imperium in Azië* (Amsterdam: Prometheus Books, 2000); Gert Oostindie, *Paradise Overseas: The Dutch Caribbean; Colonialism and Its Transatlantic Legacies* (Oxford: Macmillan, 2005).

[6] Michel Espagne and Michaël Werner, eds., *Transferts: Les relations interculturelles dans l'espace franco-allemand (XVIIIᵉ et XIXᵉ siècle)* (Paris: Éd. Recherche sur les civilisations, 1988); Patricia Clavin, "Defining Transnationalism," *Contemporary European History* 14, no. 4 (2005): 421–39; Christopher A. Bayly, et al., "AHR Conversation: On Transnational History," *American Historical Review* 111, no. 5 (2006): 1440–64; Gunilla Budde, Sebastian Conrad, and Oliver Janz, eds., *Transnationale Geschichte: Themen, Tendenzen und Theorien* (Göttingen: Vandenhoeck & Ruprecht, 2006); Akira Iriye and Pierre-Yves Saunier, eds., *The Palgrave Dictionary of Transnational History: From the Mid-19th Century to the Present Day* (Basingstoke: Palgrave Macmillan, 2009).

[7] Sebastian Conrad, *What Is Global History?* (Princeton: Princeton University Press, 2016).

histories of one country, they often lead to more colorful, fancier national histories, but national histories nonetheless.[8] Methodologically speaking, the transnational approach in many cases only gestures at the global. Ultimately, whenever the transnational is invoked as a context in order to better understand a nation, it tends to reproduce the spatialities it purports to challenge.[9] Frequently, then, larger contexts serve as a foil against which to situate the nation, or indeed as a stage for the nation, rather than as the scale on which to address questions of cause and effect.

This latter strategy – using the global as a scale – is surely where the promise of global approaches lies. It is, however, important to keep in mind that global perspectives are no panacea; they are not the one superior angle that delegitimizes all others, and they work better for some themes while being less effective for others. Moreover, the appeal of global history is by no means uniform, not least because the politics of the approach vary. For some, the global appears as an arena in which to parade national significance, compiled "out of love for our country."[10] For others, it offers a corrective to national myths.[11] As a result, global perspectives are welcomed as a critical challenge in countries where traditions of national history writing are well established and (all too) firmly engrained. By contrast, such an intervention may seem less urgent in places where national historiographies were less well hedged, and where national identities seem less stable, as in some countries of the former Eastern Bloc and even in Italy. Different again is the situation when writing the history of multinational entities such as the Habsburg Empire or the Soviet Union: In a space that has been characterized as an empire of diasporas, with its long post-national (and at the same time imperial – or was it Eurasian?)

[8] Sebastian Conrad and Jürgen Osterhammel, eds., *Das Kaiserreich transnational: Deutschland in der Welt 1871–1914* (Göttingen: Vandenhoeck & Ruprecht, 2004); Thomas Bender, *A Nation among Nations: America's Place in World History* (New York: Hill and Wang, 2006); Georgiy Kasianov and Philipp Ther, eds., *A Laboratory of Transnational History: Ukraine and Ukrainian Historiography since 1991* (Budapest: Central European University Press, 2008); Vesna Drapac, *Constructing Yugoslavia: A Transnational History* (New York: Springer, 2010); "The Italian Risorgimento: Transnational Perspectives," special issue, *Modern Italy* 19, no. 1 (2014); Niall Whelehan, ed., *Transnational Perspectives on Modern Irish History* (London: Routledge, 2014); Tyler Stovall, *Transnational France: The Modern History of a Universal Nation* (New York: Routledge, 2015).
[9] Arif Dirlik, "Performing the World: Reality and Representation in the Making of World Histor(ies)," *Journal of World History* 16, no. 4 (2005): 391–410.
[10] Andrea Giardina, during the roundtable "Storia mondiale dell'Italia," Rome, 30 November 2017, online. Giardina goes on to affirm that "Italy is an extraordinary country, much better than it is usually represented" (quote at 22:10). The roundtable discusses Andrea Giardina, ed., *Storia mondiale dell'Italia* (Bari: Laterza, 2017).
[11] See the debate about Patrick Boucheron, ed., *Histoire mondiale de la France* (Paris: Éd. du Seuil, 2017), discussed in more detail in Chapter 1.

history, the call to go transnational and global comes across as much less innovative and iconoclast.[12]

For all these reasons, the degree to which the historiography of different countries (and of different topics) has undergone a global turn varies. And even where such a turn has taken place, many studies remain confined to individual nations. Nevertheless, when we take an overarching view and look at many initiatives and new forays together, a picture emerges that suggests a gradual rewriting of the European past. As far as the subject of this chapter – Europe's political history and the history of political power more broadly conceived – is concerned, this recent literature demonstrates that crucial watersheds of European history are now seen as part of larger configurations and as responses to global challenges.

Let us briefly look at some of the iconic moments of European political history. One symbolic battlefield has been the reinterpretation of the French Revolution – the moment that in standard accounts marked the rupture between tradition and modernity, and by extension between Europe and the rest of the world. In revisionist readings, the French Revolution is no longer seen as simply initiating modern ways of thinking and organizing society that then gradually radiated out from Europe. Instead, historians claim that the "causes, internal dynamics, and consequences of the French Revolution all grew out of France's increasing participation in processes of globalization."[13] Reenergized by the growing scholarship on the Atlantic waves of revolution, in particular in Haiti, the French Revolution now looks global not only in its repercussions but also in its very origins.[14]

[12] Yuri Slezkine, "The USSR as a Communal Apartment, or How a Socialist State Promoted Ethnic Particularism," *Slavic Review* 53, no. 2 (1994): 414–52; Terry Martin, *The Affirmative Action Empire: Nations and Nationalism in the Soviet Union, 1923–1939* (Ithaca, NY: Cornell University Press, 2001); Francine Hirsch, *Empire of Nations: Ethnographic Knowledge and the Making of the Soviet Union* (Ithaca, NY: Cornell University Press, 2005); Stephen Kotkin, "Mongol Commonwealth? Exchange and Governance across the Post-Mongol Space," *Kritika: Explorations in Russian and Eurasian History* 8, no. 3 (2007): 487–531; Ilya Gerasimov, Sergey Glebov, and Marina Mogilner, "The Postimperial Meets the Postcolonial: Russian Historical Experience and the Postcolonial Moment," *Ab Imperio* 2 (2013): 97–135; Lewis H. Siegelbaum and Leslie Page Moch, *Broad Is My Native Land: Repertoires and Regimes of Migration in Russia's Twentieth Century* (Ithaca, NY: Cornell University Press, 2014); Rachel Applebaum, "The Friendship Project: Socialist Internationalism in the Soviet Union and Czechoslovakia in the 1950s and 1960s," *Slavic Review* 74, no. 3 (2015): 484–507; Erik R. Scott, *Familiar Strangers: The Georgian Diaspora and the Evolution of Soviet Empire* (Oxford: Oxford University Press, 2016). For an exploration of the potential of global approaches for Russian and Soviet history, see Martin Aust, ed., *Globalisierung imperial und sozialistisch: Russland und die Sowjetunion in der Globalgeschichte, 1851–1991* (Frankfurt: Campus, 2013).
[13] Suzanne Desan, Lynn Hunt, and William Max Nelson, eds., *The French Revolution in Global Perspective* (Ithaca, NY: Cornell University Press, 2013), 4.
[14] Bailey Stone, *Reinterpreting the French Revolution: A Global-Historical Perspective* (Cambridge: Cambridge University Press, 2002); Joseph Klaits and Michael H. Haltzel, eds., *The Global Ramifications of the French Revolution* (Cambridge: Cambridge University Press,

Similarly, the Enlightenment, long celebrated as the pivotal moment that defined political and cultural modernity as European, has begun to be decentered. On the one hand, large parts of Enlightenment cosmology – debates about the character of humankind, the idea of the law of nations and an international order, the ethnological and geographical explorations of the globe, the comparative study of language and religion, the theories of free trade and the civilizing effects of commerce, the notions of race and also of cosmopolitanism – must be seen as responses to the cognitive challenge that was posed by an increasingly integrated globe. On the other hand, scholars now argue that the Enlightenment was not confined to a short period in European history but had a longer, and global, history that involved a multitude of different actors throughout the world.[15]

The organizational shape that political modernity assumed in Europe crystallized in the institution of the nation-state. In the age of high imperialism and into the twentieth century, the ethnic-cultural cohesion and bureaucratic rationality of the European nation-state were contrasted to a variety of seemingly premodern polities, ranging from the large empires of the Ottomans and the Qing to small-scale units built on personal interactions. The nation-state was seen as a European achievement, and the lack thereof elsewhere was used to legitimize interventions and empire. In recent years, however, historians have effectively reconfigured this classical field of the discipline, questioning Eric Hobsbawm's verdict that Europe was nationalism's "original home."[16] They have begun to move toward an understanding of nationalism as globally constituted and not as the natural outgrowth of prior and long-standing internal traditions. Nation-states, in such a reading, played a mediating role between the local, on the one hand, and the integration of world markets and an international order, on the other. Projecting themselves backward in time and inventing long genealogies, nineteenth-century nation-states were in fact geopolitical innovations that fundamentally altered existing conceptions of space.[17]

2002 [1994]); C. A. Bayly, *The Birth of the Modern World, 1780–1914: Global Connections and Comparisons* (Oxford: Blackwell, 2004); David Armitage and Sanjay Subrahmanyam, eds., *The Age of Revolutions in Global Context, c. 1760–1840* (New York: Red Globe Press, 2009); Alan Forrest and Matthias Middell, eds., *The Routledge Companion to the French Revolution in World History* (London: Routledge, 2016); and Bryan A. Banks and Erica Johnson, eds., *The French Revolution and Religion in Global Perspective: Freedom and Faith* (Cham: Palgrave Macmillan, 2017).

[15] Sebastian Conrad, "Enlightenment in Global History: A Historiographical Critique," *American Historical Review* 117, no. 4 (2012): 999–1027.

[16] Eric J. Hobsbawm, *Nations and Nationalism since 1780: Programme, Myth, Reality* (Cambridge: Cambridge University Press, 1990), 151.

[17] Manu Goswami, "Rethinking the Modular Nation Form: Toward a Sociohistorical Conception of Nationalism," *Comparative Studies in Society and History* 44, no. 4 (2002): 776–83; Christopher L. Hill, *National History and the World of Nations: Capital State and the*

Such a perspective opens up avenues for research that transcends the logic of states as fixed containers and traces the ways in which multidirectional forms of mobility – of things, ideas, and people – were instrumental in producing national territorialization. For nineteenth-century European history, for example, this invites us to follow the migration flows that propelled millions of people around the world. Those leaving the continent frequently engaged in "long-distance nationalism," while migrants from elsewhere who arrived in Europe were the object of exclusionary measures that helped foster a sense of national belonging.[18] Finally, European cities emerged as crucial sites for the development of colonized countries' elites and the construction of anti-colonial nationalisms.[19] Taken together, this new strand of research demonstrates that the local, nation-states, "Europe," and the global can fruitfully be seen as scales, both of historical agency and of retrospective analysis.

According to the textbook version of European history, these nation-states then reached out, spreading goods, people, institutions, and values around the world. What recent scholarship has shown, however, is that nation-states and imperialism were not simply consecutive stages. In important ways, European nationalism and state-building were synchronous, and deeply enmeshed, with imperial interventions. More generally, key institutions of political, social, and cultural modernity were made in spaces that included both metropole and colony. Historians have explored the ways in which imperial interventions were translated into metropolitan concerns and have studied the "repercussions" that practices that had originated, or had been tested, at the colonial periphery could

Rhetoric of History in Japan, France, and the United States (Durham, NC: Duke University Press, 2008); John Breuilly, "Nationalism as Global History," in *Nationalism and Globalisation: Conflicting or Complementary?* ed. Daphne Halikiopoulou and Sofia Vasilopoulou (London: Routledge, 2011), 65–83; Stephen W. Sawyer, "Ces nations façonnées par les empires et la globalisation: Réécrire le récit national du xixe siècle aujourd'-hui," *Annales HSS* 69, no. 1 (2014): 117–37.

[18] Mark I. Choate, *Emigrant Nation: The Making of Italy Abroad* (Cambridge, MA: Harvard University Press, 2008); Adam McKeown, *Melancholy Order: Asian Migration and the Globalization of Borders* (New York: Columbia University Press, 2008); and Sebastian Conrad, *Globalisation and the Nation in Imperial Germany* (Cambridge: Cambridge University Press, 2010), which was first published in 2006.

[19] Michael Goebel, *Anti-Imperial Metropolis: Interwar Paris and the Seeds of Third-World Nationalism* (Cambridge: Cambridge University Press, 2015). See also Jennifer Anne Boittin, *Colonial Metropolis: The Urban Grounds of anti-Imperialism and Feminism in Interwar Paris* (Lincoln: University of Nebraska Press, 2010); Noor-Aiman I. Khan, *Egyptian-Indian Nationalist Collaboration and the British Empire* (New York: Palgrave Macmillan, 2011); Nathanael Kuck, "Anticolonialism in a Post-Imperial Environment: The Case of Berlin, 1914–1933," *Journal of Contemporary History* 49, no. 1 (2014): 134–59; Marc Matera, *Black London: The Imperial Metropolis and Decolonization in the Twentieth Century* (Berkeley: University of California Press, 2015); Daniel Brückenhaus, *Policing Transnational Protest: Liberal Imperialism and the Surveillance of Anticolonialists in Europe, 1905–1945* (New York: Oxford University Press, 2017).

have on European societies, from the study of English literature as a field of scholarship to exclusionary measures, a racial order, and human rights.[20] While Europeans were engaged in a supposedly civilizing mission abroad, they were also, and at the same time, busy civilizing themselves.[21]

The French Revolution, the Enlightenment, nation-states, civilization: central features of the European political past have thus been fundamentally reconfigured. The result is a thorough undermining of essentialized notions of "Europe," notions that continue to pervade both historiography and public debate. Importantly, such a perspective can ultimately also change the position of Europe in the hegemonic narratives. Europe is no longer taken for granted, no longer a self-explanatory unit in which history simply unfolds. Instead of viewing European history as merely in need of globalizing, global perspectives make it easier to see the extent to which Europe – all continuities notwithstanding – was in important ways repeatedly refashioned and remade under changing global conditions. Indeed, we may say that "Europe" as we know it was essentially constituted by global conjunctures.

What this also implies is that Europe's claim to unity and cohesion was reinforced, not least, by observers from without. In the late nineteenth century, in many societies across Latin America, Africa, and Asia, contemporaries began to refer to a "Europe" that was less a specific location than a product of the imagination.[22] The result was a "hyper-real" Europe, as Dipesh Chakrabarty has called it, a reified category (akin to the "Orient") that implied less a geographical space than a set of geopolitical relations: the dominance of British capital, the colonial influence of France, the power of German heavy industry, and the presence of Prussian military advisers.[23] To a considerable

---

[20] Gauri Viswanathan, *Masks of Conquest: Literary Study and British Rule in India* (New York: Columbia University Press, 1989); Susan Buck-Morss, "Hegel and Haiti," *Critical Inquiry* 26, no. 4 (2000): 821–65.

[21] Catherine Hall, *Civilising Subjects: Colony and Metropole in the English Imagination, 1830–1867* (Chicago: University of Chicago Press, 2002).

[22] Rifāʿa Rāfiʿ al-Ṭahṭāwī, *An Imam in Paris: Account of a Stay in France by an Egyptian Cleric (1826–1831)* (London: Saqi Books, 2004); William G. Beasley, *Japan Encounters the Barbarian: Japanese Travellers in America and Europe* (New Haven: Yale University Press, 1995); Roxanne L. Euben, *Journeys to the Other Shore: Muslim and Western Travelers in Search of Knowledge* (Princeton: Princeton University Press, 2006); Christopher A. Bayly, "Rammohan Roy and the Advent of Constitutional Liberalism in India, 1800–30," *Modern Intellectual History* 4, no. 1 (2007): 25–41; David Motadel, "The German Other: Nasir al-Din Shah's Perceptions of Difference and Gender during His Visits to Germany, 1873–1889," *Iranian Studies* 44, no. 4 (2011): 563–79; Naghmeh Sohrabi, *Taken for Wonder: Nineteenth-Century Travel Accounts from Iran to Europe* (Oxford: Oxford University Press, 2012); Nile Green, *The Love of Strangers: What Six Muslims Learned in Jane Austen's London* (Princeton: Princeton University Press, 2016).

[23] Dipesh Chakrabarty, *Provincializing Europe: Postcolonial Thought and Historical Difference* (Princeton: Princeton University Press, 2000), 23.

degree, the unity of "Europe" was made from without.[24] Henceforth, it was taken as a yardstick against which social and political development could be measured.[25]

This does not mean, to be sure, that outside observers were not keenly aware of the internal differences that characterized Europe as a whole. In the early twentieth century, the Japanese art critic Okakura Tenshin assessed the situation in the following terms: "All these countries have different systems; what is right in one country is wrong in the next; religion, customs, morals, there is no common agreement on any of these. Europe is discussed in a general way, and this sounds splendid; the question remains, where in reality does what is called Europe exist?"[26]

Indeed, important divisions were obvious to contemporaries.[27] One axis was the deep gulf that emerged between the more advanced regions and those left behind. In his travelogues, Friedrich Nicolai, a well-known Protestant representative of Enlightenment Berlin, described the Catholic parts of southern Germany as an internal colony, evoking a gap between the "two Europes" that endured into the era of the *Kulturkampf* (culture wars) in the nineteenth century.[28] At the same time, whole swaths of the continent were identified with backwardness and reinvented as "Eastern Europe."[29] The fissures did not remain confined to mental maps but were repeatedly translated into imperial ventures within Europe, from Napoleon to Hitler, and, as some would claim, the European Union.[30] Consequently, who belonged to "Europe" and who did

---

[24] See "Beyond Hegemony? 'Europe' and the Politics of Non-Western Elites, 1900–1930," special issue, *Journal of Modern European History* 4, no. 2 (2006).

[25] Chakrabarty, *Provincializing Europe*; James G. Carrier, *Occidentalism: Images of the West* (Oxford: Clarendon Press, 1995).

[26] Cited in Christopher Benfey, *The Great Wave: Gilded Age Misfits, Japanese Eccentrics, and the Opening of Old Japan* (New York: Random House, 2003), 85.

[27] John G. A. Pocock, "Deconstructing Europe," *History of European Ideas* 18, no. 3 (1994): 329–45.

[28] Manuel Borutta, *Antikatholizismus: Deutschland und Italien im Zeitalter der europäischen Kulturkämpfe* (Göttingen: Vandenhoeck & Ruprecht, 2010), 49–61. See also Christopher Clark and Wolfram Kaiser, eds., *Culture Wars: Secular–Catholic Conflict in Nineteenth-Century Europe* (Cambridge: Cambridge University Press, 2003) for the emergence of discourses about the "two Spains," the "two Italies," etc.

[29] Larry Wolff, *Inventing Eastern Europe: The Map of Civilization on the Mind of the Enlightenment* (Stanford: Stanford University Press, 1994); Maria Todorova, *Imagining the Balkans* (Oxford: Oxford University Press, 1997).

[30] Michael Broers, *The Napoleonic Empire in Italy, 1796–1814: Cultural Imperialism in a European Context?* (Basingstoke: Palgrave Macmillan, 2005); Mark Mazower, *Hitler's Empire: How the Nazis Ruled Europe* (London: Penguin, 2008); Shelley Baranowski, *Nazi Empire: German Colonialism and Imperialism from Bismarck to Hitler* (Cambridge: Cambridge University Press, 2010); Jan Zielonka, *Europe as Empire: The Nature of the Enlarged European Union* (Oxford: Oxford University Press, 2006); Gary Marks, "Europe and Its Empires: From Rome to the European Union," *Journal of Common Market Studies* 50,

not remained a fraught issue, from the debate between the Slavophiles and the Westernizers in nineteenth-century Russia all the way to Brexit.

These differences notwithstanding, in their quest for modernization and "self-strengthening," as it was called in the Chinese context, politicians and reformers both in Europe and beyond continued to make references to a unified "Europe," frequently for strategic reasons. Importantly, this "Europe" cannot simply be considered the result of a long and continuous history but must be seen as a response to the global power configurations of the times. Beginning in the late eighteenth century, the interwoven processes of industrialization and globalization repeatedly reconfigured macro-regions on a global scale. Increasingly, commonalities were defined less by a shared religion and culture than by the parameters of industrialized modernity: power, wealth, and geopolitics.[31]

This fundamental shift in the notion of "Europe" implied that in theory any society could become "European," irrespective of geography or culture. In contemporary parlance, the concepts of modernization, "Westernization," and "Europeanization" were often used interchangeably. "My country is no longer in Africa; we are now part of Europe," declared the Egyptian ruler Ismail Pasha in 1878 – and in doing so referred not so much to a geographical rapprochement resulting from the opening of the Suez Canal in 1869 as to Egypt's politics of modernization.[32] In Russia, the imperial expansion into Central Asia in the late nineteenth century promised to realize the long-cherished dream of the "Westernizers" – eloquent proof of how closely conceptions of Europe there were bound up with power politics and empire. The exiled Mikhail Petrashevsky, a critic of the Tsarist regime, hoped that through its "civilizing" of the Asian peoples, Russia "was destined ... to achieve a diploma with the title of a truly European people."[33] Countries in eastern Europe felt continuously on the edge. In 1894, the popular Bulgarian writer Aleko Konstantinov had his famous satirical character Bai Ganio exclaim: "Europeans we are, but not quite."[34] And in Japan, the journalist Hinohara Shôzô mused in 1884: "Do we have to be content to belong to Asia just because the Europeans see China and also Japan as

---

no. 1 (2012): 1–20; Hartmut Behr and Yannis A. Stivachtis, eds., *Revisiting the European Union as Empire* (London: Routledge, 2015).

[31] For a related argument, see Sebastian Conrad and Prasenjit Duara, *Viewing Regionalisms from East Asia* (Washington, DC: American Historical Association, 2013).

[32] Nile Green, "Spacetime and the Muslim Journey West: Industrial Communications in the Making of the 'Muslim World'," *American Historical Review* 118, no. 2 (2013): 401–29, here p. 406.

[33] Mark Bassin, "Asia," in *The Cambridge Companion to Modern Russian Culture*, ed. Nicholas Rzhevsky (Cambridge: Cambridge University Press, 2012 [1998]), 65–93, here p. 79.

[34] Quoted in Roumen Daskalov, "Modern Bulgarian Society and Culture through the Mirror of Bai Ganio," *Slavic Review* 60, no. 3 (2001): 530–49, here p. 536.

belonging to Asia?"[35] It was a rhetorical question. Just one year later, the well-known philosopher, entrepreneur, and politician Fukuzawa Yukichi demanded that Japan should formally "quit" Asia and become part of Europe.[36]

When historians speak of the need to "provincialize" Europe today, this is the Europe they have in mind – a product of global geopolitics, not of geography or culture; otherwise, the urgency of the plea would ring hollow. This Europe emerged as a response to global challenges and continues to evolve; it was not constituted, in the nineteenth century, once and for all. Historians have studied several moments of such reterritorialization and have reinterpreted them as global conjunctures.[37] They have shown how, in the early twentieth century, large western European countries tried to refashion themselves as world empires, in competition with the United States.[38] New scholarship has turned the First World War into the *world* war that in historiography, so far, it never was. The interwar years are being rediscovered as a moment of internationalist activities. And fascism is no longer just Italian, German, or European – but also Japanese, Argentinian, and global.[39]

The postwar reinvention of a democratic, anti-fascist Europe in the 1960s, too, has now been reframed and globalized. In this way, actors come into view who did not have a place in traditional political histories of Europe. Older research had long established that "1968," and the revolutionary 1960s more generally, were linked across borders: Paris in May, sit-ins at North American

---

[35] Quoted in Urs Matthias Zachmann, "Blowing up a Double Portrait in Black and White: The Concept of Asia in the Writings of Fukuzawa Yukichi and Okakura Tenshin," *Positions: East Asia Cultures Critique* 15, no. 2 (2007): 345–68, here p. 347.

[36] Fukuzawa Yukichi, "On De-Asianization" [1885], in *Meiji Japan through Contemporary Sources*, ed. Center for East Asian Cultural Studies, 3 vols. (Tokyo: Center for East Asian Cultural Studies, 1972), 3:129–33, here p. 133.

[37] Charles S. Maier, "Consigning the Twentieth Century to History: Alternative Narratives for the Modern Era," *American Historical Review* 105, no. 3 (2000): 807–31; Maier, *Once within Borders: Territories of Power, Wealth, and Belonging since 1500* (Cambridge, MA: Harvard University Press, 2016).

[38] Sönke Neitzel, *Weltmacht oder Untergang? Die Weltreichslehre im Zeitalter des Imperialismus* (Paderborn: Schoningh, 2000); Duncan Bell, *The Idea of Greater Britain: Empire and the Future of World Order, 1860–1900* (Princeton: Princeton University Press, 2007); John Darwin, *The Empire Project: The Rise and Fall of the British World-System, 1830–1970* (Cambridge: Cambridge University Press, 2011).

[39] Hew Strachan, "The First World War as a Global War," *First World War Studies* 1 (2010): 3–14; Robert Gerwarth and Erez Manela, "The Great War as a Global War: Imperial Conflict and the Reconfiguration of World Order, 1911–1923," *Diplomatic History* 38, no. 4 (2014): 786–800; Federico Finchelstein, *Transatlantic Fascism: Ideology, Violence, and the Sacred in Argentina and Italy, 1919–1945* (Durham, NC: Duke University Press, 2010); Reto Hofmann, *The Fascist Effect: Japan and Italy 1915–1952* (Ithaca, NY: Cornell University Press, 2015); Daniel Hedinger, *Die Achse Berlin – Rom – Tokio, 1919–1946* (Munich: C. H. Beck, 2021); and Reto Hofmann and Daniel Hedinger, eds., "Axis Empires: Towards a Global History of Fascist Imperialism," special issue, *Journal of Global History* 12, no. 2 (2017): 161–5.

universities, the Prague Spring – all these events had an audience elsewhere, and were often directly connected. But what recent studies have shown is the degree to which many of the actors were informed by a global political consciousness and by a conceptualization of the globe in terms of the Three Worlds paradigm. In particular on the left, many activists perceived the world as a systemic whole that connected their own efforts at social revolution to, and rendered them equivalent with, the liberation struggles in the Third World. But such *Tiers-mondisme* was not limited to the left; it was also embraced by diverse segments of the population. Nor, as recent research has shown, was it limited to western Europe; it tapped into in Hungary, Czechoslovakia, and the Soviet Union as well.[40] Crucially, the Third World was not just an imaginary projection or a discursive referent. European activists were engaged in Algeria, Cuba, and Angola, while at the same time students from postcolonial countries were active participants in the conflicts that shook Paris, Frankfurt, and Rome.[41] In this way, the Third World was more than merely a canvas upon

[40] For eastern Europe, see Tobias Rupprecht, "Gestrandetes Flaggschiff: Die Moskauer Universität der Völkerfreundschaft," *Osteuropa* 60, no. 1 (2010): 95–114; Anne Gorsuch and Diane Koenker, eds., *The Socialist Sixties: Crossing Borders in the Second World* (Bloomington: Indiana University Press, 2013); Oscar Sanchez-Sibony, *Red Globalization: The Political Economy of the Soviet Cold War from Stalin to Khrushchev* (Cambridge: Cambridge University Press, 2014); James Mark and Péter Apor, "Socialism Goes Global: Decolonization and the Making of a New Culture of Internationalism in Socialist Hungary, 1956–1989," *Journal of Modern History* 87 (2015): 852–91; Anne E. Gorsuch, "'Cuba, My Love': The Romance of Revolutionary Cuba in the Soviet Sixties," *American Historical Review* 120, no. 2 (2015): 497–526; Tobias Rupprecht, *Soviet Internationalism after Stalin: Interaction and Exchange between the USSR and Latin America during the Cold War* (Cambridge: Cambridge University Press, 2015); Jeremy Friedman, *Shadow Cold War: The Sino-Soviet Competition for the Third World* (Chapel Hill: University of North Carolina Press, 2015); and Elidor Mëhilli, *From Stalin to Mao: Albania and the Socialist World* (Ithaca, NY: Cornell University Press, 2017); Besnik Pula, *Globalization under and after Socialism: The Evolution of Transnational Capital in Central and Eastern Europe* (Stanford: Stanford University Press, 2018); James Mark, Artemy M. Kalinovsky, and Steffi Marung, eds., *Alternative Globalizations: Eastern Europe and the Postcolonial World* (Bloomington: Indiana University Press, 2020).

[41] Important examples of this new scholarship include Quinn Slobodian, *Foreign Front: Third World Politics in Sixties West Germany* (Durham, NC: Duke University Press, 2012); Christoph Kalter, *The Discovery of the Third World: Decolonization and the Rise of the New Left in France, c.1950–1976* (Cambridge: Cambridge University Press, 2016). See also Martin Klimke, *The Other Alliance: Student Protest in West Germany and the United States in the Global Sixties* (Princeton: Princeton University Press, 2010); Alexander C. Cook, ed., *Mao's Little Red Book: A Global History* (Cambridge: Cambridge University Press, 2014); Timothy Scott Brown, *West Germany and the Global Sixties: The Anti-Authoritarian Revolt, 1962–1978* (Cambridge: Cambridge University Press, 2013); Samantha Christiansen and Zachary Scarlett, eds., *The Third World in the Global 1960s* (New York: Berghahn Books, 2013); Robert Gildea, James Mark, and Anette Warring, eds., *Europe's 1968: Voices of Revolt* (Oxford: Oxford University Press, 2013); Quinn Slobodian, ed., *Comrades of Color: East Germany in the Cold War World* (New York: Berghahn Books, 2015); and Chen Jian et al., eds., *The Routledge Handbook of the Global Sixties: Between Protest and Nation-Building* (London: Routledge, 2018).

which to project individual fantasies, "but also developed into a symbol [of] the need [for] 'peace' in Europe and a projection screen for Europe as a model for overcoming Fascism, dictatorship and imperialism."[42]

Finally, projects of political union, too, can be seen as another set of reconfigurations of Europe, each corresponding to larger processes. It would be naive to see the present-day European Union as a direct heir to the lofty ideas entertained by Richard Coudenhove-Kalergi and others in the interwar period. Instead, various incarnations of the Europe-idea served specific agendas at different times. During the Second World War, "Europe" served as a veil for Nazi expansionism.[43] In the postwar period, Eurafrica emerged as a strategy to bolster Europe vis-à-vis American hegemony by rearranging and hedging its imperial holdings in Africa.[44] The early forms of European political integration from the 1950s onwards sought to position Europe in relation to both the United States and the Soviet Union, and also to incorporate and contain a resurgent West Germany. At the same time, they need to be seen against the background of decolonization – Britain's application to join the European Community in 1961, only shortly after most of its African colonies had acquired independence, was widely perceived as a farewell to empire (just as voting "leave" in 2016 was in some quarters triggered by imperial nostalgia).[45] Lastly, the founding of the European Union in 1993 was not just the fulfillment of a long-standing promise, the pinnacle of a development that

---

[42] Kim Christiaens, "Europe at the Crossroads of Three Worlds: Alternative Histories and Connections of European Solidarity with the Third World, 1950s-80s," in "The Bonds that Unite? Historical Perspectives on European Solidarity/Les liens qui unissent? Perspectives historiques sur la solidarité européenne," special issue, *European Review of History/Revue européenne d'histoire* 24, no. 6 (2017): 932–54, here p. 947.

[43] Götz Aly and Susanne Heim, *Architects of Annihilation: Auschwitz and the Logic of Destruction* (Princeton: Princeton University Press, 2003), which was first published in 1991; and Mazower, *Hitler's Empire*.

[44] Sven Beckert, "American Danger: United States Empire, Eurafrica, and the Territorialization of Industrial Capitalism, 1870–1950," *American Historical Review* 122, no. 4 (2017): 1137–70; and Peo Hansen and Stefan Jonsson, *Eurafrica: The Untold History of European Integration and Colonialism* (London: Bloomsbury, 2014).

[45] Peo Hansen, "European Integration: European Identity and the Colonial Connection," *European Journal of Social Theory* 5, no. 4 (2002): 483–98; António de Figueiredo, "The Empire Is Dead, Long Live the EU," in *The Last Empire: Thirty-Years of Portuguese Decolonization*, ed. Stewart Lloyd-Jones and António Costa Pinto (Bristol: Intellect, 2003), 127–44; António Costa Pinto and Nuno Severiano Teixeira, "From Atlantic Past to European Destiny: Portugal," in *European Union Enlargement: A Comparative History*, ed. Wolfram Kaiser and Jürgen Elvert (London: Routledge, 2004), 112–30; Elena Calandri, ed., *Il primato sfuggente: L'Europa e l'intervento per lo sviluppo (1957–2007)* (Milan: FrancoAngeli, 2009); Marie-Thérèse Bitsch and Gérard Bossuat, eds., *L'Europe unie et l'Afrique: De l'idée d'Eurafrique à la Convention de Lomé I* (Brussels: Bruylant, 2005); Giuliano Garavini, *Dopo gli imperi: L'integrazione europea nello scontro Nord-Sud* (Florence: Mondadori, 2009); see also the informative literature review by Kiran Klaus Patel, "Europäische Integrationsgeschichte auf dem Weg zur doppelten Neuorientierung: Ein Forschungsbericht," *Archiv für Sozialgeschichte* 50 (2010): 595–642.

reached back decades, if not centuries. Instead, the Maastricht Treaty must be understood as a response to the end of the global Cold War and the demise of the bipolar world order, to the onset of globalization and the concomitant formation of larger regional entities around the world.[46]

Much of this new and exciting scholarship has begun to significantly alter our views of Europe's political past. Through studies of this kind, Europe no longer appears simply as a model for something that would happen sooner or later elsewhere, too (the pioneering role assigned by modernization theory), nor as the colonizer imposing its ways on the rest of the world (as stipulated by postcolonial studies). Moving beyond a reductive but still common paradigm of consecutive stages – European, imperial, global – "the global is now understood as the *condition* of the modern world, not its *consequence.*"[47] As a result, European societies emerge as important arenas, and indeed factors, in the constitution of the modern world, themselves co-constituted by global contexts. In a global perspective, in other words, Europe is not treated as the origin and sole motor of historical change but is more appropriately understood as just one of the sites where large-scale global processes such as industrialization or the birth of the nation-state played out. It was no doubt frequently a powerful and privileged site, and sometimes witnessed the first iteration of these processes; but its trajectory is now seen less as a model and rather as one manifestation among others.

Does this mean that the work is done? The prompt for this volume was an invitation to reflect on "European history after the global turn." But the retrospective mode may be premature; one could even ask whether in its current form the turn has gone far enough. Analytically speaking, some of the main challenges of this kind of work still lie ahead of us. One of our tasks will be to move beyond an understanding that limits "global history" to charting hitherto unknown connections and to demonstrating how entangled it all was. Instead, the theoretical promise of the concept is to move analysis beyond the dichotomy of internal and external – and thus beyond the notion of the global as something "out there," as separate and distinct from the local and

---

[46] Kiran Klaus Patel, "Germany and European Integration since 1945," in *The Oxford Handbook of Modern German History*, ed. Helmut Walser Smith (Oxford: Oxford University Press, 2011), 775–94; Peter Katzenstein, *Tamed Power: Germany in Europe* (Ithaca, NY: Cornell University Press, 1997); Mareike König and Matthias Schulz, eds., *Die Bundesrepublik Deutschland und die europäische Einigung, 1949–2000: Politische Akteure, gesellschaftliche Kräfte und internationale Erfahrungen* (Stuttgart: F. Steiner, 2004); Peter J. Katzenstein, *A World of Regions: Asia and Europe in the American Imperium* (Ithaca, NY: Cornell University Press, 2005); Martin Conway and Kiran Klaus Patel, eds., *Europeanization in the Twentieth Century: Historical Approaches* (Basingstoke: Palgrave Macmillan, 2010).

[47] Gurminder K. Bhambra, "Historical Sociology, Modernity, and Postcolonial Critique," *American Historical Review* 116, no. 3 (2011): 653–62, here p. 662 (emphasis in the original); see also Bhambra, *Connected Sociologies* (London: Bloomsbury, 2014).

the national. It is more productive to see the global not as a distinct location but as one layer of social activity among many; not as a place, in other words, but as a scale.[48] Some global historians have recently ceded to the temptation to call it quits in the face of what they perceive as a "backlash" to globalization.[49] It seems clear, however, that if we are to make sense of the present age, and of its history, the real analytical work has only just begun.

---

[48] For a delineation of global history as a distinct approach, see Conrad, *What Is Global History?*, 62–89; Romain Bertrand and Guillaume Calafat, "La microhistoire globale: affaire(s) à suivre," *Annales HSS* 73, no. 1 (2018): 1–18; Les Annales, "Les échelles du monde: Pluraliser, croiser, généraliser," *Annales HSS* 75, nos. 3/4 (2020): 465–92.

[49] For a premature obituary, see Jeremy Adelman, "What Is Global History Now?" *Aeon*, 2 March 2017, Online; see also Richard Drayton and David Motadel, "Discussion: The Futures of Global History," *Journal of Global History* 13, no. 1 (2018): 1–21.

3   Making Europe's Economy

Sven Beckert

Europe, as we know it, was made by its connections to the extra-European world.[1] Very little about the economic history of the continent during the past 500 years can be understood without looking at it from a global vantage point. The examples one could cite are almost endless: American silver lubricated the trade within Europe and between Europe and Asia that was crucial to the formation of the world economy. Plants that would become essential to European nutrition – from maize to the potato – came from other continents. Enslaved African workers produced the commodities that helped power the accelerating economic development of Europe, including sugar, tobacco, cotton, and coffee. Important technologies – from the spinning wheel to cotton printing – traveled from Asia to Europe. European connections with the Islamic world provided access to yet another body of knowledge, and European expansion into the Atlantic was at the core of a process that set the European economy on a new trajectory. By the nineteenth century, imperial domination gave Europe access to plentiful resources and markets from all corners of the world: African copper helped power the second Industrial Revolution, Latin American and Malaysian rubber provided the tires that set European armies in motion, Indian consumers purchased the cottons coming out of British factories – and all the while massive migrations out of and into Europe profoundly shaped European labor markets.

None of these observations as such are controversial, and indeed they can be found in any standard textbook on European history. And yet huge swaths of the literature on the continent's economic history have marginalized the impact of these connections and instead tried to explain European economic development out of itself; indeed, very few popular master narratives are still as Eurocentric as the one about Europe's economic development. "Economic history that was global, or at least intercontinental, was rare," observed

---

[1] My thanks to Ulbe Bosma, Alison Frank Johnson, and Eric Vanhaute for their comments on earlier versions of this chapter. The literature on European economic history is so vast that it is impossible to provide more than a first taste of some of it in this chapter. Many important books and articles will not be mentioned in the following pages.

Kenneth Pomeranz as recently as 2018.[2] When many Europeans, including many historians of that continent, think about Europe's material accomplishments, they all too often believe in the continent having pulled itself up by its own bootstraps, turning its inhabitants in the process into an example to be followed by other human communities.[3] Europe's economic ways seem to foreshadow everyone's future, as Friedrich Engels and Karl Marx argued as early as 1848.[4] It is a heroic story, one that has served many political purposes over the centuries, yet it is also fundamentally flawed.

In recent years, however, the global turn, connecting to many older streams of research, has resulted in an ever more sophisticated connected, comparative, and systemic history of European economic development. It has made older visions of European economic history as a largely insular development, drawing solely on that continent's cultural, social, political, and economic sources, unsustainable. Global economic history has shown that Europe's economic development during the past 500 years was the result of the labor, inventiveness, ecological resources, and capital of people from all continents, and the creation of a connected yet hierarchical world economy was at the very core of European economic ascendancy. As Stephen Broadberry and Steve Hindle have stated, "economic historians previously locked away in the study of their particular country and period have been forced to confront the inter-connectedness of their specialisms."[5] And they have done so with great success.

–

How could such a powerful story have been marginalized for so long? For one, as with all history, it has been a function of scale. Many of the plentiful histories of economic development written during the past century have focused on individual companies, entrepreneurs, cities, regions, and, at most, countries. Indeed, no other part of the world has been subjected to such sustained, detailed, and brilliant analysis of the development of its economy, businesses, social classes, labor regimes, migrations, and other such things as the continent of Europe. And, as is the case with almost all fields of historical study for most historians, the natural container of these inquiries was the

---

[2] Kenneth Pomeranz, "Scale, Scope and Scholarship: Regional Practices and Global Economic Histories," in *Global History, Globally: Research and Practice around the World*, ed. Sven Beckert and Dominic Sachsenmaier (London: Bloomsbury, 2018), 163–94, here p. 163.

[3] Deirdre McCloskey, *Bourgeois Equality: How Ideas, Not Capital or Institutions, Enriched the World* (Chicago: Chicago University Press, 2016), is an important example.

[4] Friedrich Engels and Karl Marx, *Manifest der Kommunistischen Partei* (London: Bildungs-Gesellschaft für Arbeiter, 1848).

[5] Stephen Broadberry and Steve Hindle, "Editor's Introduction," in "Asia in the Great Divergence," special issue, *Economic History Review* 64, no. S1 (2011): 1–7, here p. 7.

nation-state or subunits within it. Biographies, business histories, studies of urban and rural economies, and even sectoral analyses of particular industries often did not concern themselves with links to the outside world, with historians studying the *Making of the English Working Class, Les bourgeois et la bourgeoisie en France*, or *Die Industrielle Revolution in Deutschland*.[6] This tendency cuts across all political proclivities, from Robert Brenner locating the origins of capitalism in the English countryside to Douglass North and Robert Paul Thomas arguing that its peculiar institutional environment set Europe apart, through to Niall Ferguson finding the six "killer apps" of economic development deep in the fabric of Europe.[7] Just think of the myriad studies written on all aspects of the continent's cotton industry, which all too often barely mention the basic fact that the raw material, much of the technology, and eventually also the markets for the products of that crucial industry were found outside Europe. The core interest of historians was to understand the peculiar trajectory of the British, German, or French economy, respectively, its inner dynamic, and what seemed to set it apart from other national economies.

Moreover, the dynamic of the discipline itself tended to move studies of economic history toward such national or at best continental perspectives. As its professionalization claims increasingly focused on the study of primary documents, history found itself drawn to national archives, which in turn oriented research toward national history. This was particularly pronounced for economic historians who relied increasingly on quantitative data, encountering a world in which much of those data were national in scope, produced by strengthening national governments in the very effort of constituting a "national" economy.[8] This approach has been dominant at least since Simon Kuznets's invention of gross national product and Angus Maddison's focus on national growth statistics in the mid-twentieth century.[9] Indeed, the common emphasis on economic growth has contributed to specialists and nonspecialists alike "seeing" the economy as national.

---

[6] E. P. Thompson, *The Making of the English Working Class* (London: Vintage, 1963); Adeline Daumard, *Les bourgeois et la bourgeoisie en France depuis 1815* (Paris: Aubier, 1987); and Hans-Werner Hahn, *Die Industrielle Revolution in Deutschland* (Munich: Walter de Gruyter 1998).

[7] Robert Brenner, "The Origins of Capitalist Development: A Critique of Neo-Smithian Marxism," *New Left Review* 1, no. 104 (1977): 25–92; Douglass C. North and Robert Paul Thomas, *The Rise of the Western World: A New Economic History* (Cambridge: Cambridge University Press, 1973); and Niall Ferguson, *Civilization: The West and the Rest* (London: Penguin 2011).

[8] Pomeranz, "Scale, Scope and Scholarship"; and Eli Cook, *The Pricing of Progress Economic Indicators and the Capitalization of American Life* (Cambridge, MA: Harvard University Press, 2017).

[9] Simon Kuznets, Lillian Epstein, and Elizabeth Jenks, *National Income and Its Composition, 1919–1938*, vol. 1 (New York: National Bureau of Economic Research, 1941); Angus Maddison, *The World Economy: Historical Statistics* (Paris: OECD, 2003).

It was also, of course, a question of politics. As history emerged as an academic discipline in the nineteenth century, it played a crucial role in the constitution of nation-states. It moved away from its earlier, eighteenth-century cosmopolitan inclinations and increasingly tried to come to terms with the history of a bounded national community, participating in turn in the constitution of that community. The very legitimacy of history in general, and economic history in particular, derived from explaining the national community, favoring a national or even nationalist vantage point. At the same time, as global politics and the global economy rested ever more on assumptions of fundamental difference, Europeans searched for explanations for both their unusual economic ascendancy and their imperial relations to people elsewhere and increasingly found them within themselves, their societies, and their politics. This was particularly pronounced from the 1930s to the 1970s, when states aimed to encase "their" capitalists and workers within the nation – and when these capitalists and workers became ever more dependent on "their" respective nation-states, a development which in itself has a global history.[10] Across the political spectrum, and from the Soviet Union to the United States, ideas about development became more teleological and more national, with the dominant modernization theory particularly influential in western Europe, steering economic history into a parallel national focus.

Scholars heavily influenced by Max Weber thus came to see the reasons for the extraordinary economic performance of some parts of Europe as internal to the European continent, factors such as the inventiveness of its people, their religious proclivities, the climate they lived in, their racial makeup, the peculiar social structure of their societies, or the unique institutional ensemble.[11] Such emphasis on European (or British or French or German) exceptionalism not only served the agenda of imperial European statesmen but also guaranteed that the global embeddedness of these processes remained marginal to the story that Europeans told about themselves. Even when the scale of historical analysis encompassed "Europe" as a whole (or at least large regions within it) – as in work by David Landes, Joel Mokyr, Alexander Gerschenkron, Sidney Pollard, and Joseph Schumpeter – there remained very little insight into the connections between Europe and the rest of the world.[12] Indeed, a

---

[10] Sven Beckert, "American Danger: United States Empire, Eurafrica, and the Territorialization of Industrial Capitalism, 1870–1950," *American Historical Review* 122, no. 4 (2017): 1137–70.

[11] A review of these approaches can be found in Peer Vries, *Escaping Poverty: The Origins of Modern Economic Growth* (Vienna: V&R Unipress, 2013). Max Weber, *The Protestant Ethic and the Spirit of Capitalism* (London: Merchant Books, 1930), is the classic reference.

[12] David S. Landes, *The Unbound Prometheus: Technological Change and Industrial Development in Western Europe from 1750 to the Present* (Cambridge: Cambridge University Press, 1969); Landes, *The Wealth and Poverty of Nations: Why Some Are So Rich*

fundamental program of that research was to marginalize the importance of these connections – a strand of analysis that has been effectively critiqued by Patrick O'Brien.[13]

It is not, however, that European historians did not also study the international dimensions of European economic history. Indeed, especially in the core countries of European imperialism – France, the United Kingdom, and the Netherlands – hundreds if not thousands of scholars wrote about global trade, the merchant communities engaged in that trade, and the economic dimensions of empire. Yet this literature all too often unfolded without sustained attention to evolutions on the European continent itself, with the analysis of trade isolated from an analysis of domestic developments, as if trade or the colony were separate from the "national" economy. To cite just two examples: Some scholars studied the vast sugar complex of the Caribbean in almost complete isolation from its relationship to Europe; while hundreds of books focused on cotton production in the Americas without giving much thought to how that history related to European economic development.

Perhaps most consequentially, such perspectives often had the unfortunate tendency to universalize from the European example. While the empirical core of analysis remained the history of economic life in Europe, its findings were all too often presented as universal truths, or even "laws" of historical motion, with the non-European world coming into these stories principally to show what its societies were lacking. Across the political spectrum there was a tendency to see the world's future in the European past, and thus to take the European example as a tool kit that seemed to reveal policy recommendations to the rest of the world. Many an economic historian of Europe perceived his or her work as exceedingly relevant to present-day extra-European policymaking.

-

This narrative of European economic history as enclosed in national boundaries and hopelessly Eurocentric is, however, radically incomplete. Indeed, looked at from a slightly different vantage point, the field today is perhaps

and Some So Poor (New York: Norton, 1998); Joel Mokyr, *The Gifts of Athena: Historical Origins of the Knowledge Economy* (Princeton: Princeton University Press, 2004); Alexander Gerschenkron, *Economic Backwardness in Historical Perspective: A Book of Essays* (Cambridge, MA: Harvard University Press, 1962); Sidney Pollard, *Peaceful Conquest: The Industrialization of Europe, 1760–1970* (Oxford: Oxford University Press, 1981); and Joseph A. Schumpeter, *Capitalism, Socialism and Democracy* (London: George Allen & Unwin, 1976 [1943]).
[13] Patrick O'Brien, "The Deconstruction of Myths and Reconstruction of Metanarratives in Global Histories of Material Progress," in *Writing World History, 1800–2000*, ed. Benedikt Stuchtey and Eckhardt Fuchs (Oxford: Oxford University Press, 2003), 67–90.

more thoroughly globalized than any other in the discipline of European history. Global history itself has had a profound impact on economic history, and the historiographical rejuvenation of each is deeply connected to the other. So vibrant has global economic history become that there are already guides to the field.[14] As early as 2009, the academic publisher Brill established a series of volumes overseen by some of the main contributors to the debate, including Maarten Prak, Jan Luiten van Zanden, Gareth Austin, Johan Fourie, Christine Moll-Murata, Elise van Nederveen Meerkerk, Şevket Pamuk, Kenneth Pomeranz, Tirthankar Roy, and Peer Vries.[15] Scholars of global economic history, thus constituted as a field, have asserted, among other things, that "Western European distinctiveness needs to be proved rather than assumed"; historians (especially members of the so-called California School), are increasingly viewing the history of Europe's economy from non-European perspectives, looking at resource flows, and adopting global approaches in considering the history of Europe's economy – particularly its labor history.[16]

These global orientations connect to various traditions and, as with all global history, are not as novel as they seem at first. For one, there is a long tradition of writing European economic history from the outside in. Scholars in Africa, Asia, and Latin America have for many years stressed the influence of global connections on European economic development. One of the best-known debates concerns slavery. Historians such as Eric Williams, C. L. R. James, and W. E. B. Du Bois have insisted since the first half of the twentieth century on the economic importance of slavery, the slave trade, and the trade in slave-grown agricultural commodities to European economic modernity.[17] James, for example, emphasized that the wealth of merchants in Nantes and Bordeaux derived from the labor of enslaved Africans in the

---

[14] Peer Vries, "Global Economic History: A Survey," in *The Oxford History of Historical Writing*, vol. 5, *Historical Writing since 1945*, ed. Axel Schneider and Daniel Woolf (Oxford: Oxford University Press, 2011), 113–34, is an important example. On the vibrancy of global economic history, see Pomeranz, "Scale, Scope and Scholarship," 6.

[15] The Brill Global Economic History Series so far consists of twenty volumes.

[16] Peter A. Coclanis, "Ten Years after: Reflections on Kenneth Pomeranz's *The Great Divergence*," *Historically Speaking* 12, no. 4 (2011): 10–25, here p. 11; Ulbe Bosma, *The Sugar Plantation in India and Indonesia: Industrial Production, 1770–2010* (Cambridge: Cambridge University Press, 2013); and Sven Beckert, Ulbe Bosma, Mindi Schneider, and Eric Vanhaute, "Commodity Frontiers and the Transformation of the Global Countryside: A Research Agenda," *Journal of Global History* 16, no. 3 (2021): 435–50.

[17] C. L. R. James, *The Black Jacobins: Toussaint L'Ouverture and the San Domingo Revolution* (London: Secker and Warburg, 1938); Eric Williams, *Capitalism and Slavery* (Chapel Hill: University of North Carolina Press, 1944); and W. E. B. Du Bois, *Black Reconstruction in America: An Essay toward a History of the Part Which Black Folk Played in the Attempt to Reconstruct Democracy in America, 1860–1880* (New York: Oxford University Press, 2007), which was first published in 1935.

Caribbean, while for Williams profits from the slave trade funded Britain's Industrial Revolution.[18] These scholars' work did not enter the mainstream of the profession when it was first published, but in recent years it has been rediscovered by a new generation of historians who have built upon their insights and largely confirmed many, though not all, of their arguments.[19]

Similarly, historians in the formerly colonial world, such as Abdoulaye Ly in Senegal, have long highlighted the economic importance of colonialism to the development of the European economy. Ly argued already in 1955 that France's position within the "Atlantic economy" affected its own political-economic structure.[20] For him, "the African trade, beyond the direct contribution to the accumulation of precious metal, had ... a prominent and growing place in the European capitalistic accumulation as a whole."[21] Indian historians, in roughly similar ways, insisted on the crucial role of what they called the "drain of wealth" from India to the United Kingdom, with Romesh Chunder Dutt examining the effect of British economic policies on India as early as 1902. He noted a concerted effort to deindustrialize the subcontinent through prohibitions and tariffs: "the policy of the ruling nation was to convert India into a land of raw produce only ... until they had crushed the Manufacturing Power of India, and reared their own Manufacturing Power."[22] This argument became a mainstay of Indian historiography, represented more recently, for example, in the works of Aditya Mukherjee and Mridula Mukherjee.[23] In 1950, Argentinian economist Raúl Prebisch developed an early version of dependency theory, arguing that the world economy was constituted by "centers" and "peripheries," with the peripheries

---

[18] James, *The Black Jacobins*, 47–50.

[19] Nick Draper, *The Price of Emancipation: Slave-Ownership, Compensation, and British Society at the End of Slavery* (Cambridge: Cambridge University Press, 2009); Matthias von Rossum, "Beyond Profitability: The Dutch Transatlantic Slave Trade and Its Economic Impact," *Slavery and Abolition* 36, no. 1 (2015): 63–83; Pepijn Brandon, *War, Capitalism, and the Dutch State (1588–1795)* (Leiden: Brill, 2015); Sven Beckert and Seth Rothman, eds., *Slavery's Capitalism: A New History of American Economic Development* (Philadelphia: University of Pennsylvania Press, 2016); and Walter Johnson, *River of Dark Dreams: Slavery and Empire in the Cotton Kingdom* (Cambridge, MA: Harvard University Press, 2013); see also the important arguments in Daron Acemoglu, Simon Johnson, and James Robinson, "The Rise of Europe: Atlantic Trade, Institutional Change, and Economic Growth," *American Economic Review* 95, no. 3 (2005): 546–79.

[20] Abdoulaye Ly, *La Compagnie du Sénégal* (Bordeaux: Karthala, 1955), 59.

[21] "Le commerce d'Afrique, au delà de la contribution directe à l'accumulation de métal précieux, avait effectivement une place de choix et grandissante dans l'accumulation capitaliste européenne prise dans son ensemble," in Ly, *La Compagnie du Sénégal*, 62

[22] Romesh Chunder Dutt, *The Economic History of India under Early British Rule*, vol. 1 (London: Routledge, 1902), 299 and 302.

[23] Aditya Mukherjee, *Imperialism, Nationalism and the Making of the Indian Capitalist Class, 1920–1947* (London: Sage, 2002); and Mridula Mukherjee, *Colonizing Agriculture: The Myth of Punjab Exceptionalism* (London: Sage, 2005).

enabling the accumulation of wealth in the centers.[24] His approach found great support among Latin American historians, whose inclination was to look at European economic history as part of a larger history of the global economy. They insisted on the significance of wealth transfers from one part of the world to the other, with Fernando Henrique Cardoso and Enzo Faletto's *Dependencia y Desarrollo en America Latina* one of this current's central contributions.[25]

In the 1940s and 1950s, such ideas remained marginal to European historiography, yet they did gain some influence, perhaps none more consequential than on the French historian Fernand Braudel. The young Braudel spent the years from 1935 to 1937 teaching at the University of São Paulo. Many years later, he published *Civilisation matérielle, économie et capitalisme* – a brilliant account of the rise of capitalism – which focused, to be sure, on Europe but, drawing on his Brazilian experiences, also emphasized the importance of global connections to the European story and indeed gave non-European merchants a key role in the transition to capitalism.[26] Braudel thus argued that the incorporation of Africa and the Americas into the European economy set Europe on a peculiar developmental trajectory, even as his counterparts on both the left and the right sought to locate the reasons for European economic development in factors that were purely local – from peculiar forms of class struggle to particular cultural proclivities. His approach, in turn, influenced scholars such as Vitorino Magalhães Godinho, whose 1969 *Os Descobrimentos e a Economia Mundial* reiterated the crucial importance of the global context for European economic development.[27]

Braudel also informed a growing group of historians, sociologists, and economists in the Global North, who, under the influence of Immanuel Wallerstein, worked on rewriting European economic history from a global perspective. Taking up the idea of center and periphery developed by Prebisch,

---

[24] Raúl Prebisch, *The Economic Development of Latin America and Its Principal Problems* (New York: United Nations, 1950); Walter Rodney, *How Europe Underdeveloped Africa* (London: Verso, 2018), which was first published in 1972; Fernando Henrique Cardoso and Enzo Faletto, *Dependency and Development in Latin America* (Berkley: University of California Press, 1979); Immanuel Wallerstein, *The Modern World-System*, vol. 1, *Capitalist Agriculture and the Origins of the European World-Economy in the Sixteenth Century* (New York: Academic Press, 1974); Wallerstein, *The Modern World-System*, vol. 2, *Mercantilism and the Consolidation of the European World-Economy, 1600–1750* (New York: Academic Press, 1980); and Wallerstein, *The Modern World-System*, vol. 3, *The Second Great Expansion of the Capitalist World-Economy, 1730–1840s* (San Diego: Academic Press, 1989), are important examples.

[25] Fernando Henrique Cardoso and Enzo Faletto, *Dependency and Development in Latin America* (Berkeley: University of California Press, 1979), which was first published in 1969; see also the works of philosopher Enrique Dussel.

[26] Fernand Braudel, *Civilisation matérielle, économie et capitalisme, XVe-XVIIIe*, 3 vols. (Paris: Garnier, 1967–79).

[27] Vitorino Magalhães Godinho, *Os descobrimentos e a economia mundial* (Lisbon: Arcádia, 1963).

they explained the world economy and Europe's role within it by emphasizing post-1492 global connections and especially hierarchies. Their ideas radiated outwards, with scholars such as Terence Hopkins, Giovanni Arrighi, Dale Tomich, and Jason Moore all agreeing on the need for a global perspective in European economic history.[28] What distinguished their work was that it was not just comparative or connected history but it also tried to analyze historical capitalism from a systemic perspective – seeing the production of changing structures of the world economy as the result of systemic processes as well as local struggles. Eric Vanhaute in particular has insisted on the distinctive qualities of this perspective on European economic history, especially its ability to transcend the dangers of purely comparative frameworks "regenerat [ing] national frameworks and essentializ[ing] features of a nation's history."[29]

And then there is a long tradition among economists of studying Europe in the world economy. Guillaume Daudin has shown that overseas trade, much of it with the Caribbean, was crucial to eighteenth-century French economic development.[30] Ralph Davis has done much the same for the British economy.[31] Barbara Solow has consistently highlighted the central place of slavery in the development of the North Atlantic economy,[32] while Joseph Inikori has demonstrated in a stunning book the significance of African-made products, African workers, and African markets to the British Industrial Revolution.[33] Jeffrey Williamson has analyzed the very long history of globalization, with a particular focus on the question of when and why markets integrated.[34] Patrick O'Brien and Stanley Engerman, whose work had

[28] Terence K. Hopkins and Immanuel Wallerstein, *World-Systems Analysis: Theory and Methodology* (New York: Sage, 1982); Giovanni Arrighi, *The Long Twentieth Century: Money, Power and the Origins of Our Times* (London: Verso, 1994); Dale W. Tomich, *Slavery in the Circuit of Sugar: Martinique and the World-Economy* (Baltimore: Johns Hopkins University Press, 1990); and Jason W. Moore, *Capitalism in the Web of Life: Ecology and the Accumulation of Capital* (London: Verso, 2015).

[29] Eric Vanhaute, "Global and Regional Comparisons: The Great Divergence Debate and Europe," in *The Practice of Global History: European Perspectives*, ed. Matthias Middell (London: Bloomsbury, 2019), 183–205, here p. 192.

[30] Guillaume Daudin, *Commerce et prospérité: la France au XVIIIe siècle* (Paris: PUPS, 2005).

[31] Ralph Davis, *The Industrial Revolution and British Oversees Trade* (Leicester: Leicester University Press, 1979).

[32] See, for example, Barbara L. Solow, *The Economic Consequences of the Atlantic Slave Trade* (Lanham: Rowman, 2014).

[33] Joseph E. Inikori, *Africans and the Industrial Revolution in England: A Study in International Trade and Economic Development* (Cambridge: Cambridge University Press, 2002).

[34] Jeffrey G. Williamson, *Trade and Poverty: When the Third World Fell behind* (Cambridge, MA: Harvard University Press, 2011), as well as Jeffrey G. Williamson and Philippe Aghion, *Growth, Inequality, and Globalization* (Cambridge: Cambridge University Press, 1998); Jeffrey G. Williamson and Kevin O'Rourke, *Globalization and History* (Cambridge, MA: Harvard University Press, 1999); and the chapters in Jeffrey G. Williamson, Michael D. Bordo, and Alan M. Taylor, eds., *Globalization in Historical Perspective* (Chicago: University of Chicago Press, 2003).

a profound influence on generations of students of European economic history, also pointed out the importance of exports to British industrialization, as did, more recently, Daron Acemoglu and James Robinson.[35] And Ronald Findlay and Kevin O'Rourke have demonstrated the great role that international trade played in the development of the domestic European economy.[36]

The work of these scholars was connected to that of early historians of the Industrial Revolution, who had likewise emphasized the importance of foreign trade – especially with the Americas. Arnold Toynbee in his *Industrial Revolution* of 1884 already observed the "all-corroding force of foreign trade" on the British economy, as did Elizabeth Gilboy in her 1932 article "Demand as a Factor in the Industrial Revolution" and John A. Hobson in his 1894 *The Evolution of Modern Capitalism*, where he argued that the "colonial economy must be regarded as one of the necessary conditions of modern capitalism."[37] Eric Hobsbawm, in his 1968 *Industry and Empire*, similarly emphasized the global embeddedness of the British economy as crucial to its industrial development.[38]

Among today's historians, global perspectives have taken center stage when it comes to rewriting the history of the European economy, with comparative, connected, and systemic approaches fully embraced. Undeniably the most influential intervention came from a historian of China, Pomeranz, whose *The Great Divergence* has become a field-defining book and generated much follow-up research since its publication in 2000.[39] Pomeranz argues that until the late eighteenth century, the most developed regions of Europe and China were broadly speaking at similar stages of economic development. They diverged thereafter, and, according to this account, the ability of some regions

---

[35] Patrick O'Brien and Stanley L. Engerman, "Export and the Growth of the British Economy from the Glorious Revolution to the Peace of Amiens," in *Slavery and the Rise of the Atlantic System*, ed. Barbara Solow (Cambridge: Cambridge University Press, 1991), 177–209; and Daron Acemoglu, Simon Johnson, and James Robinson, "The Rise of Europe: Atlantic Trade, Institutional Change, and Economic Growth," *American Economic Review* 95, no. 3 (2005): 546–79.

[36] Ronald Findlay and Kevin O'Rourke, *Power and Plenty: Trade, War, and the World Economy in the Second Millennium* (Princeton: Princeton University Press, 2007).

[37] Arnold Toynbee, *Lectures of the Industrial Revolution in England: Popular Addresses, Notes and Other Fragments* (Cambridge: Cambridge University Press), 56, which was first published in 1884; Elizabeth Waterman Gilboy, "Demand as a Factor in the Industrial Revolution," in *Facts and Factors in Economic History: Articles from former Students of Edwin Frances Gay*, ed. Arthur H. Cole, A. L. Dunhman, and N. S. B. Gras (Cambridge, MA: Harvard University Press, 1932), 620–39; and John A. Hobson, *The Evolution of Modern Capitalism: A Study of Machine Production* (London: Allen and Unwin; New York: Macmillan; 1926 [1894]), 13.

[38] Eric Hobsbawm, *Industry and Empire: From 1750 to the Present Day* (London: The New Press, 1968).

[39] Kenneth Pomeranz, *The Great Divergence: China, Europe, and the Making of the Modern World Economy* (Princeton: Princeton University Press, 2000).

of Europe to embark upon a trajectory of modern economic growth was the result of their unusual capacity to escape its resource constraints. Fortuitous access to coal and resources from colonial peripheries, especially in the Americas, was crucial. Along with other members of the "California School," such as Roy Bin Wong, Li Bozhong, Andre Gunder Frank, and Jack Goldstone, to name but a few, Pomeranz adopted comparative approaches to consider the question from alternate, primarily Asian, perspectives, recasting Europe from main star to bit player in the world economy.[40]

The debate surrounding this book has raised many disagreements – with some historians seeing earlier differences emerging between these regions and others emphasizing that the "great divergence" is better explained by foregrounding other factors. Vries, for example, has stressed the comparative history of the state, while Kaoru Sugihara has emphasized the differences between a (European) capital-intensive path toward industrialization and an (Asian) labor-intensive path.[41] Yet despite these differences, all these authors converge on embracing a comparative and connected perspective to better understand European economic development.

---

[40] Jack Goldstone, *Why Europe? The Rise of the West in World History, 1500–1850* (New York: McGraw-Hill Education, 2008), is an example.

[41] A small sampling of these works needs to include Peer Vries, "Are Coal and Colonies Really Crucial? Kenneth Pomeranz and the Great Divergence," *Journal of World History* 12 (2001): 407–46; Philip C. C. Huang, "Development or Involution in Eighteenth-Century Britain and China," *Journal of Asian Studies* 61 (2002): 501–38, which sharply critiques Pomeranz's views on British and Chinese agriculture in the eighteenth century; Robert C. Allen, "Agricultural Productivity and Rural Incomes in England and the Yangtze Delta, c. 1620-c. 1820," *Economic History Review* 62 (2009): 525–50, which offers a more nuanced assessment of Pomeranz's contentions regarding comparative agricultural productivity; Jan Luiten van Zanden and Eltjo Buringh, "Charting the 'Rise of the West': Manuscripts and Printed Books in Europe, a Long-Term Perspective from the Sixth through the Eighteenth Centuries," *Journal of Economic History* 69, no. 2 (2009): 409–45; and Peer Vries, "The California School and beyond: How to Study the Great Divergence," *History Compass* 8 (2010): 730–51, appearing first in the *Journal für Entwicklungspolitik* 24, no. 4 (2008): 6–49, which argues that the Californians often exaggerate the resemblances between western Europe and East Asia and should be more specific when it comes to time, place, and the differing historical trajectories of various regions; Jean-Laurent Rosenthal and Roy Bin Wong, *Before and beyond Divergence: The Politics of Economic Change in China and Europe* (Cambridge, MA: Harvard University Press, 2011); Prasannan Parthasarathi, *Why Europe Grew Rich and Asia Did Not: Global Economic Divergence 1600–1850* (Cambridge: Cambridge University Press, 2011); Williamson, *Trade and Poverty*; Bozhong Li and Jan Luiten van Zanden, "Before the Great Divergence? Comparing the Yangzi Delta and the Netherlands at the Beginning of the Nineteenth Century," *Journal of Economic History* 72, no. 4 (2012): 956–89; Peer Vries, *State, Economy and the Great Divergence: Great Britain and China, 1680s-1850s* (London: Bloomsbury, 2015); Leonid Grinin and Andrey Korotayev, *Great Divergence and Great Convergence: A Global Perspective* (Berlin: Springer, 2015); Peer Vries, "What We Do and Do Not Know about the Great Divergence at the Beginning of 2016," *Historische Mitteilungen der Ranke-Gesellschaft* 28 (2016): 249–97; Paul Warde, *Energy Consumption in England and Wales, 1560–2000* (Rome: Consiglio Nazionale delle Ricerche, 2007); and E. A. Wrigley, *Energy and the English Industrial Revolution* (Cambridge: Cambridge University Press, 2010).

A second example of the impact of global perspectives on European economic history is a debate initiated by Marcel van der Linden at the Institute for Social History in Amsterdam, which in effect defined a new field: global labor history. Drawing on the work of scholars such as Dipesh Chakrabarty and Samir Amin, who questioned the universal validity of the western European path of industrial working-class formation, van der Linden critiqued traditional labor history – an important part of the economic history of Europe – for its focus on formal employment in industry of mostly male workers.[42] He argued that such a narrow focus had in fact left out the vast amount of work done outside the Global North, outside industry, and outside the classical wage–labor relationship. The new global labor history that grew out of these observations has carefully delineated how the expansion of capitalism has gone along with the development of a diversity of labor regimes. It has questioned whether wage labor has been the true labor of capitalism and has connected the expansion of wage labor in some parts of the world, such as Europe, to the expansion of forms of unfree labor in others.[43] In its most ambitious undertaking to date, labor historians are in the process of creating a global inventory of labor relations over the past 500 years. And such a rethinking of labor history has also generated an even larger project, globalizing social history, which has led to innovative work, for example, on the "global bourgeoisie."[44]

Many more debates have emerged in this most dynamic field, some emphasizing its connected, others its comparative, and yet others its systemic dimensions. Vanessa Ogle's writings on offshore jurisdictions such as Bermuda or the Cayman Islands have opened new vistas on Europe's twentieth-century political economy.[45] Histories of trade in extra-European commodities have traced how textiles, porcelain, and spices, for example, have shaped the cultures, tastes, fashions, and interior design of Europeans.[46] Acemoglu and

---

[42] Samir Amin, *L'eurocentrisme: Critique d'une idéologie* (Paris: Anthropos, 1988), 119–22; and Dipesh Chakrabarty, *Rethinking Working-Class History: Bengal 1890–1940* (Princeton: Princeton University Press, 1989), 222–3.

[43] Marcel van der Linden, *Workers of the World: Essays toward a Global Labor History* (Leiden: Brill, 2008).

[44] Christof Dejung, David Motadel, and Jürgen Osterhammel, eds., *The Global Bourgeoisie: The Rise of the Middle Classes in the Age of Empire* (Princeton: Princeton University Press, 2019).

[45] Vanessa Ogle, "Archipelago Capitalism: Tax Havens, Offshore Money, and the State, 1950s–1970s," *American Historical Review* 122, no. 5 (2017): 1431–58.

[46] Robert Finlay, *The Pilgrim Art: Cultures of Porcelain in World History* (Berkeley: University of California Press, 2010); Hanna Hodacs, *Silk and Tea in the North: Scandinavian Trade and the Market for Asian Goods in Eighteenth-Century Europe* (New York: Palgrave, 2016); Giorgio Riello, *Cotton: The Fabric that Made the Modern World* (Cambridge: Cambridge University Press, 2013); and Maxine Berg, "Britain's Asian Century: Porcelain and Global History in the Long Eighteenth Century," in *The Birth of Modern Europe: Essays in Honour of Jan de Vries*, ed. Laura Cruz and Joel Mokyr (Leiden: Brill, 2010), 133–56, are important examples.

Robinson's writings on the "reversal of fortunes" embed European history deeply into global history, comparing the institutional setup of economies all around the world over five centuries.[47] Alexander Anievas and Kerem Nisancioglu's *How the West Came to Rule* emphasizes the geopolitical dimensions of European economic ascendancy, especially by focusing on the Ottoman Empire's changing fortunes.[48] Commodity histories – of sugar, tobacco, and cotton, among others – have emphasized the connectedness of the European economy to other parts of the world and the impact of resource transfers on European economic development.[49] Jürgen Kocka's concise *Geschichte des Kapitalismus* glances in insightful ways beyond the European horizon.[50] Other historians have continued to work on the importance of the colonial world to European economic development.[51] Last but not least, in a body of work that is both connected and comparative history, Robert Allen has argued that the British Industrial Revolution was the result of that country's high level of wages (and cheap energy), which, in turn, resulted from its maritime activities that depended on vast labor input elsewhere.[52]

All these works – along with many others that could not be mentioned here – show that the modern European economy was produced by interactions with other parts of the world. To be sure, Europe had a huge impact on economic development elsewhere. But Europe itself was made in a real and material sense by the extra-European world; what is allegedly distinctly "European" is the result of interactions between particular European regions and other parts of the world. Efforts to write a history of Europe confined to its own ill-defined boundaries might serve particular political needs but are, in

---

[47] Daron Acemoglu and James A. Robinson, *Economic Origins of Dictatorship and Democracy* (Cambridge: Cambridge University Press, 2006); Daron Acemoglu and James A. Robinson, *Why Nations Fail: The Origins of Power, Prosperity, and Poverty* (New York: Crown, 2012).

[48] Alexander Anievas and Kerem Nisancioglu, *How the West Came to Rule: The Geopolitical Origins of Capitalism* (London: Pluto Press, 2015).

[49] See for example: Sidney Mintz, *Sweetness and Power: The Place of Sugar in Modern History* (New York: Penguin, 1985); Iain Gately, *Tobacco: A Cultural History of How an Exotic Plant Seduced Civilization* (New York: Grove Press, 2001); and Sven Beckert, *Empire of Cotton: A Global History* (New York: Random House, 2014).

[50] Jürgen Kocka, *Geschichte des Kapitalismus* (Munich: C. H. Beck, 2013).

[51] Inikori, *Africans and the Industrial Revolution in England*; Mauricio Drelichman, "The Curse of Moctezuma: American Silver and the Dutch Disease," *Explorations in Economic History* 42 (2005): 349–80; Stephen Broadberry and Kevin O'Rourke, *The Cambridge Economic History of Modern Europe* (Cambridge: Cambridge University Press, 2010); Jan Luiten van Zanden and Maarten R. Prak, "Demographic Change and Migration Flows in Holland between 1500 and 1800," in *Working on Labor: Essays in Honor of Jan Lucassen*, ed. Marcel van der Linden and Leo Lucassen (Leiden: Brill, 2012), 237–45; and Peter Foldvari, Bas van Leeuwen, and Jan Luiten van Zanden, "The Contribution of Migration to Economic Development in Holland 1570–1800," *De Economist* 161, no. 1 (2013): 1–18; and Beckert, *Empire of Cotton*.

[52] Robert Allen, *The British Industrial Revolution in Global Perspective* (Cambridge: Cambridge University Press, 2009).

fact, historically inaccurate. Indeed, large swaths of Europe were more connected to extra-European spaces than to "Europe" as such; important European
societies, such as Great Britain, were at least as much defined by networks
encompassing Asian, African, and American territories as by their "European"
connections. Likewise, Europe's economic development, its "great
divergence," cannot even begin to be understood without reference to its
connections to the rest of the world: resource transfers – including but not
limited to the slave trade, silver exports from the Americas, Malayan rubber
plantations, and the migrations of workers from the Maghreb into the
European steel and coal industries – were crucial to Europe's economic
development as Europeans incorporated the land, labor, and natural resources
of much of the rest of the world into the continent's circuits of economic
reproduction. Moreover, the bureaucratic, infrastructural, and military capacity
of European states, so important to the continent's economic development, as
Charles Tilly, Peer Vries, and William Ashworth, among others, have shown,
was decisively shaped by their imperial projects.[53] Europe was a production of
the world, and future research would do well to address both the huge range of
particular connections and the big question of how capitalism has constituted
itself as a constantly changing, but always global, system over the past
500 years if we are to understand how various parts of the European story fit
into this global history. Europe, like any other place in the world, is the result
of a whole range of interactions with peoples from around the globe over a
very long time span.[54] The continent's economy cannot be understood out of
itself only: Europe's economy was a production of the world just as much as
the world economy was a co-production of Europeans and people elsewhere.

---

[53] Charles Tilly, *Coercion, Capital, and European States, AD 990–1990* (Malden: Wiley-
Blackwell, 1990); Vries, *State, Economy and the Great Divergence*; and William J.
Ashworth, *The Industrial Revolution: The State, Knowledge and Global Trade* (London:
Bloomsbury, 2017).
[54] Pomeranz, "Scale, Scope and Scholarship," 40–1.

4   European Intellectual History after the Global Turn

Samuel Moyn

I still remember the shock I felt upon realizing that global decolonization did not appear in the story of twentieth-century European intellectual history I had received from my teachers.[1] It was simply not a set of events that mattered in the field. And no wonder, since decolonization had barely registered in the canon of modern European philosophy and social thought in the first place. Those European thinkers who lived through decolonization had entirely scanted it. Historians were simply following the orientation of their sources. As for those few canonical philosophers who did comment in real time, such as Hannah Arendt, they tended to reduce decolonization to unaccountable violence – partly because some European thinking, notably that of Jean-Paul Sartre, justified that violence – as if the same ambiguous bid for freedom intellectuals often made central to their frameworks of citizenship and modernity were not involved.[2] The Cold War as a bipolar contest over the meanings of freedom, equality, and modernity intrudes deep into both the primary and secondary literature about European intellectuals; the beneficiaries and victims of decolonization beyond the usual horizons of European social thought, and even of the Cold War itself beyond those boundaries, concerned next to no one.

In certain respects, the recognition of this omission and silence both in history and in historiography felt more serious than the "discovery" in recent years that the Enlightenment had global features or that, after a turn to empire, nineteenth-century European liberal thought so often apologized for global hierarchy in framing theories of civilization and race.[3] It even competed in

---

[1] I am grateful to David Armitage and Julian Bourg for their helpful comments. I use "decolonization" even though the term was itself a European creation to make sense of a confusing set of developments that could have been imagined some other way, see Stuart Ward, "The European Provenance of Decolonization," *Past & Present*, no. 230 (2016): 227–60.

[2] Hannah Arendt, *On Violence* (New York: Houghton Mifflin Harcourt, 1970), 19–21, commenting on Jean-Paul Sartre, "Preface," in Frantz Fanon, *The Wretched of the Earth* (New York: Grove Press, 1963), 7–31, which was first published in 1961.

[3] On the global Enlightenment, major recent contributions include Alexander Bevilacqua, *The Republic of Arabic Letters: Islam and the European Enlightenment* (Cambridge, MA: Harvard University Press, 2018); and Jürgen Osterhammel, *Unfabling the East: The Enlightenment's Encounter with Asia* (Princeton: Princeton University Press, 2018), which was first published in

moral significance with the findings of the now voluminous scholarship showing that twentieth-century extremism attracted some of Europe's great minds in its time. For it looked as though European thought, which before the twentieth century had congratulated itself for chronicling the adventures of "the world spirit," had simply paid the most liberatory event in human history no mind – even though G. W. F. Hegel had taken "world history" as his theme and "progress in the consciousness of freedom" as his thesis.[4] And its historians had followed suit.

For a long time, modern European intellectual historians could rest content with the thought that they were the cosmopolitans in their guild, blissfully free of the nationalizing defaults of their colleagues. Given the continental ramifications of the Enlightenment, it was normal to frame it supra- and transnationally.[5] It required no deep insight to place the international circulation of intellectual movements – and their human representatives, thanks to the waves of exile that followed political repression in both the nineteenth and twentieth centuries – center stage in a host of studies. "Ideas are the most migratory things in the world," Arthur O. Lovejoy commented in 1940.[6] The configuration of modern European history in leading centers in the United States typically involved a series of experts in national historiographies and, if departments were lucky, an intellectual historian – who typically felt an enduring sense of marginality while the mainstream of European history engaged in successive fashions of political, social, and cultural history. From their peripheral vantage point, these intellectual historians could at least boast more literacy when it came to different places in Europe and across the Atlantic, while other Europeanists carved up the continent among themselves at its national joints.

But the truth is that the mainstream of the field of modern European intellectual history was never really cosmopolitan. Lovejoy, the great founder in the United States, hardly tracked migratory ideas beyond their transatlantic circuits. Opposing the disembodiment of Lovejoy's approach, Quentin Skinner spawned a school of (chiefly British) followers committed to studying ideas in

---

1998. On liberalism and empire, the best overview is Jennifer Pitts, "Political Theory of Empire and Imperialism: An Appendix," in *Empire and Modern Political Thought*, ed. Sankar Muthu (Cambridge: Cambridge University Press, 2012), 351–87.

[4] G. W. F. Hegel, *Introduction to the Philosophy of History* (Indianapolis: Hackett, 1988), 21–2, which was first published in 1882.

[5] Not so long ago, it was a novel move to reconsider the Enlightenment "in national context," see Roy Porter and Mikuláš Teich, eds., *The Enlightenment in National Context* (Cambridge: Cambridge University Press, 1981).

[6] Arthur O. Lovejoy, "Reflections on the History of Ideas," *Journal of the History of Ideas* 1 (1940): 3–23, here p. 4, cited in David Armitage, "The International Turn in Intellectual History," in *Rethinking Modern European Intellectual History*, ed. Darrin M. McMahon and Samuel Moyn (Oxford: Oxford University Press, 2013), 232–52, here p. 232.

intra-European context, while his fellow founder of the Cambridge school
J. G. A. Pocock situated them in an "Atlantic republican tradition."[7]
European intellectual history encompasses a zone that is "neither world-wide
nor national," H. Stuart Hughes explained a generation after Lovejoy in a
trendsetting intervention for Americans occupied with more modern topics
than the Cambridge school usually took up. Hughes's approach isolated a
"core" Europe on the basis of "shared institutions and an intellectual heritage –
in philosophy, in law, and in the structure of higher education – that presented
their leading social thinkers with a similar set of problems."[8] The same was
true of fellow titans of modern European intellectual history Peter Gay and
Carl Schorske.[9] If any of these figures who lived through decolonization so
much as mentioned it, I have not located the passage. For all their default
internationalism, then, modern European intellectual historians saw no need
for global consciousness. That has been changing recently, partly out of the
decentering trends of global history but also out of the necessity that all
historians of European society currently face to make themselves relevant.
Fortunately, it is not hard to defend the proposition that modern European
intellectual history can not only survive but thrive after a "global turn."[10]

-

We are only a few years into the unsettlement of modern European intellectual
history. Before its stabilization in more globally sensitive form, the moment
seems right to offer some examples of early pathways that the field might take.
One is the inestimably important recovery of the global contexts and sources
of the continuously reconstructed canon of "European thought." A second
route is to recapture the global imaginations of modern European thinkers.

[7] J. G. A. Pocock, *The Machiavellian Moment: Florentine Political Thought and the Atlantic Republican Tradition* (Princeton: Princeton University Press, 1975). The late Émile Perreau-Saussine contended subversively that Skinner's intra-European framing of the history of ideas was in reaction to the trauma of decolonization: Perreau-Saussine, "Quentin Skinner in Context," *Review of Politics* 69, no. 1 (2007): 106–22. Whether or not this is true, there is clearly much more to be said about the colonial origins of the Cambridge school, whose founders were born in South Asia (John Dunn), the son of a colonial administrator in Africa (Skinner), and the descendant of settler-colonialism in the Pacific (Pocock). Pocock did write an early comparative essay on Chinese notions of tradition in chapter 7 of Pocock, *Politics, Language and Time: Essays on Political Thought and History* (New York: Athaneum, 1971).
[8] H. Stuart Hughes, *Consciousness and Society: The Reorientation of European Social Thought, 1890–1930* (New York: Knopf, 1958), 12–14.
[9] Gay's work concerned continental Europe, reaching across the Atlantic in *The Enlightenment: An Interpretation*, 2 vols. (New York: Knopf, 1966–1969), while Schorske's was not geographically ambitious, launching in his extraordinary *Fin-de-Siècle Vienna* (New York: Knopf, 1979) a historiography set at the level of European cities.
[10] For the profound risks inherent in talk of "turns," see Judith Surkis, "When Was the Linguistic Turn? A Genealogy," *American Historical Review* 117, no. 3 (2012): 700–22.

A third and more difficult possibility is to track how European concepts and traditions were received and remade as they traveled the globe, even as complex feedback networks blurred the line between the European and the extra-European. The fourth and most controversial final mode is to insist that the modern European canon is of prime significance in understanding historical and contemporary global relations – and that part of its value lies in helping undo the exclusions that its own historians have colluded in visiting on that canon by misrepresenting European thought as a merely European affair.

It is dawning more or less suddenly on the field that the global was always inherent in modern European intellectual history, even if the way it was canonized and taught did not reflect this fact. The Enlightenment understanding of "religion" in general and Islam in particular occurred thanks to an unprecedented amount of global knowledge about belief and practice, however (mis)interpreted by European audiences.[11] A whole debate has erupted on whether Hegel himself had the revolt of Black and mixed-race Haitians in mind in his revolutionary depiction of the relation between freedom, recognition, and violence.[12] The origins of European social theory – certainly in the writings of Émile Durkheim, which drew on ethnographies of criminal punishment and religious life in specific worldwide locales, or of Max Weber, which depended on information transmitted to him regarding China, India, and elsewhere – turn out to be unthinkable outside its global setting. And so on. Down to the birth of deconstruction, recent scholarship is showing, it is pressing to reconstruct how thought once quarantined as "European" almost unfailingly presupposed a historically specific set of global entanglements, both intellectual and practical.[13]

Finding the world in the European text has been answered by the second project: finding European texts that imagine the world. The global imaginations of intellectuals localized in Europe has been one area of new interest, sometimes to celebrate their prescient brilliance in anticipating "globalization," but more often to understand their parochial limitations. After the long-standing tradition of universal history, the Enlightenment allowed for framing a capaciously global understanding of what "universality" might cover.[14]

---

[11] Bevilacqua, *The Republic of Arabic Letters*, offers a striking account of these exchanges.
[12] Susan Buck-Morss, *Hegel, Haiti, and Universal History* (Pittsburgh: University of Pittsburgh Press, 2009).
[13] Harry Liebersohn, *The Return of the Gift: European History of a Global Idea* (Cambridge: Cambridge University Press, 2010); and Gili Kliger, "Humanism and the Ends of Empire, 1945–1960," *Modern Intellectual History* 15, no. 3 (2018): 773–80.
[14] David Armitage, *Foundations of Modern International Thought* (Cambridge: Cambridge University Press, 2013), chapter 10; Jennifer Pitts, *A Turn to Empire: The Rise of Imperial Liberalism in Britain and France* (Princeton: Princeton University Press, 2005), chapter 1; and

To take an example of the more enthusiastic approach, Maya Jasanoff has highlighted how Joseph Conrad was an avatar of globalization, and thus anticipated our contemporary reckoning with many aspects of its interconnection and upheaval, from trade to terrorism.[15] Duncan Bell, more skeptical about the necessarily particular and specific vantage point from which the globe is construed as a unified space in various intellectual projects, proposes to study "world-making practices that articulate forms of universality." Alternative or even competing visions of globality are all there have been – or, one might surmise, can ever be.[16] From the ancient world on, there have been plural cosmopolitanisms, Sheldon Pollock famously noted, and each of these has usually turned out in retrospect to be produced by "intellectuals" connecting local ambitions of empire with grandiose dreams of moral order at the largest possible scale.[17] Adapting his claim for the modern times of the global, it follows that there are only plural globalizations, and for intellectual historians these are most usefully studied as the series of alternative and competing visions they are, without misguided efforts to test their truth or validity. "Worlds are construed or conceptualized with a particular interest or purpose in mind," Bell comments.[18] Not infrequently, intellectuals make worlds only as part of larger projects to alter the global order in a specific fashion, something hardly unknown to modern European history. And as Benjamin Lazier has so intrepidly shown, the appearance of the literally visible globe in the age of space flight – which intersected with the decolonization process – provoked not a unified vision of the world among European intellectuals but an open-ended struggle over the terms of coexistence on a small planet that continues to this day.[19]

Both of these ways of globalizing modern European intellectual history could be accused of looking like strategies to conserve a preexisting canon as is, disturbing it mainly to document its global sources or even confining

Sankar Muthu, *Global Connections in Enlightenment Thought* (Princeton: Princeton University Press, forthcoming).

[15] Maya Jasanoff, *The Dawn Watch: Joseph Conrad in a Global World* (New York: Penguin, 2017).

[16] Duncan Bell, "Making and Taking Worlds," in *Global Intellectual History*, ed. Samuel Moyn and Andrew Sartori (New York: Columbia University Press, 2013), 254–81, here p. 272.

[17] Sheldon Pollock, "Cosmopolitanism and Vernacular in History," in *Cosmopolitanism*, ed. Carol A. Breckinridge, Homi Bhabha, Dipesh Chakrabarty, and Sheldon Pollock (Durham, NC: Duke University Press, 2012), 15–53. See also Myles Lavan, Richard E. Payne, and John Weisweiler, eds., *Cosmopolitanism and Empire: Universal Rulers, Local Elites, and Cultural Integration in the Ancient Near East and Mediterranean* (Oxford: Oxford University Press, 2016).

[18] Bell, "Making and Taking Worlds," 261.

[19] Benjamin Lazier, "Earthrise, or the Globalization of the World Picture," *American Historical Review* 116, no. 3 (2011): 602–30. See also Michael Lang, "Mapping Globalization or Globalizing the Map: Heidegger and Planetary Discourse," *Genre* 36, nos. 3/4 (2003): 239–50.

attention to the way the texts of that canon projected supralocally. In the eyes of their worst critics, such historiographical strategies are little more than barely disguised attempts to recenter European thought and ratify business as usual. One is about receiving the world and the other about producing it – but both usually focus on how European intellectuals did so locally. At stake is not so much Haiti but what Hegel knew of it and what European frames were applied to it; not so much Indigenous peoples but how European ethnography transported its own understanding of them for social theorists such as Durkheim or Marcel Mauss to think about in the Parisian armchairs they never left. The far-flung itineraries of intellectuals a historian might track – placed at the center of Jasanoff's study of Conrad or comparable literature on the natural sciences or even earlier literary figures such as Herman Melville – most often confirms Michel de Montaigne's withering remark upon hearing that someone learned nothing from his travels: "I should think not . . . he took himself along with him."[20] Still, the renovations of an intellectual history reconstituting the European reception and production of the globe have been nothing if not exciting and are likely to be pursued much further. Most generously, they offer two important modes of scholarly response to the global setting of European thought that requires the development of others.

-

A much more ambitious task, for those who can undertake it, is to refuse the geographical constraints that have traditionally defined European thought. Jack Goody has asked whether there was a singular (European) Renaissance or many intellectual parallels across the globe.[21] The Enlightenment, as it has been perhaps the chief virtue of Jonathan Israel's writings to document, ramified to the ends of the earth in its own early bout of globalization.[22] Christopher Bayly famously traced the career of South Asian analogies to European liberalism.[23] When it comes to later stages of European intellectual

---

[20] Michel de Montaigne, *The Complete Essays* (Stanford: Stanford University Press, 1965), 176; see also Harry Liebersohn, *The Travelers' World: Europe to the Pacific* (Cambridge, MA: Harvard University Press, 2006); and Charles Roberts Anderson, *Melville in the South Seas* (New York: Columbia University Press, 1939).

[21] Jack Goody, *Renaissances: One or Many?* (Cambridge: Cambridge University Press, 2010).

[22] Jonathan I. Israel, *Democratic Enlightenment: Philosophy, Revolution, and Human Rights, 1750–1790* (Oxford: Oxford University Press, 2011), especially part 3; and Israel, *The Expanding Blaze: How the American Revolution Ignited the World, 1775–1848* (Princeton: Princeton University Press, 2017). Even more boldly, see Sebastian Conrad, "The Enlightenment in Global History: A Historiographical Critique," *American Historical Review* 117, no. 4 (2012): 999–1027.

[23] C. A. Bayly, *Recovering Liberties: Indian Thought in the Age of Liberalism and Empire* (Cambridge: Cambridge University Press, 2011).

history, scholars track how concepts and movements traditionally studied in narrow contexts found wide application and dissemination, often because they resonated with analogous preexisting currents of thought. In leading studies, scholars such as Alison Bashford, Joyce Chaplin, Yoav Di-Capua, Marwa Elshakry, Omnia El Shakry, and Kris Manjapra have traced the reception of "European" thought as it was remade thanks to imperial circuitry and global interconnections.[24] An even wider group are forging a golden age of what one might call anti- and post-European intellectual history, with chronicles abounding of attempts made within existing networks and in new ones across the "Global South" to respond to northern currents of thought by deploying local intellectual resources or synthesizing new intellectual combinations. Often these took place between metropole and colony, but they were just as frequent in colonial and postcolonial settings whose intellectuals were to make common cause in imagining a nonimperial modernity – one that did not merely accept the vision presented to them by modern Europe.[25]

All of the new works of global intellectual history that track the canon globally or induct new members into it by virtue of an expanded frame must determine whether their stories are comparative, diffusionist, or interactional. Comparisons do not actually establish a global intellectual history except insofar as their authors juxtapose elements that are internal and external to Europe for the sake of illumination. The models of diffusion and interaction, by contrast, concentrate on connections that were actually made rather than ones the historian establishes in retrospect. Indeed, rather than insist on a general choice between these two options, it is better to envision a continuum from the one to the other. Different stories will rightly fall at distinct points along it. Sometimes a globalizing European intellectual history will address the full-fledged origination of a concept or school in one place and trace its reception elsewhere. Reception itself is always active, but only in some cases does it reshape and retransmit in powerful ways. Other times the reputation of a "European" tradition turns out to be misplaced, for it involves knowledge

---

[24] Alison Bashford and Joyce E. Chaplin, *The New Worlds of Thomas Robert Malthus* (Princeton: Princeton University Press, 2016); Yoav Di-Capua, *No Exit: Arab Existentialism, Jean-Paul Sartre, and Decolonization* (Chicago: University of Chicago Press, 2018); Marwa Elshakry, *Reading Darwin in Arabic, 1860–1950* (Chicago: University of Chicago Press, 2013); Omnia El Shakry, *The Arabic Freud: Psychoanalysis and Islam in Modern Egypt* (Princeton: Princeton University Press, 2017); and Kris Manjapra, *Age of Entanglement: German and Indian Intellectuals across Empire* (Cambridge, MA: Harvard University Press, 2014).

[25] Cemil Aydin, *The Politics of Anti-Westernism in Asia: Visions of World Order in Pan-Islamic and Pan-Asianist Thought* (New York: Columbia University Press, 2007); Cemil Aydin, *The Idea of the Muslim World: A Global Intellectual History* (Cambridge, MA: Harvard University Press, 2017); Janaki Bakhle, "Putting Global Intellectual History in Its Place," in Moyn and Sartori, *Global Intellectual History*, 228–53; and Pankaj Mishra, *From the Ruins of Empire: The Intellectuals Who Remade Asia* (New York: Farrar, Strauss, and Giroux, 2012).

from elsewhere, relying on Europe merely for its fame. Isaiah Wilner turns in a brilliant version of this kind of argument when he contends that Franz Boas's notion of the plurality of cultures, while bearing his signature for a global audience, in fact was taught to him by his Indigenous contacts.[26] Most often, the truth will turn out to lie somewhere between these two extremes, and teasing apart where European intellectual history ends and global intellectual history begins is what makes the study of both enticing.

For all the relative decentering that the European canon experiences in the historiographical present and future, however, it seems as if its place is ultimately secure. And given an ambitious last approach, it may even win back in a new form some of the centrality it has lost in a global age, once it is clearer how profoundly European thought has informed many of the most important ideologies of modern emancipation. Whether by dint of the forcible imposition of its values worldwide, or the lasting appeal they have held for all kinds of people, it does not seem that the contemporary provincialization of Europe is the last word in its legacy. On the contrary, one final pathway for globalizing European thought is to insist, however unfashionably, that its trajectory into supra-European relevance fulfilled some of its main impulses in spite of itself.

For all his faults, Hegel remains a touchstone figure for the very reason that his script of history rules out his own exclusions.[27] The globalization of collective emancipation through the nation channeled a philosophically idealist spirit for most of the nineteenth century and into the twentieth. For those, such as Andrew Sartori, who feel that Hegel's great successor Karl Marx provides the superior framework for understanding both the past and the future of global freedom, there is much evidence of the increasingly broad appeal of his doctrines.[28] It may well turn out to be true, after the most recent crisis of capitalism, that a new generation of Marxist radicals is on the march that will vindicate the relevance of this strand of European thought to global affairs once again, regardless of Marx's personal failures as a theorist of colonialism and capitalism across the world in his time. For that matter, European intellectuals devised resistance of various kinds to their own local schemes of global or universal emancipation – Hegelian, Marxist, or other – and this resistance has also since gone global. (Who invented "ethnonationalism," or even the

---

[26] Isaiah Lorado Wilner, "Transformation Masks: Recollecting the Indigenous Origins of Global Consciousness," in *Indigenous Visions: Rediscovering the World of Franz Boas*, ed. Ned Blackhawk and Isaiah Lorado Wilner (New Haven: Yale University Press, 2018), 3–41; see also Gili Kliger, "Colonial Reformation: Religion, Empire and the Origins of Modern Social Thought" (PhD diss., Harvard University, 2022).

[27] Sanjay Subrahmanyam, "Global Intellectual History beyond Hegel and Marx," *History & Theory* 54, no. 1 (2015): 126–37.

[28] Andrew Sartori, *Bengal in Global Concept History: Culturalism in the Age of Capital* (Chicago: University of Chicago Press, 2008); and Sartori, *Liberalism in Empire: An Alternative History* (Berkeley: University of California Press, 2014).

"populism" feared as a global scourge today?) European thought is not a bloc but itself a bitterly divided tradition whose arguments and tools served a multitude of contending agendas worldwide – and continue to do so.

-

As Richard Drayton and David Motadel have argued, our discipline is only at the beginning of where global history will take it, and premature doubts about this renovation are misplaced: It is a mistake to call off a venture when it has barely been tried.[29] It should be acknowledged that those who decide to embrace the significance of the globe in both the origins and ramifications of European intellectual history are hard-pressed to do much about it mid-career. The discovery of the importance of empire and decolonization in making sense of canonical social theory as well as creative arts has generally led to homespun and tentative attempts to place European and transatlantic ideas in their properly global setting and to interpret how the existence of the globe and its peoples might expand more traditional stories told about freedom, justice, nation, and rights.[30] And scholars are starting to embark on ambitious projects that investigate possibilities from a global Enlightenment to global existentialism and modernism.

Clearly, feints in the direction of the global on the basis of little to no prior training come with the risk of ignorance and superficiality. Literary critics, who are more apt to construct their accounts on the basis of singular examples rather than painstaking research into arcane sources, are far ahead of European intellectual historians in inventing (or reviving) a burgeoning field of world literature – and can thus provide both cause for inspiration and reasons for caution to anyone who would follow suit in globalizing European intellectual history.[31] For young people entering that field, meanwhile, it is unclear what training is needed to track modern European ideas or

---

[29] Richard Drayton and David Motadel, "The Futures of Global History," *Journal of Global History* 13, no. 1 (2018): 1–21.

[30] For my own such tries, see Samuel Moyn, *The Last Utopia: Human Rights in History* (Cambridge, MA: Harvard University Press, 2010), chapter 4; Moyn, "On the Non-Globalization of Ideas," in Moyn and Sartori, *Global Intellectual History*, 187–204; and Moyn, *Not Enough: Human Rights in an Unequal World* (Cambridge, MA: Harvard University Press, 2018), chapters 4 and 6.

[31] David Damrosch, *What Is World Literature?* (Princeton: Princeton University Press, 2003); David Damrosch, ed., *World Literature in Theory* (New York: Wiley-Blackwell, 2014); Martin Puchner, *The Written World: The Power of Stories to Shape People, History, Civilization* (New York: Random House, 2017); and Emily Apter, *Against World Literature: On the Politics of Untranslatability* (New York: Verso, 2013); see also the brilliant sociological account in Pascale Casanova, *The World Republic of Letters* (Cambridge, MA: Harvard University Press, 2004).

intellectuals once they have been let out of the cage in which their historiography has so often confined them. But then, it is still not entirely clear what it means with finite abilities, time, and energy to set out to study global history more generally – and it surely should not involve learning fewer languages than before or risking the loss of mastery of the arcana of local settings, and of rich literatures about them, that was once commonplace. Even so, it is hard to believe it is taking so long for graduate and undergraduate teaching to reflect the expansion of our conscience and consciousness: I do not know of new textbooks that globalize modern European intellectual history in the way they present it to students, or even of individual teachers who routinely do so.[32]

The safest conclusion is the most tentative one. We are still at an early stage in the reckoning of European intellectual history with the unfamiliar truth that the "theater" of history is not Europe alone but, as Hegel originally claimed, the world.[33] I have identified four current approaches that may help European intellectual history bring the sideshow it has hitherto magnified in importance into an unknown future on a larger stage. Yet this reckoning need not mean the field's deflation, let alone disappearance. No one really knows what will occur. But it is likely to be exciting to find out.

---

[32] There are, however, essay collections for scholars: Moyn and Sartori, *Global Intellectual History*; and Margrit Pernau and Dominic Sachsenmaier, eds., *Global Conceptual History: A Reader* (London: Bloomsbury, 2016).

[33] Hegel, *Introduction to the Philosophy of History*, 58.

5   Religion and the Global History of Europe

Abigail Green

European history has been defined as a field by a notion of Europe – its borders, values, civilization, and nationalities – that is structured by Christianity and its secular legacies.[1] Christianity has been intertwined with European imperialism since the early modern era, while the concept of "Europe" remains unavoidably shaped by its long association with Latin Christendom.[2] When the historian Robert Bartlett wrote of the "Europeanisation of Europe," he described a process whereby "a culture or society ... that had its centres in the old Frankish lands, ... Latin and Christian but not synonymous with Latin Christendom," expanded into the surrounding regions during the High Middle Ages, changing as it did so.[3] Today, Christianity remains the religious heritage of the overwhelming majority of even "secular" Europeans. Arguably, Jean-Jacques Rousseau's 1761 observation that "Europe, even now, is indebted more to Christianity than to any other influence for the union ... which survives among her members" still holds true.[4] Certainly, in global historical terms, Europe continues to figure as "Christian." The global turn has therefore

---

[1] I would like to thank Martin Conway, David Feldman, Emily Greble, and Ruth Harris for their feedback and support during the writing of this chapter.

   On the Christianity of secularism, see Talal Asad, *Formations of the Secular: Christianity, Islam, Modernity* (Stanford: Stanford University Press, 2003); and the contributions in Ari Joskowicz and Ethan Katz, eds., *Secularism in Question: Jews and Judaism in Modern Times* (Philadelphia: University of Pennsylvania Press, 2015).

[2] On Europe and Latin Christendom, see for instance Robert Bartlett, *The Making of Europe: Conquest, Colonization and Cultural Change, 950–1350* (London: Penguin, 1993), especially chapter 11; William Chester Jordan, "'Europe' in the Middle Ages," in *The Idea of Europe: From Antiquity to the European Union*, ed. Anthony Pagden (Cambridge: Cambridge University Press, 2002), 72–90. On the shift from Christendom to a more geographical conception of Europe, see John Hale, *The Civilization of Europe in the Renaissance* (London: HarperCollins, 1993), 3–50. On the emergence of a more secular conception of Europe linked to particular political forms, see the discussion in Anthony Pagden's introduction to Pagden, *The Idea of Europe*, 1–32, especially pp. 1–4.

[3] Bartlett, *The Making of Europe*, 160–1.

[4] Jean-Jacques Rousseau, "Extrait du projet de paix perpétuelle de monsieur l'abbé de Saint-Pierre" [1761], *Œuvres complètes*, vol. 4, *Mélanges*, part 1 (Paris: Lefèvre, 1839), 259, cited in Anthony Pagden, "Europe: Conceptualising a Continent," in Pagden, *The Idea of Europe*, 33–54, here p. 43.

prompted historians to think anew about the outward-facing dynamic of European religious energies in the modern era – not just the relationship between missions and empire but also the relationship between Christianity and the politics of anti-slavery and humanitarianism.[5] But thinking about how European Christianity impacted other parts of the world – and was impacted by them – has so far done nothing to unsettle the dominant narrative.

We might do better to ask how the historiography of Europe can be integrated with the historiographies of Europe's historic non-Christian populations, more specifically Jews and Muslims. This is a different undertaking from diversifying our understanding of individual European states through a focus on religious and ethnic minorities – a project that remains rooted within a national framework.[6] Jews and Muslims have lived in Europe (and been Europeans) for centuries, but they also belong to religious worlds that have historically transcended both the continent and its nation-states. If we take this as our starting point, we can engage their European histories on more challenging terms, as one component in a differently configured global geography. For while "Europe" has long been part of the Jewish and Muslim worlds, it is not necessarily center stage: These are historiographies with their own particular rhythms, conceptual frameworks, and geographies; they are historiographies in which Europe – as a continent, a civilization, and an idea – carries quite different connotations. Transcending the interface between the "European" and the "global," they allow us to rethink what that interface might mean.

---

[5] Indicative of new work on missions and empire are Andrew Porter, *Religion versus Empire? British Protestant Missionaries and Overseas Expansion, 1700–1914* (Manchester: Manchester University Press, 2004); and J. P. Daughton, *An Empire Divided: Religion, Republicanism, and the Making of French Colonialism, 1880–1914* (Oxford: Oxford University Press, 2006). On the mobilization of faith communities around secular causes, see Abigail Green and Vincent Viaene, eds., *Religious Internationals in the Modern World: Globalization and Faith Communities since 1750* (Basingstoke: Palgrave Macmillan, 2012). Michael Barnett, *Empire of Humanity: A History of Humanitarianism* (Ithaca, NY: Cornell University Press, 2011), 49–94, reflects the direction of travel on humanitarianism, but see the critique offered in Abigail Green, "Humanitarianism in Nineteenth Century Context: Religious, Gendered, National," *Historical Journal* 57, no. 4 (2014): 1157–75.

[6] On Jews in national contexts, see Pierre Birnbaum and Ira Katznelson, eds., *Paths of Emancipation: Jews, States, and Citizenship* (Princeton: Princeton University Press, 1995). Recent work has been more locally focused, see Till van Rahden, *Jews and Other Germans: Civil Society, Religious Diversity and Urban Politics in Breslau, 1860–1925* (Madison: University of Wisconsin Press, 2008). A not wholly dissimilar literature on Muslims has begun to emerge, for instance Nathalie Clayer and Eric Germain, eds., *Islam in Inter-War Europe* (New York: Hurst and Company, 2008), part 4. Humayun Ansari, *"The Infidel within": Muslims in Britain since 1800* (London: Hurst, 2004) is a model of how to write such a study. For a more imperial take, see Naomi Davidson, "Muslim Bodies in the Metropole: Social Assistance and 'Religious' Practice in Interwar Paris," in *Muslims in Interwar Europe: A Transcultural Historical Perspective*, ed. Bekim Agai, Umar Ryad, and Mehdi Sajid (Leiden: Brill, 2016), 105–23.

To begin with, thinking about Jews and Muslims imposes a different geography because they have, until relatively recently, been located primarily on the European "periphery": in medieval Spain and, later, in the Mediterranean and in eastern Europe.[7] In this sense, the histories of both groups challenge the notion of Christian Europe that underpins modern European history. They shift our focus from west to east, and highlight the persistence of an older geography structured not by land but rather around the "Middle Sea" of Fernand Braudel in which "the Turkish Mediterranean lived and breathed with the same rhythms as the Christian, [and] the whole sea shared a common destiny."[8] The importance of Jews as a Mediterranean diaspora highlights the problematic nature of these overly prescriptive terms of reference and the need to consider the dynamic relationship between all three religious cultures.

Yet the historical evolutions of these groups as European minorities have been so divergent that we need to consider them separately. On the one hand, we have the project of making Jews European, which, seventy-five years after the Holocaust, has largely succeeded and no longer entails any kind of quid pro quo signifying the rejection or denigration of "traditional" Jewish culture (previously regarded as "Oriental," "medieval," and "uncivilized"). On the other, we have the project of making the Balkans Christian within the emerging nation-states of southeast Europe and despite the continued presence of large numbers of Muslims.[9] Antisemitism is far from dead, but except on the far right the Europeanness of Jews is now accepted almost without question. In the antisemitism on the left, it is now axiomatic that Jews are historically European and should be regarded as "white". The Europeanness of Islam has, in contrast, vanished from view – or even been completely denied.[10] Consequently, Jewish and Muslim geographies raise different questions about the interface between "Europe" and "the world."

---

[7] On the relative novelty of this periphery, see Larry Wolff, *Inventing Eastern Europe: The Map of Civilization on the Mind of the Enlightenment* (Stanford: Stanford University Press, 1994).

[8] Fernand Braudel, preface to the English edition of *The Mediterranean and the Mediterranean World in the Age of Philip II*, 2 vols. (Berkeley: University of California Press, 1995–6 [1972–3]), 1:13–14, here p. 14, which was first published in 1949. On the Mediterranean as a modern unity, see Julia A. Clancy-Smith, *Mediterraneans: North Africa and Europe in an Age of Migration, c. 1800–1900* (Berkeley: University of California Press, 2010); Maurizio Isabella and Konstantina Zanou, eds., *Mediterranean Diasporas: Politics and Identity in the Long 19th Century* (London: Bloomsbury, 2015); James McDougall, "Modernity in 'Antique Lands': Perspectives from the Western Mediterranean," *Journal of the Economic and Social History of the Orient* 60, nos. 1/2 (2017): 1–17.

[9] Ben Gidley and James Renton, eds., *Antisemitism and Islamophobia in Europe: A Shared Story?* (London: Palgrave Macmillan, 2017).

[10] Tharik Hussain, *Minarets in the Mountains: A Journey into Muslim Europe* (Chesham: Bradt Travel Guides, 2021).

Jewish history was until recently a profoundly Eurocentric field, driven by the apparently divergent dilemmas modernity posed for Jews living in western and eastern Europe, by the devastation of the Holocaust, and by the Zionist promise of redemption – a promise that was quintessentially European in both its nationalist and its settler-colonial dimensions, even if the descendants of Jews forced to leave their homelands in the Middle East and North Africa now form a majority in Israel. Yet the global turn currently taken by Jewish history speaks to a rather different historical trajectory, in which the distinction between Europe and the rest of the world that animates both European and global history only really acquired relevance for Jews with the Enlightenment. Rather, the Sephardi–Ashkenazi divide – arguably the most important divide in the Jewish world even today – cut right across Europe dividing north from south, although cities such as Venice, Amsterdam, and London provided crucial points of contact. Even in the late eighteenth century the Italian Jew Samuele Romanelli operated within a Sephardic world order comprising the Mediterranean, pockets of northern Europe, and America. He and his Moroccan patrons belonged to the same Jewish, halachic world and "shared the same transnational identity in which being Jewish transcended any type of national affiliation – in Europe as well as the Maghreb."[11] Jewish history in this reading was neither European nor global but something else entirely. Jews led diasporic lives, and the shape of the Western Sephardi diaspora reflected the rise of world maritime empires: Venetian, Portuguese, Spanish, Dutch, English, and French. Indeed, it was precisely the ability to transcend divides that mattered to others that rendered Jews such important agents of early modern globalization. As Jonathan Israel has argued, Jewish "diasporas within a diaspora" linked all the continents and bridged all four religious spheres – Protestant, Catholic, Orthodox, and Muslim – in Europe and the Near East, with the divide between Christendom and Islam forming a central axis of activity.[12] This Jewish world was itself fragmented and divided. Yet recent research emphasizes too the importance of this period in generating structures of solidarity, religious authority, and subversion that bridged internal divides within the Jewish world in ways that point to a certain trans-Judaic cohesion.[13]

---

[11] Daniel J. Schroeter, "Orientalism and the Jews of the Mediterranean," *Journal of Mediterranean Studies* 4, no. 2 (1994): 183–96, here p. 185.

[12] Jonathan I. Israel, *Diasporas within a Diaspora: Jews, Crypto-Jews and the World Maritime Empires (1540–1740)* (Leiden: Brill, 2002).

[13] Notably Elisheva Carlebach, *The Pursuit of Heresy: Rabbi Moses Hagiz and the Sabbatian Controversies* (New York: Columbia University Press, 1990); Matthias B. Lehmann, *Emissaries from the Holy Land: The Sephardic Diaspora and the Practice of Pan-Judaism in the Eighteenth Century* (Stanford: Stanford University Press, 2014); Adam Teller, *Rescue the Surviving Souls: The Great Jewish Refugee Crisis of the Seventeenth Century* (Princeton: Princeton University Press, 2020).

These structures remained relevant even as the "great divergence" erected a distinction, more familiar to both European and global historians, between the West and the rest of the world. In a sense, this was the moment when Jewish history became properly European: First, because modern Jewish history was invented by *maskilic* Jews who were products of the Jewish Enlightenment, conceived of themselves as Europeans, and thereby helped shape what that meant; second because the disintegration of the *ancien régime* made it possible for Jews in western Europe to enter the social and political mainstream. Jews had lived on the fringes of "European" politics and culture; now through emancipation – and new patterns of Jewish migration – the histories of these interrelated societies gradually began to merge. In reality, however, European Jewry was only one element in a broader picture, and Jews in large swathes of North Africa, the Middle East, and even South Asia continued to lead non-European lives.

Modern Jewish history is only just beginning to incorporate these Jews into a narrative that was created to fit a European mould. In this context, global history has proved a very useful framework for rethinking the Jewish encounter with modernity, both through its imperial preoccupations and through the study of what I and others have termed "Jewish internationalism."[14] The divide between "Europeans" and "Orientals" which animates this new historiography operated differently in the Jewish world.[15] Here too it reflected the disparities and priorities of western European imperialism. Yet "Oriental" Jews were as likely to live in eastern Europe as the Middle East and North Africa, while the birth of global civil society and a set of interlocking global publics provided a space in which the Jews of "East" and "West" could connect in transformative ways.[16] The migrations and traumatic upheavals of the twentieth century have further complicated this picture. Western European ideologues such as Romano Prodi may celebrate Jews as "the first Europeans,"[17] but the identification of Jews with contemporary Europe – expressed in the 1968 slogan *nous sommes tous des juifs*

---

[14] Lisa Moses Leff, *Sacred Bonds of Solidarity: The Rise of Jewish Internationalism in Nineteenth-Century France* (Stanford: Stanford University Press, 2006); Abigail Green, "Nationalism and the 'Jewish International': Religious Internationalism in Europe and the Middle East c. 1840–c. 1880," *Comparative Studies in Society and History* 50, no. 2 (2008): 535–58.

[15] Ivan Davidson Kalmar and Derek J. Penslar, eds., *Orientalism and the Jews* (Waltham: Brandeis University Press, 2005).

[16] Eli Bar-Chen, *Weder Asiaten Noch Orientalen: Internationale Jüdische Organisationen und die Europäisierung "Rückständiger" Juden* (Würzburg: Ergon, 2005); Abigail Green, "The 'West' and the Rest: Jewish Philanthropy and Globalization to c. 1880," in *Purchasing Power: The Economics of Modern Jewish History*, ed. Rebecca Kobrin and Adam Teller (Philadelphia: University of Pennsylvania Press, 2015), 155–70.

[17] Romano Prodi, "A Union of Minorities" [2004], in *The Jewish Contribution to European Integration*, ed. Sharon Pardo and Hila Zahavi (London: Lexington Books, 2020), 85–92, here p. 85; cited in Matti Bunzl, "Between Anti-Semitism and Islamophobia: Some Thoughts on the New Europe," *American Ethnologist* 32, no. 4 (2005): 499–508, here p. 502.

allemands – is an appropriation that denies Jewish difference. Prodi's assertion reflects an essentially Christian reading of the European past, structured by European boundedness and the problems posed by "multiple allegiances" for the modern nation-state. In fact, after 1945 Judaism ceased to be a predominately European faith or culture. Most Jews now live elsewhere, in the United States and in Israel – a country in the eastern Mediterranean understood in the Arab world as a European colonial outpost and occasionally treated as such within frameworks such as the Eurovision Song Contest or sporting events, and yet also seen by many Europeans as an essentially exotic Middle Eastern state.

These realities have shaped the new international Jewish history, which has both transatlantic and Mediterranean dimensions even as it incorporates European Jews as actors and beneficiaries of transnational Jewish activism.[18] Unlike their predecessors, these historians are relatively unconcerned by the problem of the European nation-state. Nor are they overly preoccupied with what Malachi Hacohen has termed "a European cosmopolitan project that left only limited room for traditional Jews."[19] The challenge, for European history, is to recognize the extent to which the new Jewish history changes the terms of debate. By showing that the "burdens of brotherhood" shared by North African Jews and Muslims living in France were quite as significant as those which bound Jews to the nation-states of Christian Europe (and arguably deeper-rooted), it reminds us that Jews living in Europe cannot simply be categorized as European.[20] By imposing a different geography it obliges us to recognize that the Jewish world never fitted neatly into a European framework even though Europe was, for centuries, its center of gravity. Finally, by emphasizing the need for traditional Jewish culture to become part of European history on equal terms – alongside the better-known integrationist trajectory of assimilation and radical secularization – it challenges complacent assumptions about the evolution of Europe as a continent, a civilization, and an idea, forcing us to confront the diversity that has always existed within it.[21]

-

[18] For good case studies, see Jaclyn Granick, *International Jewish Humanitarianism in the Age of the Great War* (Cambridge: Cambridge University Press, 2021); Nathan Kurz, *Jewish Internationalism and Human Rights after the Holocaust* (Cambridge: Cambridge University Press, 2020).

[19] Malachi Haim Hacohen, *Jacob and Esau: Jewish European History between Nation and Empire* (Cambridge: Cambridge University Press, 2019), xi. Hacohen's attempt to produce a "Jewish European history" represents a less globally framed alternative to this approach.

[20] Ethan B. Katz, *The Burdens of Brotherhood: Jews and Muslims from North Africa to France* (Cambridge, MA: Harvard University Press, 2015).

[21] As a corrective to the Germanocentric narrative of Jewish modernity, see Eliyahu Stern, *The Genius: Elijah of Vilna and the Making of Modern Judaism* (New Haven: Yale University Press, 2013).

Writing Islam and Europe's Muslims into European history poses similar challenges in a different key. Like Jewish history, thinking about Muslims undermines our conventional understanding of Europe as a conceptual and geographical category, drawing our attention to the importance of Mediterranean, Balkan, and Russian borderlands as unities in their own right and to the continuous presence of Muslims in western Europe, albeit in very small numbers. More fundamentally, it enjoins us to embrace the Ottoman Empire as a properly European state, building on recent work pointing to its hybrid nature and the importance of Eastern Christianity and the Byzantine past in making and shaping the Ottoman world.[22] Just as Renaissance thinkers such as Thomas More were forced to accept that there was more to Europe than "those parts where the faith and religion of Christ prevails," so European historians need to think harder about what this means for our field.[23]

Ottoman Europe is not a contradiction in terms. If we agree with Maria Todorova that "the conclusion that the Balkans are the Ottoman legacy is not an overstatement," we need to see the Ottoman Empire (and the Muslim world in which it loomed so large) as constitutive forces within Europe – not just outsiders against whom Europe has defined itself, but insiders too.[24] This means more than simply appreciating the role of Muslims and Islam in the making of early twentieth-century nation-states such as Yugoslavia and Albania, the only European country with a Muslim majority.[25] Bosnia and Albania were not peripheral to the Ottoman Empire. They were core parts of the Ottoman state whose notables formed part of the religious and political establishment. That the early nineteenth-century founder of modern Egypt, Mehmed Ali, was in fact an Albanian speaks to the place of southeast Europe and European Muslims within this other world. Even as the Ottoman Empire retreated from the Balkans, informal ties of family, business, education, and trade continued to connect Bosnia-Herzegovina's 400,000 Muslims to the new Ottoman heartlands, while the religious freedoms accorded by the Habsburgs cemented their identity as Muslims and fostered a different kind of connection

---

[22] See Daniel Goffman, *The Ottoman Empire and Early Modern Europe* (Cambridge: Cambridge University Press, 2002); Suraiya Faroqhi, *The Ottoman Empire and the World around It* (London: I. B. Tauris, 2004); and the contributions to Pascal Firges, Tobias Graf, and Gülay Tulasoğlu, eds., *Well-Connected Domains: Towards an Entangled Ottoman History* (Leiden: Brill, 2014).

[23] Thomas More, *Utopia* [1516], cited in Hale, *The Civilization of Europe*, 38.

[24] Maria Todorova, *Imagining the Balkans* (Oxford: Oxford University Press, 2009 [1997]), 12.

[25] Edin Hajdarpasic, *Whose Bosnia? Nationalism and Political Imagination in the Balkans 1840–1914* (Ithaca, NY: Cornell University Press, 2015); Emily Greble, "Hierarchies of Citizenship: Islam, the Yugoslav State, and Continuities of Empire," working paper, University of Washington-Seattle, 9 February 2017, Online; Nathalie Clayer, "Behind the Veil: The Reform of Islam in Inter-War Albania or the Search for a 'Modern' and 'European' Islam," in Clayer and Germain, *Islam in Inter-War Europe*, 128–55.

to the sultan-caliph, whose name they continued to mention in Friday prayers. Nor did the emerging Islamic reform movement overlook this new reality. Writing in 1909 in his Egyptian journal *al-Manar*, the influential Syrian-born pan-Islamist Muhammad Rashid Rida engaged with the problems of Muslim life under Christian rule raised by a Bosnian student but concluded that *hijra* (religiously motivated migration) was not an obligation because Bosnian Muslims were free to practice their faith.[26] During the interwar period, Mustafa Kemal Atatürk's secularist attack on Islamic institutions in Turkey only reinforced the networks that continued to link the Balkans and the Arab world. Al-Azhar University in Cairo now became the center of religious learning for European Muslims, who also forged new connections with their brethren in India, testifying to the increasingly global nature of twentieth-century Islam.[27]

Europe was of course not the heart of this Muslim world, although it had always been part of it. (Indeed, the symbolic importance and political reach of the sultan-caliph suggest that we would be wrong to see Europe as peripheral in this context.) Yet thinking about its contours confronts us with a radically different geography which provincializes Europe in unsettling ways. The Ottoman Empire was a European state; it was also a Middle Eastern and a western Asian one. Thus Lâle Can has highlighted the way Russian imperial expansion in the later nineteenth century helped bring broader segments of Central Asian society into sustained contact with Ottoman society: the creation of new railroads and steamship routes made travel to Ottoman cities more accessible, rerouting the *hajj* via Odessa and Istanbul and swelling the number of Central Asian pilgrims. Even as the Tanzimat reforms of 1839 to 1876 created a concept of Ottoman citizenship that included Jews and Christians but excluded non-Ottoman Muslims previously subject to the sultan-caliph's authority, new *hajj* hubs emerged and Muslims from so-called peripheries became more connected to the central Islamic lands.[28] Abdülhamid II built on these expanding Ottoman networks as he sought to fashion an Islamist modernity in opposition to the West, emphasizing his role as caliph and protector of Muslims worldwide. European colonial expansion in southeastern Europe, Algeria, Tunisia, Egypt,

---

[26] Leyla Amzi-Erdoğdular, "Afterlife of Empire: Muslim-Ottoman Relations in Habsburg Bosnia-Herzegovina, 1878–1914" (PhD diss., Columbia University, 2013), 94. See also Catherine Mayeur-Jaouen, "'À la poursuite de la réforme': renouveaux et débats historiographiques de l'histoire religieuse et intellectuelle de l'islam, xvᵉ-xxıᵉ siècle," *Annales HSS* 73, no. 2 (2018): 317–58.

[27] See Nathalie Clayer and Eric Germain, "Muslim Networks in Christian Lands," in Clayer and Germain, *Islam in Inter-War Europe*, 22–31.

[28] Lâle Can, "Connecting People: A Central Asian Sufi Network in Turn-of-the-Century Istanbul," *Modern Asian Studies* 46, no. 2 (2012): 373–401; Lâle Can, "The Protection Question: Central Asians and Extraterritoriality in the Late Ottoman Empire," *International Journal of Middle East Studies* 48, no. 4 (2016): 679–99.

India, Central Asia, Indonesia, and Malaysia meant that by the early 1900s the Ottoman Empire was the only major Muslim state apart from Iran to have preserved its independence. The historically fissiparous and heterogeneous Muslim world became more unipolar, as Muslims now living under European colonial rule increasingly looked to the sultan-caliph for guidance and support. This fostered a pan-Islamic sentiment combining the long-standing Islamic notion of *umma* with appeals to nascent anti-colonial nationalism. One reading of this development might be that it cemented the divide between Christian Europe and an increasingly extra-European "Muslim world" more focused on Istanbul than ever before – a process enhanced by the massacre and expulsion of Muslims from most of the emerging nation-states in the Balkans. Another reading radically relativizes the importance of Balkan and Mediterranean contact zones in what was a global encounter between Muslims and European imperialism. In this reading, India – not the boundary between Christian Europe and the Ottoman world – was now "the frontline of . . . Muslim interaction with Christian power."[29] Such a reading turns the bread-and-butter assumptions of European history on their head.

Yet Europe as a place loomed surprisingly large in the international Muslim networks of the modern era. The bonds of empire and the magnetic attraction of European culture and power drew increasing numbers of Muslim travelers, intellectuals, students, and political exiles from Turkey, the Middle East, and India in particular, alongside the burgeoning communities of migrant laborers that arrived in France and elsewhere. Meanwhile, as Nile Green has argued, their encounters and experiences of travel and of life in Europe created new conceptions of geography and history that came to cluster around the notion of a "Muslim world": "It was in the age of industrialized communications that the Muslim world was made. And it was made in Europe as much as Asia."[30] By the interwar period, western Europe had emerged as a different kind of Muslim space: one that became a target for innovative forms of Muslim missionary activity originating in India, Algeria, and Singapore; but also one in which the old, primarily religious transnational networks linking southeast Europe to the rest of the Muslim world were revitalized in the context of European colonial expansion and secularization by new sociopolitical networks that began to promote reformist and pan-Islamic ideologies.[31] The

[29] Nile Green, *Terrains of Exchange: Religious Economies of Modern Islam* (Oxford: Oxford University Press, 2015), 19.

[30] Nile Green, "Spacetime and the Muslim Journey West: Industrial Communications in the Making of the 'Muslim World'," *American Historical Review* 118, no. 2 (2013): 401–29, here p. 429; see also David Motadel, "The Making of Muslim Communities in Western Europe, 1914–1939," in *Transnational Islam in Interwar Europe: Muslim Activists and Thinkers*, ed. Götz Nordbruch and Umar Ryad (London: Palgrave Macmillan, 2014), 13–43.

[31] For a transnational approach, see Agai, Ryad, and Sajid, *Muslims in Interwar Europe*.

European Muslim Congress held in Geneva in 1935 reflected this new reality, symbolically establishing Islam as a European religion while defining the contours of European Islam in a way that denied its historic bonds with now secular Turkey. But this event too might be read differently, as a recognition of the new place a post-Ottoman "Europe" occupied within the *Dar al-Islam*. Indeed, Europe also became a place where dissident Muslim thinkers and conservative Islamists were able to develop political movements more freely than in their home countries.[32]

Talal Asad has rightly observed that "although the West contains many faces at home it presents a single face abroad."[33] Writing European history in a postcolonial world, we need to deconstruct that single face in a way that allows us to appreciate the implications of Europe's religious diversity: We need to write the history of Europe itself against the grain. By challenging the conventional idea of Europe – as a continent, a civilization, and an idea – and denying its inevitable centrality, the modern histories of Europe's Muslims and Jews expose the assumptions that underpin our field. After the global turn, European history must take account of such alternate readings and geographies. Writing connected history is not just about uncovering the connections between "Europe" and "the world"; it also entails connecting the overlapping histories we may find in Europe itself – both with each other and within divergent global frameworks. As I recently discovered, this poses fundamental conceptual and institutional challenges. At Oxford, European history and the history of Islam are both core areas for our library, but (like Hebrew and Jewish studies) the latter remains the remit of what was, until very recently, our Oriental Studies Faculty (now renamed Asian and Middle Eastern Studies); the history of Muslims in western Europe has consequently fallen through the cracks. Wheels are now being set in motion, but this particular historian has grasped that when it comes to "religion," reframing the history of Europe is both harder – and more urgent – than it looks.[34]

---

[32] As described in Gerhard Höpp, "Zwischen Moschee und Demonstration: Muslime in Berlin, 1920–1930," *Moslemische Revue* 3 (1990): 135–46; 4 (1990): 230–8; and 1 (1991): 13–19. On the social interaction and accommodations between Muslims and non-Muslim Europeans, see for instance David Motadel, "Islamische Bürgerlichkeit: Das soziokulturelle Milieu der muslimischen Minderheit in Berlin 1918–1939," *Tel Aviver Jahrbuch für Deutsche Geschichte* 37 (2009): 103–21.

[33] Asad, *Formations of the Secular*, 13.

[34] Talal Asad, "Muslims and European Identity: Can Europe Represent Islam?" in Pagden, *The Idea of Europe*, 209–27.

6   European Social History and the Global Turn

Richard Drayton

"Ideas [are] conveyd to the minde noe other way but by the senses them selves . . . I demand whether after all the descriptions a traveller can give of the tast of that delicious fruit cald a pine apple a man who hath never had any of it in his mouth hath any Idea of it or noe?" asked John Locke in the *Essay Concerning Human Understanding*.[1] How should we read this eruption of the pineapple into Locke's theory of mind? Was the Caribbean fruit merely an ornamental topos for a proposition arising out of the internal necessities of European thought? The global turn proposes, instead, that we recognize it as a sign of how in 1689 the extra-European had penetrated and changed what it meant to be European. A range of twenty-first-century studies in intellectual and cultural history have argued, in this spirit, that commercial and colonial expansion rewired modern European thought and sensibility.[2]

But is this "turn" new? No, to the extent that the problem space of modern European history has always been defined by the frame of the extra-European, known or imagined, whether "Moslems" or Africans, Montaigne's cannibals or Montesquieu's Persians.[3] The unity of European history, Leopold von

---

[1] John Locke, *Drafts for the Essay concerning Human Understanding, and Other Philosophical Writings*, ed. Peter H. Nidditch and G. A. J. Rogers (Oxford: Clarendon Press, 1990), 7.

[2] Michael Wintroub, *A Savage Mirror: Power, Identity, and Knowledge in Early Modern France* (Stanford: Stanford University Press, 2006); Michael Wintroub, *The Voyage of Thought: Navigating Knowledge across the Sixteenth-Century World* (Cambridge: Cambridge University Press, 2017); Richard Drayton, *Nature's Government: Science, Imperial Britain, and the "Improvement" of the World* (New Haven: Yale University Press, 2000); Richard Drayton, "Empire and Knowledge," in *The Oxford History of the British Empire*, vol. 2, *The Eighteenth Century*, ed. P. J. Marshall and Alaine Low (Oxford: Oxford University Press, 1998), 231–52; Nicholas Dew, "*Vers la ligne*: Circulating Measurements around the French Atlantic," in *Science and Empire in the Atlantic World*, ed. James Delbourgo and Nicholas Dew (New York and London: Routledge, 2008), 53–72; Miguel de Asúa and Roger French, *A New World of Animals: Early Modern Europeans on the Creatures of Iberian America* (London: Routledge, 2017); Brian Cowan, *The Social Life of Coffee: The Emergence of the British Coffee House* (New Haven: Yale University Press, 2005); and Marcy Norton, "The Chicken and the *Iegue*: Human–Animal Relations and the Columbian Exchange," *American Historical Review* 120, no. 1 (2015): 28–60.

[3] For an earlier discussion of the importance of the implicit and tacit "global" in the construction of history at the scales of Europe and the nation, see Richard Drayton, "Where Does the World

Ranke argued, even at its birth as a modern discipline, lay in three common "external" enterprises, the "three great respirations of this incomparable union": continental migrations, the Crusades, and overseas colonization.[4] Within such a view, it was possible to see European society as radiating outwards into the world, from Percy Schramm's Hamburg or Huguette and Pierre Chaunus's Seville.[5] What is fresh, however, is our contemporary insistence that for social forms, as much as ideas, Europe's history is, *pace* Ranke, comparable, and that colonizer and colonized, European and extra-European, were in a dynamic relationship of reciprocal influence. To this extent, the global turn cannot be compared, as it sometimes thoughtlessly is, with the cultural or linguistic or imperial turn. For these amount merely to temporary shifts in the focus of research onto particular genres of sources or aspects of the past. The new attention to the global can only be compared to the rise of awareness of the centrality of gender in the way that it interrupts every mode of historical investigation. We should not, of course, exaggerate how far anything has turned. There remain many who refuse to abandon the diffusionist idea that Europe has played a special, sacred or secular, providential role in human history.[6] The majority of European historians continue to seek historical problems, sources, and explanations in the terrain of that western peninsula of Eurasia. Most remain loyal servants of the national and continental paradigm.

Social history, so keenly linked to national(ist) historiography, lagged behind intellectual and economic history in responding to the global. It is true that the rise of "history from below," in social and then in cultural history, was an important influence in the emergence of contemporary forms of global history.[7] But it is important to remember that the new social history of the post-1960 period looked out from Europe, working strictly within the national paradigm and often leaving even the colonial offshore of the European nation off the historical balance sheet. Whatever its subsequent global life,

Historian Write from? Objectivity, Moral Conscience and the Past and Present of Imperialism," *Journal of Contemporary History* 46, no. 3 (2011): 671–85.
[4] Leopold von Ranke, *History of the Latin and Teutonic Nations, from 1494 to 1514* (London: George Bell and Sons, 1887), 1–19, here p. 19, which was first published in 1824.
[5] Percy Schramm, *Hamburg, Deutschland und Die Welt* (Munich: Callwey, 1943); and Huguette Chaunu and Pierre Chaunu, *Séville et l'Atlantique, 1504–1650*, 8 vols. (Paris: Armand Colin, 1955–9).
[6] Niall Ferguson, *Civilization: The West and the Rest* (London: Penguin, 2011); and Ricardo Duchesne, *The Uniqueness of Western Civilization* (Leiden: Brill, 2011). On Ferguson, see Pankaj Mishra, "Watch This Man," *London Review of Books* 33, no. 21 (3 November 2011): 10–12. In 2011, Duchesne's book had the distinction of being included in a list of "books recommended for White Nationalists" on the neo-Nazi website *Stormfront*: see post by "Knight Ops," 8 December 2011.
[7] Richard Drayton and David Motadel, "The Futures of Global History," *Journal of Global History* 13, no. 1 (2018): 1–21, here p. 5.

E. P. Thompson's *The Making of the English Working Class* (1963) uses the word "colony" and its cognates to describe only communities of Irish or English exiles.[8] He quotes the "New Jerusalemite" prophecy that the "British Empire is the peculiar possession of Messiah, and his promised naval dominion," without any exegesis of how an imperial view was held from below as well as above.[9] Charles Tilly's *The Vendée: A Sociological Analysis of the Counter-Revolution of 1793* (1964) ignores the exact contemporaries of the events he describes: that alliance of slave insurrection, loyalism, and Spanish intervention on the other side of the Atlantic which in 1792–3 formed the first stage of the Haitian Revolution.[10] The famous *colloque* held in Saint-Cloud in May 1965, which launched a generation of work in social history in France, was keenly European in its priorities.[11] Its successor in 1989, despite its promising title "Histoire Sociale, Histoire Globale?" continued this focus, intending "global" only in the *Annales*'s sense of total history.[12] In Germany, the problem of imperialism was a central concern of the Bielefeld school that pioneered the new social history, but it reduced it to a *Strategie herrschender Eliten* in which the extra-European was a mere object of the ruling elite's manipulation of domestic politics.[13] In Christopher Hill's history-from-below classic *The World Turned Upside Down* (1972), all six mentions of "slavery" refer to its "neo-Roman" usage as the opposite of liberty, and none to the slaves of 1640s Barbados and 1660s Jamaica.[14] In Joan Scott's classic 1986 discussion of gender as a category of analysis, the non-West erupts only

---

[8] E. P. Thompson, *The Making of the English Working Class* (New York: Vintage, 1963), 82, 214, 286, and 400. On the later global influence of Thompson's history from below, see the articles in "The Global E. P. Thompson," special issue, *International Review of Social History* 61, no. 1 (2016).

[9] Thompson, *The Making of the English Working Class*, 382.

[10] Charles Tilly, *The Vendée: A Sociological Analysis of the Counter-Revolution of 1793* (London: Edward Arnold, 1964). For this view of the origins of the Haitian Revolution, see Antonio Jesús Pinto Tortosa, *Santo Domingo: Una colonia en la encrucijada 1790–1820* (Madrid: Foro para el Estudio de la Historia Militar de España, 2017).

[11] *L'Histoire sociale, sources et méthodes: Colloque de l'École normale supérieure de Saint Cloud, 15–16 mai 1965* (Paris: PUF, 1967).

[12] Christophe Charle, ed., *Histoire Sociale, Histoire Globale?* (Paris: MSH, 1993).

[13] Hans-Ulrich Wehler, *Bismarck under Imperialismus* (Cologne: Kiepenheuer und Witsch, 1969); Wehler, "Sozialimperialismus," in *Imperialismus*, ed. Hans-Ulrich Wehler (Cologne: Kiepenheuer und Witsch, 1970), 86; Hans-Ulrich Wehler, "Bismarck's Imperialism 1862–1890," *Past & Present*, no. 48 (1970): 119–55; Hans-Ulrich Wehler, *Das Deutsche Kaiserreich, 1871–1918* (Göttingen: Vandenhoeck and Ruprecht, 1973); and Jürgen Kocka, *Klassengesellschaft im Krieg: Deutsche Sozialgeschichte, 1914–1918* (Göttingen: Vandenhoeck and Ruprecht, 1973).

[14] Christopher Hill, *The World Turned Upside Down: Radical Ideas during the English Revolution* (London: Maurice Temple Smith, 1972), 46, 53, 115, 156, 214, 224, and 351. On the neo-Roman use of this concept, see Quentin Skinner, *Liberty before Liberalism* (Cambridge: Cambridge University Press, 1998).

in one reference to Ayatollah Khomeini's uses of masculinity.[15] As late as 1990, Shula Marks, in the very first article to address "empire" explicitly in *History Workshop Journal*, the flagship of British social history, had to scold social historians for the "distorting insularity" of the way they addressed national identity.[16] The new social history not only paid scant attention to the world beyond Europe, it largely ignored the non-European impact on European class and society.

The national paradigm in social history was linked to the assumptions of both Marxists and "modernization theory" liberals that European social forms represented a vanguard of human development. An unexamined diffusionist view of modernity, with its attention focused on social formations for which the periphery was peripheral, kept the extra-European in its place. The Annales school, so influential for later work on world history, and even Fernand Braudel, held Europe and France at the center of comparative logics, with a colonial imaginary of peoples without history at their foundation.[17] Thompson's "Time, Work-Discipline, and Industrial Capitalism" (1967), with its turn to anthropological accounts of twentieth-century African and Latin American society and its explosive concluding reflections on the postcolonial and the postindustrial, might appear to be an exception.[18] But there, too, a temporality of modernization was being rehearsed, in which the social forms of the later non-West were scrutinized for clues to the earlier West. This structural Eurocentrism remains in its pristine form in the view of the origins of capitalism espoused by Robert Brenner and Ellen Meiksins Wood.[19] Diffusionism, of course, in the interstices of multiple heroic "rise of the West" interpretations, continues to meet the demands of many of the West's historians and their publics.[20]

---

[15] Joan W. Scott, "Gender: A Useful Category of Historical Analysis," *American Historical Review* 91, no. 5 (1986): 1053–75, here p. 1072.

[16] Shula Marks, "History, the Nation and Empire: Sniping from the Periphery," *History Workshop Journal* 29, no. 1 (1990): 111–19.

[17] Florence Deprest, "Fernand Braudel et la géographie 'algérienne': Aux sources coloniales de l'histoire immobile de la Méditerranée?" *Matériaux pour l'histoire de notre temps* 99, no. 3 (2010): 28–35; and John Strachan, "The Colonial Cosmology of Fernand Braudel," in *The French Colonial Mind*, ed. Martin Thomas (Lincoln: University of Nebraska Press, 2011), 72–95.

[18] E. P. Thompson, "Time, Work-Discipline, and Industrial Capitalism," *Past & Present*, no. 38 (1967): 56–97.

[19] Robert Brenner, "Agrarian Class Structure and Economic Development in Pre-industrial Europe," *Past & Present*, no. 70 (1976): 30–75; and Ellen Meiksins Wood, *The Origins of Capitalism* (New York: Monthly Review Press, 1999). For a penetrating discussion of Brenner and Wood, see James M. Blaut, *Eight Eurocentric Historians* (New York: Guilford Press, 2000).

[20] See, for example, the oeuvre of David Landes; or more recently Joel Mokyr, *A Culture of Growth: The Origins of the Modern Economy* (Princeton: Princeton University Press, 2016).

It was colonials, it bears repeating, who first challenged Eurocentric European social history, insisting that class formations in the imperial core were connected to their contemporaries at the colonial peripheries. For the Trinidadians C. L. R. James and Eric Williams in the 1930s, diffusionism was linked to how Britain and France now justified colonial domination through the export of liberty and material progress. Against this, James's *Black Jacobins* of 1938 argued for the role of Saint-Domingue's slaves in making eighteenth-century France's economy, contending that when they rose in revolt they became crucial allies and arguably, as they distracted British military aggression from 1794 to 1798, the saviors of French Revolution in Europe, while later giving Napoleon his first military defeat.[21] In *Capitalism and Slavery* (1944), Williams similarly argued for the crucial contribution of the slave and plantation trades to the making of economy and society in Britain, including the production of the social classes and material interests which, in a sublime dialectical way, would underpin both the triumph of liberal political economy and an abolitionist movement in which slave rebels participated.[22] James and Williams offered a radical view of the imperial periphery as simultaneous with, and even in some ways in advance of, the European core: African slaves in the modern Americas were for them the partners of the emergent bourgeoisie and proletariat of Europe.[23] Their arguments met with decades of resistance (and indeed perhaps are still resisted): the *Black Jacobins* was out of print from 1938 to 1963, while it took twenty years for a British edition of *Capitalism and Slavery* to be published.[24] It would take much longer before Europeans began to see their societies in these bold transnational terms.

But over the long 1970s the global began, gradually, to intrude into thinking about European society. Eric Hobsbawm in the preface of *Industry and Empire* (1968) acknowledged "the impact of the great movements of political decolonization," even if in practice "Industry" figured far more than "Empire" in his analysis.[25] The Cuban Revolution, the Vietnam War, and the rise of the "Third World" had forced new attention to the colonial. Perspectives that had arisen in the Americas in the 1950s suddenly found

---

[21] C. L. R. James, *The Black Jacobins: Toussaint L'Ouverture and the San Domingo Revolution* (London: Secker and Warburg, 1938).

[22] Eric Williams, *Capitalism and Slavery* (Chapel Hill: University of North Carolina Press, 1944).

[23] For an extension of this argument to include those east Europeans submitted to the "second serfdom" in the slave-capitalist complex, see Richard Drayton, "The Collaboration of Labour: Slaves, Empires and Globalizations in the Atlantic World, c. 1600–1850," in *Globalization in World History*, ed. A. G. Hopkins (London: W. W. Norton, 2002), 98–114, here p. 102.

[24] For a devastating critique of that resistance, see Cedric J. Robinson, "Capitalism, Slavery and Bourgeois Historiography," *History Workshop Journal* 23 (1987): 122–40.

[25] Eric J. Hobsbawm, *Industry and Empire: From 1750 to the Present Day* (London: Weidenfeld and Nicholson, 1968), xii.

wider purchase, in particular "dependency theory," which grew out of scrutiny of Latin America's neocolonial predicament, and an American Marxist current around the journal *Monthly Review*, which looked at Europe from the outside.[26] In this tradition, the sociologist Immanuel Wallerstein, under the influence of Frantz Fanon (whom Wallerstein credited with making him see the modern from the perspective of the periphery), proposed his "World Systems Theory" within which the European core of capitalism was coproduced with its extra-European hinterlands.[27] The anthropologist Eric Wolf, in *Europe and the People without History* (1982), similarly argued that modern European society was inextricably entangled in the global.[28] In 1980, Christopher Hill explored his 1972 hunch that the West Indies might be a place to look for overseas extensions of English "lower-class radicalism" in his seminal essay "Radical Pirates?"[29] Over the decade that followed, postcolonial British imperial historians – trained from the 1960s in the "area studies" model of African and Asian history – led a revolution in which the periphery drove change in metropolitan society and politics.[30] By 1987, Richard J. Evans had turned to Eugene Genovese's *The World the Slaveholders Made* (1969) and Charles van Onselen's "The World the Mineowners Made" (1979) as a model for his portrait of the Hamburg merchant bourgeoisie.[31] By the 1990s, even Robert

---

[26] Alvin Y. So, *Social Change and Development: Modernization, Dependency, and World-Systems Theory* (Newbury Park: Sage, 1990); J. F. J. Toye and Richard Toye, "The Origins and Interpretation of the Prebisch-Singer Thesis," *History of Political Economy* 35, no. 3 (2003): 437–67; and Paul Baran, *The Political Economy of Growth* (New York: Monthly Review Press, 1957).

[27] Immanuel Wallerstein, *The Modern World-System*, vol. 1, *Capitalist Agriculture and the Origins of the European World-Economy in the Sixteenth Century* (New York: Academic Press, 1974); vol. 2, *Mercantilism and the Consolidation of the European World-Economy, 1600–1750* (New York: Academic Press, 1980); vol. 3, *The Second Great Expansion of the Capitalist World-Economy, 1730–1840s* (San Diego: Academic Press, 1989); and vol. 4, *Centrist Liberalism Triumphant, 1789–1914* (Berkeley: University of California Press, 2011). For his expression of his debt to Fanon, see Immanuel Wallerstein, "The Development of an Intellectual Position," 2000, Online.

[28] Eric R. Wolf, *Europe and the People without History* (Berkeley: University of California Press, 1982).

[29] For Hill's guess that the subject deserved research, see *The World Turned Upside Down*, 255 note 120; "Radical Pirates?" appears in *The Collected Essays of Christopher Hill*, vol. 3, *People and Ideas in 17th Century England* (Brighton: Harvester Press, 1986), 161–87.

[30] John M. Mackenzie, *Propaganda and Empire: The Manipulation of British Public Opinion, 1880–1960* (Manchester: Manchester University Press, 1984) and his "Studies in Imperialism" book series; C. A. Bayly, *Imperial Meridian: The British Empire and the World, 1780–1830* (London: Routledge, 1989); and P. J. Cain and A. G. Hopkins, *British Imperialism, 1688–1990*, 2 vols. (London: Longman, 1993).

[31] Eugene D. Genovese, *The World the Slaveholders Made: Two Essays in Interpretation* (New York: Pantheon Books, 1969); Charles van Onselen, "The World the Mineowners Made: Social Themes in the Economic Transformation of the Witwatersrand, 1886–1914," *Review (Fernand Braudel Center)* 3, no. 2 (1979): 289–302; Richard J. Evans, *Death in Hamburg: Society and Politics in the Cholera Years, 1830–1910* (London: Penguin, 2006 [1987]), 571–2.

Brenner, despite his diffusionist ideology, ended up offering a view of the
English economy and society remade by the pull and push of extra-European
influences.[32]

The 1980s and 1990s were also when the question of race in European
social history began to emerge. Critical to this were immigrant intellectuals
from the postcolonies such as Stuart Hall, Peter Fryer, and David Dabydeen.[33]
Out of Hall's Centre for Contemporary Cultural Studies in Birmingham came
the bellwether collection *The Empire Strikes Back* (1982) and the work of Paul
Gilroy and Bill Schwarz.[34] Under its influence, *History Workshop Journal*
begin to address race and empire.[35] By the 1990s, Catherine Hall's and
Antoinette Burton's connected body of groundbreaking work brought race
into dialogue with class and gender and opened the path for a globalized
British social and cultural history which would brand itself "a new imperial
history."[36] In parallel, Atlantic and African diaspora history opened up a
multiethnic, transnational social history which included Europe, but not as
its center.[37] Of this tradition, Peter Linebaugh and Marcus Rediker's seminal
The Many-Headed Hydra deserves special attention for its break with

[32] Robert Brenner, *Merchants and Revolution: Commercial Change, Political Conflict, and London's Overseas Traders, 1550–1653* (Cambridge: Cambridge University Press, 1993).

[33] Stuart Hall, "Race, Articulation and Societies Structured in Dominance," in *Sociological Theories: Race and Colonialism*, ed. UNESCO (Paris: UNESCO, 1980), 305–45; Peter Fryer, *Staying Power: The History of Black People in Britain* (London: Pluto Press, 1984); and David Dabydeen, *Hogarth's Blacks: Images of Blacks in Eighteenth-Century English Art* (London: Dangaroo Press, 1985). On Hall's enormous impact, see John Solomos, "Stuart Hall: Articulations of Race, Class and Identity," *Ethnic and Racial Studies* 37, no. 10 (2014): 1667–75.

[34] Centre for Contemporary Cultural Studies, *The Empire Strikes Back: Race and Racism in 70s Britain* (London: Routledge, 1982); Paul Gilroy, *"There Ain't No Black in the Union Jack": The Cultural Politics of Race and Nation* (London: Unwin Hyman, 1987); and Bill Schwarz, "'The Only White Man in There': The Re-racialisation of England, 1956–1968," *Race and Class* 38, no. 1 (1996): 65–78.

[35] The earliest article in the *History Workshop Journal* (founded in 1976) to explicitly address race is Jennifer Davis, "From 'Rookeries' to 'Communities': Race, Poverty and Policing in London, 1850–1985," *History Workshop Journal* 27, no. 1 (1989): 66–85.

[36] Catherine Hall, *White, Male and Middle-Class: Explorations in Feminism and History* (Cambridge: Polity Press, 1992); Catherine Hall, *Civilising Subjects: Metropole and Colony in the English Imagination, 1830–1867* (Cambridge: Polity Press, 2002); Antoinette M. Burton, *Burdens of History: British Feminists, Indian Women, and Imperial Culture, 1865–1915* (Chapel Hill: University of North Carolina Press, 1994); Antoinette M. Burton, ed., *At the Heart of the Empire: Indians and the Colonial Encounter in Late Victorian Britain* (Berkeley: University of California Press, 1998); Antoinette M. Burton, *After the Imperial Turn: Thinking with and through the Nation* (Durham, NC: Duke University Press, 2003); and the contributions to Kathleen Wilson, ed., *A New Imperial History: Culture, Identity and Modernity in Britain and the Empire, 1660–1840* (Cambridge: Cambridge University Press, 2004).

[37] Joseph C. Miller, *The Way of Death: Merchant Capitalism and the Angolan Slave Trade, 1750–1830* (Madison: University of Wisconsin Press, 1988); and David Hancock, *Citizens of the World: London Merchants and the Integration of the British Atlantic Community, 1735–1785* (Cambridge: Cambridge University Press, 1995).

modernization theory and diffusionism as much as for its influence.[38] In its narration of waves of slave, Native American, convict, and worker struggle, connected but dispersed in space and time, it points to a fractured temporality very different from that of the rise and fall of revolutions bounded in specific temporal and national contexts presented in the latter-day stadial history of Hill or Thompson.

From 2000, as the global turn crested to visibility, there was a flowering of new European social history. It is impossible, here, to do more than point to a few currents. Boundary-changing contributions came from Jürgen Osterhammel and Victor Lieberman, historians who began as extra-European specialists before annexing Europe to monumental global syntheses.[39] The old questions of the once "new social history" began to receive new transnational attention, in particular as historians sought out the global entanglements of European social classes.[40] Marcel van der Linden, for example, took up the threads left by James and Williams, and via his Brill series "Studies in Global Social History" has engaged European labor and working-class history with global approaches "freed from Eurocentrism and methodological nationalism."[41] Merry Wiesner-Hanks, Imaobong Umoren, and others have similarly located Europe in a global history of gender meshed with race and class.[42] The question of race, once exclusively an Anglophone problematic,

---

[38] Peter Linebaugh and Marcus Rediker, *The Many Headed Hydra: Sailors, Slaves, Commoners, and the Hidden History of the Revolutionary Atlantic* (London: Beacon Press, 2000).

[39] Jürgen Osterhammel, *The Transformation of the World: A Global History of the Nineteenth Century* (Princeton: Princeton University Press, 2014); and Victor B. Lieberman, *Strange Parallels: Southeast Asia in Global Context, c. 800–1830*, vol. 1, *Integration on the Mainland*; vol. 2, *Mainland Mirrors: Europe, Japan, China, South Asia, and the Islands* (Cambridge: Cambridge University Press, 2003; 2010).

[40] David Motadel, "Qajar Shahs in Imperial Germany," *Past & Present*, no. 213 (2011): 191–235; and the chapters in A. Ricardo López-Pedreros and Barbara Weinstein, eds., *The Making of the Middle Class: Toward a Transnational History* (Durham, NC: Duke University Press, 2012); and Christof Dejung, David Motadel, and Jürgen Osterhammel, eds., *The Global Bourgeoisie: The Rise of the Middle Classes in the Age of Empire* (Princeton: Princeton University Press, 2019).

[41] Marcel van der Linden, *Workers of the World: Essays toward a Global Labor History* (Leiden: Brill, 2008), 9. See also Holger Weiss, ed., *International Communism and Transnational Solidarity: Radical Networks, Mass Movements and Global Politics, 1919–1939* (Leiden: Brill, 2016); and the contributions to John Donoghue and Evelyn P. Jennings, eds., *Building the Atlantic Empires: Unfree Labor and Imperial States in the Political Economy of Capitalism, ca. 1500–1914* (Leiden: Brill, 2015); and Fabrice Bensimon, Quentin Deluermoz, and Jeanne Moisand, eds., *"Arise Ye Wretched of the Earth": The First International in a Global Perspective* (Leiden: Brill, 2018).

[42] Merry E. Wiesner-Hanks, *Mapping Gendered Routes and Spaces in the Early Modern World* (London: Routledge, 2016); and the contributions to Merry E. Wiesner-Hanks, ed., *Women and Gender in the Early Modern World* (London: Routledge, 2015); Joanne Miyang Cho and Douglas T. McGetchin, eds., *Gendered Encounters between Germany and Asia: Transnational Perspectives since 1800* (New York: Palgrave Macmillan, 2017); and Magaly Rodríguez García, Lex Heema van Voss, and Elise van Nederveen Meerkerk, eds., *Selling Sex*

has emerged in French and German social history.[43] New global urban and rural histories have shown how, as commodities, people, ideas, and politics moved, Europe and the rest of the world became inextricably entangled.[44] Most strikingly, historians have even applied global approaches to European societies such as Switzerland, situated far from the ocean.[45]

Still, we are only beginning to get our heads around the pineapple's tang; we are in the midst of the global turn rather than "after" it. Beyond the discovery of new exotic causes or measures of social change, there are internal reasons for European historians to seek to push "the global" further. For the flip side of historical Eurocentrism has been nation-centric history, and with it the under-development of a European history which is multi-perspectival, multilingual, and based on a trans-European archival research program.[46] Asking the comparative and connective questions of global history goes hand in hand with the exploration of the social phenomena and sources that lie below, above, and across the political boundaries of the continent. Their connected promise is a postcolonial European social history that is genuinely pan-European in its engagement and more than a federation of national specializations.

A decolonized European history might then begin to challenge some of the distortions within the field that arose from the long dominance of the continent's western maritime façade in defining its modernity. For example, might the focus of a twenty-first-century European social history swing to the continent's east for its key questions?[47] Were we to take Austria-Hungary, Russia, and the Ottoman Empire as the center of the field, might questions of religion, ethnicity, and engagement with the Islamic societies to Europe's east and south take precedence, for example, for social historians over the problem of class? Might new geographies of European social forms and

in the City; as well as Imaobong D. Umoren, *Race Women Internationalists: Activist-Intellectuals and Global Freedom Struggles* (Berkeley: University of California Press, 2018).

[43] Pap N'Diaye, "Pour une histoire des populations noires en france: préalables théoriques," *Le Mouvement Social* 213, no. 4 (2005): 91–108; and the contributions to Wulf D. Hund, Christian Koller, and Moshe Zimmermann, eds., *Racisms Made in Germany* (Berlin: LIT Verlag, 2011).

[44] Sven Beckert, *Empire of Cotton: A Global History* (New York: Vintage, 2014); Minkah Makalani, *In the Cause of Freedom: Radical Black Internationalism from Harlem to London, 1917–1939* (Chapel Hill: University of North Carolina Press, 2011); and Michael Goebel, *Anti-Imperial Metropolis: Interwar Paris and the Seeds of Third World Nationalism* (Cambridge: Cambridge University Press, 2015).

[45] Patricia Purtschert and Herald Fischer-Tiné, eds., *Colonial Switzerland: Rethinking Colonialism from the Margins* (Basingstoke: Palgrave Macmillan, 2015).

[46] For an example of what is possible from European historians sensitized to global and transnational history, see Christophe Charle, *La Crise des sociétés impériales: Allemagne, France, Grande Bretagne (1900–1940) – Essai d'histoire sociale comparée* (Paris: Éd. du Seuil, 2001); and Christopher M. Clark, *The Sleepwalkers: How Europe Went to War in 1914* (London: Allen Lane, 2012).

[47] The reflections in this paragraph I owe to Christophe Charle's response to an earlier draft of this chapter.

cultural processes, pulled to the west by forms of offshore capitalism and settler-colonial enclaves, and to the east by an ancient conversation with Asia and North Africa, become visible? Are there, lastly, in these reimagined spaces of history, new ways of mapping Europe's time, as comparing and connecting Europe to its peripheries drives new perspectives and new periodizations? A new continent of modern European history awaits discovery.

7 Europe's Place in Global Environmental History

J. R. McNeill

One of the unsung antecedents of the American Revolution was the Pine Tree Riot of 14 April 1772 in Weare, New Hampshire, about 100 km north-northwest of Boston. Beginning in 1690, the British Crown had reserved tall white pine in its American colonies for mast timber for the Royal Navy. Yankee loggers routinely ignored the law and the "king's broad arrow" used to mark suitable trees. A zealous Surveyor of the King's Woods began to try to enforce the law in the 1760s, and when his deputy noticed 270 white pine logs in Weare's sawmills, the local sheriff, Benjamin Whiting, soon visited the village with arrest warrants in his saddlebag. Not long after Whiting settled into a tavern, the good citizens of Weare "caught him, took away his small guns, held him by his arms and legs up from the floor, his face down, two men on each side, and with their rods beat him to their hearts' content. They crossed out the account against them of all logs cut, drawn and forfeited, on his bare back ... They made him wish he had never heard of pine trees fit for masting the royal navy."[1] They beat the deputy sheriff with tavern floorboards and mutilated the horses on which the forces of law and order had just arrived in the inhospitable hamlet.

Tussles over the tall white pines of New Hampshire were a small part of a bigger story, a story of the many environmental relationships between Europe and the rest of the world. Europe and Europeans, and Europe's flora and fauna as well, altered environments on other continents. The content of other continents' biosphere, and their soils, seas, and mineral veins, affected Europe too. These sorts of connections, involving animals, plants, microbes, minerals – and many other components of the natural world – had occasionally powerful impacts on European and indeed world history. They began many millennia ago.

For the purposes of this chapter, "Europe" refers to the lands from the Urals to the Atlantic, and from the Arctic Ocean to the Mediterranean Sea. However,

---

[1] Thanks to Ramachandra Guha for suggestions on the first draft of this chapter. William Little, *History of Weare, New Hampshire 1735–1888* (Lowell: S. W. Huse & Co., 1888), 189. Weare was incorporated in 1764 and officially had 1,924 residents by the first US census in 1790.

within this European space, environmental historians have allotted their attention very unevenly, geographically, chronologically, and thematically. With respect to the last 500 years, roughly speaking, an attention gradient slopes downward from the shores of the North Sea to the shores of the Black Sea and eastern Mediterranean, although not without anomalies such as the paucity of Irish environmental history.[2] As is common within environmental history elsewhere, in Europe more recent periods have inspired more work than earlier ones. This chapter reflects those inequities and has more to say about northwestern than southeastern Europe, and about modern than ancient history.

By and large, Europeanist environmental historians, like most of their colleagues elsewhere, have preferred to work within national or local boundaries. That allows them to make the most of hard-won expertise but, as environmental historians never tire of pointing out, ignores the obvious fact that most environmental issues and processes ooze across borders with ease. Nonetheless, an active minority of Europeanist environmental historians, whether themselves European or not, have sought to illuminate Europe's myriad environmental connections to other parts of the world, whether nearby North African shores or remote oceanic islands.

This chapter is concerned with the subjects brought into focus by this minority. In every case, it ruthlessly compresses complex matters. It begins with an overview of Europe's distinctive environmental features. It then turns to four broad and overlapping categories, all considered only as regards European connections to other world regions: Europe's history of biological exchanges and its imperial environmental history, industrial environmental history, and intellectual environmental history.

-

Every part of the world has its environmental and geographical distinctions that affect its history. In Europe's case, most of them have been in place at least since the early Holocene. The first of these is a temperate climate in a northern land, delivered by the warm waters of the Gulf Stream, or, as specialists would prefer, the Atlantic Meridional Overturning Circulation. Just as Egypt is the "gift of the Nile" (Herodotus), so northwestern Europe is the gift of the Gulf Stream. Palm trees grow on the west coast of Scotland, further north than Kodiak Island in Alaska or the tip of Kamchatka. Athens is further north than Tokyo; Rome northward of Chicago and Beijing; Paris of

---

[2] Admittedly Ireland is not on the North Sea, but its historiographic traditions are strongly influenced by those of the rest of the British Isles, where environmental history took root much earlier than in Ireland. This attention gradient would be reversed for the ancient world, with more inquiry devoted to southeastern and less to northwestern Europe.

Montreal and Vladivostok. The peculiarly warm climate (for its latitude) allowed agricultural yields and population densities that no other lands so close to the Arctic have sustained. Humid air accompanying the Gulf Stream led to adequate and reliable rainfall, meaning that irrigation played a smaller role in Europe, especially northern Europe, than in any other major centers of population around the world. All these effects diminish as one goes east, away from the influence of the Atlantic. Since the end of the frosty phase known as the Younger Dryas, about 11,700 years ago, the Gulf Stream has reliably delivered warmth and moisture to Europe. In recent decades its flow has begun to weaken, raising concerns that some new version of the Younger Dryas may lie ahead.[3]

The Younger Dryas was the last gasp of glacial cold that, as recently as 23,000 years ago, covered one-third of Europe with ice, and almost another third with tundra. The retreat of the ice invited animals and plants to colonize Europe, creating new ecosystems. So the forests and meadows, lakes and rivers, of Europe are in most cases comparatively young, like those of northern North America which was also under ice until roughly the same time. Human occupation is also comparatively recent; in Britain for example, homo sapiens' continuous presence dates only from 12,000 years ago, in contrast to Africa (300,000 years), southwest Asia (100,000 years), or Australia (50,000 or more years). This means, among other things, that the historical relationships among plants, animals, and humans are less likely to be stable in Europe than elsewhere.

A third eccentricity of Europe, at least since the retreat of the ice, is the abundance of convenient water transport. Navigable rivers such as the Rhine, Po, Danube, or Volga (and dozens of others) give access to broad swathes of Europe. The coastline pattern of countless bays and peninsulas achieves the same effect. Compared to Africa, Australia, and much of Asia and the Americas, Europe is better provided with waters suited to transport, and thus was more easily enmeshed in webs of trade, at least in bulk goods that cannot justify the cost of overland transport except locally.[4]

Lastly, Europe's mines provided abundant supplies of copper, tin, iron, and coal. Copper and tin are required for making bronze, important in weaponry

---

[3] Monica Ionita, Viorica Nagavciuc, Patrick Scholz, and Mihai Dima, "Long-term Drought Intensification over Europe Driven by the Weakening Trend of the Atlantic Meridional Overturning Circulation," *Journal of Hydrology* 42 (2022), Online; Michael Vellinga and Richard A. Wood, "Impacts of Thermohaline Circulation Shutdown in the Twenty-First Century," *Climatic Change* 91, nos. 1/2 (2008): 43–63; and Laura C. Jackson, Ron Kahana, Trevor A. Graham, Mark A. Ringer, Tim Woollings, Jennifer V. Mecking, and Robert A. Wood, "Global and European Climate Impacts of a Slowdown of the AMOC in a High Resolution GCM," *Climate Dynamics* 45, no. 11 (2015): 3299–316.

[4] Parts of Asia to which this comparison would not apply include Mesopotamia, the Gangetic plain, and the north China plain.

and art for millennia. Iron, in most parts of the world, replaced bronze in weaponry (but not art) and replaced wood and stone in the making of many tools. Iron is widely distributed over the earth's surface, and Europe's abundance in this respect was not eccentric. Its coal seams, on the other hand, were. A carboniferous crescent, stretching from Scotland to Silesia, provided coal at accessible depths with powerful consequences for European, and indeed world, history from about 1780 to about 1980. Comparatively cheap coal did not matter much at all before steam engines matured in the late eighteenth century, and mattered less and less after oil and other energy sources proved practical in the twentieth century. But for roughly two centuries, Europeans converted coal into power, both in the energetic and political senses of that word. For European history, it often mattered that Germany had coal and Italy did not, or that Sweden had iron ore and the Netherlands did not. But for world history what mattered more was that Europeans, until the post-1950 age of oil, lacked none of the minerals important for amassing wealth and power.

The environmental features of any landscape exercise some influence, large or small, over its historical trajectories. Some prominent scholars, such as Eric L. Jones or Jared Diamond, emphasized that influence in trying to explain Europe's early modern rise.[5] But environmental factors alone determine rather little, and probably less and less over time. Nonetheless, even today it matters that Europe is not half-covered in ice despite its latitude, or that for 200 years it prospered on the basis of cheap coal.

-

For almost all of human history, useful energy came not from coal or oil but in the form of sunshine, plants, and animals. People everywhere took an active interest in acquiring new plants and animals that, they hoped, would ease their lives, resulting in a long history of biological exchanges. They also, without taking an active interest, accidentally acquired parasites and pathogens that affected their health. Europe's participation in that history began with the acquisition of dogs some point after 25,000 years ago. More fundamentally, in a slow process beginning about 7000 BCE, Europe acquired the Neolithic complex of crops and domesticated animals (wheat, barley, peas, lentils, beans, carrots, grapes, cattle, sheep, pigs, goats, horses) from southwest Asia. It reached Britain about 4000 BCE. This suite of plants and animals

---

[5] Eric L. Jones, *The European Miracle: Environments, Economies and Geopolitics in the History of Europe and Asia* (Cambridge: Cambridge University Press, 1981); and Jared Diamond, *Guns, Germs, and Steel: The Fates of Human Societies* (New York: Norton, 1997). Diamond addresses Europe's case mainly in the final chapter.

provided the basis for European agrarian life to the present. All the important crops and farm animals in European history are imports.[6]

Biological exchanges of course continued after the durable components of European farming were in place. In the heyday of the ancient Silk Road, the Roman Mediterranean acquired cherries, peaches, apricots, pears, cucumbers, walnuts – and perhaps smallpox too – from various lands to the East. As Andrew Watson and others showed, another era of heightened trade and travel, that of the Abbasid Caliphate, the Crusades, and the Pax Mongolica, brought another surge of biological exchange ca. 800 to 1350 CE. Sugar, citrus fruits, eggplant, cotton, and rice came from South Asia, often via Egypt, to Mediterranean shores including those of southern Europe. Sugar and cotton production could flourish even with unskilled and unmotivated slave labor, perhaps quickening the slave-raiding that long characterized Mediterranean littorals. Rice, sugar, and cotton prospered best with irrigation techniques that Europeans, especially in Spain, Italy, and Crete, learned from Arabs.[7] The Pax Mongolica also created conditions conducive to the transmission of pathogens such as the plague bacillus. It originated somewhere in Central Asia, entered Europe in 1347, and in the next five years killed around one-third to one-half of Europeans.[8]

Aside from the Black Death, these exchanges, from 7000 BCE to 1350 BCE, were comparatively slow. In any given locale new crops or animals might usher in revolutionary changes; for Europe as a whole their impact, because so gradual, was never revolutionary. Nor was any plant, animal, or microbe exported from Europe revolutionary anywhere in the world. That changed in 1492.

The spurt of biological exchange following in the wake of Columbus's voyages is the only one to which historians apply a name: the Columbian Exchange, a term coined in the early 1970s by Alfred Crosby, whose book of

[6] Barry Cunliffe, *Europe between the Oceans* (New Haven: Yale University Press, 2008). Expert opinion differs on the degree to which farming came to Europe with people who replaced prior Europeans as opposed to as an idea adopted by prior Europeans. Current genomic evidence favors the replacement hypothesis.

[7] Andrew M. Watson, *Agricultural Innovation in the Early Islamic World: The Diffusion of Crops and Farming Techniques, 700–1100* (Cambridge: Cambridge University Press, 1983). See the reconsideration of Watson's work by Paolo Squatriti, "Of Seeds, Seasons, and Seas: Andrew Watson's Medieval Agrarian Revolution Forty Years Later," *Journal of Economic History* 74, no. 4 (2014): 1205–20. An important dissent regarding the Arab role is Karl W. Butzer, Juan Mateu, Elisabeth Butzer, and Pavel Kraus, "Irrigation Agrosystems in Eastern Spain: Roman or Islamic Origins?," *Annals of the Association of American Geographers*, 75, no. 4 (1985): 479–509. A recent conspectus is Helena Kirchner, "Water Management and Irrigation in Medieval Mediterranean Societies: An Overview," in *Convivencia and Medieval Spain: Essays in Honor of Thomas F. Glick*, ed. Mark T. Abate, (London: Palgrave Macmillan 2019), 65–98.

[8] Evidence concerning plague's fourteenth-century transmission is reviewed most recently in James Belich, *The World the Plague Made: The Black Death and the Rise of Europe* (Princeton: Princeton University Press, 2022), 33–73.

that title is a landmark in environmental history.[9] Prior to 1492 the important biotic connections for European history had been with Asia, mainly southwest Asia, and, to a lesser extent, with Africa. After 1492 European mariners linked the world's coastlands together as never before, inaugurating a burst of biological traffic. In this case, unlike the earlier eras of heightened biological exchange, Europe exported more than it imported, although most of the important exports were in fact prior imports from Asia.

The crops Europeans carried to the Americas after 1492 originally came from all over Eurasia – and from Africa as well. The cereals, all originally from southwest Asia, and sugarcane (from southeast Asia) were the most important. Later, as Judith Carney has shown, Africans on board European shipping (mainly slaving vessels) brought several African crops, including West African rice, to the Americas.[10] The important animals brought to the Americas were those of the Neolithic complex: sheep, goats, pigs, cattle, and horses. The diseases introduced into the Americas, which together with various forms of violence killed off 70–95 percent of Amerindian populations within 150 years, were those common throughout the densely populated regions of Eurasia: smallpox, influenza, typhus, measles, mumps. Slave traders also imported two African diseases, malaria and yellow fever, which added to the Americas' demographic catastrophe in warm lowlands where their mosquito vectors thrived.[11] The Indigenous peoples of the Americas, not having encountered these diseases in childhood, lacked acquired immunities and suffered accordingly after 1492. As Crosby explained in a subsequent book, the diseases, animals, crops, and weeds combined with human effort in (mostly unconscious) teamwork to bring an ecological as well as social, economic, and political makeover to the Americas, one in which European rulers and settlers dominated the remaining Indigenous populations and that of enslaved Africans.[12]

The Americas, in turn, exported several crops, but no animals of significance and at most one important disease. It is possible, but uncertain, that syphilis arrived in Europe, Africa, and Asia from the Americas. It is certain,

[9] Alfred W. Crosby, *The Columbian Exchange: Biological and Cultural Consequences of 1492* (Westport: Greenwood, 1972).
[10] Detailed in Judith A. Carney, *Black Rice: The American Origins of Rice Cultivation in the Americas* (Cambridge, MA: Harvard University Press, 2002) and Judith A. Carney and Richard Nicholas Rosomoff, *In the Shadow of Slavery: Africa's Botanical Legacy in the Atlantic World* (Berkeley: University of California Press, 2009).
[11] A recent summary is J. R. McNeill, "Disease Environments of the Caribbean, 5000 BCE to 1850 CE," in *Sea and Land: An Environmental History of the Caribbean*, ed. Philip Morgan, J. R. McNeill, Stuart Schwartz, and Matthew Mulcahy (New York: Oxford University Press, 2022), 130–86.
[12] Alfred W. Crosby, *Ecological Imperialism: The Biological Expansion of Europe, 900–1900* (New York: Cambridge University Press, 1986).

and far more consequential historically, that maize, potatoes, tomatoes, tobacco, peanuts, cassava (manioc), sweet potatoes, and a score of less important crops spread from their American homes to the shores of Africa and Eurasia in the holds of European ships. These crops helped spur population growth, especially in Europe and China, by their suitability to environments in which Old World crops did not thrive and by their high yields. The potato wrought a revolution in northern European agriculture because of its extraordinary per acre yields and its success in sandy soils. It flourished in combination with cultivated clover, imported from Islamic Andalucía a few centuries before. Bacteria associated with clover's roots fix nitrogen from the air into soils, and potatoes are especially nitrogen-hungry crops.[13] In southern Europe, especially the Balkans, northern Italy, and southwestern France, maize had an impact parallel to that of potatoes in northern Europe. It yielded well and coped admirably with summer heat and drought.[14] Maize proved even more consequential in Africa, where it eventually became the single most important crop.[15]

As historians since Crosby have noted, the Columbian Exchange was part of a rapid, ongoing globalization of the world's flora, fauna, and microbes, all of which was initiated and most of it sustained by European mariners. Whereas prior to the 1490s great oceans stood as barriers separating some of the world's main biogeographic provinces, between 1492 and the settlement of Australia in 1788, European sailors charted every coastline on the habitable earth and undertook to ferry plants and animals wherever they could find advantage in doing so. And they unwittingly carried pathogens as well, sometimes to their cost, more often to someone else's. Europeans played an outsized role in all this, not so much because of the character of their flora and fauna but because they were the ones doing most of the oceanic navigating.[16]

Taken together, the whirlwind of intercontinental biological exchange in the centuries between 1500 and 1800 brought astounding changes around the world. It led to demographic catastrophes in lands such as the Americas and Australia. It eventually improved the quantity and reliability of food supplies almost everywhere. In cases where horses were new, such as the North American Great Plains, it reshuffled political relations by providing a new basis for warfare, giving rise to powerful new confederations such as the

---

[13] Thorkild Kjaergaard, "A Plant that Changed the World: The Rise and Fall of Clover, 1000–2000," *Landscape Research* 28, no. 1 (2003): 41–9.

[14] Traian Stoianovich, "Le maïs dans les Balkans," *Annales ESC* 21, no. 5 (1966): 1026–40.

[15] James McCann, *Maize and Grace: Africa's Encounter with a New World Crop, 1500–2000* (Cambridge, MA: Harvard University Press, 2005).

[16] This theme is emphasized in J. R. McNeill, "Biological Exchange in Global Environmental History," in *A Companion to Global Environmental History*, ed. J. R. McNeill and Erin Stewart Mauldin (Oxford: Wiley-Blackwell, 2012), 433–52.

Comanche and Lakota Sioux. European imperialism in the Americas, Australia, South Africa, and New Zealand simultaneously promoted and was promoted by the spread of European (or more usually Eurasian) animals, plants, and diseases. Europeans brought a biota that in myriad ways favored the spread of European settlers, European power, and Eurasian species.[17]

In the Columbian Exchange, sailing ships linked the continents as never before, uniting what had previously been separate biogeographical provinces. But sailing vessels did not prove hospitable to every form of life. They filtered out a few species that could not, for one reason or another, survive a journey of weeks or months. The age of steam, and then of air travel, broke down most remaining barriers to biological exchange, accelerating the dispersal of species as never before.

Although its greatest impacts came in the sixteenth and seventeenth centuries, in a sense the Columbian Exchange never ended. American raccoons, gray squirrels, and muskrats for example colonized parts of Europe in the nineteenth and twentieth centuries. European starlings spread throughout North America. In the eighteenth and nineteenth centuries deliberate introductions became an increasingly institutionalized enterprise. Botanical gardens undertook to spread useful plants far and wide, especially within the confines of European empires. In the most famous example, British plant prospectors took seeds of the rubber tree from their native turf in Brazilian Amazonia to Kew Gardens outside London, and from there to British Malaya. A rubber plantation economy soon blossomed in Malaya, undermining the rubber-tapping business in Brazil by 1912. Dutch authorities managed to get seeds of cinchona trees (native to the eastern slopes of the Peruvian Andes) to Java, where by the 1870s they were producing commercial quantities of quinine, a drug that offered protection against malaria. Cheap quinine made the European empires, and briefly in the early 1940s the Japanese empire too, far more practical in malarial lands than they could otherwise have been. In Australia and New Zealand, settlers organized societies dedicated to the purpose of importing familiar plants and animals from Britain, which they typically regarded as superior to the native species of the Antipodes. As historians such as Lucile Brockway, Warren Dean, Richard Drayton, and others have shown, botanical gardens, plant prospectors, and acclimatization societies all combined with improved transportation technology to sustain biological exchanges in the nineteenth and twentieth centuries.[18]

---

[17] Crosby, *Ecological Imperialism.*
[18] Lucile H. Brockway, *Science and Colonial Expansion: The Role of the British Royal Botanic Gardens* (New Haven: Yale University Press, 1979); Warren Dean, *Brazil and the Struggle for Rubber: A Study in Environmental History* (New York, Cambridge University Press, 1987); Richard Drayton, *Nature's Government: Science, Imperial Britain, and the "Improvement" of the World* (New Haven: Yale University Press, 2000); Michael Osborne, *Nature, the Exotic,*

Inevitably, accidental and unwelcome biological exchange continued as well. Pests such as coffee rust or phylloxera (a menace to grape vines) circulated around the world thanks to improved and intensified transport in the nineteenth century. Cholera escaped from its native haunts around the Bay of Bengal in the early nineteenth century and became a global scourge, conveyed largely by British imperial military migrations. At the end of the century rinderpest, an extremely lethal cattle virus, spread from British India to east and southern Africa, wiping out as much as 90 percent of the herds and bringing destitution to pastoral peoples (and opening larger niches for wildlife). Around 1880 someone brought the colorful Amazonian flower known as water hyacinth to the Bengal Delta, where it colonized and clogged the waterways by 1910, impeding both navigation and cultivation of rice and jute. A Central American ornamental shrub, lantana, arrived in India around 1800, and Australia and South Africa by about 1850. From the 1920s it proved a notorious weed, outcompeting local vegetation, covering fields and disturbed forests. Today it is among the ten costliest invasive species worldwide. The demobilization of millions of soldiers and sailors after the First World War, and their quick movements around the world by steamship, spread an influenza virus that killed 15–50 million people, most of them in India. The influenza killed many more people than did the war itself. Faster and more frequent transport in the age of steam opened floodgates anew for biological exchanges.[19]

Giant tankers that carried great quantities of ballast water proved efficient conveyors of aquatic species to and from Europe by the late twentieth century. In recent decades the Black Sea, Caspian Sea, Sea of Marmara, and Aegean Sea have come to host the comb jelly (*Mnemiopsis ledyi*), a voracious predator

and the Science of French Colonialism (Bloomington: Indiana University Press, 1994); Christophe Bonneuil, "Mettre en ordre et discipliner les tropiques: les sciences du végétal dans l'Empire français, 1870–1940" (PhD diss., Université Paris VII, 1997); Harriet Ritvo, "Going Forth and Multiplying: Animal Acclimatization and Invasion," *Environmental History* 17, no. 2 (2012): 404–14; Pete Minard, *All Things Harmless, Useful, and Ornamental: Environmental Transformation through Species Acclimatization, from Colonial Australia to the World* (Chapel Hill: University of North Carolina Press, 2019); and Jackson Perry, "The Gospel of the Gum: Eucalyptus Enthusiasm and the Modern Mediterranean, ca. 1848–1900" (PhD diss., Georgetown University, 2021).

[19] Stuart McCook, "Global Rust Belt: Hemileia vastatrix and the Ecological Integration of World Coffee Production since 1850," *Journal of Global History* 1, no. 2 (2006): 177–95; McCook, *Coffee Is Not Forever: A Global History of the Coffee Leaf Rust* (Athens: Ohio University Press, 2019); Christopher Hamlin, *Cholera: The Biography* (Oxford: Oxford University Press, 2009); Iftekhar Iqbal, "Fighting with a Weed: Water Hyacinth and the State in Colonial Bengal, c. 1910–1947," *Environment and History* 15, no. 1 (2009): 35–59; Shonil A. Bhagwat et al., "A Battle Lost? Report on Two Centuries of Invasion and Management of *Lantana camara L.* in Australia, India, and South Africa," *PLOS One* 7, no. 3 (2012), Online; and Peter Spreeuwenberg, Madelon Kroneman, and John Paget, "Reassessing the Global Mortality Burden of the 1918 Influenza Pandemic," *American Journal of Epidemiology* 187, no. 12 (2018): 2561–7.

of fish eggs and larvae native to warm waters of the Atlantic coasts of North and South America. It has destroyed fisheries and radically reorganized the food web of the Black Sea. Meanwhile in 1988 European waters donated zebra mussels (*Dreissena polymorpha*) to North American rivers and lakes. They have colonized all the Great Lakes and hundreds of lesser lakes and rivers, bringing dramatic changes to aquatic biota, including extinctions. They also cost billions of dollars annually by clogging up the water intake pipes of power stations and municipal water filtration systems. So while at the moment it continues mainly in estuaries and lakes, the Columbian Exchange in the twenty-first century is still ongoing.[20]

-

Biological exchange, as Crosby emphasized, coincided with the establishment of European overseas empires. Those empires were another way in which Europeans influenced environments around the world.[21] Collectively, the British, Dutch, French, Spanish, and Portuguese maritime empires, and the Russian terrestrial empire, directly or indirectly produced massive ecological changes around the world, above and beyond biological exchanges.

They provided the framework for an invigorated fur trade in Siberia and North America, a subject that has attracted serious historical investigation since the work of Innis and Fisher nearly a century ago.[22] Russian expansion into Siberia from the 1580s, and French, Dutch, and British forays into

[20] David L. Strayer, "Twenty Years of Zebra Mussels: Lessons from the Mollusk That Made Headlines," *Frontiers in Ecology and the Environment* 7, no. 3 (2009): 135–41. The Global Invasive Species Database lists 215 animals and 210 plants that are invasives in Europe. See Global Invasive Species Database (2021), Online.

[21] While no single book galvanized this field as Crosby's *Columbian Exchange* did for the history of biological exchanges, perhaps the closest equivalent would be Crosby's *Ecological Imperialism* of 1986; or perhaps John F. Richards, *Unending Frontier: An Environmental History of the Early Modern World* (Berkeley: University of California Press, 2003), although it is not confined to European empires; or William Beinart and Lotte Hughes, *Environment and Empire* (Oxford: Oxford University Press, 2009), which is confined to the British Empire. More recently, and dealing with more recent history, the most influential work is probably Corey Ross, *Ecology and Power in the Age of Empire: Europe and the Transformation of the Tropical World* (Oxford: Oxford University Press, 2017).

[22] Harold Innis, *The Fur Trade in Canada: An Introduction to Canadian Economic History* (New Haven: Yale University Press, 1930); Raymond H. Fisher, *The Russian Fur Trade, 1550–1700* (Berkeley: University of California Press, 1943). More recent work often emphasizes the roles of Indigenous populations. Arthur J. Ray, *The Canadian Fur Trade in the Industrial Age* (Toronto: University of Toronto Press, 1990); the chapters in Susan-Sleeper Smith, ed., *Rethinking the Fur Trade: Cultures of Exchange in an Atlantic World* (Lincoln: University of Nebraska Press, 2009); Eric Jay Dolin, *Fur, Fortune, and Empire: The Epic History of the Fur Trade in America* (New York: Norton, 2011); and Jonathan Schlesinger, *A World Trimmed with Fur: Wild Things, Pristine Places, and the Natural Fringes of Qing* (Stanford: Stanford University Press, 2017).

northern North America soon thereafter, ignited a relentless hunt for fur-bearing mammals in higher latitudes where pelts were thicker. Beaver, sable, marten, fox, and other creatures suffered dramatic population declines over the next three centuries at the hands of trappers. In the case of North America's beavers, which had served as hydraulic engineers in their environments for at least 7.5 million years, their drastic decline in the eighteenth and nineteenth centuries led to a revamping of the hydrosphere: a landscape that had been "castorized" since the Miocene was suddenly decastorized by human hands. Tens of millions of beaver dams and ponds decayed and vanished as the beaver neared extinction by 1850; wetlands, which covered perhaps a tenth of North America,[23] dried out; undammed streams flowed more freely, forcing the aquatic biota to adjust. Streams and rivers carried more sediment to lowlands and seashores. In addition, beaver ponds had formerly released millions of tons of methane, a potent greenhouse gas, into the atmosphere each year, so the near-destruction of the North American beaver population also brought a modest reduction in global methane emissions and contributed in a small way to climatic cooling toward the end of the Little Ice Age.[24]

European overseas empires also quickened the world's mining frontiers, with attendant environmental changes. Beginning in the mid-sixteenth century, silver mining in Spanish Mexico and the high Andes, especially at Potosí in today's Bolivia, brought acute deforestation (for fuelwood and pit props) and mercury pollution (silver amalgamation required mercury). Gold mining in colonial Brazil, and in the nineteenth century in British Australia, New Zealand, South Africa, and the Yukon territory – not to mention California – led to dramatic local changes in vegetation cover and, once hydraulic mining became routine, in landforms and waterways, often in the form of enormous increases in sediment flows and downstream siltation and alluviation. The dumping of mining debris regularly led to conflict between miners and aggrieved farmers and ranchers over land and water rights. In the twentieth century, central African copper mining, undertaken in the Belgian Congo and northern Rhodesia (Zambia), carried similar consequences, including, in addition, local air pollution due to on-site smelting.[25]

---

[23] Alice Outwater, *Water: A Natural History* (New York: Basic Books, 1996), 32–3, says beaver wetlands once covered a tenth of the United States. They probably covered a larger proportion of Canada. On the longer history of *Castor canadensis*, Tessa Plint et al., "Evolution of Woodcutting Behavior in the Early Pliocene Beaver Driven by Consumption of Woody Plants," *Scientific Reports* 10, no. 1 (2020), Online.

[24] Johan C. Varekamp, "The Historic Fur Trade and Climate Change," *Eos* 87, no. 52 (2006): 593–7; and Colin J. Whitfield et al., "Beaver-mediated Methane Emission: The Effects of Population Growth in Eurasia and the Americas," *Ambio* 44, no. 1 (2015): 7–15.

[25] Daviken Studnicki-Gizbert, *The Three Deaths of Cerro de San Pedro: Four Centuries of Extractivism in a Small Mexican Mining Town* (Chapel Hill: University of North Carolina

Mining was only one enterprise that put pressure on forests within Europe's empires. Naval construction was another, recognized by historians since Albion a century ago.[26] The teak forests of India's Malabar coast had supported shipbuilding for millennia when Portuguese mariners took control of Goa and other ports in the sixteenth century. Teak's resistance to water and rot, its hardness, and its superior shrinkage ratio (it scarcely shrinks at all when dried, which is crucial in shipbuilding) recommended it for naval use. More than two centuries later, the British also established a naval shipbuilding program using Malabar teak and some from elsewhere in South Asia. From about 1810 to 1860, the Bombay shipyard was one of the major construction sites for the Royal Navy. The cedars of Cuba also made excellent ship timber, resistant to shipworm rot and twice as durable as naval timber from Iberia. Spain opened a naval shipyard in Havana in 1555 in order to exploit cedar's merits, and over the course of the next three centuries built a large proportion of its naval vessels, including the largest ones, of Cuban timber. Cedar in western Cuba began to run short, inspiring the efforts at forest conservation by 1749. Mexican timber also went into Spanish naval shipbuilding in the eighteenth century. Canadian timber, particularly its white pine that made ideal masts, sustained Britain's Royal Navy in the eighteenth and first half of the nineteenth century. After 1860, European navies built fewer and fewer wooden ships, and their interest in colonial timber fell sharply.[27]

Press, 2022); Studnicki-Gizbert, "The Environmental Dynamics of a Colonial Fuel-Rush: Silver Mining and Deforestation in New Spain, 1522 to 1810," *Environmental History* 15, no. 1 (2010): 94–119; Nicholas A. Robins, *Mercury, Mining and Empire: The Human and Ecological Cost of Colonial Silver Mining in the Andes* (Bloomington: Indiana University Press, 2011); Nicholas A. Robins, *Santa Bárbara's Legacy: An Environmental History of Huancavelica, Peru* (Leiden: Brill Publishers, 2017); Andrew Isenberg, *Mining California: An Ecological History* (New York: Hill & Wang, 2006); Terry Hearn, "Mining the Quarry," in *Environmental Histories of New Zealand*, ed. Eric Pawson and Tom Brooking (Oxford: Oxford University Press, 2002), 84–99; Ross, *Ecology and Power in the Age of Empire*; Fei Sheng, "Environmental Experiences of Chinese People in the Mid-Nineteenth Century Australian Gold Rushes, *Global Environment* 7, no. 8 (2011): 98–127. The early chapters of John Sandlos and Arn Keeling, *Mining Country: A History of Canada's Mines and Mining* (Toronto: James Lorimer & Company, 2021) include environmental perspectives on colonial Canadian mining.

[26] Robert G. Albion, *Forests and Sea Power: The Timber Problem of the Royal Navy, 1652–1862* (Cambridge, MA: Harvard University Press, 1926). In the same vein, see Paul Walden Bamford, *Forests and French Sea Power, 1660–1789* (Toronto: University of Toronto Press, 1956); John T. Wing, *Roots of Empire: Forests and State Power in Early Modern Spain, c.1500–1750* (Leiden: Brill, 2015); and Jan Glete, *Swedish Naval Administration, 1521–1721: Resource Flows and Organisational Capacities* (Leiden: Brill, 2010), 313–448.

[27] K. S. Mathew, *Shipbuilding, Navigation and the Portuguese in Pre-modern India* (Abingdon: Routledge, 2018), chapter 4; Andrew Lambert, "Strategy, Policy and Shipbuilding: The Bombay Dockyard, the Indian Navy and Imperial Security in Eastern Seas, 1784–1869," in *The Worlds of the East India Company*, ed. H. V. Bowen, Margarette Lincoln, and Nigel Rigby (Woodbridge: Boydell Press, 2002), 137–51; Ovidio Ortega Pereyra, *El Real Arsenal de La Habana: La construcción naval en La Habana bajo la dominación colonial española* (Havana: Letras Cubanas, 1998); Reinaldo Funes Monzote, *From Rainforest to Cane Field in*

Figure 7.1 The boiling house of a sugar plantation on Antigua (British Caribbean), 1823. Heavy fuelwood use, for boiling cane syrup, was one of the environmental effects of sugar plantations. Drawing by William Clark.
Source: British Library, CC0 1.0 Universal Public Domain.

Another phenomenon characteristic of European imperialism helped to shape environmental history on several continents: plantation agriculture (Figure 7.1). The plantation format, borrowed from the Islamic world, flourished on the small Atlantic islands of Madeira, the Canaries, and São Tomé by the sixteenth century. Entrepreneurs, and their mainly enslaved labor force, installed it in coastal Brazil at the same time, and a century later in the eastern Caribbean. By the eighteenth century, large plantations had also become commonplace on the bigger islands of the western Caribbean such as Jamaica, Hispaniola, and Cuba. Plantations soon appeared on island shores in the Indian and Pacific oceans too, in Mauritius and Réunion, Fiji and

Cuba: An Environmental History since 1492 (Chapel Hill: University of North Carolina Press, 2008), 20–66 passim; Antonio Béthencourt Massieu, "El real astillero de Coatzacoalcos (1720–1735)," *Anuario de Estudios Americanos* 15 (1958): 371–428; Arthur R. M. Lower, *Great Britain's Woodyard: British America and the Timber Trade, 1763–1867* (Montreal: McGill-Queen's University Press, 1973); and Graeme Wynn, *Timber Colony: A Historical Geography of Early Nineteenth Century New Brunswick* (Toronto: University of Toronto Press, 1981).

Hawaii, and several other islands besides; and on Australia's Queensland coast and Natal in South Africa.[28]

Everywhere that sugar, cotton, indigo, coffee, rice, tea, and other plantation crops took root, laborers first had to cut and burn forest or bush. Replacement of forest by cropland or fallow led to a suite of environmental transformations, beginning with accelerated soil erosion and siltation. It included reduction of habitat, and therefore populations, of forest species. Barbados, for example, lost most of its forest and songbirds within a generation after sugar planting began in the 1640s. Sugar planting in the Caribbean and Natal created local environments extremely propitious for populations of *Aedes aegypti*, the mosquito species that serves as a vector for yellow fever, chikungunya, Zika, and dengue, leading to new and dangerous disease regimes in these regions. Rice plantations had a parallel effect for the mosquito genus *Anopheles*, which includes several vectors of malaria. In some arid or semi-arid environments, plantation agriculture also required extensive new irrigation networks, as in the cotton precincts of imperial Russian and later Soviet Central Asia or the Gezira scheme in the Anglo-Egyptian Sudan. Plantation agriculture, while not confined to the lands of European imperialism, was characteristic of many of them, and everywhere it existed its requirements proved environmentally consequential.[29]

European imperialism shaped urban environmental history too. Whereas before 1600, most cities of the world had grown up chaotically over centuries and often amounted to agglomerations of villages, colonial settings offered the opportunity and sometimes the resources to plan cities carefully. Philip II of Spain in 1573 required cities in Spanish America to conform to an ideal of gridded streets and plazas, something hard to find in Spain itself. For Europeans, especially Iberians, French, and Italians conscious of their

---

[28] Philip D. Curtin, *The Rise and Fall of the Plantation Complex: Essays in Atlantic History* (New York: Cambridge University Press, 1990); J. H. Galloway, *The Sugar Cane Industry: An Historical Geography from Its Origins to 1914* (Cambridge: Cambridge University Press, 1989).

[29] Among the works addressing these themes, see Philip Morgan, "The Caribbean Environment to 1850," in *Sea and Land*, ed. Philip Morgan, J. R. McNeill, Stuart Schwartz, and Matthew Mulcahy, 19–129; Lydia M. Pulsipher, *Seventeenth-century Montserrat: An Environmental Impact Statement* (Norwich: Geo Books, 1986); Funes Monzote, *From Rainforest to Cane Field*; Warren Dean, *With Broadaxe and Firebrand: The Destruction of the Brazilian Atlantic Forest* (Berkeley: University of California Press, 1997); Richard Grove, *Green Imperialism: Colonial Expansion, Tropical Island Edens and the Origins of Environmentalism 1600–1860* (New York: Cambridge University Press, 1995); David Watts, *The West Indies: Patterns of Development, Culture, and Environmental Change since 1492* (Cambridge: Cambridge University Press, 1987); J. R. McNeill, *Mosquito Empires: Ecology and War in the Great Caribbean, 1620–1914* (New York: Cambridge University Press, 2010); Philip D. Rotz, "Vectors and Viruses in Southeast Africa and the Indian Ocean World: Aedes aegypti, Chikungunya, and Dengue in Durban, Natal" (PhD diss., Boston University, 2021); and Maya K. Peterson, *Pipe Dreams: Water and Empire in Central Asia's Aral Sea Basin* (New York: Cambridge University Press, 2019).

Roman heritage, this amounted to an invitation to inscribe gridded patterns upon landscapes in the Americas, Africa, and Asia.[30] Occasionally that involved creating cities from scratch, but more often it required obliterating prior settlements in order to create a system of squares, blocks, and right-angled streets. Colonial (and contemporary) Mogadishu, Melbourne, Toronto, or Buenos Aires, and dozens of other cities, as well as the former "European quarter" of Algiers, Chennai (Madras), or Nairobi, show this impulse to geometrically ordered cities.[31]

-

Industrialization after 1780 or so marked a new era in world history. It also reconfigured ecology far and wide, within and without Europe. The history of European industrialization's impact on Europe's own environment is well told in a handful of pollution studies. The full history of European industrialization's impact on the global environment remains to be told, although fragments of the story are available: for example, the cases of Lebanon's silk, Argentina's quebracho, and Indonesia's gutta percha.

Nineteenth-century Mount Lebanon, an Ottoman province, had produced small amounts of silk since Byzantine times. In 1801, tinkerers in Lyon invented a mechanical silk loom, sharply reducing the cost of weaving silk. By 1835, regular steamship traffic linked Beirut and Marseille, making Lebanese silk cheap in France. By 1910, 90–93 percent of Lebanese raw silk went to France. Meanwhile, the extent of silk production in Lebanon multiplied in response to the opportunities presented by the export trade. Raising silkworms and their sole food, mulberry leaves, suited the soils and climate of Lebanon nicely. But extracting silk thread from cocoons required boiling water, and therefore fuel, which on Mount Lebanon came mainly in the form of firewood from the fabled cedar forests. Village entrepreneurs placed boiling houses next to forests for fuel. By 1869, fuelwood was sufficiently scarce that conservation measures were attempted. By 1910 imported British coal was cheaper than fuelwood on Mount Lebanon. The silk trade had rapidly shrunk the cedar forests, opening the slopes to accelerated soil erosion and lowering the water table. Per-hectare yields of raw silk fell, due in part, perhaps, to soil impoverishment in the 35 percent of arable devoted to mulberry trees. About

---

[30] Orthogonal grids were used in ancient cities in China, the Indus Valley, and Mesoamerica as well as by the Romans. Chicago is probably the most orthogonally regular big city in the world.

[31] The chapters in Carlos Nunes Silva, ed., *Urban Planning in Sub-Saharan Africa: Colonial and Post-colonial Planning Cultures* (New York: Routledge, 2015); Richard Morse, *From Community to Metropolis: A Biography of São Paulo, Brazil* (Gainesville: University of Florida Press, 1958); and Eric Lewis Beverley, "Colonial Urbanism and South Asian Cities," *Social History*, 36, no. 4 (2011): 482–97.

150,000 emigrants left for the Americas between 1887 and 1913, despairing of their prospects at home. (The population of Mount Lebanon at the time was about 400,000.)[32]

Leather manufacture stood among Europe's major industries from 1750 to 1940. Most of the necessary raw materials, such as hides and tannin from tree bark, could be found locally, although both were also imported from other continents. In 1867, a discovery was made that for the next several decades linked Europe's leather industry to the Chaco, a semi-arid district in the interior of South America, straddling the border between Argentina and Paraguay. The heartwood of the *quebracho colorado* tree, if ground up into powder and boiled, made a superb vegetal tannin and dyestuff, ideal for soft leather manufacture. It made its reputation in industrial expositions in Barcelona and Paris. Although it took decades for railroads and other infrastructure to connect the Chaco to the port of Buenos Aires, by 1895 quebracho was the world's leading source of vegetal tannin, with about 170,000 tons of quebracho heartwood per year sent to Europe.[33] Unfortunately, harvesting it required felling mature trees over 200 years old. The quebracho boom by 1940 cost Argentina almost all its quebracho forest and about 10 percent of its national forest area. The industry limped on for a few more decades before chemical dyes and shortage of quebracho killed it off.[34]

Like quebracho dye, gutta percha came from trees. In the mid-nineteenth century chemical engineers, notably Werner Siemens, discovered that a refined sap from a tree species (*Palaquium gutta*) found in the Dutch East Indies and the southernmost Malay peninsula made an excellent insulation for undersea telegraph cables. Gutta percha did not corrode in saltwater and retained strength and flexibility in the cold waters of the ocean floor – unlike rubber. By 1860, private companies, spurred on by navies and strategists in the corridors of power, began a forty-year frenzy of laying submarine cables. By 1903, when the frenzy ceased, a neural network of copper cable conducted electrons bearing information around the world, and every inch of the 265,000 miles of cable was coated in gutta percha, as were another 30,000 miles of

---

[32] Kais Firro, "Silk and Agrarian Changes in Lebanon, 1860–1914," *International Journal of Middle East Studies* 22, no. 2 (1990): 151–69; Gaston Ducousso, *L'industrie de la soie en Syrie et au Liban* (Beirut: Imprimerie Catholique, 1913); Marvin W. Mikesell, "The Deforestation of Mount Lebanon," *Geographical Review* 59, no. 1 (1969): 1–28; and, above all, Graham A. Pitts, "Fallow Fields: Famine and the Making of Lebanon" (PhD diss., Georgetown University, 2016).

[33] Charles T. Davis, *The Manufacture of Leather* (Philadelphia: H. C. Baird & Co, 1897), 40.

[34] The quebracho story appears in part in Juergen Bünstorf, "Tanningewinnung und Landerschliessung im Argentinischen Gran Chaco," *Geographische Zeitschrift* 59, no. 3 (1971): 177–204; Lucas A. Tortorelli, *Maderas y bosques argentinos* (Buenos Aires: Editorial Acme, 1956); Adrián Gustavo Zarrilli, "El oro rojo: la industria del tanino en la Argentina (1890–1950)," *Silva Lusitania* 16, no. 2 (2008): 239–59.

cable beneath the soggy streets of London. Obtaining gutta percha required locating the right trees amid the rainforests of Borneo, Sumatra, or Malaya, felling them, incising them, and draining their sap – work all done by Indigenous populations such as the Iban, Punan, or Binua. Chinese traders acquired the raw gutta percha, ferried it to Batavia or Singapore for shipment to Rotterdam or London, where it would be heated, treated chemically, and converted into just the thing for coating submarine cables. About ninety million trees were cut for this purpose from 1851 to 1903, leading to "scarcity, and threatened extinction," of the species.[35] Many contemporaries found the assault on gutta trees wasteful. Attempts at growing the trees on plantations, undertaken in the Philippines, Vietnam, Sumatra, and Malaya, yielded meager results. As with quebracho, technological change eased pressure on a dwindling resource: by the 1920s wireless radio eliminated interest in laying further undersea cables.[36]

Lebanese silk, Argentine quebracho, and southeast Asian gutta percha are three of dozens of examples of a general process by which European industrialization altered ecologies around the world. In some cases, such as gutta percha, the entire business took place within the confines of European empires. In others, such as quebracho, it did not. In any case, imperialism and industrialization were deeply intertwined, exerting environmental impacts in far-flung lands (and seas).

The production of silk, quebracho, and gutta percha all involved the destruction of trees, either as fuelwood or as a source of an industrial raw material. As a result, the proportion of the planet's carbon sequestered in vegetation declined, and the proportion in soils and the atmosphere rose. About one-third of the carbon added to the atmosphere since 1850 derives from the loss of vegetation rather than fossil fuel use. In a modest way, the trees burned or felled in pursuit of silk, quebracho, and gutta percha contributed to the carbon loading of the atmosphere and the destabilization of the modern climate system.

-

[35] Charles Bright, *Submarine Telegraphs: Their History, Construction and Working* (London: Crosby Lockwood & Son, 1898), 258 for the quotation. Today the world loses about ten billion trees annually. T. W. Crowther et al., "Mapping Tree Density at a Global Scale," *Nature* 525, no. 7568 (2015): 201–5.

[36] Helen L. Godfrey, *Submarine Telegraphy and the Hunt for Gutta Percha: Challenge and Opportunity in a Global Trade* (Leiden: Brill, 2018); Lesley M. Potter, "A Forest Product out of Control: Gutta Percha in Indonesia and the Wider Malay World, 1845–1915," in *Paper Landscapes: Explorations in the Environmental History of Indonesia*, ed. Peter Boomgaard, Freek Colombijn, and David Henley (Leiden: KITLV Press, 1997), 281–308; and John Tully, "A Victorian Ecological Disaster: Imperialism, the Telegraph, and Gutta-Percha," *Journal of World History* 20, no. 4 (2009): 559–79; Bright, *Submarine Telegraphs*.

Over the past 500 years, at least, European thinkers and scientists have hatched ideas that, sooner or later, proved environmentally consequential both within Europe and without. The important ones are well known and I will not belabor them here. Chronologically speaking, the first of these comprised the so-called Scientific Revolution of the early modern period, itself partly a product of intellectual exchanges between Europeans and populations elsewhere. Whether or not the Scientific Revolution invited people (men in particular) to take a cold, calculating, and instrumentalist outlook with respect to nature, as Carolyn Merchant argued, it without doubt empowered people to understand and more efficiently alter environments.[37] Subsequent European science, whether thermodynamics, germ theory, genetics, or nuclear physics, raised human capabilities to alter environments by several orders of magnitude. Not all science with this power was undertaken in Europe or by Europeans but between 1700 and 1940 or so most of it was.

Two other subsequent strands of European thought also played strong roles in shaping global environments: economics and environmentalism. In the nineteenth century, various thinkers, most of them British, crystallized what has become the modern discipline of economics, with its uncompromising commitment to economic growth as the source of human welfare. This iron commitment stood at the foundation of both capitalist and communist economics. Only a tiny platoon of heretical thinkers, ecological economists, questioned it – and they never got near the seats of power. As a consequence, wherever states and societies took the wisdom of economists, they sought to maximize production and discounted almost all ecological consequences as, in the jargon of the profession, externalities. Moreover, the adherents to the dogmas of economics dismissed the prospect of raw material shortages, confident that – as indeed happened with quebracho and gutta percha – substitutes would appear should the supply of anything desirable diminish. This set of ideas, hatched mainly in the nineteenth century, acquired global reach in the twentieth, and since about 1930 governed the outlook and conduct of almost everyone in or adjacent to the corridors of power – whether or not they considered themselves capitalists.[38]

At the same time that science empowered endless alterations to the global environment, and economics justified them as appropriate measures in the advance of social welfare, environmental anxieties emerged in several parts of the world, not least Europe and its empires. According to Richard Grove,

---

[37] Carolyn Merchant, *The Death of Nature: Women, Ecology, and the Scientific Revolution* (New York: Harper & Row, 1980).

[38] Marco P. Vianna Franco and Antoine Missemer, *A History of Ecological Economic Thought* (London: Routledge, 2022) explains the intellectual evolution of ecological economics with due attention to eastern and central European contributions.

the roots of modern environmentalism lie in the observations of colonial administrators and scientists posted to island and imperial backwaters of the British and French empires in the seventeenth and eighteenth centuries.[39] In the nineteenth century, dominant and durable ideas concerning forest conservation emerged from German, French, and British experts. Their institutions became models elsewhere, and not only in European colonies, whether or not they fit forest realities around the world.[40] Reigning ideas about soil science and soil conservation came from Russia beginning in the 1870s, the British Empire, as well as by the 1920s from the United States. Most of the science underlying anxieties about the atmosphere and climate originated in Europe, beginning with the Swede Svante Arrhenius in the 1890s. The vigor and global prestige of European science between about 1850 and 1950 ensured that a disproportionate share of the ideas behind modern environmentalism were European, and that they traveled readily to the four corners of the earth.

Thanks, in short, to the power and influence of Europe in recent centuries, ideas that originated mainly in Europe exercised an outsized influence over the course of global environmental history from 1800 if not before. And, in attenuated ways, they still do.

-

This sketch aims to illustrate several of the many pathways by which Europe and Europeans have influenced, and been entangled in, global environmental history. Through biological exchanges, imperial, industrial, and intellectual impacts, all of which overlapped and intertwined at times, Europeans participated in transnational and intercontinental environmental histories. Most environmental historians, like most historians in general, remain more comfortable working within national or at most continental frameworks, as Germanists or Europeanists for example. But much (not all) of the subject matter of environmental history, whether the ecological consequences of plantation economies, the ideas behind forest conservation, or a thousand other topics, flows readily across borders and leaps oceans in a single bound. The training and ambition of environmental historians, like that of all historians, are still adjusting to that challenge.

It may seem from these pages that Europeans get more than their due as agents of environmental change in world history. If so, that is a result of the emphasis placed here on the years between 1500 and 1950. An earlier focus would yield a different perspective with less intercontinental environmental influence in general, and with a much smaller role for Europeans within it.

---

[39] Richard Grove, *Green Imperialism.*
[40] Joachim Radkau, *Wood: A History* (Cambridge: Polity Press, 2011).

A later focus, post-1950, would feature North Americans and (post-2000) Chinese more prominently as shapers of global environmental history. But in the early modern centuries when oceanic navigation came of age, and in the first centuries of the industrial era (1750–1950), Europe and Europeans altered global environmental history through transnational and transcontinental interactions more than anyone else.

8   Global Turns in European History and the History of Consumption

Maxine Berg

Perhaps the key area where global history has affected European history has been the study of the trade in commodities and its impact on European consumer behavior. This is a long-standing interest among those who studied Europe's encounters with the wider world. Fernand Braudel included non-European foods, drinks, spices, and stimulants as well as furniture and textiles in his chapters on material life in the first volume of his *Civilization and Capitalism, 15th–18th Century*.[1] At the time he wrote in the later 1970s these were an add-on, a superfluity in everyday life, not the source of a key transformation of consumer cultures in the way we have come to see them today. It remains the case, however, that the study of wider world commodities and their impact on Europe has taken less from global approaches than it could do. In the cases of many of these commodities there remains a divide between the study of the production and distribution of goods, from coffee and sugar to porcelain and muslins, and the study of how these goods became desirable then embedded in European consumption and everyday life. In 1997 Sanjay Subrahmanyam published his "Connected Histories," arguing for transition across the regional boxes that have confined historians. He argued for applying global dimensions to the necessary local and microhistorical base of historical research.[2] After nearly twenty-five years of engaging in global history historians are still in the early stages of applying connected histories to their methods. At a time now of historians uncovering Europe's slavery past and enquiring further into coerced and low-wage labor systems, we have separate histories of slavery and slave plantations from those of Europe's consumer cultures of sugar, coffee, and cotton.

Consumption became a leading subject among European social and cultural historians during the 1980s and 1990s. Many studied the probate inventories

---

[1] Fernand Braudel, *Civilization and Capitalism, 15th–18th Century*, vol. 1, *The Structure of Everyday Life: The Limits of the Possible* (London: Collins, 1981), which was first published in 1967.

[2] Sanjay Subrahmanyam, "Connected Histories: Notes towards a Reconfiguration of Early Modern Eurasia," *Modern Asian Studies* 31, no. 3 (1997): 735–62.

left in the wills of ordinary householders in communities across northwestern Europe and colonial North America. They identified a transition in the quantity and character of possessions starting during the later seventeenth century and gathering pace in the eighteenth. There were more furnishings and material objects, special front stage rooms for display and sociability, and more things from outside the local region, and even from outside Europe.[3] Historical debate during this period focused on identifying the timing, places, and sources of a "consumer revolution" that predated or accompanied an industrial revolution. Some connected this focus on early consumerism as an aspect of postwar and Cold War policies of promoting mass consumer societies that would underpin new industrial growth and modernization.[4] Whatever the political origins of the subject, social and cultural historians delved into the meaning and significance of the goods, their gender characteristics, their role in gift and credit relations, and their markers of status and life cycle. Fashionability and novelty accompanied family heritage.[5]

British studies demonstrated an expansion of the world of goods in ordinary and middle-class households at a time that economic historians were arguing for a prolonged period of static or falling real wages during the period of the Industrial Revolution. There was little conversation between the two groups.[6] There was little serious discussion, furthermore, of the sources and routes of distribution of many of the new goods, notably ceramics and some textiles, among social and cultural historians. Economic historians, in their turn, gave little credence to the part played by foreign trade in Britain's and wider Europe's eighteenth-century economic growth. Agricultural transformation,

---

[3] For an early statement of this see Lorna Weatherill, *Consumer Behaviour and Material Culture in Britain 1660–1760* (London: Routledge, 1988). See Anne E. C. McCants, "Poor Consumers as Global Consumers: The Diffusion of tea and Coffee Drinking in the Eighteenth Century," *Economic History Review* 61, no. S1 (2008): 172–200 on the Dutch; Daniel Roche, *The Culture of Clothing: Dress and Fashion in the Ancien Regime* (Cambridge: Cambridge University Press, 1994) on the French; and Lois Green Carr and Lorena S. Walsh, "Changing Lifestyles and Consumer Behavior in the Colonial Chesapeake," in *Of Consuming Interests: The Styles of Life in the Eighteenth Century*, ed. Cary Carson, Ronald Hoffman, and Peter J. Albert (Charlottesville: University Press of Virginia, 1994), 59–166 on colonial North America.

[4] John Brewer, "The Error of Our Ways: Historians and the Birth of Consumer Society," working paper no. 12, 23 September 2003 <www.consume.bbk.ac.uk/working_papers>; and Frank Trentmann, *Empire of Things: How We Became a World of Consumers, from the Fifteenth Century to the Twenty-First* (London: Allen Lane, 2016), 3–16.

[5] John Brewer and Roy Porter, eds., *Consumption and the World of Goods* (London: Routledge, 1993), especially the chapters by Jan de Vries, Lorna Weatherill, Cissie Fairchilds, T. H. Breen, and Amanda Vickery. Also see Beverly Lemire, *Fashion's Favourite: The Cotton Trade and the Consumer in Britain, 1660–1800* (Oxford: Oxford University Press, 1991).

[6] Charles H. Feinstein, "Pessimism Perpetuated: Real Wages and the Standard of Living in Britain during and after the Industrial Revolution," *Journal of Economic History* 58, no. 3 (1998): 625–58.

demographic transition, and energy sources dominated discussion.[7] Study of the household and labor markets generated in an older debate on proto-industrialization was, however, connected by Jan de Vries with the many probate inventory studies to yield the concept he developed of the "industrious revolution." In a key article first published in 1993, then in his book *The Industrious Revolution*, published fifteen years later, he set out the part played by colonial groceries and material goods in a northern European "industrious revolution." The "industrious revolution" describes a change in the behavior of men, women, and children within the household. Demand for new commodities persuaded them to work for cash, for the market, instead of, and in addition to, subsistence work for the household. New goods, de Vries thus argued, stimulated a greater market orientation and greater intensity of labor in the century preceding industrialization.[8]

The global turn in the study of European consumption really emerged only late in the 1990s as some historians moved on from consumption to study the role of luxury and superfluous goods in European elite and nonelite house-holds.[9] This coincided with new comparative research of Chinese and Indian historians on the "great divergence" in economic pathways between Asia and Europe.[10] There was a turn to the study of "global commodities" – colonial groceries on the one hand (coffee, tobacco, chocolate, tea) and Asian luxury manufactures on the other, especially ceramics and cotton textiles.

Jan de Vries's later article on the "Limits of Globalization" shows the comparative growth of imports to Europe from Asia and the New World, demonstrating the dramatic growth of Atlantic world imports. Imports,

---

[7] E. A. Wrigley, *Continuity, Chance and Change: The Character of the Industrial Revolution in England* (Cambridge: Cambridge University Press, 1988); Robert C. Allen, *The British Industrial Revolution in Global Perspective* (Cambridge: Cambridge University Press, 2009).

[8] Jan de Vries, "Between Purchasing Power and the World of Goods: Understanding the Household Economy in Early Modern Europe," in *Consumption and the World of Goods*, ed. John Brewer and Roy Porter (London: Routledge, 1993), 85–132; and Jan de Vries, *The Industrious Revolution: Consumer Behavior and the Household Economy, 1650 to the Present* (Cambridge: Cambridge University Press, 2008).

[9] Maxine Berg and Helen Clifford, eds., *Consumers and Luxury: Consumer Culture in Europe, 1650–1850* (Manchester: Manchester University Press, 1999); Maxine Berg and Elizabeth Eger, eds., *Luxury in the Eighteenth Century: Debates, Desires and Delectable Goods* (London: Palgrave Macmillan, 2003); and Maxine Berg, *Luxury and Pleasure in Eighteenth-Century Britain* (Oxford: Oxford University Press: 2005). On English seventeenth-century elite luxury consumption, see Linda Levy Peck, *Consuming Splendor: Society and Culture in Seventeenth-Century England* (Cambridge: Cambridge University Press, 2005).

[10] Kenneth Pomeranz, *The Great Divergence: China, Europe, and the Making of the Modern World Economy* (Princeton: Princeton University Press, 2000); Roy Bin Wong, *China Transformed: Historical Change and the Limits of European Experience* (Ithaca, NY: Cornell University Press, 1997); and David Washbrook, "India in the Early Modern World Economy: Modes of Production, Reproduction and Exchange," *Journal of Global History* 2, no. 1 (2007): 87–111.

produced largely by African enslaved labor, paralleled a rise in the supply of enslaved peoples by over 2 percent per annum over the whole period 1525–1790, accelerating after 1650.[11] De Vries clearly demonstrated that this rate of growth of trade was double that of the trade with Asia, but it was to Asia rather than the New World that many European historians of consumption turned. The Asian manufactured goods left material traces in probate inventories, customs accounts, records of criminal theft, correspondence and diaries, pattern books, and family and museum collections. The Asian focus on the global turn also coincided with emerging studies in material culture. Historians from Kirti Chaudhuri to Robert Finlay found that a great expansion in long-distance maritime trade from the sixteenth century brought Asian luxury goods, already desired among the elites, in much larger quantities than hitherto, and fostered many East India Companies, especially the Portuguese Estado da India, the Dutch East India Company (VOC), and the English East India Company, as well as smaller French, Danish, Swedish, Austrian, and Prussian companies.[12] My own investigation of the types of goods imported – the Chinese and Japanese porcelain and lacquerware, printed Indian calicoes and fine muslins, and Indian acacia wood furnishings – and how they were used and displayed was soon followed by study of their social and economic impact.[13] Textiles and porcelain made up most of the manufactured imports: 1.3 million pieces of Indian cotton textiles reached Europe by the late 1680s, and 24.3 million over the period 1665–1799, and these came in at least fifty different types. The Dutch imported forty-three million pieces of porcelain from China from the early seventeenth century to the end of the eighteenth century, and the English, French, Danish, and Swedish companies imported another thirty million pieces. Most of these goods were brought to Europe by monopoly-chartered companies, but many private commissions were also taken by ships' captains and merchants for a great variety of porcelains and some fine textiles such as figured muslins.[14]

---

[11] Jan de Vries, "The Limits of Globalization in the Early Modern World," *Economic History Review* 63, no. 3 (2010): 710–33.

[12] K. N. Chaudhuri, *Trade and Civilisation in the Indian Ocean: An Economic History from the Rise of Islam to 1750* (Cambridge: Cambridge University Press, 1985); K. N. Chaudhuri, *Asia before Europe: Economy and Civilisation of the Indian Ocean from the Rise of Islam to 1750* (Cambridge: Cambridge University Press, 1990); Robert Finlay, "The Pilgrim Art: The Culture of Porcelain in World History," *Journal of World History* 9, no. 2 (1998): 141–87; and Robert Finlay, *The Pilgrim Art: Cultures of Porcelain in World History* (Berkeley: University of California Press, 2010).

[13] Maxine Berg, "In Pursuit of Luxury: Global History and British Consumer Goods in the Eighteenth Century," *Past & Present*, no. 182 (2004): 85–142; and the chapters in Maxine Berg, with Felicia Gottmann, Hanna Hodacs, and Chris Nierstrasz, eds., *Goods from the East, 1600–1800: Trading Eurasia* (Basingstoke: Palgrave Macmillan, 2015).

[14] The chapters in Anne Gerritsen and Giorgio Riello, eds., *The Global Lives of Things: The Material Culture of Connections in the Early Modern World* (London: Routledge, 2016).

These Asian goods were to have a profound impact on European material cultures and industrialization. Painted and printed calicoes were popular for furnishing and fashion fabrics, but these were adapted to meet European taste: prints made on light rather than deep-colored backgrounds, and designs based on European floral motifs. Printed calicoes succeeded as a fashion textile, widely used in the dress of the middle classes and the elites, then imitated in Europe and traded widely across classes and down to the poor.

This extensive maritime trade in cotton textiles with India found its parallel in the trade with China in porcelain. An extensive factory production developed in Jingdezhen for standardized goods produced to Western taste, in much the same way in which it had produced for the diverse tastes of the East and Southeast Asian trade and for the Islamic world long before this. Histories of the production processes in China, Japan, and India have thus recently brought historians of Asia into dialogue with European historians. The extensive factory complexes of Jingdezhen producing porcelain for the world, and complex networks and subdivisions of labor among Indian cotton spinners, weavers, and printers, responded to large-scale buyers at European autumn and spring company auctions. These were affected in turn by the choices of the small retailers and even peddlers they sold on to.[15]

Beyond charting the quantities of Asian goods brought to Europe, historians have also asked whether these Asian goods were irresistible and, if so, how long they remained so.[16] We cannot class these commodities with the addictive colonial groceries of tobacco, sugar, coffee, and tea, but they had an inherent aesthetic appeal across Europe and its social fabric. Indian cotton textiles and Chinese porcelain were part of a new widespread fashionable and breakable fragile material culture. East India Companies and private traders working with Asian merchants succeeded in adapting qualities and designs to attract European consumers. Some of the markets they developed, centered on courts, elites, and luxury display, but increasingly they shifted toward middle- and even lower-class consumers seeking fashion, civility, status, and respectability. That civility connected with what Norbert Elias called "the civilizing process" extended far deeper than the elites. "Manners" and "politeness" became an international code.[17]

---

[15] Giorgio Riello, *Cotton: The Fabric that Made the Modern World* (Cambridge: Cambridge University Press, 2013); and Anne Gerritsen, *The City of Blue and White: Chinese Porcelain and the Early Modern World* (Cambridge: Cambridge University Press, 2020).

[16] Jan de Vries, "Understanding Eurasian Trade in the Era of the Trading Companies," in *Goods from the East*, ed. Berg, with Gottmann, Hodacs, and Nierstrasz, 7–44.

[17] Norbert Elias, *The Civilizing Process*, 2 vols. (Oxford: Blackwell, 1994), which was first published in 1939; Lawrence E. Klein, "Politeness and the Interpretation of the British Eighteenth Century," *Historical Journal* 43, no. 4 (2002): 869–98; Woodruff D. Smith, *Consumption and the Making of Respectability, 1600–1800* (London: Routledge, 2002).

We find some evidence of the material culture of these aspirations across classes in museum collections but much more in sources such as the inventories of the Amsterdam Orphanage, in the records of theft recorded in the archives of the Old Bailey, and in the textile token identifiers attached to the individual records of 5,000 babies left in Thomas Coram Foundling Hospital in London between 1740 and 1761. The inventories of the Amsterdam Orphanage show the deep penetration of Chinese porcelain, as well as a considerable amount of Japanese porcelain. They also show textiles of many different qualities and varieties from Asia.[18]

Other wider questions about European culture were raised by Lynn Hunt.[19] She asked what it was in European cultures that inspired this wider global interaction in their construction of their everyday lives? Europeans developed a culture in which exotic goods made sense. From the early seventeenth century, small numbers of Turkish carpets were brought into Europe, but their significance was high. They were not rarities exclusive to the small elites, but they were expensive and were used as table coverings. Seventeenth-century Dutch artists included them in their paintings of "interiors," as did early eighteenth-century English painters of "conversation pieces." They appealed to the imagination, and they enhanced the value of other Asian goods. Another important factor set out by Hunt was choice. Larger populations, especially in specific places with higher discretionary incomes, wanted more choice; individuals expressed a psychology of "the self" in new commodities. Different varieties of goods, and individual choices among them, demarcated new social groups. Goods associated with long-distance trade and especially the exotic East were valued for their craftsmanship, their variety, and their unique characteristics as much as for the high transaction costs involved in acquiring them.[20]

Recent work has delved into the varieties of goods carried in those East India Company cargoes and constantly sought in East India Company orders. This was no random collection of goods but one constantly responding to large-scale buyers at the autumn and spring company auctions; these closely affected in turn the choices of all the small retailers and peddlers they sold on to. French colorways dictated Swedish silk imports from China; East India Company orders went out with letters criticizing the colors of earlier cargoes and demanding dynamic, responsive, and intuitive designs and patterns. Dutch

---

[18] John Styles, *The Dress of the People: Everyday Fashion in Eighteenth-Century England* (New Haven: Yale University Press, 2007); Anne E. C. McCants, "Exotic Goods, Popular Consumption, and the Standard of Living: Thinking about Globalization in the Early Modern World," *Journal of World History* 18, no. 4 (2007): 433–62.
[19] Lynn Hunt, *Writing History in the Global Era* (New York: W. W. Norton & Co., 2014).
[20] Ibid., 114–41.

and English East India Companies and private European and Indian merchants competed vigorously for the finest figured jamdani muslins.[21]

The fashion demand that underlay the issues of agency and identity also developed in a social framework. Cities were a part of this story. The close urban integration of towns and cities in the Low Countries and Britain provided a context for the sociability that fostered new experiences of consuming Asian goods. Asia's "exotic East" was deeply embedded in the European imagination. It conveyed the "East" encountered by classical and early Christian Europe. It was the destination of ambassadorial missions and gift exchanges and brought back to Europe curiosities, fine arts, and material craftsmanship of which little was hitherto known.[22] It was, above all, the object of trade. The objects and foodstuffs merchants traded also signaled cosmopolitan social cultures. Europeans adopted colonial groceries in new structures and timing of meals and drinking hot beverages in new settings of sociability. The Dutch consumed enough hot drinks, porcelain, and Indian printed calicoes by the mid-eighteenth century to generate half the VOC sales in Amsterdam. The goods consumed and displayed were also cosmopolitan: A single room might display exotic Spanish American wood furniture upholstered in Chinese silk or Indian chintzes. Chinese porcelain might sit on tables covered in Persian carpets, and a Japanese lacquer nanban screen might be decorated with images of American maize.[23]

These goods of fragility, novelty, and fashion also stimulated the invention of European substitutes. My own work on product innovation highlighted this. The craft of Indian textiles and Chinese porcelain provoked a continually expressed aim among inventors to improve the quality of their European counterparts. European porcelain works arose to fill the desires introduced by Asian ceramics, but much more significant were the quality developments in the earthenware sector. Josiah Wedgwood's fine earthenware manufacture undertook the challenge posed by Europe's new taste for Asia by producing a high-quality ceramic body and decorating this in new glazes and classical themes. Likewise for cotton textiles, only a few Indian cottons featured among the textile swatches for identifying babies submitted to the London Foundling Hospital, but there were many printed calicoes from English workshops and

[21] Hanna Hodacs, *Silk and Tea in the North: Scandinavian Trade and the Market for Asian Goods in Eighteenth-Century Europe* (London: Palgrave Macmillan, 2016); and Maxine Berg, "'The Merest Shadows of a Commodity': Indian Muslins for European Markets 1750–1800," in Berg, *Goods from the East*, 119–38, ed. Berg, with Gottmann, Hodacs, and Nierstrasz.

[22] Zoltán Biederman, Anne Gerritsen, and Giorgio Riello, "Introduction," in *Global Gifts: The Material Culture of Diplomacy in Early Modern Eurasia*, ed. Zoltán Biederman, Anne Gerritsen, and Giorgio Riello (Cambridge: Cambridge University Press, 2018), 1–33.

[23] De Vries, *The Industrious Revolution*, 122–66; McCants, "Poor Consumers as Global Consumers," 172–200.

factories made in imitation of them. They demonstrate how quickly a new industry producing printed calicoes was established in Britain in the wake of this trade with India. Britain also developed new machinery to produce cotton yarn, especially high-quality and muslin yarn. Further in-depth research by John Styles has demonstrated the continued and innovative parts played by linen and silk. Britain and Europe's own production of cotton yarn to substitute for Indian imports relied on new imports of raw cotton, first from the Levant, but soon rapidly overtaken by imports from the Caribbean, Brazil, and colonial North America.[24] These New World imports relying on enslaved labor are treated later in the chapter.

Over the long run these Asian long-distance maritime trade goods seamlessly embedded themselves within the material cultures of those who acquired them. Printed calicoes became quintessentially English – Paisley shawls, then Liberty and Laura Ashley – or French, in the well-known toile de Jouy fabric. Tea drinking and tea services lost their identity with China; tea and coffee drinking were fitted into a preexisting culture of drinking and dining around silver, glassware, and maiolica. Asia was thus neutralized and domesticated in its European frameworks, her products disconnected from their Indian Ocean and Asian seas origins.

-

Colonial groceries, long before the global turn, featured as a cornerstone of the consumer revolution. The British consumer imports that Timothy H. Breen identified as the "baubles of Britain" and provoked the American Revolution came with a tea culture.[25] I spent many years arguing the case for the wide impact of imports of Asian manufactured goods on material culture and consumer demand; I argued that these stimulated adaptive and inventive products and technologies, leading into Britain's Industrial Revolution.

Now I think we need to ask about the key components of what economic historians call colonial groceries: What of the impact of food and drink? Tea drinking changed Europe's China trade from a luxury silk trade to a major commodity trade in tea and the porcelain ceramics associated with it. Most

---

[24] Berg, "In Pursuit of Luxury"; Berg, *Luxury and Pleasure in Eighteenth-Century Britain*, 85–153; Styles, *The Dress of the People*, 109–34; and John Styles, "The Rise and Fall of the Spinning Jenny: Domestic Mechanisation in Eighteenth-Century Cotton Spinning," *Textile History* 51, no. 2 (2020): 195–236.

[25] T. H. Breen, "'Baubles of Britain': The American and Consumer Revolution of the Eighteenth Century," *Past & Present*, no. 119 (1988): 73–104; and T. H. Breen, *The Marketplace of Revolution: How Consumer Politics Shaped American Independence* (Oxford: Oxford University Press, 2004).

colonial groceries, apart from tea, and in the early stages, coffee, however, came from the New World. First a point on historiography: Brewer and Porter's pathbreaking *Consumption and the World of Goods* (1993) contained significant chapters by Carole Shammas on early modern English and Anglo-American consumption, with a section on colonial groceries including sugar, and a chapter by Sidney Mintz on the role of food in consumer society, which also included a restatement of his iconic work on sugar, *Sweetness and Power* (1985).[26] This was also the place where Jan de Vries first set out his theory of the "industrious revolution."[27] Yet for all the research on ceramic and glass vessels in Europe, there was much less on the colonial groceries brought from the New World. There was a long-standing historiography of these goods but little of this until recently connected with a global framework.

Tobacco and chocolate (cacao) were incorporated early into European consumer practices. Historians of encounters detailed their transition from Indigenous cultures to Europe. Spanish conquistadors accepted tobacco and cacao or chocolate as gifts at meetings with Meso-American groups. They signaled diplomacy and hospitality. Marcy Norton developed the story in the early 2000s.[28] Chocolate was derived from the cacao tree of the upper Amazon basin and Meso-America. Mixed with water and spice it was an esteemed beverage to Meso-American societies. It was part of religious ritual, where it was considered as the food of the gods and a sacred substance. Though early Spanish explorers and conquerors did not find it appealing, it was soon to be incorporated into the daily life of Spanish Americans. By the seventeenth century, settlers over wide social groups drank it. Cacao trees for chocolate production were soon cultivated in Central America, the Caribbean, Brazil, Venezuela, and Ecuador. Chocolate entered Spain as a desirable commodity associated with the Indies. There it was drunk hot, sweetened with cane sugar, and flavored with vanilla or cinnamon. By the late sixteenth century, it was used in Spain, Italy, and Flanders, especially at court, and taken up by the Habsburg monarchs. By the eighteenth century, chocolate was widely consumed throughout Spain. Northern Europeans came to associate chocolate with Catholicism, Spanish qualities, and the feminine; by the time of the Enlightenment, they connected it with luxury and absolutism. What had

---

[26] Brewer and Porter, eds., *Consumption and the World of Goods*; Carole Shammas, "Changes in English and Anglo-American consumption from 1550 to 1800," in Brewer and Porter, *Consumption and the World of Goods*, 177–205; Sidney W. Mintz, "The Changing Roles of Food in the Study of Consumption," in Brewer and Porter, *Consumption and the World of Goods*, 261–73; and Sidney W. Mintz, *Sweetness and Power: The Place of Sugar in Modern History* (New York: Viking, 1985).

[27] De Vries, "Between Purchasing Power and the World of Goods."

[28] Marcy Norton, *Sacred Gifts, Profane Pleasures: A History of Tobacco and Chocolate in the Atlantic World* (Ithaca, NY: Cornell University Press, 2009).

become a common beverage in Spain was viewed in other parts of Europe as a decadent luxury.[29]

Coffee consumption also increased rapidly, but earlier historiography focused less on its consumption and production than on the politics of the coffee house. Samuel Pepys and Robert Hooke visiting their London coffee houses in the 1660s and 1670s drank sugared coffee, but there were a number of other beverages on offer including ales, wine, distilled liquors, and another plantation crop, chocolate.[30] Coffee consumption was slower to take off than were the coffee houses. Brian Cowan and Steve Pincus explored the cultural and political settings of coffee's consumption, and Simon Smith the state tax regimes that helped to explain the greater taste for it in wider Europe than in Britain.[31]

Coffee remained a rare and exotic beverage. Initially it was brought from the Levant and Mocha, but it became a colonial plantation crop harvested by enslaved labor from the late seventeenth century, cultivated especially by the Dutch and the French. Coffee cultivation did not start in the British West Indies until 1728, on Montserrat, then Jamaica. It was always sugar's "poor relation" in the British plantation system and never contributed more than 5 percent of British coffee imports before the 1750s. Arabian coffee was still preferred by British coffee drinkers and tea much preferred to coffee.[32] By mid-century, Saint-Domingue had become the world's leading coffee producer, supplying France and much of the rest of Europe. From the Haitian Revolution of 1791, however, Jamaica took the lead in world coffee production for a few decades, adding to the continued profitability of the British Caribbean into the early nineteenth century.[33]

---

[29] Rebecca Earle, "Chocolate in the Historical Imagination," in *Luxury and the Ethics of Greed in Early Modern Italy*, ed. Catherine Kovesi (Turnhout: Brepolis, 2019), 95–118.

[30] Phil Withington, "Where Was the Coffee in Early Modern England?," *Journal of Modern History* 92, no. 1 (2020): 40–75.

[31] Brian Cowan, *The Social Life of Coffee: The Emergence of the British Coffeehouse* (New Haven: Yale University Press, 2005); Steve Pincus, "'Coffee Politicians Does Create': Coffee Houses and Restoration Political Culture," *Journal of Modern History* 67, no. 4 (1995): 807–83; and S. D. Smith, "Accounting for Taste: British Coffee Consumption in Historical Perspective," *Journal of Interdisciplinary History* 27, no. 2 (1996): 183–214.

[32] Mark Pendergrast, *Uncommon Grounds: The History of Coffee and How It Transformed Our World* (London: Texere, 2001).

[33] David P. Geggus, "Sugar and Coffee Cultivation in Saint Domingue and the Shaping of the Slave Labor Force," in *Cultivation and Culture: Labor and the Shaping of Slave Life in the Americas*, ed. Ira Berlin and Philip D. Morgan (Charlottesville: University Press of Virginia, 1993), 73–98; Aaron Graham, review of *Plantation Coffee in Jamaica, 1790–1848*, by Kathleen Monteith (Kingston: University of the West Indies Press, 2019), *Economic History Review* 74, no. 2 (2021): 570–1; S. D. Smith, "Sugar's Poor Relation: Coffee Planting in the British West Indies 1720–1833," *Slavery & Abolition* 19, no. 3 (1998): 68–89; and Christine Fertig and Ulrich Pfister, "Coffee, Mind and Body: Global Material Culture and the Eighteenth-Century Hamburg Import Trade," in Gerritsen and Riello, *The Global Lives of Things*, 221–40.

Tobacco use spread by Spanish merchants and sailors to ports and large towns. It was widely consumed in western and central Europe by the seventeenth century and spread through the movement of armies in the Thirty Years' War (1618–48). Tobacco became the first mass consumer export to Europe; by 1670, 25 percent of the English population was using it – mainly men who smoked it in clay pipes in taverns and coffee houses. Tobacco was distributed through state monopolies in France, Spain, Portugal, Russia, Sweden, and many German and Italian states. Its trade was in private hands in Britain, Ireland, the Northern Netherlands, and the Hanseatic ports, but it was heavily taxed. In the eighteenth century it was consumed as snuff as well as pipe smoking. Tobacco was equally popular in Russia but smoked in very different ways. Though banned in Russia for much of the seventeenth century, its markets were eagerly developed by Dutch and English traders, and it was eventually legalized by Peter the Great in the early eighteenth century. European Russia adopted the Dutch and English habit of pipe smoking; the inhabitants of Eastern Siberia preferred water pipes, and those of Eastern Siberia adopted the Chinese method of sweetened ball tobacco in their pipes.[34]

The key New World grocery to transform everyday life in Europe was sugar. Yet the impact of sugar consumption on British and European society did not figure as a major subject in the ensuing long historiography of consumer culture. Neither did it feature much in the writing on global history that developed from 2000 onwards, nor in the food budgets constructed by economic and demographic historians that now tell us of real wages and the standard of living.[35] Very recently food history has entered histories of consumer culture, best exemplified by the notable studies by Jan de Vries on bread in the Dutch Republic, Rebecca Earle on the potato in Europe, and Emma Spary on the sciences of food in France; but there is nothing for sugar that reaches in breadth and analysis beyond Mintz's classic *Sweetness and Power*.[36]

---

[34] Jordan Goodman, *Tobacco in History: The Cultures of Dependence* (London: Routledge, 1994); on the global history of smoking see Sander L. Gilman and Zhou Xun, *Smoke: A Global History of Smoking* (Chicago: University of Chicago Press; London: Reaktion Books, 2004); and Matthew P. Romaniello, "Customs and Consumption: Russia's Global Tobacco Habits in the Seventeenth and Eighteenth Centuries," in Gerritsen and Riello, *The Global Lives of Things*, 183–97.

[35] On budgets, consumption, and standards of living see Sara Horrell, "Consumption, 1700–1870," in *The Cambridge Economic History of Modern Britain*, vol. 1, *Industrialisation, 1700–1870*, ed. Roderick Floud, Jane Humphries, and P Johnson (Cambridge: Cambridge University Press, 2014), 237–63.

[36] Jan de Vries, *The Price of Bread: Regulating the Market in the Dutch Republic* (Cambridge: Cambridge University Press, 2019); Rebecca Earle, *Feeding the People: The Politics of the Potato* (Cambridge: Cambridge University Press, 2020); E. C. Spary, *Eating the Enlightenment: Food and the Sciences in Paris, 1670–1760* (Chicago: University of Chicago Press, 2012); and Mintz, *Sweetness and Power*.

Britain's sugar culture was closely connected with the earlier rapid spread of its tobacco culture. Tobacco plantations in the Chesapeake developed on indentured and then enslaved labor, and in the West Indies also provided both a mass consumer market in Britain by the mid-seventeenth century as well as a rapid expansion in reexports to Europe in the eighteenth century. Tobacco was the pioneer crop, but while British consumption of tobacco leveled off, the consumption of the other great plantation crop, sugar, started to grow from the mid-seventeenth century and experienced a revolutionary increase from the early eighteenth century. Sugar products were, moreover, used in making a number of new alcoholic intoxicants – gin, rum, and punches – popularized in seventeenth- and eighteenth-century Europe and added to wine as "sack."[37]

All of these addictive consumables were, apart from tea, produced on North and South American and Caribbean colonial plantations with enslaved labor. The levels of growth in Europe's trade with the New World in these commodities corresponded to the growth of the slave trade between Africa and the New World. Yet historians have until recently separated their study of European consumer culture from that of slavery and the slave trade. This connection is only now being developed in global history, and the key case is sugar.

–

We can look first to the levels of imports of sugar into Europe, then set this alongside the growth of the Caribbean plantation system. Sugar production in the Western hemisphere was 54,000 tons in 1700; this figure doubled by 1740, and tripled by 1776. The value of British cane sugar imports from the Caribbean between 1670 and 1820 far surpassed that of imports of any other commodity in Britain's world trade.[38] Sugar consumption in England increased rapidly over the course of the eighteenth century, much faster than on the European mainland, due both to rising real incomes and to a shift in consumer preferences for the new hot sugared beverages of tea, coffee, and chocolate, along with new tastes for distilled liquors relying on sugar: rum, punch, and gin. In 1700 per capita consumption of sugar in England was around 7 lb; in the 1790s, it was 24 lb.[39]

---

[37] Phil Withington, "Intoxicants and the Invention of 'Consumption'," *Economic History Review* 73, no. 2 (2020): 384–408.

[38] Barbara L. Solow, "Capitalism and Slavery in the Exceedingly Long Run," in *British Capitalism and Caribbean Slavery: The Legacy of Eric Williams*, ed. Barbara L. Solow and Stanley L. Engerman (Cambridge: Cambridge University Press, 1987), 51–78, here pp. 70–2.

[39] Barbara L. Solow, *Slavery and the Rise of the Atlantic System* (Cambridge: Cambridge University Press, 1991); and Nuala Zahedieh, "Overseas Trade and Empire," in Floud, Humphries, and Johnson, *The Cambridge Economic History of Modern Britain*, 1:392–420.

The sugar imports of other European countries take a different trajectory. Arrivals of mostly finer "clayed" sugars at the French ports rose from 60 million lb to 180 million lb over the course of the eighteenth century. The English consumed most of the sugar they brought from their Caribbean colonies and between two and three times more sugar than the French over the period. The French reexported large proportions of their colonial sugar. The various Italian states took thirteen million lb of fine clayed sugar, including two million to Venice and three million to Naples and Sicily. Spain took another one million lb and the Levant three million lb. Hamburg took over four-fifths of the French sugar redistributed to northern Europe. The Dutch were the highest takers, their 145 sugar refineries relying for over two-thirds of their imports on the French and the rest on the Dutch plantations.[40]

These histories of European sugar consumption need to be put together with histories of the plantations that produced these levels of output and exports. The part played by the slave trade and plantation slavery so powerfully set out in 1944 in Eric Williams's *Capitalism and Slavery* is now once again central to historical debate.[41] A global perspective shows the extent to which the turning point in European consumer cultures relied on the great growth in enslaved labor and slave plantations. In 1763 Britain owned eleven "sugar islands" in the West Indies plus the rice, indigo, and tobacco colonies on the North American mainland. Five other European powers owned extensive sugar colonies. Saint-Domingue (French), the "pearl of the Antilles," then exported 31.7 percent of West Indian sugar even though the colony also produced cotton, coffee, and indigo. Jamaica (British) came next with 18.7 percent, followed by Antigua (British), Saint Christopher (British), Martinique (French), Saint Croix (Danish), Guadeloupe (French), Barbados (British), and Grenada (French), all of which exported between 8 and 11 percent of the total. Cuba (Spanish), which was to become the main exporter of sugar after the decline of other parts of the West Indies in the early nineteenth century, ranked tenth at this time with just 2.7 percent of all sugar exports. The Caribbean on the eve of the American Revolution had an estimated 3,900 sugar plantations, of which 1,830 were British, 1,350 French, 475 Spanish, 195 Danish, and 50 Dutch. The sugar was produced from an early stage in the plantation system using Black African enslaved labor; labor cost and race determined this system. British traders were the leading players in the Atlantic slave trade as early as the 1670s; they dominated the trade in the last

---

[40] Robert Stein, "The French Sugar Business in the Eighteenth Century: A Quantitative Study," *Business History* 22, no. 1 (1980): 3–17; and Ad van der Woude and Jan de Vries, *The First Modern Economy: Success, Failure, and Perseverance of the Dutch Economy, 1500–1815* (Cambridge: Cambridge University Press, 1997), 472–7.

[41] Eric Williams, *Capitalism and Slavery* (London: Penguin Classics, 2022), which was first published in 1944.

quarter of the eighteenth century, when they accounted for more than half of total shipments from Africa, with all European shipments peaking at 80,000 a year.[42]

France's involvement in the slave trade and the import of slaves to its islands increased dramatically in the decades between the mid-eighteenth century and 1790. Annual slave imports to its islands doubled from the 1760s and 1770s to the 1780s, and indeed the rapid expansion of the sugar trade in the 1780s was only possible because of the vast number of enslaved peoples brought into the French West Indies over these decades. In the 1780s, Saint Domingue had 700,000 and Jamaica 600,000 enslaved people; slaves constituted 90 percent of the population of Saint Domingue, compared with 84 percent in Jamaica and 80 percent in Barbados.[43] The high levels and rapid growth of sugar imports into Europe and the parallel rapid growth of the slave trade and slave plantations to produce this sugar were remarkable. Yet historians have to a great degree ignored the extent to which colonial groceries (still considered rare luxuries by many economic historians) had become embedded in foodways by the later eighteenth century. Few recent historians have incorporated into estimates of diets, calories, and agricultural output the pioneering work carried out especially by Carol Shammas from the 1980s onwards on the output, import, and consumption of colonial groceries.[44] Sugar was the major component in the early stages of what the global historian of the "great divergence" Kenneth Pomeranz referred to as "ghost acres."[45] Slave-produced foodstuffs from plantations in the Caribbean, the Carolinas, and Georgia provided "ecological" relief as Britain's population growth pressed against the limits of her domestic food production. Those Caribbean islands were Europe's "ghost" food frontiers. Sugar contributed energy and calories, tea and coffee were stimulants, and tobacco an appetite suppressant. All were

---

[42] Richard B. Sheridan, "The Plantation Revolution and the Industrial Revolution, 1625–1775," *Caribbean Studies* 9, no. 3 1969: 5–25, here pp. 21–2.

[43] Stein, "The French Sugar Business in the Eighteenth Century"; and Thomas Piketty, *Capital and Ideology* (Cambridge, MA: Harvard University Press, 2020).

[44] The arguments of this paragraph are based on Maxine Berg and Pat Hudson, *Slavery, Capitalism and the Industrial Revolution* (Cambridge: Polity Press, 2023). Recent statements on consumption and diet can be found in Horrell, "Consumption, 1700–1870"; Craig Muldrew, *Food, Energy and the Creation of Industriousness: Work and Material Culture in Agrarian England, 1550–1780* (Cambridge: Cambridge University Press, 2011); for the contrast with findings in the 1980s and early 1990s, see Mintz, *Sweetness and Power*; Carole Shammas, "Food Expenditures and Economic Well-Being in Early Modern England," *Journal of Economic History* 43, no. 1 (1983): 89–100; and Carole Shammas, *The Pre-industrial Consumer in England and America* (Oxford: Oxford University Press, 1990).

[45] The term referring to the divergence in development and economic growth between western Europe and Asia seen to have taken place at some point between the seventeenth century and 1800, see Pomeranz, *The Great Divergence*, who identified the turning point at around 1800.

addictive. Sugar promoted the consumption of inferior grains such as oats and rice to supplement wheat.

Just how sugar became part of European everyday life remains an open question. Many decades ago Mintz analyzed the cultural processes by which sugar became part of European and especially British foodways. An exotic commodity, which first entered the social lives of the powerful, became a type of "kingly" luxury for commoners. But sugar was probably less about kings than we once thought. It was already an everyday commercial commodity in both British and colonial North American foodways from the mid-seventeenth century. Its use included the high end of the social scale, where it was a key part of the gum paste of the confectioner's art in the making of sweet condiments and sugar sculptures to decorate the dessert tables of the rich. It was also the treacle added to the poor man's porridge in English workhouses and the syrup that went into popular Neapolitan street food and ice cream.[46]

There was also a clear link between the rapid growth of sugar imports and East India Company tea imports in the first half of the eighteenth century. The East India Company fostered a taste for tea associated with sugar; sugar consumed in this way became "virtuous," as opposed to the extravagance of sugar decorations. Grocers as well as tea dealers sold tea and sugar together, often in small quantities, such as an ounce of tea and a small pinch of sugar (taken from sugar loaves with nippers).[47]

Colonial groceries, and especially sugar, probably stimulated northern Europe's "industrious revolution" as much or even more so than did Asian manufactured luxuries. In the 1770s, Adam Smith wrote in *The Wealth of Nations* that rum, sugar, and tobacco had become objects "of almost universal consumption."[48] What is the story for other parts of Europe? Did France's different experience – of reexporting much of its sugar, and consuming what it

---

[46] Mimi Goodall, "The Rise of the Sugar Trade and Sugar Consumption in Early British America, 1650–1720," *Historical Research* 93, no. 262 (2020): 678–91; and Melissa Calaresu, "Making and Eating Ice Cream in Naples: Rethinking Consumption and Sociability in the Eighteenth Century," *Past & Present*, no. 220 (2013): 35–78.

[47] Markman Ellis, Richard Coulton, and Matthew Mauger, *Empire of Tea: The Asian Leaf that Conquered the World* (London: Reaktion Books; Chicago: Chicago University Press, 2015); Troy Bickham, "Eating the Empire: Intersections of Food, Cookery and Imperialism in Eighteenth-Century Britain," *Past & Present*, no. 198 (2008): 71–109, here p. 76; Jon Stobart, *Sugar and Spice: Grocers and Groceries in Provincial England, 1650–1830* (Oxford: Oxford University Press, 2012), 55, 60, 220; and Ralph A. Austen and Woodruff D. Smith, "Private Tooth Decay as Public Economic Virtue: The Slave–Sugar Triangle, Consumerism, and European Industrialization," *Social Science History* 14, no. 1 (1990): 95–115, here pp. 102–4.

[48] Adam Smith, *The Wealth of Nations*, cited in Richard B. Sheridan, *Sugar and Slavery: An Economic History of the British West Indies, 1623–1775* (Baltimore: Johns Hopkins University Press, 1974), 347, which was first published in 1776.

kept in such a socially and geographically divisive manner – negatively affect ongoing economic development?[49]

-

The new history of capitalism arose in recent years alongside the global history-centered explanation of industrialization in Europe and of the cotton industry and the slave trade in America. Sven Beckert's *Empire of Cotton* (2014) called cotton the "first global commodity," the key commodity that resulted in the industrialization and transformation of the West.[50] The reach and impact of cotton in turn rested upon the greatly intensified work of enslaved labor in the American South producing the raw cotton for Europe's and America's textile factories in the first half of the nineteenth century. A focus not on Asian manufactured goods, nor New World groceries, but on New World raw materials and American cotton plantations has shifted debate on the global origins of industrialization. The American focus of this history of capitalism takes the study of cotton away from its long and wide Asian, African, European, and American history. By contrast, Giorgio Riello's *Cotton: The Fabric that Made the Modern World* demonstrates this long and wide history.[51] *Empire of Cotton*'s periodization is too late to account for key technological transformations in the British cotton industry and furthermore narrows the global framework away from the significance of raw cotton in the Caribbean and Brazil as sources of raw cotton. It also weakens the place of Asian trade and the East India Companies during the preceding century in making cotton fabric the global commodity so desired in Europe. In new research by John Styles demonstrates the connections between cotton's mechanized technologies – the spinning jenny, the water frame, and the spinning mule – and a particular type of high-quality long-staple raw cotton (*Gossypium barbadense*) grown with enslaved labor in the Caribbean and Brazil. This was the cotton imported at the time of the crucial innovations leading to mechanization in the industry; this was the cotton used to produce the high-quality fabrics that were easy to print and geared to Atlantic markets.[52] Sources of cotton from the American South reinforced British textile industrialization only from the turning of the nineteenth century.

Global history, now combined with the recent rise of the history of capitalism, challenges European historians of consumer culture and industrialization to connect the European reception of wider world goods and raw materials to

---

[49] Guillaume Daudin, "How Important Was the Slavery System to Europe?," *Slavery & Abolition* 42, no. 1 (2021): 151–7.

[50] Sven Beckert, *Empire of Cotton: A New History of Global Capitalism* (New York: Penguin, 2014); see the critique by Trevor Burnard and Giorgio Riello, "Slavery and the New History of Capitalism," *Journal of Global History* 15, no. 2 (2020): 225–44.

[51] Riello, *Cotton.*   [52] Styles, "The Rise and Fall of the Spinning Jenny."

the Americas and to slavery. This is a key new direction in historical research. Furthermore, despite decades of research on consumer culture, we still know little of the capitalist organization of the production, trade, and distribution of the wider world goods that transformed European diets and material culture. New research will go forward on the social and economic histories of just "how it was done."

9   Global Material Culture in Early Modern and Modern Europe

Anne Gerritsen

Gallery 1.5 of the national museum of the Netherlands, the Rijksmuseum in Amsterdam, holds an extraordinary mixture of eighteenth-century objects. Among the sixty-six objects on display are portraits of famous Dutch officials, a framed oil painting depicting a scene from the sixteenth-century pastoral play *Aminta* by Torquato Tasso, a wooden box decorated with the crest of one of the richest men of the Dutch Republic, a teak chair, a silver tray, plates in various materials, wine glasses, a nightlight in the shape of a cat, a bronze and wood cannon (Figure 9.1), and so on. Surely, these are all examples of European, in fact Dutch, visual and material culture. They represent the wealth and power of the members of the Dutch elite, displaying their command over resources and technologies from all over the world. Described in a different way, however, the objects in this gallery would not be identified as European or Dutch at all. There are paintings and sculptures by Asian artists, including the Canton-based artist Chitqua (Tan-Che-Qua); there are enameled plaques and reverse glass paintings, lacquered boxes, porcelain plates, an ivory fan, and a bejeweled cannon.[1] These exotic objects were almost all made in Asia, in places such as Masulipatnam, Batavia, and Canton, Sri Lanka, China, and Japan.[2] The materials and designs signal precisely their extra-Europeanness, but all of them are also closely associated with "the Dutch overseas," which is the name of the gallery.[3] The question this chapter considers is if, and if so how, such objects form part of European material culture. What can their inclusion or exclusion tell us about the global turn in European history?

---

[1] Natasha Eaton, "Glimmer of Empire: Academy, 'Alchemy,' Exotic," *Eighteenth-Century Studies* 52, no. 1 (2018): 13–18; see also references to Chitqua in Peter J. Kitson, *Forging Romantic China: Sino-British Cultural Exchange 1760–1840* (Cambridge: Cambridge University Press, 2013).

[2] Karina H. Corrigan, Jan van Campen, and Femke Diercks, eds., *Asia in Amsterdam: The Culture of Luxury in the Golden Age* (Salem, MA: Peabody Essex Museum, 2015).

[3] Jan van Campen et al., *Aziatische Kunst* (Amsterdam: Rijksmuseum, 2014); Corrigan, Campen, and Diercks, *Asia in Amsterdam*; Jan van Campen and Titus M Eliëns, eds., *Chinese and Japanese Porcelain for the Dutch Golden Age* (Zwolle: Waanders Uitgevers, 2014).

Figure 9.1 Singhalese cannon, made of bronze and wood; height c. 54 cm, width c. 181 cm, depth c. 77 cm, Sri Lanka, before 1745.
Source: Rijksmuseum, Amsterdam. Inv. No. NG-NM-1015.

Objects have not always been an obvious subject of study for historians of early modern and modern Europe. Images were sooner identified as sources of interest to the historian. Peter Burke's 1991 volume *New Perspectives on Historical Writing* included a section on images, authored by Ivan Gaskell, but nothing on material culture.[4] Artifacts such as silver candlesticks, jewelry, furniture, or textiles, usually categorized as decorative art, were considered the domain of art historians (or, more likely, curators and conservators); daily-use objects with non-Western origins the domain of anthropologists; technological instruments the domain of historians of science; and anything found in the ground or at the bottom of the sea the

---

[4] Peter Burke, ed., *New Perspectives on Historical Writing* (Cambridge: Polity Press, 1991). In fact, only the third edition of Bloomsbury's *Writing History: Theory and Practice* had a section on material culture, included under the heading "the eclecticism of contemporary historical writing"; Stefan Berger, Heiko Feldner, and Kevin Passmore, eds., *Writing History: Theory and Practice*, 3rd ed. (London and New York: Bloomsbury Academic, 2020).

domain of archaeologists.[5] Material culture seemed to require special skills to study it "properly," using, for example, the steps laid out by the art historian Jules Prown.[6] Prown defined material culture as "the study through artifacts of the beliefs – values, ideas, attitudes, and assumptions – of a particular community or society at a given time," and offered a three-step method for object analysis: description, deduction, and speculation, whereby the first step focuses on the object itself, the second interprets the way the object interacts with the receiver (or viewer) of the object, and the third frames the kinds of questions that arise from the object and can be answered by bringing in external evidence.[7] Historians generally felt safer with a focus on text and considered the textual record to be the domain in which their rule was unchallenged.

Over the decades, several factors have played a part in changing the aloofness that characterized historians' views of objects. The turn to the social and the interest in history from below broadened the source base, so as to facilitate writing about those who did not necessarily have access to publishing, print, or even writing. The cultural turn allowed historians to write about all kinds of historical artifacts, including not just the (applied) arts and adornments but also what Prown calls "diversions" (such as games and toys), "modifications of the landscape" (architecture and so on), and devices of all sorts.[8] The push toward interdisciplinarity, too, eased historians gradually into new disciplinary territories. Writing about objects of all kinds and using a material culture approach to the study of the past have latterly become part of the historian's toolkit.[9]

Before the so-called global turn had become fully established within mainstream historical practice, the study of material culture in European historical scholarship focused on objects made and consumed within the European context. Brewer and Porter's classic study *Consumption and the World of Goods*, identified consumption as something mainly associated with eighteenth-century England and France, though seventeenth-century eastern Europe and eighteenth-century America also make appearances.[10] Ludmilla Jordanova's 2012 *The Look of the Past* placed the analysis of visual and

[5] Lorraine Daston, *Things That Talk: Object Lessons from Art and Science* (New York: Zone Books, 2004).

[6] Jules David Prown, "Mind in Matter: An Introduction to Material Culture Theory and Method," *Winterthur Portfolio* 17, no. 1 (1982): 1–19.

[7] Ibid., 1 and 7.   [8] Ibid., 3.

[9] Margot C. Finn, "Material Turns in British History: I. Loot," *Transactions of the Royal Historical Society* 28 (2018): 5–32.

[10] John Brewer and Roy Porter, eds., *Consumption and the World of Goods* (London: Routledge, 1993); and see the perceptive discussion of this issue in Craig Clunas, "Modernity Global and Local: Consumption and the Rise of the West," *The American Historical Review* 104, no. 5 (1999): 1497–511.

material objects at the heart of the historian's craft, but the image- and object-based essays that are interspersed between the methodological texts are all European: the Wren library in Cambridge, Bernini's *Ecstasy of St Teresa*, Renoir's portrait of Ambroise Vollard, and so on.[11] The museum loomed large in these studies, and the organization of museum objects by material within a museum such as the Victoria and Albert, with its spaces devoted to ceramics, furniture and woodwork, glass, jewelry, and metalwork, including silver and textiles, provides a key to studies of British and European material culture.[12] The same is true for American material culture: the Winterthur Museum in Delaware collected and displayed mainly American material culture, telling the story of American culture and art through objects categorized by materials such as ceramics, furniture, metalwork, textiles, and needlework.[13]

National boundaries were important in this older literature on material culture.[14] It seemed significant to identify the ways in which early modern material culture was typically Dutch or characteristically British.[15] Similarly, studies focused on the material culture of larger regions, such as Europe or Asia.[16] The contextualization of material culture within a specific national context was also visible in the ways in which material culture became identified with consumption in the modern era. Daniel Miller's work on material culture and mass consumption focused on mass consumption in contemporary Britain, and Frank Trentmann's *Oxford Handbook of the History of Consumption* reminded readers of the two important periods in the history of consumption: its emergence in the seventeenth and eighteenth centuries, and the arrival of a fully fledged consumer society after the Second World War, both with unspoken roots in Britain and North America.[17]

---

[11] Ludmilla Jordanova, *The Look of the Past: Visual and Material Evidence in Historical Perspective* (Cambridge: Cambridge University Press, 2012).

[12] Malcolm Baker, Brenda Richardson, and Anthony Burton, eds., *A Grand Design: The Art of the Victoria and Albert Museum* (London: V&A, 1997).

[13] Ann Smart Martin, *Makers and Users: American Decorative Arts, 1630–1820, from the Chipstone Collection* (Madison: Elvehjem Museum of Art, 1999).

[14] Ulrich-Christian Pallach, *Materielle Kultur und Mentalitäten im 18. Jahrhundert: Wirtschaftliche Entwicklung und Politisch-sozialer Funktionswandel des Luxus in Frankreich und im Alten Reich am Ende des Ancien Régime* (Munich: R. Oldenbourg, 1987).

[15] Annemarie Vels Heijn and Gerard van der Hoek, *Pruikentijd: Hollandse Kunst en Kunstnijverheid in de 18e Eeuw* (Amsterdam: Gravenhage: Educatieve Dienst van het Rijksmuseum, 1971); and Michael Snodin and John Styles, *Design and the Decorative Arts: Britain, 1500–1900* (London: V&A, 2001).

[16] Catherine Richardson, Tara Hamling, and David Gaimster, eds., *The Routledge Handbook of Material Culture in Early Modern Europe* (London: Routledge, 2016); and Marianne Hulsbosch, Elizabeth Bedford, and Martha Chaiklin, eds., *Asian Material Culture* (Amsterdam: Amsterdam University Press, 2009).

[17] Daniel Miller, *Material Culture and Mass Consumption* (Oxford: Blackwell, 1994); and Frank Trentmann, ed., *The Oxford Handbook of the History of Consumption* (Oxford and New York: Oxford University Press, 2012).

Of course, there was a recognition of the key importance and attraction of goods imported from beyond Europe.[18] Items such as textiles from India, porcelains from China, or silver from Batavia marked out wealth and status for their early modern European collectors.[19] But they were seen as a distinct group, with a separate space in the museum (displayed in galleries as "art and material culture from Asia") forming a story of imported luxuries that had a significant impact on the consumption practices of, again, national contexts.[20] Goods from elsewhere gained attention as objects of historical research through several separate pathways: the focus on global goods in the field of economic history on the one hand, and the growing presence of ethnographic objects and visibility of anthropological approaches in historical studies on the other.

The growing awareness of the ways in which history could and should be told from a global perspective also changed the museum world. Neil MacGregor's pathbreaking BBC program and accompanying book, for example, sought to tell the history of the world by way of 100 objects in the British Museum collection.[21] The project reached wide audiences, and the show of the British Museum's 100 objects traveled far and wide. The global turn also changed the ways in which historians approached material culture. Less focused on specifically European goods, material culture studies began to acknowledge the significance of the influx of goods from beyond European boundaries, especially the Americas and Asia.[22] Before the early modern period, precious goods arrived in Europe from distant locations through diplomatic exchange, gift giving, and collecting, but in relatively small quantities. Rich Renaissance collectors such as the Medici family in Florence amassed large collections of Chinese porcelains but they were the exception rather than the norm.[23]

The flow of goods from Asia and the Americas into early modern Europe was substantially larger and more regular, arriving on ships that sailed frequently across the Atlantic and Pacific oceans. Awareness grew of the multiple

[18] Reinier Baarsen et al., eds., *Het Nederlandse Binnenhuis Gaat Zich te Buiten: Internationale Invloeden op de Nederlandse Wooncultuur* (Leiden: Primavera Pers, 2007).

[19] Titus M. Eliëns, Erik Hesmerg, and Janey Tucker, *Zilver uit Batavia* (The Hague: Gemeentemuseum Den Haag, 2012).

[20] Maxine Berg, "In Pursuit of Luxury: Global History and British Consumer Goods in the Eighteenth Century," *Past & Present*, no. 182 (2004): 85–142.

[21] Neil MacGregor, *A History of the World in 100 Objects* (London: Allen Lane, 2010).

[22] Ina Baghdiantz McCabe, *Orientalism in Early Modern France: Eurasian Trade, Exoticism and the Ancien Régime* (Oxford: Berg, 2008); Ina Baghdiantz McCabe, *A History of Global Consumption: 1500–1800* (Abingdon: Routledge, 2015).

[23] Marco Spallanzani, *Ceramiche orientali a Firenze nel Rinascimento* (Florence: Cassa di Risparmio di Firenze, 1978); and Marco Spallanzani, *Ceramiche alla corte dei Medici nel Cinquecento* (Modena: F. C. Panini, 1994).

ways in which European interiors, from grand palaces to humble homes, were shaped by imported goods: hats made with fur from the Americas, tapestries and metal wares from the Middle East and Central Asia, porcelains and lacquerwares from East Asia, palampores from India, and so on.[24] Historians became attuned to the ways in which new beverages such as coffee, tea, and chocolate, especially in combination with Caribbean sugar, transformed not just what people drank but the vessels from which they consumed these sweet, hot drinks and the social spaces in which they consumed them.[25] New food-stuffs, brought from the Americas after the so-called Columbian Exchange, transformed culinary practices and tastes, and new materials (cottons and silk) introduced new ways of dressing. Of course, exotic and luxury goods from other parts of the world had always been part of status and hierarchy. What was new in the early modern era was the ways in which these exotica also reached lower social groups.[26] As Anne McCants showed on the basis of eighteenth-century inventories, for example, the alms houses and orphanages of Amsterdam also had access to porcelain goods, even if the quality of the porcelain was not as high as the imported porcelains that graced the canal houses of the East India traders in the same city.[27]

The scholarship that took account of this increasing ubiquity of imported goods in private and public spaces shifted from economic histories focused on the institutions of global trade, such as the East India Companies and the commodities they traded, to studies that took account of the ways in which material life in Europe changed on the basis of these imported goods.[28] Cultural-historical approaches had broadened the sources available for histor-ical study as well as the areas for investigation, such as the study of food and drink, identity and performance, distinction and taste, and domesticity and

[24] Timothy Brook, *Vermeer's Hat: The 17th Century and the Dawn of the Global World* (New York: Bloomsbury, 2008) is a good example.

[25] Timothy J. Tomasik and Juliann M. Vitullo, ed., *At the Table: Metaphorical and Material Cultures of Food in Medieval and Early Modern Europe* (Turnhout: Brepols, 2007).

[26] Giorgio Riello, "Luxury or Commodity: The Success of Indian Cotton Cloth in the First Global Age," in *Luxury in Global Perspective: Objects and Practices, 1600–2000*, ed. Bernd-Stefan Grewe and Karin Hofmeester (Cambridge: Cambridge University Press, 2016), 138–68.

[27] Anne E. C. McCants, "Asiatic Goods in Migrant and Native-Born Middling Households," in *Goods from the East, 1600–1800: Trading Eurasia*, ed. Maxine Berg, with Felicia Gottmann, Hanna Hodacs, and Chris Nierstrasz (Basingstoke: Palgrave Macmillan, 2015), 197–215; and Anne E. C. McCants, "Exotic Goods, Popular Consumption, and the Standard of Living: Thinking about Globalization in the Early Modern World," *Journal of World History* 18, no. 4 (2007): 433–62.

[28] Tânia Manuel Casimiro, "Globalization, Trade, and Material Culture: Portugal's Role in the Making of a Multicultural Europe (1415–1806)," *Post-Medieval Archaeology* 54, no. 1 (2020): 1–17.

public ritual. Imported goods from around the European empires and colonial possessions turned out to play key roles in all of these.

The scholarship on luxury that emerged from the late 1990s was significant in this wider literature.[29] The emphasis away from, for example, British or Netherlandish goods and their histories of manufacturing toward the influx and consumption of global goods produced new histories of technology and innovation based on the availability of goods such as Indian cotton textiles and Chinese porcelain.[30] Maxine Berg's work was central to this development, first in the form of "The Luxury Project" at Warwick, then in her *Past & Present* article in 2004, and finally in the book *Luxury and Pleasure in Eighteenth-Century Britain*.[31] She pointed out the profound impact of the arrival of global luxuries in Britain: on consumer desire and on the material culture landscape of eighteenth-century Britain, but also on the patterns of manufacture and the emergence of technological innovations. The European East India Companies and the opportunities for the extraction of goods and control over resources that the building of empires afforded European nations were significant in these developments. The potteries in Staffordshire and the textile mills in Lancashire would have produced very different things if it had not been for what was brought into Britain from the East India ship cargoes. Luxury goods and especially global luxuries that might previously have been dismissed as unimportant extras for a small segment of the population came to be seen as significant drivers for new patterns of consumption and innovative methods of production and marketing.[32] Even the European countries that did not have their own East India Companies and did not directly participate in the building of overseas empires saw transformations in both consumption and production after the growing availability of new materials, designs, and technologies.

Historians of collections also contributed to these developments.[33] Objects that travel bestow power and prestige onto those who own them, even if they themselves have not traveled at all. Christopher Bayly, writing about the

---

[29] Rengenier C. Rittersma, ed., *Luxury in the Low Countries: Miscellaneous Reflections on Netherlandish Material Culture, 1500 to the Present* (Brussels: Pharo, 2010).

[30] Maxine Berg and Helen Clifford, eds., *Consumers and Luxury: Consumer Culture in Europe 1650–1850* (Manchester: Manchester University Press, 1999).

[31] Maxine Berg and Elizabeth Eger, eds., *Luxury in the Eighteenth Century: Debates, Desires and Delectable Goods* (Basingstoke and New York: Palgrave, 2003); Berg, "In Pursuit of Luxury"; Maxine Berg, *Luxury and Pleasure in Eighteenth-Century Britain* (Oxford: Oxford University Press, 2010).

[32] Maxine Berg et al., eds., *Goods from the East, 1600–1800: Trading Eurasia* (Basingstoke: Palgrave Macmillan, 2015).

[33] Jessica Keating and Lia Markey, "'Indian' Objects in Medici and Austrian-Habsburg Inventories: A Case-Study of the Eighteenth-Century Term," *Journal of the History of Collections* 23, no. 2 (2011): 283–300.

history of such goods, called this "archaic globalization."[34] Spectacular collections of highly prized and exotic goods, such as those put together by the Medici family in fifteenth-century Florence and Wunderkammer throughout Europe in the sixteenth century, demonstrate the desire to display such goods as a separate collection. From the seventeenth century, when goods from Asia such as textiles and porcelains flooded into the European market in much larger quantities, such goods no longer appeared in separate, dedicated collection spaces but as part of the domestic interior. The imagination of the wider world that goods from the Americas and Asia made possible for European consumers was shared by much wider segments of the population from then onwards.[35] The significance of the work of anthropologists in these studies cannot easily be overestimated. Arjun Appadurai's work on the social lives of things shifted attention away from histories of categories of traded goods and individual pieces with established meanings and values toward the study of the trajectories of goods.[36] Objects move through various stages, Appadurai and Igore Kopytoff argued, from raw material to crafted object, from traded good to gifted item, or from inherited gift to recommercialized object.[37] As objects move through these fluid phases, their meanings and values are constantly renegotiated and reestablished, inviting historians not just to study the histories of objects but their itineraries and their social, and even global, lives.[38]

The shift to the study of global goods and their ubiquitous presence in the lives of early modern and modern Europeans led to a questioning of the relationship between object and identity. Do some objects belong in a certain place, while others do not, because they are imported, or perhaps because they

---

[34] C. A. Bayly, "'Archaic' and 'Modern' Globalization in the Eurasian and African Arena, c. 1750–1850," in *Globalization in World History*, ed. A. G. Hopkins (New York: W.W. Norton, 2002), 47–73; and C. A. Bayly, "From Archaic Globalization to International Networks, circa 1600–2000," in *Interactions: Transregional Perspectives on World History*, ed. Jerry Bentley, Renate Bridenthal, and Anand Yang (Honolulu: University of Hawai'i Press, 2005), 14–29.

[35] Anne Gerritsen and Giorgio Riello, "Spaces of Global Interactions: The Material Landscapes of Global History," in *Writing Material Culture History*, ed. Anne Gerritsen and Giorgio Riello (London: Bloomsbury, 2021), 123–42.

[36] Arjun Appadurai, ed., *The Social Life of Things: Commodities in Cultural Perspective* (Cambridge: Cambridge University Press, 1986).

[37] Igor Kopytoff, "The Cultural Biography of Things: Commoditization as Process," in *The Social Life of Things*, ed. Appadurai, 64–92.

[38] Rosemary A. Joyce and Susan D. Gillespie, eds., *Things in Motion: Object Itineraries in Anthropological Practice* (Santa Fe: School for Advanced Research Press, 2015); Hans Peter Hahn and Hadas Weiss, eds., *Mobility, Meaning and the Transformations of Things: Shifting Contexts of Material Culture through Time and Space* (Oxford: Oxbow Books, 2013); Hans Peter Hahn and Hadas Weiss, "Introduction: Biographies, Travels and Itineraries of Things," in *Mobility, Meaning and the Transformations of Things*, ed. Hahn and Weiss, 1–14; and the chapters in Pamela H. Smith, ed., *Entangled Itineraries: Materials, Practices, and Knowledges across Eurasia* (Pittsburgh: University of Pittsburgh Press, 2019).

are composite pieces that reveal a combination of elements and identities? Objects that reveal such global trajectories were sometimes marked as different from objects that seemed to belong in one place: what Homi Bhabha called "culturally hybrid" included goods distinct from what was locally made and locally consumed.[39] These might include objects perceived as foreign as well as materials and designs that had gradually become domesticated or integrated into local cultures.[40] Hybrid objects might not exactly be European, because they reveal knowledge, materials, and methods that had their origins outside of Europe, but also not exactly African, American, or Asian, because they were clearly produced for a consumer with European tastes and preferences. Lisa Jardine and Jerry Brotton talked of a "two-way material exchange across geographical and ideological boundaries," which had "an enduring influence on European cultural identity."[41] The goods produced in Canton are typically in this category of "hybrid goods": the materials are undoubtedly Asian – lacquered boxes, ivory baskets (Figure 9.2), embroidered silk coverlets, painted wallpapers, and so on – as are the designs (e.g., ladies in flowing robes with parasols; dragons, bats, and unicorns) and the shapes (e.g., vast porcelain fishbowls and planters, betel nut boxes, or kimono-style robes). But they are distinct from goods made for local markets in the ways in which they combine elements: Chinese designs on a gin bottle or butter dish, steam trains and airplanes on a silk robe, or boxes in precious woods with Western-style fixings and locks. Made to order for export, and highly suitable as souvenirs and gifts, such objects often did not rank highly in the hierarchies of (decorative) art. Peter Burke defined hybridity rather broadly, more or less on a par with the idea of cultural interaction, which he saw as "extremely positive," pointing out "that all innovation is a kind of adaptation and that cultural encounters encourage creativity."[42] Others have been rather more critical of the concept, pointing out the ways in which an emphasis on a blend of cultural characteristics as hybridity tends imply not only to suggest the potential existence of the nonhybrid (i.e., purity) but also implicitly pays lip

---

[39] Homi Bhabha referred to identities that were not fixed by characterized by a fluidity and an in-betweenness as cultural hybridity. Homi K. Bhabha, *The Location of Culture* (London: Routledge, 1994).

[40] Beverly Lemire, "Domesticating the Exotic: Floral Culture and the East India Calico Trade with England, c. 1600–1800," *Textile: Journal of Cloth and Culture* 1, no. 1 (2003): 64–85; Jeremy Prestholdt, *Domesticating the World: African Consumerism and the Genealogies of Globalization* (Berkeley: University of California Press, 2008); and Anne Gerritsen, "Domesticating Goods from Overseas: Global Material Culture in the Early Modern Netherlands," *Journal of Design History* 29, no. 3 (2016): 228–44.

[41] Lisa Jardine and Jerry Brotton, *Global Interests: Renaissance Art between East and West* (London: Reaktion, 2000), 7.

[42] Peter Burke, *Cultural Hybridity* (Cambridge: Polity Press, 2009).

Figure 9.2 Ivory stacking basket, made in Canton, c. 1795–c. 1810, height 47.5 cm, length 128.5 cm, width 20.5 cm.
Source: Rijksmuseum, Amsterdam, AK-NM-7023.

service to a hierarchical order between the two, with the hybrid as second best to or lesser than the pure.

In Carolyn Dean and Dana Leibsohn's analysis, this is particularly true for the colonial context in the Americas, where the nonhybrid art forms are those associated with the Old World, whereas the material forms associated with Spanish American Christianity involve elements of indigeneity combined with interpretations of Christian iconography.[43] A collection edited by Avtar Brah and Annie Coombes also, critiqued the notion of hybridity, with its problematic associations with race and especially racial purity and implications for notions of nation, nativism, and belonging.[44] And yet Nevertheless, the concept of hybridity has not disappeared from the scholarly apparatus. In a study of African objects in the Manchester Museum, Emma Poulter reconsiders hybridity by returning to the concept of the contact zone. Instead of identifying certain objects as hybrid because they emerge from a time and space in which cultural interactions take place, she insists on seeing the objects themselves as contact zones.[45] Invoking Mary Louise Pratt's notion as well as James Clifford's development of the concept by adapting it to museum collections, Poulter suggests that the objects themselves are sites of negotiation and interaction, dominated by power relations but also able to facilitate dialogue and new understandings.[46]

The transformation in thinking about material culture in Europe has profoundly changed with the integration of the global turn. From considering European material culture only from within a tightly bordered European perspective, approaches have shifted to not only identifying the ubiquity of non-European goods within European material landscapes but also recognizing the impossibility of maintaining a distinction between what is European and what is non-European. As we saw in the case of Gallery 1.5 in the Rijksmuseum, seventeenth- and eighteenth-century Dutch identities were forged in part overseas and in part at home, through the rich materiality of coproduced goods that signal many places within one object and within one space.[47]

Of course, our inability to identify where something was made on the basis of its design or materials is not only a feature in our approach to early modern

---

[43] Carolyn Dean and Dana Leibsohn, "Hybridity and Its Discontents: Considering Visual Culture in Colonial Spanish America," *Colonial Latin American Review* 12, no. 1 (2003): 5–35.

[44] Avtar Brah and Annie E. Coombes, eds., *Hybridity and Its Discontents: Politics, Science, Culture* (London: Routledge, 2000).

[45] Emma K. Poulter, "Hybridity – Objects as Contact Zones: A Critical Analysis of Objects in the West African Collections at the Manchester Museum," *Museum Worlds* 2, no. 1 (2014): 25–41; Mary Louise Pratt, *Imperial Eyes: Travel Writing and Transculturation* (London: Routledge, 1991).

[46] Poulter, "Hybridity – Objects as Contact Zones," 26.

[47] Benjamin Schmidt, *Inventing Exoticism: Geography, Globalism, and Europe's Early Modern World* (Philadelphia: University of Pennsylvania Press, 2015).

objects. The material world of the modern era seems to be characterized precisely by objects that appear the same, regardless of where they were made, suggesting a kind of homogeneity or loss of distinction. A pair of blue jeans, the famous Coca-Cola bottle, or the interior of a McDonalds outlet are all instantly recognizable, wherever they are situated.[48] We tend to assume that the modern world is a globalized world, in which the production of goods is entirely separated from the site of their consumption. It is a process that started, arguably, with the production of blue-and-white porcelains in Jingdezhen or the manufacture of cotton textiles in Gujarat for consumers all over the world that went on to transform the production processes of textiles and ceramics in Europe, creating goods that were hard to distinguish from or even surpassed the goods made in Asia.[49] The erasure of the Asian origins of manufacturing materials and technologies was enhanced by the expansive control that European empires exerted on the wider world in the nineteenth and twentieth centuries.

The loss of specific origin narratives for material culture of the modern era is both exemplified and enhanced by the removal of production sites from Europe to Asia in search of cheaper labor costs. Iconic goods associated with specifically European material goods became too expensive to produce in Europe in the second half of the twentieth century and their production was relocated to Asia. Wedgwood ceramics, for example, moved its production away from Staffordshire to Asia in the 1990s, as did Spode. Northampton, once home to many of the United Kingdom's prestigious and high-quality footwear manufacturers from the late nineteenth century onwards, also lost many of its brands to cheaper manufacturing sites in East and Southeast Asia.[50] Interestingly, the importance of the "Made in Britain" label for brand recognition and trust was also responsible for a gradual return to production within the United Kingdom. A brand such as Burberry is very careful about which parts of the production of its fashion clothing range are located within the United Kingdom and which parts can be outsourced to cheaper sites of production without losing the claim to Britishness.[51] Arguably, the complex, multi site production processes that are part of labor-intensive products such as footwear, clothing, and ceramics make it impossible to determine exactly where something is made, although a

---

[48] George Ritzer, *The McDonaldization of Society: An Investigation into the Changing Character of Contemporary Social Life* (Thousand Oaks: Pine Forge Press, 1993).

[49] Giorgio Riello, *Cotton: The Fabric That Made the Modern World* (Cambridge: Cambridge University Press, 2013); Anne Gerritsen, *The City of Blue and White: Chinese Porcelain and the Early Modern World* (Cambridge: Cambridge University Press, 2020).

[50] The chapters in Lois Labrianidis, ed., *The Moving Frontier: The Changing Geography of Production in Labour-Intensive Industries* (Abingdon: Routledge, 2018).

[51] Andy Pike, *Origination: The Geographies of Brands and Branding* (Chichester: Wiley Blackwell, 2015).

sophisticated advertising campaign can do a great deal to create a European or specifically British, identity for such goods.

Global labor historians have done important work to counter the assumption that goods consumed in the modern world are global goods, without a specific place of origin. Take, for example, the ubiquitous blue jeans, worn all over the world, in some places more than five out of seven days a week.[52] Anthropologists such as Daniel Miller and Sophie Woodward have done much to reveal the diversity in wearing styles, practices, and meanings associated with the wearing of jeans in different parts of the world, challenging the idea of homogeneity through patterns of consumption.[53] But labor historians such as Marcel van der Linden have shown the importance of focusing on the global trajectories of labor that form part of the production of a pair of jeans. Starting with the cotton fiber, the indigo dye, and the thread, all the way to the zips, buttons, and rivets that make up a pair of jeans, the material elements all require a separate production process. The harvesting of the cotton, the weaving and dyeing of the textile, the stitching of the pattern, the production of the zip, the placement of the rivets: each of these are completed in different places, where the production conditions are cheapest. Van der Linden's motto, "follow the traces," allows us to see the final piece of clothing not as a single item of ubiquitous casual wear but as a complex item made up from the combined work of laborers all over the world, which can reveal the trajectory of capitalism that shaped the piece.[54]

European material culture, then, turns out to be full of traces that lead back to empire, colonial oppression, and the exploitation of labor. The global turn has broadened what we might think of as European material culture; we consider it to be an inclusive category of objects that included objects that were created elsewhere for European consumers, objects that were brought to Europe by collectors and (scientific) explorers, as well as European-made objects consumed and/or recreated in other parts of the world. But that same global turn has also opened our eyes to the problematic nature of those acquisitions: collecting that consisted in fact of the acquisition of goods under unequal circumstances; colonial "gifts" that were demanded and/or received

---

[52] Daniel Miller and Sophie Woodward, *Blue Jeans: The Art of the Ordinary* (Berkeley: University of California Press, 2011), 4; and the chapters in Daniel Miller and Sophie Woodward, eds., *Global Denim* (Oxford: Berg, 2011).

[53] Miller and Woodward, *Blue Jeans*.

[54] "Follow the traces" was mentioned as a way of writing global history even from the perspective of a small village or community. Wherever the starting point is, Van der Linden recommended, we "follow the traces … wherever they might lead: across political and geographic frontiers, time frames, territories, and disciplinary boundaries." Marcel van der Linden, "The Promise and Challenges of Global Labor History," *International Labor and Working-Class History* 82 (2012): 57–76, here p. 62.

under the threat of violence; manufacture by enslaved laborers, or by free or forced labor under appalling conditions that produced the cheap goods that satisfy our every wish. The material legacy of colonial exploits that fills European museum collections, castles, grand houses, and public spaces as well as private residences, presents us with profound challenges.

The response to these challenges has been varied. In the first place, it has led to public debate about the extent to which the institutions that hold collections of colonial goods or whose financial and material fabric is the outcome of slavery need to acknowledge this legacy.[55] The National Trust, for example, or some of the Oxbridge colleges, have decided that this acknowledgment is an important first step in the direction of righting such major historical wrongs, and have invested in research projects that bring these legacies to light.[56] Similarly, in the Netherlands, a pilot project entitled Provenance Research on Objects of the Colonial Era was carried out between 2019 and 2022, with partners that included the National Institute for War, Holocaust and Genocide Studies, the Rijksmuseum Amsterdam, and the national museums of world cultures in the Netherlands (NMVW).[57] In the second place, attempts are being made all over the world to establish workable practices for the return of wrongfully obtained goods.[58] The Dutch government and the NMVW were also among the first in Europe to declare their willingness to return any colonial object in their collections to its place of origin.[59] This is, of course, easier said than done. Colonial restitution works on the assumption that the rightful owners of a piece can be identified and that their right to the object is not tainted in any way by other practices of oppression or force, though the willingness to do so is an important first step. Others have resisted these shifts toward redress and restitution and refuse to acknowledge the problematic colonial relationships that more often than not lie at the foundations of the global interactions that shape today's material legacies. Ongoing research and

---

[55] See, for example, the "Legacies of British Slavery" project, led by Professor Catherine Hall.

[56] Salle-Anne Huxtable et al., eds., *Interim Report on the Connections between Colonialism and Properties Now in the Care of the National Trust, including Links with Historic Slavery* (Swindon: National Trust, 2020).

[57] Pressing Matter: Ownership, Value and the Question of Colonial Heritage in Museums will end in 2025. The project is run by the National Museum of World Cultures and the Vrije Universiteit, Amsterdam.

[58] The discussions around the Humboldt Forum in Berlin are an example, see Johanna Di Blasi, *Das Humboldt Lab: Museumsexperimente zwischen postkolonialer Revision und szenografischer Wende* (Bielefeld: Transcript Verlag, 2019).

[59] Sarah Cascone, "The Dutch Government Just Promised to Return Any Stolen Colonial-Era Objects in Its Collections Back to Their Countries of Origin," Artnet News, 4 February 2021, Online.

the willingness to debate will undoubtedly keep moving these issues forward, though they will inevitably reveal uncomfortable truths about the centrality of the exploitation of natural resources and the enslavement of human beings in the creation of Europe's material heritage. Global history will inevitably continue to play a central role in bringing these stories to light and resisting a return to nationalist narratives of the past.

10 Migration and European History's Global Turn

Elizabeth Buettner

Research on migration has long stood at the forefront of transnational and global approaches to both contemporary social phenomena and more distant historical epochs. Having grown steadily more visible since the late 1990s, interdisciplinary interventions by Nina Glick Schiller, Linda Basch, Cristina Blanc-Szanton, Andreas Wimmer, Steven Vertovec, and Nancy Green among many others, have deeply influenced scholarly analyses of the increasing hypermobility – both within Europe and between Europe and the wider world – that has characterized recent decades.[1] Even as the citizens of an expanding European Union (EU) were able to cross its internal and external borders with considerable ease as professionals, workers, students, and tourists, Europeans simultaneously engaged in intense and often hostile debates about the impact of episodes such as the so-called "refugee crisis" that intensified from 2015 onwards as millions from Africa, the Middle East, and elsewhere risked their lives in hopes of reaching security and better prospects in Europe – often in vain. Freedom of movement within the EU, for its part, created both opportunities and challenges, not least in the eyes of the many Britons who in 2016 voted for Brexit out of resentment and fear about migration's impact on the United Kingdom. Populist nationalism relying on perceptions of unwanted migration, whether actual or potential, was a transnational phenomenon visible in varying ways from Denmark to Hungary to Italy, to name just a few examples – even while so many Danes, Hungarians, Italians, and others regularly traveled in and beyond Europe for

---

[1] Seminal contributions focusing on contemporary conditions (some also encompassing a historical perspective) include Nina Glick Schiller, Linda Basch, and Cristina Blanc-Szanton, eds., *Towards a Transnational Perspective on Migration: Race, Class, Ethnicity, and Nationalism Reconsidered* (New York: New York Academy of Sciences, 1992); Andreas Wimmer and Nina Glick Schiller, "Methodological Nationalism, the Social Sciences, and the Study of Migration: An Essay in Historical Epistemology," *International Migration Review* 37, no. 3 (2003): 576–610; Steven Vertovec, "Transnationalism and Identity," *Journal of Ethnic and Migration Studies* 27, no. 4 (2001): 573–82; and Nancy L. Green, "The Trials of Transnationalism: It's Not as Easy as It Looks," *Journal of Modern History* 89, no. 4 (2017): 851–74.

work, pleasure, or both.[2] The abrupt standstill that hundreds of millions of Europeans experienced in much of 2020 and 2021 thanks to the COVID-19 pandemic stands out as an exception that proved the rule. But even with the permissible mobility many Europeans had come to take for granted stalled in its tracks in the face of lockdowns, curfews, and severe travel restrictions, "illegal" migrants persisted in attempting to reach European shores from without.

The fever pitch that migration within Europe, and between Europe and the wider world, reached before the pandemic provides further illumination of the global context of European migration in the past and present alike. Taking the late modern era as its focus, this chapter considers how Europe's embeddedness in transatlantic, imperial, and other global arenas has been thrown into relief through journeys and relocations that brought people into direct contact with other cultures and ethnicities at both the individual and societal levels. Over the long nineteenth century and into the twentieth, faster and easier travel via rail and steamship along with modern global and imperial infrastructures created increasingly favorable conditions for Europeans themselves to cross land and sea as emigrants, settlers, or in a military, administrative, or commercial capacity. Rough estimates suggest that between 1815 and 1939 over fifty-five million people left Europe, primarily for North and South America (thirty-five million and eight million, respectively) as well as other global settings, including those that remained parts of European overseas empires.[3] European states and agents also orchestrated multiple global migrations of Africans in the era of the transatlantic trade in enslaved peoples and Asian indentured workers after slavery's formal abolition, to give just two of the most important variations. Multiethnic societies across much of the world thus bore a deep European imprint, whether or not they included substantial numbers of European-descended peoples in settler or non-settler colonial and postcolonial arenas.

Global interactions such as these correspondingly became entangled with internal European relations within and between states. Ideas about racial, civilizational, and cultural hierarchies playing out inside Europe as ethnic groups, cultures, and nationalities coalesced, transformed, and came into

---

[2] The chapters in Nicholas De Genova, ed., *The Borders of "Europe": Autonomy of Migration, Tactics of Bordering* (Durham, NC: Duke University Press, 2017); Leo Lucassen, "Peeling an Onion: The 'Refugee Crisis' from a Historical Perspective," *Ethnic and Racial Studies* 41, no. 3 (2018): 383–410; Adrian Favell, *Eurostars and Eurocities: Free Movement and Mobility in an Integrating Europe* (Malden: Blackwell, 2008); and Kathy Burrell et al., "Brexit, Race and Migration," *Environment and Planning C: Politics and Space* 37, no. 1 (2019): 3–40.

[3] Donna R. Gabaccia, Dirk Hoerder, and Adam Walaszek, "Emigration and Nation Building during the Mass Migrations from Europe," in *Citizenship and Those Who Leave: The Politics of Emigration and Expatriation*, ed. Nancy L. Green and François Weil (Urbana: University of Illinois Press, 2007), 63–90, here p. 63.

contact with one another repeatedly bore traces of wider global interactions and frames of reference.[4] In time, moreover, they intersected with responses to the growing presence on the continent of non-European-origin peoples from colonial, postcolonial, or other multiethnic societies across the world, not least as the impact of decolonization was felt in western and southern Europe as well as overseas after 1945. Some migration streams were encouraged, others strictly controlled as inducements and restrictions waxed and waned and repeatedly took racialized forms.

In many respects, the "global turn" has long been integral (if not always explicitly so) to the wider field of migration history, albeit to varying degrees depending on the places and themes in question. Historians have produced an immense literature illuminating countless manifestations of Europe's, and Europeans', migration histories and their globalized contexts and consequences. We now benefit from a substantial body of excellent, wide-ranging studies concerned with larger structures, patterns, and demographic trends that show how migration flows – outward, inward, and internal – have been central to the history of all parts of the continent.[5] Imperial/global labor migration patterns, whether "forced" or "free" (or somewhere in between); European emigration and its impact on both sending and receiving societies; Europe's internal mobilities, whether circular or permanent, as well as refugee movements and forced population transfers; and the return, arrival, and settlement of postcolonial peoples and other groups from across the world: together with considerations of ethnic diversity, racialized categorizations, "whiteness," hybridity, and other themes, these have been treated in an impressive body of scholarship continually augmented by new approaches and case studies. Some – if only a fraction – are noted in the sections that follow. Migration, in sum, is at once a shared European history and a global one with social and cultural as well as economic and political ramifications. Given the

---

[4] Tara Zahra, *The Great Departure: Mass Migration from Eastern Europe and the Making of the Free World* (New York: W. W. Norton, 2016).

[5] Essential overarching studies that have emerged since the 1990s include Klaus J. Bade, *Migration in European History* (Malden: Blackwell, 2003), which was first published in 2001; Dirk Hoerder, *Cultures in Contact: World Migrations in the Second Millennium* (Durham, NC: Duke University Press, 2002); Leslie Page Moch, *Moving Europeans: Migration in Western Europe since 1650* (Bloomington and Indianapolis: Indiana University Press, 1992); and Leo Lucassen, *The Immigrant Threat: The Integration of Old and New Migrants in Western Europe since 1850* (Urbana: University of Illinois Press, 2005) – not to mention countless articles written by Leo Lucassen and Jan Lucassen, among others, and invaluable reference books such as Klaus J. Bade et al., eds., *The Encyclopedia of Migration and Minorities in Europe: From the Seventeenth Century to the Present* (Cambridge: Cambridge University Press, 2011), and Christiane Harzig, and Dirk Hoerder with Donna Gabaccia, *What Is Migration History?* (Cambridge: Polity Press, 2009). Many of the contributions to the two volumes comprising Donna Gabaccia, ed., *The Cambridge History of Global Migrations* (Cambridge: Cambridge University Press, 2023) demonstrate how the field continues to evolve.

embarrassment of academic riches already at our disposal, what topics and perspectives stand out as areas with the potential to take European history's global turn in new directions?

This chapter departs from many treatments of migration that focus on macro-level histories, arguing that zooming in on individual interpretations and experiences can open up nuanced perspectives that are frequently sidelined in more general, broad-brush studies where, rather paradoxically, actual migrants can often find themselves submerged beneath an emphasis on migration phenomena. Historians of Europe's late modern era might take further inspiration from scholars of global microhistory, for example, many of whom have focused on earlier periods, and more generally from landmark treatments of lives lived beyond borders that use intricate evaluations of individuals and their movements to comprehend interlocking wider worlds.[6] By the same token, they can evaluate how studies such as Tara Zahra's *The Great Departure* deftly combine a far larger European and global picture with individual examples that bring it to life – a balance rarely struck within much existing historiography.[7] Not only does this approach enable time-, place-, and circumstance-specific stories to emerge; it also shows how fields of migration scholarship that have largely remained separate can be fruitfully brought together to produce new insights into the histories of Europe, Europeans, and the worlds in which they moved.

As an example of this approach, the pages that follow will trace the global implications of two lives that together span almost two centuries, using vignettes of their individual circumstances and perspectives to open out broader questions. Although born nearly eighty years and thousands of kilometers apart, Jacob Riis (1849–1914) and Gérald Bloncourt (1926–2018) were both leading documentary photographers who shared a deep commitment

---

[6] Romain Bertrand and Guillaume Calafat, eds., "Micro-analyse et histoire globale," special issue, *Annales HSS* 73, no. 1 (2018); and the contributions in John-Paul Ghobrial, ed., "Global History and Microhistory," *Past & Present*, supplement 14 (2019), offer recent overviews of global microhistory. Among the leading book-length studies centered on individuals, see Natalie Zemon Davis, *Trickster Travels: A Sixteenth-Century Muslim between Worlds* (New York: Hill and Wang, 2006); Mercedes García-Arenal and Gerard Wiegers, *A Man of Three Worlds: Samuel Pallache, a Moroccan Jew in Catholic and Protestant Europe* (Baltimore: Johns Hopkins University Press, 2007); Linda Colley, *The Ordeal of Elizabeth Marsh: A Woman in World History* (Princeton: Princeton University Press, 2007); Miles Ogborn, *Global Lives: Britain and the World, 1550–1800* (Cambridge: Cambridge University Press, 2008); Maya Jasanoff, *The Dawn Watch: Joseph Conrad in a Global World* (London: Penguin, 2017). Isabella Löhr, "Lives beyond Borders, or: How to Trace Global Biographies, 1880–1950," *Comparativ: Zeitschrift für Globalgeschichte und vergleichende Gesellschaftsforschung* 23, no. 6 (2013): 7–21, provides a valuable discussion focused on more modern examples.
[7] Zahra, *The Great Departure.*

to social reform and the amelioration of working-class conditions, bequeathing invaluable visual archives to posterity.[8] Each recorded migration histories both on camera and in writing, thereby enabling an analysis of multimedia representations emanating from the same source. That both were of migration backgrounds themselves renders the images and texts they created particularly resonant, for their own origins and mobile lives proved crucial to their heightened interactions with and perceptions of the wider flows of people that connected Europe with different global settings. Some of the countless ways that they, and their subject matter, were part of far bigger histories and bring telling intersections into sharp relief are flagged along the way.

Jacob Riis's European and American Worlds

When his book *How the Other Half Lives: Studies among the Tenements of New York* first appeared in 1890, Riis already had an established reputation as an investigative journalist and newspaper editor.[9] Through his many books, articles, and public lectures, middle- and upper-class Americans could visit the dilapidated, overcrowded tenement housing, workplaces, back-alleys, and markets of Lower Manhattan and learn second-hand about the grinding poverty, labor exploitation, and structural disadvantages suffered by much of New York City. Unlike more judgmental commentators, Riis saw New York's poor largely as victims abused by profiteering landlords and employers. The enduring power of *How the Other Half Lives* stemmed not just from its first-person textual narrative but also its illustrations – initially line engravings based on photographs taken either by Riis himself or by others more experienced in the still-emerging technologies of the camera and flash photography. It took until the mid-twentieth century for the original images to resurface and gradually gain recognition as pioneering works of visual social realism.[10] Today, Riis is often better known as an eminent documentary photographer than as a

---

[8] Many of Riis's photographs form part of the Jacob A. Riis Collection of the Museum of the City of New York (see https://collections.mcny.org/Explore/Highlights/Jacob-A-Riis), while a selection of Bloncourt's thousands of images can be viewed via https://www.bloncourt.net. For a suggestive piece on the use of photographs as a historical source, see Derek Sayer, "The Photograph: The Still Image," in *History beyond the Text: A Student's Guide to Approaching Alternative Sources*, ed. Sarah Barber and Corinna Peniston-Bird (London: Routledge, 2009), 49–71, which makes reference to Jacob Riis on pp. 50 and 55.

[9] Jacob A. Riis, *How the Other Half Lives: Studies among the Tenements of New York* (New York: Charles Scribner's Sons, 1890).

[10] The later edition used here – Jacob A. Riis, *How the Other Half Lives: Studies among the Tenements of New York*, ed. Sam Bass Warner Jr. (Cambridge, MA: Harvard University Press, 2010 [1890]) – first appeared in 1970, replacing many of the engraved images with Riis's original photographs. Though the secondary literature is extensive, particularly useful discussions of Riis and his photographs can be found in Alan Trachtenberg's introduction to the aforementioned edition as well as Edward T. O'Donnell, "Pictures vs. Words? Public History,

passionate reformer and author who successfully campaigned for improved urban conditions. In time, both the author/photographer and his subjects became an established, even canonical, part of the turn-of-the-century American story.

Yet Riis's life and work, like those of many people he wrote about and photographed, were just as much part of a transnational European global history as an unfolding American one. The vast majority of those featured in *How the Other Half Lives* were either immigrants or the children of immigrants from different parts of Europe. Like many of his contemporaries, Riis described his subjects in terms of their places of origin and ethnicity – as Italians, Irish, Polish or Russian Jews, "Bohemians" (or Czechs), and occasionally Germans and other communities who retained these identities after coming to the United States. Far from being left behind on the "old continent," European historical conditions and conflicts maintained their hold over the distinct European "races" (as Riis and others of his time typically termed them) who journeyed to America (Figure 10.1). When it was said that New York "beats the world" as a clothing manufacturer, for example, this was attributed in large part to Jewish workers pushed out by Europe's pogroms: "Every fresh persecution of the Russian or Polish Jew on his native soil starts greater hordes hitherward ... The curse of bigotry and ignorance reaches halfway across the world."[11]

Riis's descriptions contained a mixture of sympathy accentuated by contempt, certainly when his attention turned from New York's central and eastern Europeans to those from further south. "The Italian comes in at the bottom, and in the generation that came over the sea he stays there," Riis wrote

He not only knows no word of English, but he does not know enough to learn. Rarely only can he write his own language. Unlike the German, who begins learning English the day he lands as a matter of duty, or the Polish Jew, who takes it up as soon as he is able as an investment, the Italian learns slowly, if at all.[12]

Even so, "the swarthy Italian immigrant has his redeeming traits," Riis believed, being "gay, lighthearted and, if his fur is not stroked the wrong way, inoffensive as a child."[13] As was then common, Riis often described

---

Tolerance, and the Challenge of Jacob Riis," *The Public Historian* 26, no. 3 (2004): 7–26; Bonnie Yochelson and Daniel Czitrom, *Rediscovering Jacob Riis: Exposure Journalism and Photography in Turn-of-the-Century New York* (Chicago: University of Chicago Press, 2008); and Tom Buk-Swienty, *The Other Half: The Life of Jacob Riis and the World of Immigrant America* (New York: W. W. Norton, 2008).

[11] Riis, *How the Other Half Lives*, 116 and 118, see also p. 130. On garment industry workers in comparative perspective, see especially Nancy L. Green, *Ready-to-Wear and Ready-to-Work: A Century of Industry and Immigrants in Paris and New York* (Durham, NC: Duke University Press, 1997).

[12] Riis, *How the Other Half Lives*, 48–9.   [13] Ibid., 54.

Figure 10.1 Bohemian cigar makers at work in their tenement.
Source: Photograph by Jacob A. Riis, New York, c. 1890 (© Museum of the City of New York, 90.13.1.149).

migrant groups in derogatory terms emphasizing excessive numbers ("hordes"), qualities associated with animals ("fur") or children, and distinctive physical characteristics (Jews' "unmistakable physiognomy"[14] or Italians' "swarthiness") – all familiar forms of group racialization by observers who placed themselves higher in the social hierarchy. In this, his texts complicate and partly undermine the images of individuals that were meant to cultivate compassion and bolster campaigns to ameliorate slum life. Riis described New York City's poor from different parts of Europe in terms of their group identities, not as "Europeans" per se; tellingly, they were mainly referred to as "white" when evaluated alongside local Chinese and "colored" (or "Negro") populations. In these contexts, they became the "white victim[s]" or "white slaves" of opium dens, or were compared unfavorably to "colored people," who in certain respects were "immensely the superior of the lowest of the

[14] Ibid., 101.

whites, the Italians and the Polish Jews" (in other words, "the lower grades of foreign white people").[15]

Such immigrants from Europe not only lacked a secure "white" identity as groups still viewed as racially "in between," in the process of "becoming white," or "working towards whiteness" – themes that scholars including David Roediger, Matthew Frye Jacobson, and other important authors have illuminated.[16] They were also not – or not yet – American. "The one thing you shall vainly ask for in the chief city of America is a distinctively American community," Riis stated.[17] Becoming American in this view involved both learning English and moving up from the tenement slums – a path along which, of all the groups Riis considered in detail, "the Teuton" (or German) had come farthest.[18] Yet even more pertinent to his account of European newcomers in the United States were those discussed least in his classic study: Scandinavians. Swedes and Finns are occasionally mentioned but never described in depth, while Danes seem entirely absent – aside, that is, from Riis himself.

In *How the Other Half Lives*, Riis significantly did not tell his readers that their liaison into slum communities was himself an immigrant who had become an American citizen only five years before the book's publication. Born on Denmark's North Sea coast into a family with fourteen children, Riis had trained as a carpenter before leaving for the United States in 1870 at the age of twenty-one. Unlike many immigrants, he had the advantage of being able to read English well upon arrival, but he initially lived a peripatetic, hand-to-mouth existence involving periods of hunger and homelessness. He eventually made his name as a newspaper reporter and then owner, counting among those who worked hard and "made good" materially and professionally. But this was a story that he kept fully separate from that of the urban poor about whom he so famously wrote and campaigned, reserving his own experiences for another book: *The Making of an American*, published in 1901. In this memoir, Riis recounted how he retained close ties with

---

[15] Ibid., 93–4 and 142–3.

[16] Among many essential studies (including more by the authors noted here), see David R. Roediger, *Working toward Whiteness: How America's Immigrants Became White: The Strange Journey from Ellis Island to the Suburbs* (New York: Basic Books, 2018 [2005]); Matthew Frye Jacobson, *Whiteness of a Different Color: European Immigrants and the Alchemy of Race* (Cambridge, MA: Harvard University Press, 1999); Noel Ignatiev, *How the Irish Became White* (New York: Routledge, 1995); Zahra, *The Great Departure*; Karen Brodkin, *How the Jews Became White Folks and What That Says about Race in America* (New Brunswick: Rutgers University Press, 1998); Jennifer Guglielmo and Salvatore Salerno, eds., *Are Italians White? How Race Is Made in America* (New York: Routledge, 2003); and Thomas A. Guglielmo, *White on Arrival: Italians, Race, Color, and Power in Chicago, 1890–1945* (Oxford: Oxford University Press, 2003).

[17] Riis, *How the Other Half Lives*, 22.   [18] Ibid., 28.

Denmark after his initial departure, writing about American topics for the Danish press and making periodic journeys back to marry and visit family.[19] "Thirty years in the land of my children's birth left me as much of a Dane as ever," he wrote, despite becoming an American citizen in 1885. Regardless of his undying love for his native land, it was eventually through his trips back to Denmark that he realized he had "become an American in truth" and not just through his passport.[20]

By contrast, finding Riis's own story in *How the Other Half Lives* requires both reading between the lines and an awareness of the larger history of European migration to the United States. Scandinavians were more likely to be found in Chicago, Minneapolis, and other cities and rural areas of the Midwest than in New York City. But their marginality in Riis's account might also be attributed to some of these groups having come even closer than Germans to counting as "old stock" Anglo-Saxon Americans – as many who were better off and longer-settled hoped. As studies by Erika K. Jackson and Jørn Brøndal on Scandinavians and Russell A. Kazal on Germans have shown, such groups, not least if they were Protestant, occupied a far more privileged place in a racialized American ethnic hierarchy than southern and eastern Europeans, who were largely Roman Catholic or Jewish.[21]

The omission of the Danish experience and Riis's own story from *How the Other Half Lives* suggests the extent to which his own assertively "American" identity implicitly derived from the contrasts between his ultimate success and the multinational, impoverished, and unassimilated tenement population he surveyed. While he remained a parvenu with an audible foreign accent, grouping eastern and southern Europeans along with Chinese as "hopelessly isolated and ignorant of our language and our laws" bolstered his own narrative inclusion among those who could use words such as "our," "us," and "we."[22] His admiration of "the Negro's" advancement in the face of immense prejudice since slavery's abolition brought this home: "with fair treatment," he hoped, "the Negro" could do "quite as well as the rest of us, his white-skinned fellow citizens, had any right to expect."[23]

[19] Jacob A. Riis, *The Making of an American* (New York: Macmillan, 1922 [1901]), 37, 57, 111, 245, 265, and 274–6. This work was translated into French a few years later, Jacob A. Riis, *Comment je suis devenu américain* (Paris: L. Michaud, 1908).
[20] Riis, *The Making of an American*, 5, 267, 274, and 283–4.
[21] Erika K. Jackson, *Scandinavians in Chicago: The Origins of White Privilege in Modern America* (Urbana: University of Illinois Press, 2019); Jørn Brøndal, "'The Fairest among the So-Called White Races': Portrayals of Scandinavian Americans in the Filiopietistic and Nativist Literature of the Late Nineteenth and Early Twentieth Centuries," *Journal of American Ethnic History* 33, no. 3 (2014): 5–36; and Russell A. Kazal, *Becoming Old Stock: The Paradox of German-American Identity* (Princeton: Princeton University Press, 2004).
[22] Riis, *How the Other Half Lives*, 100 and 138.   [23] Ibid., 149.

The figure of Riis, in sum, suggests how one could self-include as American on a level beyond formal citizenship, but also that being accepted as such by others could prove considerably more complicated. Education, speaking English, achieving a respected class and professional status, and the ability to be seen as "white" helped immensely; being able to comfortably claim multiple identities, in his instance American and Danish, was a privilege and not a given. Indeed, white Anglo-Saxon/Anglophone American nativism rose markedly during Riis's later life and after his death in 1914 – a sentiment to which selected newer arrivals like himself might also contribute at the expense of others less fortunate. This culminated in fierce new immigration restriction acts in 1921 and 1924 that used quotas to exclude many ethnonational groups, particularly those from southern and eastern Europe. For many, finding fuller acceptance as American and "white" (or "Caucasian") took considerably longer, as historians including Mary Waters and Gary Gerstle have perceptively examined.[24] Significantly, a more overarching "white" identity became consolidated in the context of mounting activism and civil rights demands by Blacks and other minority groups from the 1950s on.

Equally important, Riis's accounts illustrate how European identities survived in other places and were nourished by the direct links individuals maintained with their homelands. He was one of millions of European emigrants to North and Latin America and settler colonies across the globe who returned home either temporarily or permanently, engaging in various forms of cyclical migration that sustained connections between nations, communities, and families across time and distance.[25] Influential studies by Caroline Brettell, Marjory Harper and Stephen Constantine, Donna Gabaccia, José Moya, Michael Goebel, and many others explore how durable interpersonal and associational networks, together with remittances sent home, contributed to migration's central place in the history of sending and receiving societies alike, whether at the level of households, localities, regions, countries and their far-flung "diasporic nations," or indeed entire continents.[26] Countless destinations had transnational

---

[24] Mary C. Waters, *Ethnic Options: Choosing Identities in America* (Berkeley: University of California Press, 1990); Gary Gerstle, *American Crucible: Race and Nation in the Twentieth Century* (Princeton: Princeton University Press, 2017 [2001]); see also the references given in notes 16 and 21.

[25] Dirk Hoerder notes that approximately one-third of those who arrived in the United States around 1900 returned to Europe; see Hoerder, "European Migrations," in *The Oxford Handbook of American Immigration and Ethnicity*, ed. Ronald H. Bayor (Oxford: Oxford University Press, 2016), 34–52, here p. 42. In addition to extensive work by the authors named in this paragraph, see also Green and Weil, *Citizenship and Those Who Leave*.

[26] Caroline B. Brettell, *Men Who Migrate, Women Who Wait: Population and History in a Portuguese Parish* (Princeton: Princeton University Press, 1987); Caroline B. Brettell, *Gender and Migration* (Cambridge: Polity Press, 2016); Marjory Harper and Stephen Constantine, *Migration and Empire* (Oxford: Oxford University Press, 2010); Donna R. Gabaccia, *Foreign Relations: American Immigration in Global Perspective* (Princeton:

European-origin populations, from Brazil, Uruguay, and Argentina to French Algeria (whose French citizens also included many of Italian, Spanish, and Maltese descent), and these diverse groups might gradually converge, retain aspects of earlier identities, or a combination of both.[27] In short, the history of emigration did not just mark much of modern Europe: the fallout from Europe's population growth, uneven economic development, political transformations, and ethnic conflicts (including the recurrent persecution of Jews) had lasting demographic and cultural consequences across the world, not least when it came to entrenched racial inequality privileging whiteness.[28]

The decolonizations of the mid-to-late twentieth century that followed violent colonial insurgencies and defensive metropolitan-settler counterinsurgencies helped send some of these migration streams into reverse. Approximately 800,000 of French Algeria's *pieds-noirs* became *rapatriés* in 1962 and over 500,000 settlers from collapsed Portuguese African communities became *retornados* in 1974 and 1975, contributing to the flow of people – both former colonizers and formerly colonized – entering Europe in the decades after the Second World War.[29] It was during this era that Europe gradually transformed from a continent primarily of emigration to one where inward migration prevailed. By one calculation, while ca. 3.1 million people migrated to Europe from other continents between 1901 and 1950, nearly twenty-five million did so between 1951 and 2000.[30] In different ways, to different degrees, and at different

Princeton University Press, 2012); and José C. Moya, *Cousins and Strangers: Spanish Immigrants in Buenos Aires, 1850–1930* (Berkeley: University of California Press, 1998).

[27] Michael Goebel, "*Gauchos, Gringos*, and *Gallegos*: The Assimilation of Italian and Spanish Immigrants in the Making of Modern Uruguay 1880–1930," *Past & Present*, no. 208 (2010): 191–229; and Yuval Tal, "The 'Latin' Melting Pot: Ethnorepublican Thinking and Immigrant Assimilation in and through Colonial Algeria," *French Historical Studies* 44, no. 1 (2021): 85–118.

[28] Settler colonialism and related themes have received innovative academic treatment in many monographs and edited collections. Outstanding examples include James Belich, *Replenishing the Earth: The Settler Revolution and the Rise of the Anglo-World, 1783–1939* (Oxford: Oxford University Press, 2009); Marilyn Lake and Henry Reynolds, *Drawing the Global Colour Line: White Men's Countries and the International Challenge of Racial Equality* (Cambridge: Cambridge University Press, 2008); Lorenzo Veracini, *The World Turned Inside Out: Settler Colonialism as a Political Idea* (London: Verso, 2021); Robert A. Bickers, ed., *Settlers and Expatriates: Britons over the Seas* (Oxford: Oxford University Press, 2010); Caroline Elkins and Susan Pedersen, eds., *Settler Colonialism in the Twentieth Century: Projects, Practices, Legacies* (New York and London: Routledge, 2005); Nicola Foote and Michael Goebel, eds., *Immigration and National Identities in Latin America* (Gainesville: University of Florida Press, 2014); and the chapters in Edward Cavanagh and Lorenzo Veracini, eds., *The Routledge Handbook of the History of Settler Colonialism* (London: Routledge, 2016).

[29] Elizabeth Buettner, *Europe after Empire: Decolonization, Society, and Culture* (Cambridge: Cambridge University Press, 2016), part 2; and Peter Gatrell, *The Unsettling of Europe: The Great Migration, 1945 to the Present* (London: Allen Lane, 2019).

[30] Leo Lucassen et al., "Cross-Cultural Migration in Western Europe 1901–2000: A Preliminary Estimate," IISH research paper 52, International Institute of Social History, Amsterdam, https://pure.knaw.nl/ws/portalfiles/portal/777930/researchpaper_52_lucassen_lucassen_et.al_versie_voor_web140801.pdf, pp. 35 and 47.

times, extra-European arrivals became a significant presence not only in western and southern Europe, where they often came from former colonies, but also in Europe's north, east, and center. These shifts merged with a much longer but equally dynamic history of intra-European mobilities that also took new forms from the mid-twentieth century on.[31] The trajectories of migrants moving from one part of Europe to another overlapped and intersected with those coming from overseas, histories that Gérald Bloncourt's life and work illuminate in ways that scholarship has yet to adequately address.

Gérald Bloncourt's Lens on European and Postcolonial Transformations

In 1946, Bloncourt, a twenty-year-old Haitian, made his first journey to France – or, to be more precise, to "European" or "hexagonal" France. Although Haiti had not counted as part of France's empire since its revolution over a century earlier, other parts of the Caribbean most certainly still did: Martinique and Guadeloupe, like French Guiana, were made "overseas departments" (*départements d'outre-mer*) within the postwar French Union of 1946–58 and remain French in 2024. Bloncourt's departure was as hasty as it was forced. Having come of age as a communist in the aftermath of the United States' 1915–34 occupation, in 1946 he played a crucial role in a five-day insurgency against the Haitian government and was forced into exile when it failed. He sailed to France, where he could claim nationality through his French mother and his Guadeloupe-born father. He arrived as a committed activist championing working-class causes and social equality as well as a poet, painter, engraver, and apprentice printer. In the coming decades, he would become best known for his photojournalism over a long career working for the newspapers like *L'Humanité*, *L'Avant-garde*, and many others.[32]

---

[31] Matthew Frank and Jessica Reinisch, eds., *Refugees in Europe, 1919–1959: A Forty Years' Crisis?* (London: Bloomsbury Academic, 2017); Rita Chin, *The Guest Worker Question in Postwar Germany* (Cambridge: Cambridge University Press, 2007); Alena K. Alamgir and Christina Schwenkel, "From Socialist Assistance to National Self-Interest: Vietnamese Labor Migration into CMEA Countries," in *Alternative Globalizations: Eastern Europe and the Postcolonial World*, ed. James Mark, Artemy M. Kalinovsky, and Steffi Marung (Bloomington: Indiana University Press, 2020), 100–24; Felipe Arocena, "From Emigrant Spain to Immigrant Spain," *Race and Class* 53, no. 1 (2011): 89–99; Pamela Ballinger, *The World Refugees Made: Decolonization and the Foundation of Postwar Italy* (Ithaca, NY: Cornell University Press, 2020); Cristina Lombardi-Diop and Caterina Romeo, "Italy's Postcolonial 'Question': Views from the Southern Frontier of Europe," *Postcolonial Studies* 18, no. 4 (2015): 367–83; Ruth Ben-Ghiat and Stephanie Malia Hom, eds., *Italian Mobilities* (London: Routledge, 2016); and Elizabeth Buettner, "Europeanising Migration in Multicultural Spain and Portugal during and after the Decolonisation Era," *Itinerario* 44, no. 1 (2020): 159–77.

[32] Bloncourt's memoir, published in 2004, provides much of the biographical information that follows: Gérald Bloncourt, *Le regard engagé: Mémoires d'un franc-tireur de l'image*

Bloncourt's biography, clearly exceptional on many levels, nevertheless fits within a wider pattern of multiple mobilities that connected Europe across its internal borders and with the wider world. Migration had been part of his family history well before his expulsion from Haiti. His French mother's parents were Italian, attesting to France's long history of immigration from within and beyond Europe compared to most parts of the continent – a history so influentially charted by Gérard Noiriel, Patrick Weil, and a host of other scholars.[33] His father, meanwhile – whom Bloncourt described as a "mulatto" and whose ancestors thus included both enslaved Africans and white settlers – had traveled from Guadeloupe to France and served in the First World War before settling in Haiti. He was thus part of a multilayered francophone "Black Atlantic" history spanning nations, empires, and continents that was perpetuated in the next generation: one of his sons was killed by the Nazis for his involvement in the French resistance during the Second World War and another was studying medicine in Paris at the time of Gérald's arrival.[34] Despite being better educated and having more family resources behind him than many could claim, Bloncourt's own journey, ethnicity, and nonhexagonal background gave him something in common with the hundreds of thousands of other migrants who headed for mainland France as it gradually recovered from the Second World War and moved into an era widely remembered as *les trente glorieuses*. These "thirty glorious years" after 1945 characterized by reconstruction, economic growth, and the spread of greater affluence also saw attempts to preserve European empires superseded by widescale decolonization and Europe's gradual integration.

His vast photographic archive from the 1950s through the 1970s and beyond provides a sympathetic portrayal of migrants that was rare among

(Paris: Bourin, 2004), here 70 and 91. His other books concern Haiti in 1946 – including *Journal d'un révolutionnaire* (Montreal: Mémoire d'encrier, 2013) – and after the fall of its dictatorship in the 1980s, as well as Haitian art and culture.

[33] Gérard Noiriel, *The French Melting Pot: Immigration, Citizenship, and National Identity* (Minneapolis: University of Minnesota Press, 1996), which was first published in 1988; Patrick Weil, *La France et ses étrangers: L'aventure d'une politique de l'immigration 1938–1991* (Paris: Calmann-Lévy, 1991); Ahmed Boubeker and Abdellali Hajjat, eds., *Histoire politique des immigrations (post)coloniales: France, 1920–2008* (Paris: Éd. Amsterdam, 2008); and the chapters in Benjamin Stora and Émile Temime, eds., *Immigrances: L'immigration en France au xxe siècle* (Paris: Hachette, 2007).

[34] Paul Gilroy, *The Black Atlantic: Modernity and Double Consciousness* (Cambridge, MA: Harvard University Press, 1993). Among many outstanding treatments in English, see Charles Tshimanga, Didier Gondola, and Peter J. Bloom, eds., *Frenchness and the African Diaspora: Identity and Uprising in Contemporary France* (Bloomington and Indianapolis: Indiana University Press, 2009); Trica Danielle Keaton, T. Denean Sharpley-Whiting, and Tyler Stovall, eds., *Black France/France Noire: The History and Politics of Blackness* (Durham, NC: Duke University Press, 2012); and Michael Goebel, *Anti-Imperial Metropolis: Interwar Paris and the Seeds of Third World Nationalism* (Cambridge: Cambridge University Press, 2015).

contemporary reporters and social commentators. Bloncourt, like Riis before him, offered insights into the lives of people who did not commonly make their own stories public. He emphasized their dignity and strength in the face of tremendous adversity, focusing not only on male migrants but also women and children. Documenting a multiethnic France in the making like few others, his lens captured many different groups who together contributed to a "super-diversity" encompassing Algerians, Moroccans, Africans and Antilleans, Yugoslavs, Portuguese, and others.[35]

Yet Bloncourt's mid-twentieth-century images differed markedly from Riis's late nineteenth-century oeuvre, and not simply because photographic technologies and conventions had moved on. His politics were far more radical and militant than Riis's reformist stance, and his work sought to rouse more than the ambivalent sympathy of Riis's photographs that were juxtaposed with texts reinforcing racialized categories, hierarchies, and stereotypes. Bloncourt's repeated proclamations of fraternity and solidarity with the oppressed classes extended in no small part from empathy. Unlike Riis, who separated his own immigration story from those of the racialized tenement population, Bloncourt interwove his own circumstances with those of his subjects, emphasizing that "I, too, am an immigrant."[36] After all, on arrival he had experienced trade union representatives asking if he had only come to France for sex and talking to him as though he were Tahitian rather than Haitian, revealing racist assumptions about the mixed origins suggested by his skin color (not to mention an entitled ignorance of geography).[37]

Bloncourt emphasized a common fate that encompassed poverty, exploitation, political and economic oppression, and often racism, regardless of migrants' ethnic or national background and whether or not they held French nationality or came from elsewhere in Europe. Unlike photographers who came, snapped, and left, Bloncourt prioritized a *regard engagé*, or "committed gaze," that involved getting to know his subjects where they lived and worked, including when they demonstrated and went on strike. In May and June of 1968, for instance, he spent thirty-three days and nights alongside the strikers at the Renault factory in Billancourt, just outside Paris, considering it his responsibility to "speak, translate, and transmit the anger of these men who wanted to end their condition as slaves of capital in order to build a more just and humane society."[38] He conveyed workers' exploitation, emotions, and

---

[35] Steven Vertovec, "Super-diversity and Its Implications," *Ethnic and Racial Studies* 30, no. 6 (2007): 1024–54.

[36] Marie Poinsot and Anne Volery, "Gérald Bloncourt par lui-même: Hommage," interview with Gérald Bloncourt conducted in April 2013, *Hommes et Migrations* 1325 (2019): 137–44, here p. 144.

[37] Bloncourt, *Le regard engagé*, 81.   [38] Ibid., 201.

Figure 10.2 Workers during the strike at the Renault factory in Boulogne-
Billancourt, France; photograph by Gérald Bloncourt, 1968.
Source: Grève à Renault Billancourt, 1045/3a, © Gérald Bloncourt,
Bridgeman Images.

ambitions to a wider public through photographs that showed individuals'
expressive faces, not simply an anonymous mass (Figure 10.2). In short, as he
saw it, "it was necessary to bear witness."[39]

As his photographs cumulatively demonstrated, living in *bidonvilles* (shan-
tytown slums), toiling in factories and on construction sites, and suffering
discrimination based on ethnicity or foreign origins (if not both) were the lot of
many migrants, regardless of birthplace or ancestry. "I rubbed shoulders with
these immigrants who were the brothers of all these other exploited French,
Italians, Portuguese, Africans, or Turks. Together they formed the 'working
class' that rebuilt postwar France," he recalled. He later wondered what had
happened to "these nameless thousands, these hundreds of Mohameds,
Ricardos, [and] Miguels" who endured so much racism and scorn: "What have
they become, these women and men who built our urban landscapes?" In all
likelihood, he imagined, many would respond that their children came to

[39] Gérald Bloncourt and Johann Petitjean, "L'œil, le monde et la colère: Gérald Bloncourt et ses
images," *Cahiers d'histoire: Revue d'histoire critique* 132 (2016): 157–84, here §34 of the
online edition, https://doi.org/10.4000/chrhc.5420.

inhabit the *banlieues* on the outskirts of Paris – remaining confined, in other words, to the margins in social, economic, and often racialized ways.[40]

It is perhaps for his depictions of Portuguese migrants that Bloncourt is best remembered today, particularly in France and Portugal but also on a wider international scale.[41] He not only wanted to know (and show) how they worked and lived but also what had brought them to France in the first place. Communism became his entry ticket into Portuguese lives determined not only by poverty but also by the *Estado Novo* dictatorship, embroiled in fighting anti-colonial insurgencies in Portuguese Africa between 1961 and 1974. In Paris, he met many men who were leftist political exiles like himself as much as they were labor migrants; some were also evading military conscription in the wars of decolonization. He was inspired to chart their lives not only after their arrival in France but from their points of departure, providing a unique visual record of the migration process as it unfolded. In the mid-1960s he visited Lisbon, Porto, and the rural Chaves region in the north, photographing impoverished Portuguese villages (which many men had already left for France or other foreign destinations) and migrants' illegal journeys out of the country, accompanying them on trucks through Spain, on foot across the Pyrenees, and then on trains bound for Paris.[42]

As he came to realize, however, in France feelings of solidarity across ethnic and national lines could have decided limits, especially when it came to Algerians and others from the Maghreb. His memoir described the corrosive effects of the Algerian War within French trade unions and political organizations in the 1950s and early 1960s, and his aim to show through photographs that "we were all part of the same society in which we all had to rub shoulders, accept, and value each other." Yet he found "racism plaguing sections of the working population," and not just dividing white French from newcomers: "Sometimes [it] infect[ed] other immigrants or children of immigrants who considered themselves 'more French' than the Arabs because they themselves were European."[43]

Bloncourt's words and images do not simply reflect a particular leftist ideological perspective and an uncommon Franco-Guadeloupean-Italian-Haitian background that crossed ethnic and national lines as well as oceans.

---

[40] Bloncourt, *Le regard engagé*, 137–8.
[41] Nuno Ferreira de Carvalho, ed., *Por uma vida melhor: O olhar de Gérald Bloncourt/Pour une vie meilleure: Le regard de Gérald Bloncourt* (Lisbon/Lyon: Fondation Berardo/Fage, 2008); and Jennifer Marc, "Pictures Tell the Story of the Portuguese in France," *New York Times*, 24 May 2013.
[42] Marie Poinsot and Anne Volery, "Entretien: Gérald Bloncourt, *Les Portugais*," *Hommes et Migrations* 1302 (2013): 152–3; Bloncourt and Petitjean, "L'œil, le monde et la colère," §§32–5; Bloncourt, *Le regard engagé*, 188–9 and 209–15.
[43] Bloncourt, *Le regard engagé*, 158–9.

They also provide revealing insights into mass migration phenomena that encompassed a range of different experiences and groups, from Algerians settling into a decolonizing and then postcolonial European France to those who moved from south to north within Europe itself – mobilities that still tend to be studied separately, yet in reality were both comparable and convergent. Portuguese leaving a late colonial and ultimately decolonizing Portugal competed with Algerians for the status of France's largest group of newcomers in the 1960s, 1970s, and afterwards, but were – and remain – on the sidelines of common understandings of France's diversity, despite important studies by Victor Pereira, Marie-Christine Volovitch-Tavares, and others.[44] Although Algerians – the subject of a vibrant historiography by Benjamin Stora, Abdelmalek Sayad, Neil MacMaster, Jim House, Todd Shepard, and Paul Silverstein, to name only a few – arrived legally as French Union citizens after 1947, this did not pave the way for their public acceptance or prevent France from retreating from inclusive citizenship and severely restricting their primary migration after decolonization.[45] Many Portuguese, by contrast, arrived illegally but later had their status regularized.

As Bloncourt observed, the so-called "Arab" (often an Algerian, always a Muslim) was the main fixation, not only among native French but also among immigrant groups whose European origins, even if initially foreign, could become a form of claim-making on French national belonging. Despite distinct evidence of their racialization upon arrival, over time a sense of the shared Europeanness of groups such as the Portuguese – enhanced by Portugal's ultimate accession to the European Economic Community (EEC) after the 1974 Carnation Revolution launched its transition to democracy – rendered them "good immigrants," "like us," and "assimilated" (or assimilable) in the eyes of many observers and perhaps also themselves. The presence of Muslims

---

[44] Victor Pereira, *La dictature de Salazar face à l'émigration: L'État portugais et ses migrants en France (1957–1974)* (Paris: Presses de Sciences Po, 2012); Marie-Christine Volovitch-Tavares, *Portugais à Champigny: Le temps des baraques* (Paris: Autrement, 1995). Charting Portuguese migration histories involving France also moves beyond empire-centered histories of Portuguese mobility. See Cristiana Bastos, "Intersections of Empire, Post-empire, and Diaspora: De-imperializing Lusophone Studies," *Journal of Lusophone Studies* 5, no. 2 (2020): 27–54; and Pedro Góis and José Carlos Marques, "Portugal as a Semi-peripheral Country in the Global Migration System," in "Migration in the Lusophone World," special issue, *International Migration* 47, no. 3 (2009): 21–50.

[45] Benjamin Stora, *Ils venaient d'Algérie: L'immigration algérienne en France, 1912–1992* (Paris: Fayard, 1992); Abdelmalek Sayad, *The Suffering of the Immigrant* (Cambridge: Polity Press, 2004), which was first published in 1999; Neil MacMaster, *Colonial Migrants and Racism: Algerians in France, 1900–62* (Basingstoke: Macmillan, 1997); Jim House and Neil MacMaster, *Paris 1961: Algerians, State Terror, and Memory* (Oxford: Oxford University Press, 2006); Todd Shepard, *The Invention of Decolonization: The Algerian War and the Remaking of France* (Ithaca, NY: Cornell University Press, 2006); and Paul A. Silverstein, *Algeria in France: Transpolitics, Race, and Nation* (Bloomington: Indiana University Press, 2004).

of North and sub-Saharan African descent, cast in the role of perennially unassimilated and threatening colonial or postcolonial outsiders regardless of birthplace or nationality, afforded the luxury of invisibility to those whose whiteness and cultural attributes (especially Catholicism) appeared to facilitate acceptance. Yet this should not obscure the overlaps Bloncourt recognized or the solidarities he hoped for, even if they proved partial and difficult to sustain.[46]

Migration Histories and Contemporary Global Europe

Irrespective of their many differences, Riis and Bloncourt both provide detailed written and visual snapshots that show Europe's dense interlocking relations with multiple global locations – an inseparability with a far longer history, to be sure, but one that has taken on particular intensity since the nineteenth century. Their richness should invite historians of migration to engage in greater depth with personal narratives, written and oral, from a wider range of historical actors, including not only women and children but also those whose class and educational disadvantages have rendered their experiences far less readily accessible than those of Bloncourt or Riis.[47] Together with fiction, photographs, film, music, art, and other cultural manifestations, these life stories offer finely textured individual vantage points on Europe's global turn in many of its forms – including but certainly not limited to European emigrants' place within a dynamic "transnational America" that encompassed the United States, the Caribbean, and Latin America, or how Europeans circulated within and beyond particular overseas empires as workers or professionals, or for political or other reasons.[48]

Global turn approaches, moreover, provide fresh ways of analyzing internal European mobilities through their juxtapositions and convergences with peoples arriving from places both near and far that commonly fall outside habitual understandings of what counts as "Europe." Did Europe, for example, include overseas possessions that particular European states once considered part of their national territories rather than colonies, as was the case with French Algeria until 1962 or Portuguese Africa until the mid-1970s, when decolonization led former imperial powers to effectively "denationalize"

---

[46] Victor Pereira, "Portuguese Migrants and Portugal: Elite Discourse and Transnational Practices," in *A Century of Transnationalism: Immigrants and Their Homeland Connections*, ed. Nancy L. Green and Roger D. Waldinger (Urbana: University of Illinois Press, 2016), 56–83, here pp. 69 and 77.
[47] Katharine M. Donato and Donna R. Gabaccia, eds., *Gender and International Migration: From the Slavery Era to the Global Age* (New York: Russell Sage Foundation, 2015) constitutes one recent wide-ranging analysis.
[48] Hoerder, "European Migrations"; Green, "The Trials of Transnationalism," 851.

places and peoples that had formerly qualified as French or Portuguese and rendered them newly foreign? Does Europe extend to France's *départements d'outre-mer* or their Dutch equivalents in the Caribbean that still count as part of the Kingdom of the Netherlands? And has formal access to European nationalities (whether before decolonization or in the postcolonial era) necessarily meant a full and unproblematic acceptance as properly "European" – as legitimate co-citizens – for those not of European descent or white?[49]

Questions such as these underscore how capturing multiple migration histories entails more than surpassing a "methodological nationalism" that privileges the nation-state as an analytical container to the exclusion of habitual forms of cross-border flows with transnational and local resonances.[50] Just as importantly, they work against rigid frameworks that Peo Hansen and Stefan Jonsson have called "methodological continentalism."[51] Writing of the inseparability of the EU's mid-twentieth-century origins and the late colonial "Eurafrican" projects shared by many of its founding member states (and which ultimately became unsustainable after decolonization), they describe "the transformation of the Mediterranean from a uniting surface into a separating [moat], a transformation that both inspires and is inspired by a 'myth of continents' that disregards connections between the histories of Africa and Europe."[52] This misleading dissociation that sidelines shared (albeit vastly unequal) imperial histories had as its counterpart the gradual coalescing of a "Fortress Europe" mentality when it came to preferred or permissible migration.

As the EEC and then the EU gradually enlarged via new member states, the commitment to internal freedom of movement had as its counterpoint an increasingly exclusionary stance toward many peoples from overseas, whether from Europe's former empires or elsewhere. After earlier accessions in 1973 (Britain, Ireland, and Denmark) and the 1980s (Greece, Spain, and Portugal), the most significant expansion occurred following the end of the Cold War and the collapse of the USSR and the Eastern Bloc satellite regimes as the EU enlarged into eastern and central Europe from 2004. This occurred alongside the

49 Étienne Balibar, *We, the People of Europe? Reflections on Transnational Citizenship* (Princeton: Princeton University Press, 2004); Elizabeth Buettner, "Postcolonial Migrations to Europe," in *The Oxford Handbook of the Ends of Empire*, ed. Martin Thomas and Andrew Thompson (Oxford: Oxford University Press, 2018), 601–20; Elizabeth Buettner, "What – and Who – Is 'European' in the Postcolonial EU? Inclusions and Exclusions in the European Parliament's House of European History," *BMGN-Low Countries Historical Review* 133, no. 4 (2018): 132–48.
50 Wimmer and Schiller, "Methodological Nationalism."
51 Peo Hansen and Stefan Jonsson, *Eurafrica: The Untold History of European Integration and Colonialism* (London: Bloomsbury, 2014), 259–62.
52 Ibid., 260; see also Martin W. Lewis and Kären E. Wigen, *The Myth of Continents: A Critique of Metageography* (Berkeley: University of California Press, 1997), 35–6 and 104–8.

extended transition of many poorer European countries, and certainly those in southern Europe, from being societies mainly of emigration to societies attracting increasing numbers of newcomers in their own right.[53] As had already been the case in much of Europe's better-off northwest, these arrivals came from both inside and outside the EU. Contemplating these transformations, Adrian Favell has pondered the relationship between new "free movers" from Europe's "porous East" and its increasingly "bordered South," represented first and foremost by its increasingly fortified Mediterranean shores: "The strong suspicion is that the eastward expansion of Europe is being built with a racial logic, seeking to open borders to the East while closing them to the South."[54] At the same time, he observes, this phenomenon was rendered more complicated as newer EU citizens were "shuffled into economic roles in the West European economies assigned in the postwar period to traditional non-European immigrants" from colonies, ex-colonies, and other developing countries.[55] In this sense, they have occupied similar roles to those once played by southern Europeans such as the Portuguese in and beyond France, alongside Algerians and other groups.

In other ways, however, as with "traditional non-European immigrants," the extent to which peoples from eastern EU states deserved to be called "immigrants" at all is open to debate. Given that many from Europe's former colonies arrived as citizens, ultimately became citizens, and had children born in Europe, terms such as "immigrant/immigration" or even "migrant/migration" may well be patently incorrect, serving to reflect and reinforce their social and cultural exclusion. By the same token, the application of these labels to Europeans moving inside the EU can be contested on many grounds. Hungary's prime minister, Viktor Orbán, for instance, insisted in early

---

[53] Italy, as it shifted from being a society mainly of emigration towards one in which immigration predominated, stands out as a particularly vibrant area of study that extends not only across the Atlantic and through Europe but also involves trans-Adriatic and trans-Mediterranean mobilities. Alongside Lombardi-Diop and Romeo, "Italy's Postcolonial 'Question'"; Ben-Ghiat and Hom, eds., *Italian Mobilities*; and Ballinger, *The World Refugees Made* noted earlier, see Pamela Ballinger, "A Sea of Difference, a History of Gaps: Migrations between Italy and Albania, 1939–1992," *Comparative Studies in Society and History* 60, no. 1 (2018): 90–118, together with key collections that focus on gender issues: Donna R. Gabaccia and Franca Iacovetta, eds., *Women, Gender, and Transnational Lives: Italian Workers of the World* (Toronto: University of Toronto Press, 2002); Loretta Baldassar and Donna R. Gabaccia, eds., *Intimacy and Italian Migration: Gender and Domestic Lives in a Mobile World* (New York: Fordham University Press, 2011).

[54] Adrian Favell, "Immigration, Migration, and Free Movement in the Making of Europe," in *European Identity*, ed. Jeffrey T. Checkel and Peter J. Katzenstein (Cambridge: Cambridge University Press, 2009), 167–89; here pp. 188–9.

[55] Ibid., 172. On related themes, see also De Genova, *The Borders of "Europe"*; and Gabriele Proglio, "Is the Mediterranean a White Italian-European Sea? The Multiplication of Borders in the Production of Historical Subjectivity," *Interventions: International Journal of Postcolonial Studies* 20, no. 3 (2018): 406–27.

2016 as the Brexit referendum gathered momentum that "it is very important that we are not considered as migrants ... into the UK. We are citizens of a state that belongs to the European Union who can take jobs anywhere freely within the European Union."[56] As József Böröcz and Mahua Sarkar deduce from this, the "migrant" label contains "a palpable element of 'racial' down-grading," making Orbán "keen to extricate the ethnonational category he represents ('Hungarians') from that discounted, racialized location that it has been assigned in at least some influential west European discussions of EU policy."[57]

Apparent here is the simultaneous (re)racialization of peoples from Europe's east, a phenomenon that brings to mind not only Riis's disparaging rhetoric over a century earlier but also some Europeans' own race- and culture-based claims as "Europeans" vis-à-vis "others," particularly those not considered Christian and white – an attitude that Bloncourt would have immediately recognized (and condemned) in other contexts. Orbán's Hungary, with other member states on the EU's outer borders, has responded to the arrival of people from the Middle East, Africa, and elsewhere with anti-refugee plat-forms that extend beyond hostile exclusionary statements to building fences and walls to keep out those trying to enter the EU through its territory; in a similar way, mobile peoples from Europe's east might deploy racism against Muslims, Blacks, and other minorities they encounter after moving further west or south. Writing of "New Europeans" in early twenty-first-century, pre-Brexit Britain, Jon Fox has suggested that "[r]acism darkens others and whitens the self; if this does not actually improve the standing of East Europeans, it improves their perception of their standing."[58] Studying the many historical antecedents of this broader tendency, both within and beyond a globalized Europe, helps make sense of its recent manifestations that sadly retain such immense and destructive power today.

---

[56] Cited in József Böröcz and Mahua Sarkar, "The Unbearable Whiteness of the Polish Plumber and the Hungarian Peacock Dance around 'Race'," *Slavic Review* 76, no. 2 (2017): 307–14, here pp. 312–13.

[57] Ibid. On Hungary and the history of migrations, see also Nora Berend, "Les récits de la migration dans la Hongrie médiévale," *Annales HSS* 76, no. 3 (2021): 457–88.

[58] Jon E. Fox, "The Uses of Racism: Whitewashing New Europeans in the UK," *Ethnic and Racial Studies* 36, no. 11 (2013): 1871–89, here pp. 1881–82.

11   Race in the Global History of Europe

Priya Satia

Since 2022, when Russia invaded Ukraine, we have witnessed the social construction of race in real time: European media deny Russian whiteness with Orientalizing imagery of a Mongol polity and bestow whiteness upon Ukrainians, a multiethnic people whose whiteness has often been questioned. Waves of Ukrainian refugees trigger emotional media commentary about the suffering of people "who look like us."[1] This discourse reifies whiteness as integral to European identity, despite the long presence of nonwhite people in the subcontinent that we call "Europe." It highlights the importance of contingently bestowed whiteness to imaginaries of European geography and identity.

Race is central to Europe's history and has been central to the "global turn" in European history. And yet that importance may be unclear in many of the considerations of European history here. In this chapter I discuss the literature produced by the global turn on the place of race and racism in European history and reflect, in conclusion, on its persistent marginalization in narratives of European history.

We know how much modern European intellectual history depended on deeply racialized notions of its key words and concepts – freedom, sensibility, history, civilization, improvement, and so on – as they evolved in an era of European encounters abroad.[2] The Enlightenment's classificatory impulse

---

[1] On this phenomenon, see, for instance, Moustafa Bayoumi, "They Are 'Civilised' and 'Look Like Us': The Racist Coverage of Ukraine," *The Guardian*, 2 March 2022, On the orientalizing of Russia, see, for instance, the circulation in 2022 of this 2018 image: https://twitter.com/raceip/status/1499048665486352386/photo/1.

[2] Ivan Hannaford, *Race: The History of an Idea in the West* (Washington, DC: Woodrow Wilson Center Press; Baltimore: Johns Hopkins University Press; 1996); Emma Rothschild, *The Inner Life of Empires: An Eighteenth-Century History* (Princeton: Princeton University Press, 2011); Tony Ballantyne, *Orientalism and Race: Aryanism in the British Empire* (Basingstoke: Palgrave Macmillan, 2002); Susan Buck-Morss, "Hegel and Haiti," *Critical Inquiry* 26, no. 4 (2000): 821–65; Tyler Stovall, *White Freedom: The Racial History of an Idea* (Princeton: Princeton University Press, 2021); Christopher Leslie Brown, *Moral Capital: Foundations of British Abolitionism* (Chapel Hill: University of North Carolina Press, 2006); Emmanuel Chukwudi Eze, "The Color of Reason: The Idea of 'Race' in Kant's Anthropology," in *Postcolonial African Philosophy: A Critical Reader*, ed. Emmanuel Chukwudi Eze (Cambridge: Wiley-Blackwell, 1997), 103–40; Emmanuel Chukwudi Eze, *Race and the Enlightenment: A Reader* (Malden: Blackwell, 2009 [1997]); George L. Mosse, *Towards the Final Solution: A History of European*

included the production of an enduring racial taxonomy and hierarchy. Stadial thinking about races evolved in a context of the waning authority of biblical genealogies and environmentalist explanations of human differences.[3] The hardening of racial categories was integral to new understandings of selfhood.[4] The social shame people of mixed-race heritage experienced in Europe in this period has been studied.[5] Views of Africans in Europe (a category dating to ancient times) shifted in the eighteenth century and were bound up with the slave trade.[6] This racism blinded many Europeans to the meaning of Black resistance, which they saw as a kind of savagery, as Cedric Robinson pointed out long ago.[7]

Scholars have shown that the foundational notion of the "state of nature" that man was destined to improve was racialized from the outset: Thomas More's Utopians celebrated their transformation of a "pack of ignorant savages" into a "civilized nation." "If the natives won't do what they are told," he wrote, "they are expelled from the area marked out for annexation."[8] War was justified "when one country denies another its natural rights to derive nourishment from any soil which the original owners are not using themselves." The "nature" on which the language of rights was grounded depended on racist understandings of savage and native in the era of New World settlement. The savage's natural state, his refusal of history, was what made conquest thinkable.

Enlightenment thinkers ordered humankind in new, racial terms partly to resolve the paradox posed by the idea of "natural rights": If they were universal because we all possess the capacity for reason, then why were some humans

Racism (Madison: University of Wisconsin Press: 2020); and Kehinde Andrews, *The New Age of Empire: How Racism and Colonialism Still Rule the World* (London: Allen Lane, 2021).

[3] Silvia Sebastiani, *The Scottish Enlightenment: Race, Gender and the Limits of Progress* (New York: Palgrave Macmillan, 2013); and Devin Vartija, "Revisiting Enlightenment Racial Classification: Time and the Question of Human Diversity," *Intellectual History Review* 31, no. 4 (2020): 603–25.

[4] Dror Wahrman, *The Making of the Modern Self: Identity and Culture in Eighteenth-Century England* (New Haven: Yale University Press, 2006); and Kathleen Wilson, ed., *A New Imperial History: Culture, Identity, and Modernity in Britain and the Empire, 1660–1840* (Cambridge: Cambridge University Press, 2004).

[5] Deborah Cohen, *Family Secrets: Shame and Privacy in Modern Britain* (Oxford: Oxford University Press, 2013).

[6] Olivette Otele, *African Europeans: An Untold History* (New York: Basic Books, 2021).

[7] Cedric Robinson, *Black Marxism: The Making of the Black Radical Tradition* (Chapel Hill: University of North Carolina Press, 2020), which was first published in 1983.

[8] Thomas More, *Utopia* (London: Penguin Classics, 2003), 50 and 60, which was first published in 1516; see also David Armitage, *The Ideological Origins of the British Empire* (Cambridge: Cambridge University Press, 2000); George Behlmer, *Risky Shores: Savagery and Colonialism in the Western Pacific* (Stanford: Stanford University Press, 2018); Martti Koskenniemi, *To the Uttermost Parts of the Earth: Legal Imagination and International Power, 1300–1870* (Cambridge: Cambridge University Press, 2021); and Priya Satia, "Risking a Colonial Anticolonialism: Chapter 10: Global Law: Ruling the British Empire," *European Journal of International Law* 32, no. 3 (2021): 1017–26.

"savages" and some worthy of enslavement? Ideas of biological inferiority, a denial of human fellowship, provided an answer. "Humanity exists in its greatest perfection in the white race," wrote Immanuel Kant.[9] "The yellow Indians have a smaller amount of Talent. The Negroes are lower and the lowest are a part of the American peoples." These ideas were integral to the Enlightenment effort to understand and prescribe the processes that, they felt, gave meaning to worldly life. Scholarship on European fascination with Indigenous visitors (some willing, others not) from the New World and the South Pacific has made clear their importance to European conversations about commercial empire.[10]

It is difficult to separate this intellectual history from Europe's political history, both at home and abroad. The founding liberal philosopher John Locke wrote key provisions of colonial governing documents that consolidated Black enslavement, though he also became a critic of slavery.[11] Racial thought was important to both the formulation and interpretation of his work. His ideas about English prosperity depended on racist understandings of Native American wildness that justified displacement. Whatever Locke's own evolving views, the United States' founding fathers saw no contradiction in drawing on Lockean ideas of liberty while pointing to the king's effort "to bring on the inhabitants of our frontiers, the merciless Indian Savages" as proof of British despotism.[12] Transatlantic Enlightenment thought enabled them to accommodate racial slavery and Native expropriation into a constitution for a new nation based on natural rights and representative government.

Racial notions shaped imaginaries even of the geography typically represented by the term "Europe," making the dichotomy of savage and civilized crucial to nation-building and border-setting within the subcontinent. Civilizational discourses about culture depended on ideas about race. Both the Irish and Slavic peoples to the east and south of the subcontinent were constructed as racially Other, as were European Jews.[13] Today's discourse about Russia and Ukraine echoes this history. The literature on the fragile nature of European belonging that Sebastian Conrad cites in Chapter 2 in fact

[9]   Immanuel Kant, cited in Eze, "The Color of Reason," 112, 118.
[10] Kate Fullagar, *The Savage Visit: New World People and Popular Imperial Culture in Britain, 1710–1795* (Berkeley: University of California Press, 2012); and Caroline Pennock, *On Savage Shores: How Indigenous Americans Discovered Europe* (New York: Knopf, 2023).
[11] Robert Bernasconi and Anika Maaza Mann, "The Contradictions of Racism: Locke, Slavery, and the Two Treatises," in *Race and Racism in Modern Philosophy*, ed. Andrew Valls (Ithaca, NY: Cornell University Press, 2005), 89–107; Domenico Losurdo, *Liberalism: A Counter History* (London and New York: Verso, 2014); and Holly Brewer, "Slavery, Sovereignty, and 'Inheritable Blood': Reconsidering John Locke and the Origins of American Slavery," *American Historical Review* 122, no. 4 (2017): 1038–78.
[12] Thomas Jefferson, et al., "The Declaration of Independence," 1776, Online.
[13] George Fredrickson, *Racism: A Short History* (Princeton: Princeton University Press, 2015), which was first published in 2002.

understands those limits as a function of *racial* views of eastern and south-eastern Europeans.[14]

Those limits found a source and echo in the civilization versus barbarism dichotomy that structured interactions between the northern and southern coasts of the Mediterranean and the broader, geographically indistinct categories of "East" and "West." The religious distinction of Christendom and Islam incorporated a powerful sense of racial distinction. Leaving aside the work of anti-colonial scholars a century ago, even since Edward Said's *Orientalism* we've known how essential racialized notions of the Other were to European self-understanding and European political and economic activities in the world.[15]

Separation of these racial notions from economic history is as untenable as the separation from intellectual and political history. Though the term "racial capitalism" does not appear in Sven Beckert's chapter on economic history in this volume, it is a key portmanteau concept through which the global turn has allowed us to understand the relations between the plantation economy and the constructions of whiteness and its Others on which it depended within the framework of European empire.[16] Coined by Robinson in 1983, the term drew on the very work of earlier Black thinkers, such as Eric Williams and C. L. R. James, that, Beckert notes, has been long marginalized in European history.

That "the Enlightenment had global features," as Samuel Moyn writes in Chapter 4 on intellectual history, is interesting and important, but the crux of the global turn's revelations is that this totemic subject of European history was bound up with the generation and spread of ideas of white supremacy (varied as Enlightenment notions of race were), based on the notion that the default or universal human being at its heart was a white man – and that this intellectual project served the destructive activities of European colonialism. As Conrad helpfully observes in Chapter 2, "large parts of Enlightenment cosmology," including "the ethnological and geographical explorations of the globe ... the notions of race and also of cosmopolitanism – must be seen as responses to the cognitive challenge that was posed by an increasingly integrated globe."

[14] Larry Wolff, *Inventing Eastern Europe: The Map of Civilization on the Mind of the Enlightenment* (Stanford: Stanford University Press, 1994); and Maria Todorova, *Imagining the Balkans* (New York: Oxford University Press, 1997).

[15] Edward Said, *Orientalism* (New York: Vintage Books, 1978).

[16] Satnam Virdee, "Racialized Capitalism: An Account of Its Contested Origins and Consolidation," *The Sociological Review* 67, no. 1 (2019): 3–27; Catherine Hall, "Racial Capitalism: What's in a Name?," *History Workshop Journal* 94 (2022): 5–21; Kris Manjapra, *Colonialism in Global Perspective* (Cambridge: Cambridge University Press, 2020); Erika Rappaport, *A Thirst for Empire: How Tea Shaped the Modern World* (Princeton: Princeton University Press, 2017); and Corey Ross, *Ecology and Power in the Age of Empire: Europe and the Transformation of the Tropical World* (Oxford: Oxford University Press, 2017).

To be sure, the Enlightenment also generated resources for criticizing slavery and racism. It did so partly thanks to Black thinkers such as Olaudah Equiano and Ottobah Cugoano involved in abolitionism.[17] White thinkers also turned the Enlightenment's critical spirit against its monstrous products. In 1775, Samuel Johnson diagnosed the hypocrisy of American colonial rebels against tyranny: "How is it we hear the loudest yelps for liberty from the drivers of negroes?"[18] But abolitionism was also no guarantor of anti-racist sentiment. The prominent abolition leader Thomas Clarkson supported colonialism in Africa and the deportation of London's poor Blacks to the colony of Sierra Leone.[19]

By the nineteenth century, the very success of colonial expansion invested emerging European national identities with racial meaning. The forging of Scots, Welsh, English, and Irish into "Britons" during the Napoleonic Wars grounded British identity in race and the common project of empire abroad.[20] If, as Conrad explains, "[t]he organizational shape that political modernity assumed in Europe crystallized in the institution of the nation-state," racial othering figured centrally in the creation of its borders.

Ideas of race evolved in the nineteenth century in the context of increasingly powerful and rivalrous European empires. As Moyn notes, liberal thought apologized for global hierarchy with theories of civilization and race. Recent work on iconic figures such as Thomas Macaulay, John Stuart Mill, and Henry Maine, British thinkers whose work and influence evolved through careers in imperial policymaking, shows how central racial thought was to liberalism's ideas of human development (framed as civilization, modernization, progress, and so on).[21]

Major concepts of liberal political-economic thought derived from racist perceptions of peoples abroad: The Scottish thinker John Rae developed the

---

[17] See Marlene Daut, *Baron de Vastey and the Origins of Black Atlantic Humanism* (New York: Palgrave Macmillan, 2017).

[18] Samuel Johnson, *Taxation No Tyranny: An Answer to the Resolutions and Address of the American Congress* (London: T. Cadell, 1775).

[19] See also Kris Manjapra, *Black Ghost of Empire: The Long Death of Slavery and the Failure of Emancipation* (New York: Scribner, 2022).

[20] Linda Colley, *Britons: Forging the Nation, 1707–1837* (New Haven: Yale University Press, 1992).

[21] Catherine Hall, *Macaulay and Son: Architects of Imperial Britain* (New Haven: Yale University Press, 2012); Karuna Mantena, *Alibis of Empire: Henry Maine and the Ends of Liberal Imperialism* (Princeton: Princeton University Press, 2010); Priya Satia, *Time's Monster: History, Conscience and Britain's Empire* (London: Allen Lane, 2020); Thomas McCarthy, *Race, Empire, and the Idea of Human Development* (Cambridge: Cambridge University Press, 2009); Theodore Koditschek, *Liberalism, Imperialism, and the Historical Imagination: Nineteenth Century Visions of a Greater Britain* (Cambridge: Cambridge University Press, 2011); James Epstein, *Scandal of Colonial Rule: Power and Subversion in the British Atlantic during the Age of Revolution* (Cambridge: Cambridge University Press, 2012).

concept of time-discounting by comparing Europeans, Asians, and Indigenous peoples in the Americas, while also assembling a "history of humanity" through study of the Polynesian "race."[22] Scholars such as Norbert Finzsch, Tony Barta, and Dirk Moses have shown how European racism of this era produced genocidal effects in America and Australia – with a later impact in Europe, too.[23] The presumption of racial difference permanently undercut the claim that European empire put peoples on the *same, universal* path of historical evolution that Europe was on. Liberal imperialism was premised on the racist notion that benighted peoples around the world, lacking conscience and virtue, required paternalistic imperial government by Europeans. Race, Amitav Ghosh helpfully observes, was "the silenced term" in liberalism: "the unstated term through which the gradualism of liberalism reconciled itself to the permanence of empire."[24]

Such ideas profoundly shaped events within Europe. The mid-century crises in the British Empire – the Maori wars, Opium Wars, First Anglo-Afghan War, Indian rebellion, Jamaican rebellion, Irish rebellion, and more – mattered in British workers' successful campaign for the vote in 1867. "Whiteness," Catherine Hall has shown, defined citizenship; and nonwhiteness, subject-hood.[25] Racism also inhibited understanding of such rebellions and justified their brutal crushing.[26] When crisis put Canada on the path of "responsible self-government" and India and Jamaica under firmer Crown control, it was clear that the fate of majority-white British colonies (in which Indigenous peoples had been displaced and destroyed) diverged from majority nonwhite colonies. These crises inspired a turn to indirect colonial rule, based on the new realization of the racial limits to the civilizing mission. The object of colonialism was now to rule discreetly behind the scenes and preserve indigenous African and Asian societies in a museum-like manner to facilitate the exploitation of their resources for Europe's "development." Such were the global political consequences of European racial thinking.

---

[22] Priya Satia, "The Way We Talk about Climate Change Is Wrong," *Foreign Policy*, 11 March 2022, Online.

[23] Dirk Moses and Dan Stone, eds., *Colonialism and Genocide* (Abingdon: Routledge, 2007); and Dirk Moses, ed., *Genocide and Settler Society: Frontier Violence and Stolen Indigenous Children in Australian History* (New York: Berghahn Books, 2004).

[24] Amitav Ghosh and Dipesh Chakrabarty, "A Correspondence on *Provincializing Europe*," *Radical History Review* 83 (2002): 146–72, here p. 148.

[25] Catherine Hall, *Civilising Subjects: Colony and Metropole in the English Imagination, 1830–1867* (Chicago: University of Chicago Press, 2002).

[26] Ibid.; Antoinette M. Burton, *The Trouble with Empire: Challenges to Modern British Imperialism* (New York: Oxford University Press, 2015); Heather Streets, *Martial Races: The Military, Race and Masculinity in British Imperial Culture, 1857–1914* (Manchester: Manchester University Press, 2010); and Scott Eastman, *A Missionary Nation: Race, Religion, and Spain's Age of Liberal Imperialism, 1841–1881* (Lincoln: University of Nebraska Press, 2021).

Scholars have examined how these shifting notions of race shaped European ideas of freedom and colonial policies.[27] Victorian women's movements traded on racialized notions of civilized womanhood.[28] Major strands of the history of medicine, including hydrotherapy and climatology, depended on European racial thought, producing their own racial tensions in the spas and hill stations French and British colonizers built.[29] Race was central to the quarantine practices that enabled early European integration.[30] Psychology's complex role in shaping attitudes toward the racial hierarchies that supported empire has also been studied.[31]

The scientific racism of the second half of the century bridged activity in a range of emerging disciplines: biology, sociology, anthropology, criminology, history, economics, and so on. Social Darwinists argued that the principles of evolution, including natural selection, apply to human societies, classes, and individuals in historical time as much as to biological species in geological time. This notion resonated with the political-economic faith in the market's ability to justly reward the deserving over time. The idea that progress depended on the "survival of the fittest" fueled the notion of competitive struggle between not only individuals but nations and races. Earlier, liberal universalism had affirmed that there was a racial and cultural hierarchy, with Britain at the top (or France, from the French point of view), but that all races *could* become civilized, namely British (or French); now, the idea of humans' inherent and permanent biological inequality – differing degrees of fitness – cast a shadow over the intellectual, political, and economic history of the rest of the modern era.

Human exhibitions – the display of people from the colonies – were entertainments of major commercial and cultural importance, producing lasting effects on attitudes toward empire, race, and anthropological inquiry.[32] Mass media representations of European empire, including its racial

---

[27] Thomas C. Holt, *The Problem of Freedom: Race, Labor, and Politics in Jamaica and Britain, 1832–1938* (Baltimore: Johns Hopkins University Press, 1992).

[28] Antoinette M. Burton, *Burdens of History: British Feminists, Indian Women, and Imperial Culture, 1865–1915* (Chapel Hill: University of North Carolina Press, 1994); see also Richard J. Evans, *The Feminists: Women's Emancipation Movements in Europe, America, and Australasia, 1840–1920* (Abingdon: Routledge, 2012 [1977]).

[29] Eric T. Jennings, *Curing the Colonizers: Hydrotherapy, Climatology, and French Colonial Spas* (Durham, NC: Duke University Press, 2006); and Eric T. Jennings, *Imperial Heights: Dalat and the Making and Undoing of French Indochina* (Berkeley: University of California Press, 2011).

[30] Alex Chase-Levenson, *The Yellow Flag: Quarantine and the British Mediterranean World, 1780–1860* (Cambridge: Cambridge University Press, 2020).

[31] Erik Linstrum, *Ruling Minds: Psychology in the British Empire* (Cambridge, MA: Harvard University Press, 2016).

[32] Sadiah Qureshi, *Peoples on Parade: Exhibitions, Empire, and Anthropology in Nineteenth-Century Britain* (Chicago: University of Chicago Press, 2011).

hierarchies, shaped knowledge formation in European societies riven by class and political differences, informing notions of "the global."[33] In the Netherlands and France, anxieties over national identity were fueled by the métis populations empire produced in southeast Asia; fears of moral, physical, and cultural contamination stoked anxieties that white men living with native women might become degenerate and lose their Europeanness.[34]

Geological discoveries about the earth's age and human antiquity intensified debates about what it meant to be human and what racial distinctions signified, consolidating the view that people elsewhere were trapped in prehistoric time and that some were "doomed to die."[35] The discovery of ancestral extinctions helped justify the devastating effects of European settler colonialism on Indigenous peoples. At the same time, racial views fed paternalist efforts at the conservationist protection of aboriginal people in a manner that led to greater control.[36]

For Europeans, then, travel was time-travel. Philosophy buttressed this outlook: As this volume attests, we are still struggling to abandon the Hegelian conviction that "the History of the World travels from East to West, for Europe is absolutely the end of History."[37] In perhaps the most literal application of this notion, settlers strove to recreate European civilization in New Zealand and Australia, a colony perceived as a blank slate, devoid of history.

Charles Darwin's cousin Francis Galton, partly out of vain fascination with his own lineage, took racial ideas of social evolution into an even darker direction, in what was one of the most consequential strands of European intellectual history. According to "eugenics" (a term he coined in 1883),

[33] John Phillip Short, *Magic Lantern Empire: Colonialism and Society in Germany* (Ithaca, NY: Cornell University Press, 2012); John M. Mackenzie, *Propaganda and Empire: The Manipulation of British Public Opinion, 1880–1960* (Manchester: Manchester University Press, 1984); and the chapters in John M. Mackenzie, ed., *Imperialism and Popular Culture* (Manchester: Manchester University Press, 1986).

[34] Ann Stoler, "Sexual Affronts and Racial Frontiers: European Identities and the Cultural Politics of Exclusion in Colonial Southeast Asia," *Comparative Studies in Society and History* 34, no. 3 (1992): 514–51; Ann Stoler, *Carnal Knowledge and Imperial Power: Race and the Intimate in Colonial Rule* (Berkeley: University of California Press, 2010 [2002]).

[35] Sadiah Qureshi, "Looking to Our Ancestors," in *Time Travelers: Victorian Encounters with Time and History*, ed. Adelene Buckland and Sadiah Quereshi (Chicago: University of Chicago Press, 2020), 3–23; Patrick Brantlinger, *Dark Vanishings: Discourse on the Extinction of Primitive Races, 1800–1930* (Ithaca, NY: Cornell University Press, 2003).

[36] Jane Samson, *Imperial Benevolence: Making British Authority in the Pacific Islands* (Honolulu: University of Hawaii Press, 1998).

[37] G. W. F. Hegel, *Lectures on the Philosophy of History* (London: George Bell and Sons, 1902), which was first given in German between 1822 and 1930; see also Dipesh Chakrabarty, *Provincializing Europe: Postcolonial Thought and Historical Difference* (Princeton: Princeton University Press, 2000).

humanity would evolve best through controlled breeding designed to increase the incidence of desirable hereditary traits: encouraging the reproduction of healthy stock, promoting social hygiene, and preventing the "multiplication of the unfit."[38] Politicians and scientists drew on eugenicist ideas as a sense of racial vulnerability afflicted western European powers. Eugenics was important in the struggle for women's reproductive rights.[39] Many Britons clung to a race-based dream of a global "Greater Britain," encompassing settler colonies such as Australia and Canada.[40] The prosperous career of "Aryanism" in this period has also been studied.[41]

The new race science informed and was supported by the practices of colonial sociology, which classified subjects racially as criminal, martial, effeminate, and so on, introducing racial understandings of categories such as caste and tribe.[42] As these categories suggest, discourses about race were also about gender, as many scholars have shown.[43] Colonial officials conducted ethnographic and anthropometric surveys delineating the racial composition of their subjects to advance the pseudo-science of race: the colonies were laboratories of this primary preoccupation of European intellectual, cultural, political, and scientific life in this period. We know, too, how racial thinking informed European military recruitment in colonies, with profound consequences.[44] Scholars have examined how the global pattern of racial

---

[38] Philippa Levine, *Eugenics: A Very Short Introduction* (New York: Oxford University Press, 2017).

[39] Richard A. Soloway, "The 'Perfect Contraceptive': Eugenics and Birth Control Research in Britain and America in the Interwar Years," *Journal of Contemporary History* 30, no. 4 (1995): 637–64, for example.

[40] Duncan Bell, *The Idea of Greater Britain: Empire and the Future of World Order, 1860–1900* (Princeton: Princeton University Press, 2007); and John Darwin, *The Empire Project: The Rise and Fall of the British World-System, 1830–1970* (Cambridge: Cambridge University Press, 2011).

[41] Tony Ballantyne, *Orientalism and Race: Aryanism in the British Empire* (Basingstoke: Palgrave Macmillan, 2002); Kris Manjapra, *Age of Entanglement: German and Indian Intellectuals across Empire* (Cambridge, MA: Harvard University Press, 2014); and David Motadel, "Iran and the Aryan Myth," in *Perceptions of Iran: History, Myths and Nationalism from Medieval Persia to the Islamic Republic*, ed. Ali Ansari (London: I. B. Tauris, 2014), 119–45.

[42] Thomas R. Metcalf, *Ideologies of the Raj* (Cambridge: Cambridge University Press, 1997); Bernard Cohn, *Colonialism and Its Forms of Knowledge: The British in India* (Princeton: Princeton University Press, 1996); Nicholas B. Dirks, *Castes of Mind: Colonialism and the Making of Modern India* (Princeton: Princeton University Press, 2001); Streets, *Martial Races*; and Mark Doyle, *Communal Violence in the British Empire: Disturbing the Pax* (London and New York: Bloomsbury Academic, 2016).

[43] Mrinalini Sinha, *Colonial Masculinity: The "Manly Englishman" and the "Effeminate Bengali" in the Late Nineteenth Century* (Manchester: Manchester University Press, 1995).

[44] Kate Imy, *Faithful Fighters: Identity and Power in the British Indian Army* (Stanford: Stanford University Press, 2019).

subordination and conflict that was imperialism itself strengthened the appeal of scientific racism and overrode ideas of racial egalitarianism.[45]

Such thinking informed the destructive European conquest of Africa and the evolution of legal thought and practice.[46] It supported fresh settler-colonial projects and the policing of nomadic and communal peoples and prevented even critics of empire such as E. D. Morel from imagining Africa ruled by Africans.[47] The goal of promoting peace among European powers (and the United States) rested on racist understandings of "civilized" warfare, which simultaneously underwrote constant "small wars" against colonized people represented as collectively militant, devoid of civilians.[48] Societies that remained constantly at war with one another (up to our time) strove to convince themselves that common whiteness could paper over other fractures.

Speaking of peace and humanity among themselves, European imperialists defended spectacular violence as the most efficient way to discipline others in the name of peace. That permissive window for violence abroad left the door open to grotesque mass violence in Europe too. In 2006, Isabel Hull's *Absolute Destruction* pivotally traced the way German military practices honed in southwest Africa were applied in Europe in the world wars.[49] More recently, we have learned how European racism informed the brutal labor policies that followed in diamond mines there – again foreshadowing the coercive labor

---

[45] Douglas Lorimer, *Science, Race Relations and Resistance: Britain, 1870–1914* (Manchester: Manchester University Press, 2013).

[46] Dan Hicks, *The Brutish Museums: The Benin Bronzes, Colonial Violence and Cultural Restitution* (London: Pluto Press, 2020); Steven Press, *Rogue Empires: Contracts and Conmen in Europe's Scramble for Africa* (Cambridge, MA: Harvard University Press, 2017); Nasser Hussain, *Jurisprudence of Emergency: Colonialism and the Rule of Law* (Ann Arbor: University of Michigan Press, 2003); Lauren Benton and Lisa Ford, *Rage for Order: The British Empire and the Origins of International Law* (Cambridge, MA: Harvard University Press, 2018); Peter Karsten, *Between Law and Custom: "High" and "Low" Legal Cultures in the Lands of the British Diaspora – The United States, Canada, Australia, and New Zealand, 1600–1900* (Cambridge: Cambridge University Press, 2002); and Philippa Levine, *Prostitution, Race and Politics: Policing Venereal Disease in the British Empire* (New York: Routledge, 2013).

[47] Satia, *Time's Monster*; Priya Satia, "The Myths of British Imperial Benevolence and Palestine," *Al Jazeera*, 16 June 2021, Online; and Benjamin D. Hopkins, *Ruling the Savage Periphery: Frontier Governance and the Making of the Modern State* (Cambridge, MA: Harvard University Press, 2020).

[48] Priya Satia, "Not Humane, Just Invisible: A Counternarrative to Samuel Moyn's 'Humane'," *LA Review of Books*, 3 December 2021, Online. On race in European diplomacy around eastern European minorities, see Carole Fink, *Defending the Rights of Others: The Great Powers, the Jews, and International Minority Protection, 1878–1938* (Cambridge: Cambridge University Press, 2006).

[49] Isabel V. Hull, *Absolute Destruction: Military Culture and the Practices of War in Imperial Germany* (Ithaca, NY: Cornell University Press, 2005). See also Volker Langbehn and Mohammad Salama, eds., *German Colonialism: Race, the Holocaust, and Postwar Germany* (New York: Columbia University Press, 2011).

camps under the Third Reich.[50] Racism also made French colonial Africa a nightmarish hellscape, whatever its humanitarian claims.[51] In French Indochina, racist understandings of criminality shaped the purpose of imprisonment away from the European idea of rehabilitation.[52]

Conrad writes that imperialist forays also fundamentally transformed European societies – the "empire at home" – but, as the literature he cites testifies, they did so partly via racial thinking.[53] As Richard Drayton writes in Chapter 6, scholars have located Europe in a global history of gender and class that is enmeshed with race.[54] Racial thinking informed European efforts to study and uplift Europe's own poor, who were anthropologized as racial Others – "street arabs," in the London context.[55] Understandings of motherhood and nutritional science evolved out of concern for the survival of the imperial race.[56] The growing presence of eastern European Jews among western Europe's urban poor intensified this exoticism and provoked antisemitic pushback.[57] In general, hardening racial beliefs transformed once

---

[50] Steven Press, *Blood and Diamonds: Germany's Imperial Ambitions in Africa* (Cambridge, MA: Harvard University Press, 2021); and David Ciarlo, *Advertising Empire: Race and Visual Culture in Imperial Germany* (Cambridge, MA: Harvard University Press, 2011).

[51] J. P. Daughton, *In the Forest of No Joy: The Congo-Océan Railroad and the Tragedy of French Colonialism* (New York: W. W. Norton, 2021).

[52] Peter Zinoman, *The Colonial Bastille: A History of Imprisonment in Vietnam, 1862–1940* (Berkeley: University of California Press, 2001).

[53] Catherine Hall and Sonya O. Rose, eds., *At Home with the Empire: Metropolitan Culture and the Imperial World* (Cambridge: Cambridge University Press, 2006); Patrizia Palumbo, ed., *A Place in the Sun: Africa in Italian Colonial Culture from Post-unification to the Present* (Berkeley: University of California Press, 2003); Ruth Ben-Ghiat and Mia Fuller, eds., *Italian Colonialism* (New York: Palgrave Macmillan, 2005); Gauri Viswanathan, *Masks of Conquest: Literary Study and British Rule in India* (New York: Columbia University Press, 1989); and Harald Fischer-Tiné, *Low and Licentious Europeans: Race, Class and "White Subalternity" in Colonial India* (New Delhi: Orient Black Swan, 2009).

[54] Joanne Miyang Cho and Douglas T. McGetchin, eds., *Gendered Encounters between Germany and Asia: Transnational Perspectives since 1800* (Cham: Palgrave Macmillan, 2017); Magaly Rodríguez García, Lex Heerma van Voss, and Elise van Nederveen Meerkerk, eds., *Selling Sex in the City*; and Imaobong Umoren, *Race Women Internationalists: Activist-Intellectuals and Global Freedom Struggles* (Oakland: University of California Press, 2018); see also Ann Laura Stoler, *Race and the Education of Desire: Foucault's History of Sexuality and the Colonial Order of Things* (Durham, NC: Duke University Press, 1995).

[55] Seth Koven, *Slumming: Sexual and Social Politics in Victorian London* (Princeton: Princeton University Press, 2006); Judith R. Walkowitz, *City of Dreadful Delight: Narratives of Sexual Danger in Late-Victorian London* (Chicago: University of Chicago Press, 1992); and Anne McClintock, *Imperial Leather: Race, Gender, and Sexuality in the Colonial Contest* (New York: Routledge, 1995).

[56] Anna Davin, "Imperialism and Motherhood," *History Workshop Journal* 5 (1978): 9–65; and James Vernon, *Hunger: A Modern History* (London: Harvard University Press, 2007).

[57] David Feldman, "The Importance of Being English: Jewish Immigration and the Decay of Liberal England," in *Metropolis: London: Histories and Representations since 1800*, ed. David Feldman and Gareth Stedman Jones (London: Routledge, 1989), 72–8; Deborah Cohen, "Who Was Who? Race and Jews in Turn-of-the-Century Britain," *Journal of British Studies* 41, no. 4 (2002): 460–83.

generous British attitudes toward provision of refuge.[58] Today's racialized conversations about refugees in western Europe derive from this history.

Intensifying fear and criminalization of homosexuality was tied to fear of racialized Others. As Anne McClintock puts it: "The invention of race in the urban metropolis . . . became central not only to the self-definition of the idle class but also to the policing of the 'dangerous classes': the working class, the Irish, Jews, prostitutes, feminists, gays and lesbians, criminals, the militant crowd and so on."[59] Homophobia and antisemitism were critical in the infamous Dreyfus Affair in France.[60] All these groups would also be targets of Nazism: Jews, homosexuals, nonwhite Europeans such as the Roma. Scholars have begun to study these racisms under a single rubric in the German context.[61]

Jews were seeking refuge in western Europe to escape violence against them further east. Steven Zipperstein has studied the transnational reaction to the antisemitic rampage at Kishinev in 1903, which became the prototype of the "pogrom," with enormous effects around the globe.[62] The history of Russian racism toward migrants from the south and east from the tsarist era has been a subject of recent study.[63]

European social history in this period includes workers from the colonies who traveled to Britain and racialized responses to their presence.[64] In Britain, the Irish Catholic Other remained a potent racial bogey.[65] Henry Strickland Constable's confident 1888 commentary on Celtic peoples articulated the perceived connection between racialized colonial subjects and Britain's poor'

[58] Caroline Shaw, *Britannia's Embrace: Modern Humanitarianism and the Imperial Origins of Refugee Relief* (Oxford: Oxford University Press, 2015); and Prakash Shah, *Refugees, Race and the Legal Concept of Asylum in Britain* (London: Cavendish, 2000).

[59] McClintock, *Imperial Leather*, 5. See also Frederick Cooper and Ann Laura Stoler, eds., *Tensions of Empire: Colonial Cultures in a Bourgeois World* (Berkeley: University of California Press, 1997); and Julia Rodriguez, "South Atlantic Crossings: Fingerprints, Science, and the State in Turn-of-the-Century Argentina," *American Historical Review* 109, no. 2 (2004): 387–416.

[60] Jack Fischel, "Review: The Dreyfus Affair in Retrospect," *Shofar* 30, no. 2 (2012): 119–22.

[61] Wulf D. Hund, Christian Koller, and Moshe Zimmermann, eds., *Racisms Made in Germany* (Berlin: LIT Verlag, 2011); see also Mark Mazower, *Inside Hitler's Greece: The Experience of Occupation, 1941–44* (New Haven: Yale University Press, 2001).

[62] Steven Zipperstein, *Pogrom: Kishinev and the Tilt of History* (New York: Liveright, 2018).

[63] Eugene Avrutin, *Racism in Modern Russia: From the Romanovs to Putin* (London: Bloomsbury Academic, 2022); and Robert Geraci, "Genocidal Impulses and Fantasies in Imperial Russia," in *Empire, Colony, Genocide: Conquest, Occupation, and Subaltern Resistance in World History*, ed. A. Dirk Moses (New York: Berghahn Books, 2008), 343–71.

[64] Arunima Datta, "Responses to Traveling Indian Ayahs in Nineteenth and Early Twentieth Century Britain," *Journal of Historical Geography* 71 (2021): 94–103; Andrew Thompson, *The Empire Strikes Back? The Impact of Imperialism on Britain from the Mid-nineteenth Century* (Harlow: Pearson Longman, 2005).

[65] Mary J. Hickman and Bronwen Walter, "Deconstructing Whiteness: Irish Women in Britain," *Feminist Review* 50 (1995): 5–19.

The Iberians are believed to have been originally an African race, who thousands of years ago spread themselves through Spain over Western Europe. Their remains are found in the barrows, or burying places, in sundry parts of these countries. The skulls are of low prognathous type. They came to Ireland and mixed with the natives of the South and West, who themselves are supposed to have been of low type and descendants of savages of the Stone Age, who, in consequence of isolation from the rest of the world, had never been out-competed in the healthy struggle of life, and thus made way, according to the laws of nature, for superior races.[66]

The "exclusionary measures" that fostered a sense of national belonging in European nations, as Conrad says, were, importantly, racial and racist – as Conrad's own work has shown.[67]

At the same time, anti-colonial thinkers in Europe influenced radical and anti-racial thought there – scholarship that should be acknowledged as part of the global turn in European intellectual history.[68] Figures such as the British MP and anti-colonial activist Dadabhai Naoroji, who were racially Othered while also helping to strengthen working-class and feminist causes, make it impossible to separate colonial and metropolitan history.[69] Black Germans challenged racial definitions of national identity.[70] Irish anti-colonialism developed in dialogue with anti-colonialism well beyond Europe.[71] The very blurriness of "Europe," in fact, complicated French missionaries' understandings of the religious and racial sources of human difference.[72] It also makes it impossible to separate the history of race in European history from Ottoman history.[73]

As this history attests, whiteness was a highly unstable category. European national identities were grounded in racial notions about the distinctions

---

[66] H. Strickland Constable, *Ireland from One or Two Neglected Points of View* (London: "The Literary Review" Pub. Co., 1888).

[67] Sebastian Conrad, *Globalisation and the Nation in Imperial Germany* (Cambridge: Cambridge University Press, 2010); see also Judith R. Walkowitz, *Nights Out: Life in Cosmopolitan London* (New Haven: Yale University Press, 2012).

[68] Priyamvada Gopal, *Insurgent Empire: Anticolonial Resistance and British Dissent* (London and New York: Verso, 2019).

[69] Dinyar Patel, *Naoroji: Pioneer of Indian Nationalism* (Cambridge, MA: Harvard University Press, 2020); Priya Satia, "A Few Heroic Men," *London Review of Books* 43, no. 17, 9 September 2021.

[70] Kira Thurman, *Singing like Germans: Black Musicians in the Land of Bach, Beethoven, and Brahms* (Ithaca, NY: Cornell University Press, 2021).

[71] Kate O'Malley, *Ireland, India and Empire: Indo-Irish Radical Connections, 1919–1964* (Manchester: Manchester University Press, 2009).

[72] J. P. Daughton, *An Empire Divided: Religion, Republicanism, and the Making of French Colonialism, 1880–1914* (Oxford: Oxford University Press, 2006). On British missionaries' views of race in southern Africa earlier in the century, see Richard Price, *Making Empire: Colonial Encounters and the Creation of Imperial Rule in Nineteenth-Century Africa* (Cambridge: Cambridge University Press, 2008).

[73] Marc David Baer, *The Ottomans: Khans, Caesars, and Caliphs* (New York: Basic Books, 2021).

between Gauls, Celts, Teutons, and Anglo-Saxons. The First World War was the product not only of European nationalist rivalries but racial ones, as the British, French, and Germans denounced one another's racial degeneracy and inferiority. Henri Bergson spoke for France's Academy of Moral and Political Sciences in diagnosing Germany's "regression to a state of savagery."[74] In the Balkans, too, the national aspirations that triggered the conflict were articulated in terms of race and ethnicity, despite centuries of mixing in the region.

Richard Evans concludes this volume by describing racism and Social Darwinism as "ideologies spawned by the imperial experience" that began to fuel "antagonisms within Europe itself" in the twentieth century. In fact, these ideologies were spawned as much by *European* experience and also *produced* imperial experience. There is, we have seen, a long lineage to racial othering within Europe and recurring concern with racial degeneration. As McClintock writes, "imperialism is not something that happened elsewhere – a disagreeable fact external to Western identity. Rather, imperialism *and the invention of race* were fundamental aspects of Western, industrial modernity."[75]

The First World War brought masses of nonwhite troops to Europe, and scholars have studied both their experiences in the subcontinent and white perceptions of them.[76] In the Middle East theater, British racial thinking about Arabs informed military innovations, such as the use of airpower and deception, that became highly influential in later conflicts.[77] The breakup of the Ottoman Empire and revolution in Imperial Russia unleashed fears of the breakdown of the racial and cultural divide between Europe and Asia. Race and ethnicity were critical to the revolutionary climate of postwar Paris.[78] In Yugoslavia racism against Muslims was pervasive.[79] Historians have studied the Soviet state's shifting understandings of ethnicity in the context of the

[74] Cited in Stéphane Audoin-Rouzeau and Annette Becker, *14–18: Understanding the Great War* (New York: Hill and Wang, 2014).

[75] McClintock, *Imperial Leather*, 5, emphasis added.

[76] Santanu Das, ed., *Race, Empire and First World War Writing* (Cambridge: Cambridge University Press, 2011); Joe Lunn, *Memoirs of the Maelstrom: A Senegalese Oral History of the First World War* (Portsmouth: Heinemann, 1999); David Omissi, *Indian Voices of the Great War: Soldiers' Letters, 1914–18* (New York: St Martin's Press, 1999); Richard Smith, *Jamaican Volunteers in the First World War: Race, Masculinity and the Development of National Consciousness* (Manchester: Manchester University Press, 2004); Timothy C. Winegard, *Indigenous Peoples of the British Dominions and the First World War* (Cambridge: Cambridge University Press, 2012); and David Olusoga, *Black and British: A Forgotten History* (London: Pan Macmillan, 2017). This was not the first time non-European troops had fought in Europe.

[77] Priya Satia, *Spies in Arabia: The Great War and the Cultural Foundations of Britain's Covert Empire in the Middle East* (New York: Oxford University Press, 2008).

[78] Tyler Stovall, *Paris and the Spirit of 1919: Consumer Struggles, Transnationalism and Revolution* (Cambridge: Cambridge University Press, 2012).

[79] Emily Greble, *Muslims and the Making of Modern Europe* (New York: Oxford University Press, 2021).

growing German and Japanese threat.[80] Various racial lenses shaped the League of Nations' mandate system, through which European powers governed newly acquired territories.[81] Global ties also made European cities key sites of interwar movements, challenging not only colonialism, as Conrad notes, but racism.[82]

The most epoch-making event in the political, military, economic, intellectual, and cultural history of the continent was a culmination of the racial thinking that had informed European interactions within and beyond the subcontinent for the modern period: the rise of Nazism. A growing body of scholarship has examined the way racial thinking enabled the development abroad of destructive visions and practices that were applied in Europe from the 1930s through the Second World War (Figure 11.1).[83] Conrad helpfully acknowledges the way the global turn has widened our lens on fascism and anti-fascism and the way fissures within the concept of Europe underwrote imperial ventures in the subcontinent, including Nazism. Anti-colonial thinkers such as

---

[80] Francine Hirsch, *Empire of Nations: Ethnographic Knowledge and the Making of the Soviet Union* (Ithaca, NY: Cornell University Press, 2007); and Kate Brown, *A Biography of No Place: From Ethnic Borderland to Soviet Heartland* (Cambridge, MA: Harvard University Press, 2005).

[81] Susan Pedersen, *The Guardians: The League of Nations and the Crisis of Empire* (New York: Oxford University Press, 2017); and Priya Satia, "Guarding *The Guardians*: Payoffs and Perils," *Humanity* 7, no. 3 (2016): 481–98.

[82] Susan Pennybacker, *From Scottsboro to Munich: Race and Political Culture in 1930s Britain* (Princeton: Princeton University Press, 2009); Mrinalini Sinha, *Specters of Mother India: The Global Restructuring of an Empire* (Durham, NC: Duke University Press, 2006); Michael Goebel, *Anti-Imperial Metropolis: Interwar Paris and the Seeds of Third World Nationalism* (Cambridge: Cambridge University Press, 2015); Jennifer Anne Boittin, *Colonial Metropolis: The Urban Grounds of Anti-Imperialism and Feminism in Interwar Paris* (Lincoln: University of Nebraska Press, 2010); Noor-Aiman I. Khan, *Egyptian-Indian Nationalist Collaboration and the British Empire* (New York: Palgrave Macmillan, 2011); Marc Matera, *Black London: The Imperial Metropolis and Decolonization in the Twentieth Century* (Oakland: University of California Press, 2015); Daniel Brückenhaus, *Policing Transnational Protest: Liberal Imperialism and the Surveillance of Anticolonialists in Europe, 1905–1945* (New York: Oxford University Press, 2017); Nathanael Kuck, "Anticolonialism in a Post-imperial Environment: The Case of Berlin, 1914–1933," *Journal of Contemporary History* 49, no. 1 (2014): 134–59; and Tyler Stovall, *Paris Noir: African Americans in the City of Light* (Boston: Houghton Mifflin, 1996).

[83] Hull, *Absolute Destruction*; Aidan Forth, *Barbed-Wire Imperialism: Britain's Empire of Camps, 1876–1903* (Oakland: University of California Press, 2017); Mahmood Mamdani, *Neither Settler Nor Native: The Making and Unmaking of Permanent Minorities* (Cambridge, MA: Harvard University Press, 2020); Kim Wagner, "Savage Warfare: Violence and the Rule of Colonial Difference in Early British Counterinsurgency," *History Workshop Journal* 85 (2018): 217–37; Mark Mazower, *Hitler's Empire: How the Nazis Ruled Europe* (New York: Penguin Press, 2008); A. Dirk Moses, *The Problems of Genocide: Permanent Security and the Language of Transgression* (New York: Cambridge University Press, 2021); and Sven Lindqvist, *"Exterminate All the Brutes": One Man's Odyssey into the Heart of Darkness and the Origins of European Genocide* (New York: New Press, 1997), which was first published in 1992.

Figure 11.1 German anthropologist Eva Justin making facial measurements
of a Romani woman as part of her race studies, 1938.
Source: German Federal Archives.

Aimé Césaire discerned this long ago, as did postwar thinkers such as Hannah
Arendt, who in 1951 connected the dots between antisemitism, imperialism, and
totalitarianism.[84] In 1952, drawing on his global experiences, Frantz Fanon
described the construction of whiteness and Blackness inherent to and pervasive
in situations of colonial domination.[85] It is surprising that this watershed
moment is not more prominent in this volume, given its importance in triggering
a global turn in European history. Indeed, the volume opens with David
Motadel's invocation of a text from this very moment – Lucien Febvre and
François Crouzet's unpublished 1950 global history of France, which, among
other things, challenged the idea of French whiteness. This outlook was of its

[84] Aimé Césaire, *Discourse on Colonialism* (New York: Monthly Review Press, 2000), which was
first published in 1955. Hannah Arendt, *The Origins of Totalitarianism* (New York: Harcourt,
Brace and Company, 1951). The Nazi regime also seemed anti-imperial in ways that appealed to
some anti-colonial activists of the time; see David Motadel, "The Global Authoritarian Moment
and the Revolt against Empire," *American Historical Review* 124, no. 3 (2019): 843–77.

[85] Frantz Fanon, *Black Skin, White Masks* (New York: Grove Press, 1968), which was first
published in 1952.

time, a product of postwar awareness of the folly of race-based nationalism, but, as Motadel explains, that nationalism and the notion of European supremacy still retained enough power to prevent publication of this extraordinary work, so that it only appeared as part of our current global turn in 2012.

Today, we also know that anti-fascist refugees from Vichy France learned from Black anti-colonialists in French Martinique, yielding a rich current of anti-racist thought.[86] Scholars have shown the pragmatism of racist states such as Nazi Germany in dealing with racial matters when it came to alliances.[87] We know of the diversity of manpower and refugees in the European theaters of the Second World War and the complex perceptions of them.[88] Across the century, refugee camps shaped dialogues about culture and race in Britain.[89] Fascism intensified the racial understanding of French identity and citizenship in a manner that galvanized anti-colonial movements.[90] In the Balkans, wartime violence itself produced new perceptions of ethnicity.[91] In the Soviet Union, too, mass evacuation changed racial attitudes.[92]

After the war, the influence of socialist internationalism inspired East German solidarity with the nonwhite world.[93] Racial perceptions mattered in Soviet relations with Cuba and other formerly colonized parts of the world.[94] The role of students from the new "Third World" and of the African American

---

[86] Eric T. Jennings, *Escape from Vichy: The Refugee Exodus to the French Caribbean* (Cambridge, MA: Harvard University Press, 2018).

[87] David Motadel, *Islam and Nazi Germany's War* (Cambridge, MA: Harvard University Press, 2014); and Motadel, "The Global Authoritarian Moment and the Revolt against Empire."

[88] Wendy Webster, *Mixing It: Diversity in World War Two Britain* (Oxford: Oxford University Press, 2018); Sonya O. Rose, *Which People's War?: National Identity and Citizenship in Wartime Britain, 1939–1945* (Oxford: Oxford University Press, 2003); and Eric T. Jennings, *Free French Africa in World War II: The African Resistance* (New York: Cambridge University Press, 2015).

[89] Jordanna Bailkin, *Unsettled: Refugee Camps and the Making of Multicultural Britain* (Oxford: Oxford University Press, 2018)

[90] Eric T. Jennings, *Vichy in the Tropics: Petain's National Revolution in Madagascar, Guadeloupe, and Indochina* (Stanford: Stanford University Press, 2001); and Frederick Cooper, *Citizenship between Empire and Nation: Remaking France and French Africa, 1945–1960* (Princeton: Princeton University Press, 2016).

[91] Max Bergholz, *Violence as a Generative Force: Identity, Nationalism, and Memory in a Balkan Community* (Ithaca, NY: Cornell University Press, 2016).

[92] Rebecca Manley, *To the Tashkent Station: Evacuation and Survival in the Soviet Union at War* (Ithaca, NY: Cornell University Press, 2009).

[93] Quinn Slobodian, ed., *Comrades of Color: East Germany in the Cold War World* (New York: Berghahn Books, 2015).

[94] Anne E. Gorsuch, "'Cuba, My Love': The Romance of Revolutionary Cuba in the Soviet Sixties," *American Historical Review* 120, no. 2 (2015): 497–526; Tobias Rupprecht, *Soviet Internationalism after Stalin: Interaction and Exchange between the USSR and Latin America during the Cold War* (Cambridge: Cambridge University Press, 2015); Jeremy Scott Friedman, *Shadow Cold War: The Sino-Soviet Competition for the Third World* (Chapel Hill: University of North Carolina Press, 2015); and James Mark, Artemy M. Kalinovsky, and Steffi Marung, eds., *Alternative Globalizations: Eastern Europe and the Postcolonial World* (Bloomington: Indiana University Press, 2020).

civil rights struggle in German and French radicalism, including views of race, has been studied.[95] Black anti-colonial thinkers in Europe and elsewhere were not concerned only or even primarily with nation-building but with racial equality at the level of the world, Adom Getachew has shown. Their visions of a postimperial world were integral to the structures that shaped Europe's history, too, including the United Nations and the postwar economic order.[96]

Scholars have also shown how the European idea of "race as an ordering system of the world cut through the universalist claims regarding human rights" in this era, enabling the intense and racist violence of conflicts in Algeria and Kenya.[97] The racial categories of European colonial rule profoundly shaped the dynamics of struggles for decolonization.[98] The very imaginariness of "Europe" matters here: Algeria was an *integral* department of France, and so the violent racism of French counterinsurgency there is Europe's history too. Todd Shepard has shown how the amputation of Algeria from the French body politic fed racial and religious tensions in postwar France.[99]

Meanwhile, postwar reconfigurations of citizenship, along with displacements caused by the war and decolonization, drew masses of refugees and immigrants (actually citizens, in the British case) to Europe, intensifying debates about race, belonging, and identity that were also responding to the loss of empire.[100] New studies have revealed the global forces that shaped postwar welfare, uncovering the "afterlife of empire" in the experiences of Black and brown students and

[95] Quinn Slobodian, *Foreign Front: Third World Politics in Sixties West Germany* (Durham, NC: Duke University Press, 2012); Christoph Kalter, *The Discovery of the Third World: Decolonization and the Rise of the New Left in France, c.1950–1976* (Cambridge: Cambridge University Press, 2016); and Martin Klimke, *The Other Alliance: Student Protest in West Germany and the United States in the Global Sixties* (Princeton: Princeton University Press, 2010).

[96] Adom Getachew, *Worldmaking after Empire: The Rise and Fall of Self-determination* (Princeton: Princeton University Press, 2020); and Mark Mazower, *No Enchanted Palace: The End of Empire and the Ideological Origins of the United Nations* (Princeton: Princeton University Press, 2013).

[97] A. Dirk Moses, Marco Duranti, and Roland Burke, eds., *Decolonization, Self-Determination, and the Rise of Global Human Rights Politics* (Cambridge: Cambridge University Press, 2020). On racist counterinsurgency in Kenya, see Caroline Elkins, *Imperial Reckoning: The Untold Story of Britain's Gulag in Kenya* (New York: Henry Holt, 2005).

[98] Bart Luttikhuis and Dirk Moses, eds., *Colonial Counterinsurgency and Mass Violence: The Dutch Empire in Indonesia* (London: Routledge, 2014).

[99] Todd Shepard, *The Invention of Decolonization: The Algerian War and the Remaking of France* (Ithaca, NY: Cornell University Press, 2008).

[100] Robert Gildea, *Empires of the Mind: The Colonial Past and the Politics of the Present* (Cambridge: Cambridge University Press, 2019); Ian Sanjay Patel, *We're Here Because You Were There: Immigration and the End of Empire* (London: Verso, 2021); Wendy Webster, *Englishness and Empire, 1939–1965* (Oxford: Oxford University Press, 2007); Tyler Stovall, *France since the Second World War* (Harlow: Longman, 2001); Tyler Stovall, *Transnational France: The Modern History of a Universal Nation* (New York: Routledge, 2015); Chris Waters, "'Dark Strangers' in Our Midst: Discourses of Race and Nation in Britain, 1947–1963," *Journal of British Studies* 36, no. 2 (1997): 207–38; James Vernon, "Heathrow and the Making of Neoliberal Britain," *Past*

migrants, white Britons in former colonies, and Irish people suspected of terrorism.[101] The transnational anti-racist efforts of Black German women have also received attention.[102] Historians have analyzed the role of racial whiteness in Russian identity.[103] Drawing on the work especially of Caribbean intellectuals, scholars have pushed back on understandings of white European identity by calling for "creolizing Europe" as necessary decolonial thinking.[104]

Ultimately, racial thinking was the backbone of (and was in turn strengthened by) the European economic transformations that, Beckert affirms, depended on access to African, Latin American, and Asian resources and consumers and a "diversity of labor regimes." It was also the cause and source of exploding European military capacity. It is important to ask, in light of this past and the current climate crisis, whether the language of "development" that Beckert employs is appropriate. Can we describe material prosperity derived from slave ownership as "development," given its destructive nature (including destruction of the humanity of those who ostensibly benefited materially)? Surely the global turn is not merely a matter of acknowledging Europe's debts and ties to other parts of the world: Once we recognize how much of European culture and economy depended on slavery and colonialism, we must question the very concept of European "development." In persisting with that narrative, we fall into the same habit of universalizing from the European example that Beckert so deplores. As Amitav Ghosh observes, "Western intellectual and academic discourse is so configured that it is easier to talk about abstract economic systems than it is to address racism, imperialism, and the structures of organized violence that sustain global hierarchies of power."[105] If "Europe" became a yardstick against which social and political development could be measured, as Conrad writes, the idea that "any society could become 'European'" was most seriously challenged by European racial thinking. The concepts of modernization, "Westernization," and "Europeanization" remained racially charged for Europeans, even as figures such as Hinohara Shôzô, Ismail Pasha, and Mikhail Petrachevsky took them as their patrimony.

& Present, no. 252 (2021): 213–47; and Kieran Connell, Black Handsworth: Race in 1980s Britain (Oakland: University of California Press, 2019).

[101] Jordanna Bailkin, The Afterlife of Empire (Berkeley: University of California Press, 2012). Gurminder K. Bhambra, "Relations of Extraction, Relations of Redistribution: Empire, Nation, and the Construction of the British Welfare State," British Journal of Sociology 73:1 (2022): 4–15.

[102] Tiffany Nicole Florvil, Mobilizing Black Germany: Afro-German Women and the Making of a Transnational Movement (Urbana: University of Illinois Press, 2020).

[103] Nikolay Zakharov, Race and Racism in Russia (Basingstoke: Palgrave Macmillan 2015).

[104] The chapters in Encarnación Gutiérrez Rodríguez and Shirley Anne Tate, eds., Creolizing Europe: Legacies and Transformations (Liverpool: Liverpool University Press, 2015).

[105] Amitav Ghosh, The Nutmeg's Curse: Parables for a Planet in Crisis (London works. Allen Lane, 2021), 120.

If eastern Europeans remained on edge, it was because they recognized the racial precariousness of the European construct.

All this scholarship helps us understand contemporary phenomena such as British ambivalence toward the EU (and why many history departments in the Anglophone world consider "Europe" as distinct from "Eastern Europe and Russia" and "Britain"). As Evans writes, the 2008 crash produced an anti-immigrant backlash and poisonous racial hatred. But it is the literature covered in this chapter that can explain the history of that xenophobia and racial feeling. In the Brexit movement, the reaction to Slavic peoples (especially Poles) and nonwhite citizens and migrants was central. (Pro-Brexit forces at the same time played on Asian Britons' criticism of the way European membership enhanced racial disparities for migrants to Britain, easing the entry of Poles and Germans while maintaining high barriers for Asians.) As Russia invaded Ukraine in 2022, the media announced the "first" European war since the Second World War, erasing the intervening conflicts in Europe's never-quite-white borderlands: Greece and Yugoslavia. At the same time, Ukrainian refugees received a welcome in many European countries that made racial prejudice against Asian and African refugees – and seemingly nonwhite Ukrainians (Tatars, Roma, Afro-Ukrainians, or Indians and Africans in Ukraine) – starkly apparent. "Buffers" have long been essential to the construction of European whiteness, the legal scholar Anjali Vats recently observed.[106] Racial understandings of Islamophobia make it possible to exclude Bosnians and Syrians. The idea that war is not normal in Europe – despite the *well-known* history of incessant conflict in the subcontinent – is a product of European racialization of war dating to the nineteenth-century pacifist movement, which made Asia and Africa domains of constant conflict stoked by Europeans and Americans. It is the mark of Europe's persistent Orientalism.

The scholarship here also helps us understand why it took the global turn for scholars to begin to properly attend to the place of race in European history. Despite the victories of anti-colonialism after the Second World War, European racism continued to shape the writing of history. Hugh Trevor-Roper proclaimed in the 1960s that "Africa has no history." As other chapters here have noted, the counternarratives of nonwhite anti-colonial thinkers were long marginalized. Even the arguments that historians are making today about European art's ties to racial capitalism were made a century ago by nonwhite scholars in Europe, who remain marginalized. The structures of racial

[106] Catherine Baker, "The Contingencies of Whiteness: Gendered/Racialized Global Dynamics of Security Narratives," *Security Dialogue* 52, no. S1 (2021): 124–32; Anjali Vats, Twitter thread, 1 March 2022, Online; and Kimberly St. Julian-Varnon, Twitter thread, 26 February 2022, Online.

capitalism that we study today caused this marginalization, explains Edwin Coomasaru.[107]

It is difficult to understand European political, economic, intellectual, social, migration, and religious history, and the history of European material culture, without the coeval understandings of race. An essay on Europe's history of ethnicity, race, and racism ought to be redundant with understandings of these histories, and yet, in this volume, race is an uneven presence in these narratives, and barely mentioned in many, despite excellent scholarship on its importance. "Racism" remains a much-silenced term. The chapters here powerfully remind us of the contingent geographical reality of Europe, but we have long known how much that construct has been defined in opposition to Others; we have long known how much it was defined by race.

This volume thus testifies to the persistent marginalization of questions about race in European history. The topic is siloed into a separate chapter, though it is central to the major thematics of political, economic, social, religious, and intellectual history and a subject that chapters on those thematics ought to address explicitly (as Chapter 6 on social history, exceptionally, does). Separating the story of race out may misleadingly suggest that race was not constitutive of and central to narratives of European political, economic, and intellectual history. But in fact, as I hope this chapter has shown, it is impossible to write an essay on race in European history that is not at once an essay on European intellectual, economic, political, migration, religious, and social history. I am myself not a historian especially of race or racial thought; my work has been in economic and military history, the history of technology, and intellectual history. But I have found it impossible to work in those areas without addressing race.

Omitting eugenics from a narrative of European intellectual history is an act of erasure, as is consideration of Hegel's or Joseph Conrad's global preoccupations without mention of the racial outlooks that shaped that engagement. So intimate and obvious was European intellectual history's entanglement with race that radical historians in the age of decolonization turned to working-class intellectual history in search of redemption – to recover alternative European values.[108] Unfortunately, this inward turn, despite its acknowledgment of the problem with canonical European thought, itself abetted amnesia about Europe's cosmopolitan past and the presence and influence of nonwhite peoples in Europe's history.

---

[107] Edwin Coomasaru, "Art Histories of Corporate Imperialism and Racial Capitalism," *Oxford Art Journal* 44, no. 3 (2022): 481–8; and Sria Chatterjee, "The Arts, Environmental Justice, and the Ecological Crisis," *British Art Studies* 18 (2020), Online.
[108] Priya Satia, "History from Below," *Aeon*, 18 December 2020, Online.

Richard Drayton rightly argues that the global turn is not a methodological shift akin to the cultural or linguistic turn but a paradigmatic shift recalling the impact of awareness of gender's role in history.[109] Central to that shift is what the global turn reveals about race in all the forces of modern history – including the very writing of history. Drayton goes on to point out the importance of nonwhite intellectuals in work on race that emerged in European social history after the 1990s. The increased attention to race since then is, certainly, related to the increasing numbers of nonwhite scholars in the discipline – as the notes in this chapter testify. And yet, here again (perhaps because of this demographic makeup), this important work has been largely quarantined away from the main lines of intellectual, economic, and political history.

And then there is the question of this scholarship's effectualness in the world. As Conrad points out, perceived threats by migration have provoked renewed and defensive emphasis on Europe's uniqueness as a site of science, secularism, Enlightenment, and so on – despite the scholarship that has destroyed this myth. This, too, is a measure of the continued marginalization of work dominated by scholars from minoritized groups. The long neglect of scholarship on Europe by nonwhite scholars was integral to the colonial project, and its stickiness is a measure of the incompleteness of decolonization.

The Martinican thinker Edouard Glissant pithily summarized that the West is "a project, not a place." We might equally understand Europe in this light – as a project, not a place, and a project in which race has been crucial. Going forward, scholars must integrate what the global turn has taught us about race in modern European history with the grand narratives of European political, intellectual, cultural, and economic history. Abigail Green's call for greater integration of scholarship on European Jews and Muslims with the rest of European historiography on religion is excellent advice but depends on the integration of the history of European race thinking with the history of religion. Drayton's concluding query about how Europe's history would look if it were recentered is profoundly intriguing in this light: Centering Europe southward or eastward may help put questions of race and ethnicity more squarely where they belong, at the heart of European history. But such a recentering would disrupt the very myth of the continent – our very sense of Europe's separateness from Asia and Africa. It may be that the myth of Europe remains too powerful to allow that shift, but the historical impact of such a move would be profound.

---

[109] Richard Drayton and David Motadel, "The Futures of Global History," *Journal of Global History* 13, no. 1 (2018): 1–21.

12   Globalizing European Gender History

Lucy Delap

"European" boundaries and values, and Europe's entanglement with wider global landscapes and power blocs, are starkly urgent contemporary questions, witnessed in the surging violence in Ukraine after the 2022 Russian invasion, the refugee crises of the 2010s, the debt and banking crises of 2008–9, and the Balkan conflicts of the 1990s, among many other recent moments of contestation of the borders and perceived character of "Europe." These crises have punctuated and accompanied the historiographical shifts that emerged through the global, postcolonial, and archival turns of the past three decades. The carnage in Ukraine prompts reflections on who belongs to Europe and what is owed between its peoples and nations. Much of this has been cast in Eurocentric terms which refuse to acknowledge the global dimensions of this conflict – its entanglement with strategies and military strikes in Syria and Afghanistan for example, or global strategic alliances and trade. Euro-American commentators on Ukraine, mostly white, have repeatedly demonstrated deeply troubling racialized and civilizational assumptions, seeing the war as "out of place" in Europe. Emotive reactions to the agony of people claimed to be "European like us" has demonstrated the rhetorical power of parochial, racist, and exceptionalist ideas of "Europe." The effects of this discursive move are not just rhetorical but grant "power over life and death, power to cripple and rot certain worlds while overinvesting others with wealth and hope."[1]

The ethnic character of Russia's invasion of Ukraine intersects with gender and sexuality in ways that are much less remarked in media coverage; forbidding Ukrainian men aged eighteen to sixty to leave the country while ushering women and children out of the conflict has been broadly accepted as an appropriate gender division in times of war. Yet images of Ukrainian women handling guns and wearing fatigues have been widely featured across media coverage, and the war has quickly engulfed attempts to create clear dividing

---

[1] Elizabeth A. Povinelli, *The Empire of Love: Toward a Theory of Intimacy, Genealogy, and Carnality* (Durham, NC: Duke University Press, 2008), 10.

lines of gender.[2] Not all men with Ukrainian citizenship have wanted to fight, and border guards have been arresting or turning them back. Male carers have been offered a degree of exemption, recognizing the ways in which gender fails as a workable shorthand for care responsibilities. Sexuality has also been thrown into view as LGBTQ+ Russians flee the authoritarian nationalism of Putin's rule, and as militaries and militias variously absorb or refuse the participation of sexual minorities. Nonbinary people or those who have transitioned have also found Ukrainian and Russian borders to be places of violence and immobility.[3]

   These divisions and conundrums, born of violence, illustrate the intersectional work of race, gender, and sexuality in historically dynamic processes of social positioning. They give urgency and meaning to historical scholarship; as Judith Butler observed in the early 2000s, "[t]heory emerges from location, and location itself is under crisis in Europe, since the boundaries of Europe are precisely what is being contested in quarrels over who belongs … and who does not."[4] Nonetheless, the placemaking, internal dynamics, and border-work of "Europe" have not been very visible in existing histories of gender and sexuality. Scholars in these fields have been more likely to turn their gaze inwards to scrutinize and contest the operations of gender in local and national perspective. In 2016, Joanne Cho and Douglas McGetchin's account of gendered encounters between Asia and Germany since 1800 argued that historians of gender in modern Germany had shown only limited interest in global dimensions.[5] Similarly, Merry Wiesner-Hanks reflected in the same year on the global turn in the field of early modern gender history and noted the lack of convergence between histories of the global and of gender. The lack of interest is surprising, she argued, given the similar mode of history writing in global and gender histories – both stress fluid exchanges, hybridity, intersections, and entanglement. Wiesner-Hanks perceived a tendency for gender historians to focus on local specificity, to step back from grand narratives, pointing in the opposite direction from the expansive global perspectives that have recently reshaped histories of regions such as Europe.[6]

   Those scholars who have registered global dimensions to histories of gender and sexuality in Europe have largely focused on colonial or missionary encounters. They have sometimes characterized global gender encounters as

[2] Siobhán O'Grady and Kostiantyn Khudov, "Ukrainian Woman Stand Strong Against Russian Invaders," *Washington Post*, 18 March 2022, Online.
[3] Lorenzo Tondo, "'I Will Not Be Held Prisoner': The Trans Women Turned Back at Ukraine's Borders," *Guardian*, 22 March 2022, Online.
[4] Judith Butler, *Undoing Gender* (New York: Routledge, 2004), 201.
[5] The chapters in Joanne Miyang Cho and Douglas T. McGetchin, eds., *Gendered Encounters between Germany and Asia: Transnational Perspectives since 1800* (Cham: Palgrave Macmillan, 2017).
[6] Merry E Wiesner-Hanks, ed., *Mapping Gendered Routes and Spaces in the Early Modern World* (London: Routledge, 2016).

European-led, a one-way process of colonization and influence understood as one of European expansion.[7] Ilse Lenz's 2017 historical overview of feminist mobilization in a global framework, for example, acknowledges the significance of anti-colonial women's organizing as one of the long-range "intellectual orientations" that produced gender politics. Nonetheless, Lenz still maintains that "[d]iscourses [on women, gender and society] were spread internationally in a *unilateral* way: they were received in anti-colonial and national resistance movements of women." She concedes that "new, blended, transcultural meanings" could result in creative recombination at the non-European periphery.[8] Nonetheless, there is little space here for more than a reactive response to encounters with European gendered activism. In other histories of gender and sexuality, the inclusion of a non-European perspective has been tokenistic, relegated to the margins of accounts of women's suffrage, women's liberation, queer activism, or the gendered elements of families, welfare states, and workplaces – to be found in a few chapters often located toward the end of an edited collection. The direction of travel in recent historiography, however, lies in a more expansive, globalized European history where the movements of people, objects, and ideas can be used to retell existing stories of sexual morality, the policing of sex and gender, and the activism of those seeking inclusive or heterodox versions of sexual difference.[9] The colonial and missionary realms remain crucial sites for this historiography and continue to offer rich insights. But religion can be approached as a broader field than that of missions, and the evolving literature on non-Christian faiths has been important in extending the field.[10] Similarly, the colonial has been investigated through new dimensions – recognizing the unfinished business of decolonization, postcolonial migrations and complex forms of citizenship entitlement that spanned pre- and post-independence for former colonies.

---

[7] An exception is Kristen Ghodsee's investigation of the influence of Islamic Aid and its fostering of conservative gender norms amongst Muslims in post-socialist Bulgaria, an account which is alert to the global and multidirectional dimensions of religious fundamentalism, see Kristen Ghodsee, *Muslim Lives in Eastern Europe: Gender, Ethnicity, and the Transformation of Islam in Postsocialist Bulgaria* (Princeton: Princeton University Press, 2009).

[8] Ilse Lenz, "Equality, Difference and Participation: The Women's Movements in Global Perspective," in *The History of Social Movements in Global Perspective: A Survey*, ed. Stefan Berger and Holger Nehring (London: Palgrave Macmillan, 2017), 449–83, here p. 462, emphasis added.

[9] An example is the reworking of gendered ideas of embodiment and entrepreneurialism amongst Brazilian female migrants to Berlin explored in Maria Lidola, "Negotiating Integration in Berlin's Waxing Studios: Brazilian Migrants' Gendered Appropriation of Urban Consumer Spaces and 'Ethnic' Entrepreneurship," *Journal of Contemporary History* 49, no. 1 (2014): 228–51.

[10] Shoshana Keller, "Trapped between State and Society: Women's Liberation and Islam in Soviet Uzbekistan, 1926–1941," *Journal of Women's History* 10, no. 1 (1998): 20–44; and Myriam Everard and Francisca de Haan, eds., *Rosa Manus (1881–1942): The International Life and Legacy of a Jewish Dutch Feminist* (Leiden: Brill, 2017).

It has been supplemented by the study of enslavement, understood as a global mode of economic organization that powerfully shaped ideologies, mentalities, family forms, and the everyday life of those who benefited from or inhabited its structures, including through the regulation of gender, reproduction, and sexuality.[11] Moreover, the study of the Cold War and the European coordination of industry, trade, defense, and energy after the Second World War that evolved into the European Union offer new avenues for the exploration of global and transnational influences on gender and sexual difference.[12]

-

Scholarship on precolonial non-European societies has been a significant source of innovation in the study of gender, revealing them to be gender-heterodox, marked variously by matrilineal kinship, complex and shared practices in relation to childcare, fluid gender norms, or possibilities for political activity and economic agency for those designated females.[13] A thriving historiographical field has demonstrated that experiences of enslavement, colonial rule, or contact with Europeans stigmatized or erased these structures and typically imposed gendered and sexed social and political infrastructures that reinforced and policed a heterosexual, binary, and cis-gendered patriarchal order that intersected with racial inequities. As Oyèrónkẹ́ Oyěwùmí noted in 1997: "The emergence of women as an identifiable category, defined by their anatomy and subordinated to men in all situations, resulted, in part, from the imposition of a patriarchal colonial state."[14] A series of landmark texts in the 1990s and early 2000s explored these

---

[11] Catherine Hall and Daniel Pick, "Thinking about Denial," *History Workshop Journal* 84, no. 1 (2017): 1–23; Catherine Hall et al., *Legacies of British Slave-Ownership: Colonial Slavery and the Formation of Victorian Britain* (Cambridge: Cambridge University Press, 2014); Pamela Scully and Diana Paton, eds., *Gender and Slave Emancipation in the Atlantic World* (Durham, NC: Duke University Press, 2005).

[12] Joanna Regulska and Bonnie G. Smith, eds., *Women and Gender in Postwar Europe: From Cold War to European Union* (London and New York: Routledge, 2012); Philip E. Muehlenbeck, *Gender, Sexuality, and the Cold War: A Global Perspective* (Nashville: Vanderbilt University Press, 2017); Laura Levine Frader, "International Institutions and Domestic Reform: Equal Pay and British Membership in the European Economic Community," *Twentieth Century British History* 29, no. 1 (2018): 104–28; and Maud Anne Bracke, "Labour, Gender and Deindustrialisation: Women Workers at Fiat (Italy, 1970s–1980s)," *Contemporary European History* 28, no. 4 (2019): 484–99.

[13] See for example Catherine Coquery-Vidrovitch, *African Women: A Modern History* (Boulder: Westview Press, 1997); and Christine Whyte, "Mothering Solidarity: Infant-Feeding, Vulnerability and Poverty in West Africa since the Seventeenth Century," *Past & Present*, no. 246, supplement 15 (2020): 54–91.

[14] Oyèrónkẹ́ Oyěwùmí, *The Invention of Women: Making an African Sense of Western Gender Discourses* (Minneapolis: University of Minnesota Press, 1997), 124.

Figure 12.1 Hutgohsodoneh/Louis Bennett, 1862, unknown photographer
Source: Public domain.

forms of violence and erasure.[15] A dynamic sense of colonial and postcolonial relations has raised questions as to how gendered and sexualized ways of exerting power – with their accompanying conceptual, material, and governmental violences – spilled out into European societies and continue to do the work of what Ann Laura Stoler terms "slow violence" through the "imperial debris" of the aftermath of colonial rule.[16] Historians have thus continued to find a rich seam in making visible colonial rule as deeply interventionist and brutal in the organization and policing of sex and gender.

They have also, however, explored the forms of agency, emotional connection, and intimacy that were possible despite the pervasive violence of

---

[15] Antoinette M. Burton, *Burdens of History: British Feminists, Indian Women, and Imperial Culture, 1865–1915* (Chapel Hill: University of North Carolina Press, 1994); Ann Laura Stoler, *Carnal Knowledge and Imperial Power: Race and the Intimate in Colonial Rule* (Berkeley: University of California Press, 2010); and Luise White, *The Comforts of Home: Prostitution in Colonial Nairobi* (Chicago: University of Chicago Press, 1990).

[16] Ann Laura Stoler, *Duress: Imperial Durabilities in Our Times* (Durham, NC: Duke University Press., 2016), 368.

European encounters with colonized peoples.[17] This extended to global movements and encounters, as charted in accounts of encounters between Europeans and Indigenous peoples of the Americas; historians of the "Red Atlantic" have turned to the diplomacy, trade, and petition rights that saw native Americans travel willingly or unwillingly across the Atlantic and make an active impact upon European society.[18] In the sixteenth century, women and children were the majority enslaved by European colonizers of the Americas; they were traded for sexual and domestic labor and created Indigenous diasporas on the Iberian peninsula.[19] Older Eurocentric accounts of the Atlantic as a European invention and site of expansion have given way to alternatives that stress Indigenous cosmologies, movements, and practices of cultural exchange. Recent contributions in this field have expanded beyond the Atlantic to trace the movement of both privileged and dispossessed people backward and forward between "peripheries" and "metropoles," or between "peripheries" in a literature that has deeply destabilized or abandoned these slippery hierarchical labels.[20]

Subnational or interstitial spaces such as port cities emerge as significant foci of historical research. Coll Thrush's *Indigenous London*, for example, explores the presence of Hutgohsodoneh/Louis Bennett in the London suburbs of the 1860s (Figure 12.1). A member of the Seneca Nation who competed in suburban running races under the stage name Deerfoot, Hutgohsodoneh's strong physique and stature were given a powerful gendered significance in juxtaposition to the feared demasculinization of "nervous" manhood in London's peripheries. Hutgohsodoneh also drew large crowds of fans, and prompted women to swoon and claim "love at first sight."[21] Sport and spectacle could thus showcase the intersection of gendered, sexed, and racialized social positioning and place non-European peoples at the center of European affairs. But like Hutgohsodoneh, Indigenous people have often been read as a fleeting presence, relatively marginal figures who could only unsettle the edges of the established European social order. A stronger focus on peoples of the

---

[17] Will Jackson and Emily J. Manktelow, eds., *Subverting Empire: Deviance and Disorder in the British Colonial World* (Basingstoke: Palgrave Macmillan, 2015); Durba Ghosh, *Sex and the Family in Colonial India: The Making of Empire* (Cambridge: Cambridge University Press, 2006).

[18] Jace Weaver, *The Red Atlantic: American Indigenes and the Making of the Modern World, 1000–1927* (Chapel Hill: University of North Carolina Press, 2014).

[19] Caroline Dodds Pennock, "Aztecs Abroad? Uncovering the Early Indigenous Atlantic," *American Historical Review* 125, no. 3 (2020): 787–814.

[20] Fullagar, Kate, *The Warrior, the Voyager, and the Artist: Three Lives in an Age of Empire* (New Haven: Yale University Press, 2020); David Motadel, "The German Other: Nasir al-Din Shah's Perceptions of Difference and Gender during His Visits to Germany, 1873–89," *Iranian Studies* 44, no. 4 (2011): 563–79.

[21] Coll Thrush, *Indigenous London: Native Travelers at the Heart of Empire* (New Haven: Yale University Press, 2016), 183.

Arctic such as the Sámi would recognize a more long-standing presence and bring into view the connections between Canada, Greenland, Russia, and Scandinavia as hosting the Indigenous peoples of a shared Arctic. Historians might learn from literatures generated in other disciplines that have explored the Arctic as a site of feminist campaigning over the disproportionate violence and state-led abuse suffered by Indigenous women and children, including their specific experiences of the loss of land and hunting rights and the cultural violence of language restriction.[22] The historiographical overemphasis on the Indigenous peoples of the Americas risks obscuring the colonial rule of Denmark in Greenland and the Faroes, as well as the long-running marginalization of Sámi people in Sweden, Norway, Finland, and Russia.

The historiography of non-European peoples has also contributed to the exploration of gender as a more capacious, queer category than a simple binary of male and female. In 2001, Joan Scott proposed that historians might usefully switch from gender to sexual difference as a central category of historical analysis, in order to better represent the embodied basis of gender and its spectrum of gendered performances.[23] Further contributions to the field of gender history have continued to problematize and provincialize binary gender, arguing that even Scott's more fluid talk of a spectrum risks maintaining the fundamental poles of gender as male and female. Jean Boydston's 2008 methodological discussion of gender argued for a local, historically contingent approach, recognizing that gender was not universally experienced as a fundamental organizing principle of human society. Where binary gender was discernible, Boydston argued, it did not always map on to female subordination and male empowerment. She drew on Afsaneh Najmabadi's work on Qajar Iran to situate binary gender as a production that must be established, rather than a natural default.[24] The field has seen further work on queer people and nonbinary gender within spaces colonized and settled by Europeans, within informal empires and sites of encounter, and also within the gender discourses and governing structures of European settings. The presence of queer people such as the *hijra*, recently explored by Jessica Hinchy, has emerged as a powerful influence on the policymaking of British colonial

---

[22] Ina Knobblock and Rauna Kuokkanen, "Decolonizing Feminism in the North: A Conversation with Rauna Kuokkanen," *NORA : Nordic Journal of Women's Studies* 23, no. 4 (2015): 275–81.

[23] Joan W. Scott, "Millennial Fantasies: The Future of Gender in the 21st Century," in *Gender, die Tücken einer Kategorie: Joan W. Scott, Geschichte und Politik; Beiträge zum Symposion anlässlich der Verleihung des Hans-Sigrist-Preises 1999 der Universität Bern an Joan W. Scott*, ed. Claudia Honegger and Caroline Arni (Zurich: Chronos, 2001), 39–64.

[24] Jeanne Boydston, "Gender as a Question of Historical Analysis," *Gender & History* 20, no. 3 (2008): 558–83; and Afsaneh Najmabadi, *Women with Mustaches and Men without Beards: Gender and Sexual Anxieties of Iranian Modernity* (Berkeley: University of California Press, 2005).

officials.[25] Kath Weston's work on the penal settlements of the Andaman Islands has argued that the "queered bodies of inmates" who were punished for "unnatural offences" helped to establish attitudes to and regulation of male same-sex desire that prompted and made meaningful sex scandals in European cities. Offshore incarceration did not banish queer sexual practices, she argues, but made them "an administrative obsession."[26] This has led to more sustained explorations of nonbinary and unstable forms of gender within Europe. Trans historiography has begun to make visible the border crossing for gender-affirming surgery that European individuals undertook, particularly to Casablanca's Clinique du Parc from the 1950s to 1970s.[27] Jen Manion's 2020 *Female Husbands* has explored the growing visibility of people who lived outside of the gender they were assigned at birth from the mid-eighteenth century in Britain and the United States, through practices that Manion terms "transing gender." This has enabled an important shift of approach away from "the sapphist paradigm" that explained such practices as an expression of sexuality.[28] While ideas of sexual inversion emerged in late nineteenth-century sexology, Manion observes and historicizes such categories and holds open a more expansive reading of the transgressive practices sexologists documented.

-

One subfield that neatly displays histories of European gender and sexuality closely in dialogue with colonial and global themes has been the historical investigation of buying and selling sex. Sex was a currency of colonial encounters, and its sale enabled or compelled engagement across lines of race, religion, caste, and class. Sex workers traveled within, to, and from colonized territories, and in doing so brought dependents, diseases, policies, pimps, and economic opportunities with them. Selling sex could be a temporary toehold occupation for those impoverished by crossing borders; it could stimulate and structure forms of (state) violence, intimacy, and dependency. Historians have revealed British policies and laws, for example, to be deeply indebted to the experiences of regulating and policing paid-for sex in colonial and dominion territories. Philippa Levine's account of colonial policymaking

[25] Jessica Hinchy, *Governing Gender and Sexuality in Colonial India: The Hijra, c.1850–1900* (Cambridge: Cambridge University Press, 2019).
[26] Kath Weston, "A Political Ecology of 'Unnatural Offences': State Security, Queer Embodiment, and the Environmental Impacts of Prison Migration," *GLQ* 14, nos. 2/3 (2008): 217–37, here p. 233.
[27] Nikolaos Papadogiannis, "Greek Trans Women Selling Sex, Spaces and Mobilities, 1960s–80s," European Review of History/Revue Européene d'histoire 29, no. 2 (2022): 331–62.
[28] Jen Manion, *Female Husbands: A Trans History* (Cambridge: Cambridge University Press, 2020), 9.

in the British Empire has demonstrated the early evolution of compulsory inspection and regulation of those deemed prostitutes in Hong Kong, India, Singapore, and Australia, which in turn influenced policymaking in Britain. The association between colonized peoples and disease, as well as their sexual objectification and exoticization, prompted intrusive policies that impacted predominantly on impoverished girls, women, and nonbinary people of color from the late eighteenth century.[29] Histories of the regulation and policing of paid-for sex have revealed a variety of approaches developed in colonial settings; policies veered between gendered or nongendered terminology for sellers of sex, and adopted inspection and certification regimes, practices of contact tracing, and allocation of public resources for treatment which shaped the systems legislated for and implemented in European contexts. Ida Blom's comparative account of Britain, Germany, and Scandinavia offers a productive example of how colonial perspectives are central to European histories. Blom's conclusion, however, shies away from this, citing what she describes as the depth of racial difference which led to "glaring polarization between 'us' in the West and 'the other' in the East and in Africa."[30] An alternative approach would note that racial difference informed and shaped the policies across the Global North and South, as policymakers, police, and activists shared knowledge and techniques of intervention and consistently failed to address the health and well-being of non-European populations.[31]

Julia Laite's microhistory of a trafficked young woman, Lydia Harvey, has brilliantly tracked the migrations of sex work that, in Harvey's early twentieth-century case, spanned New Zealand and Australia, as well as well-established centers of selling sex: London, Buenos Aires, and Paris. The "informal empire" that linked Britain and Argentina in the early twentieth century included sex alongside other commodities of the global economy.[32] The intensified paper trails of shipping, commerce, and criminal justice systems, as well as the twenty-first century digitization of such sources, have enabled these kinds of global histories that disrupt national and regional framings in relation to the sex economy.[33]

---

[29] Philippa Levine, *Prostitution, Race, and Politics: Policing Venereal Disease in the British Empire* (London: Routledge, 2003).

[30] Ida Blom, "Gender, Class, Race and Sexuality: A Transnational Approach to Legislation on Venereal Diseases, 1880s–1940s," in *Gender History in a Transnational Perspective: Networks, Biographies, Gender Orders*, ed. Oliver Janz and Daniel Schönpflug (New York: Berghahn Books, 2014), 200–18, here p. 211.

[31] Carina Ray, "World War II and the Sex Trade in British West Africa," in *Africa and World War II*, ed. Judith A. Byfield et al. (Cambridge: Cambridge University Press, 2015), 339–56.

[32] Julia Laite, *The Disappearance of Lydia Harvey: A True Story of Sex, Crime and the Meaning of Justice* (London: Profile Books, 2021).

[33] Julia Laite, "The Emmet's Inch: Small History in a Digital Age," *Journal of Social History* 53, no. 4 (2020): 963–89; and Lara Putnam, "The Transnational and the Text-Searchable: Digitized Sources and the Shadows They Cast," *American Historical Review* 121, no. 2 (2016): 377–402.

Selling and buying sex can also reveal global links established outside of colonial and postcolonial relationships. Pataya Ruenkaew, for example, has traced the migration of Thai women to Germany from the mid-1970s in a sharply feminized migrant labor market. Their experiences spanned sex work, precarious labor in catering or massage parlors, and "mail order marriages." The choices of Thai women were mostly oriented to the support of dependent children who remained in Thailand or might sometimes be brought to Germany. Ruenkaew describes the "shuttling prostitution" of repeated moves back and forth between Germany and Thailand, shaped by the three-month visa regime available until 1988. She also notes the internal movements of Thai women who were twice-migrants, mobile in Thailand from rural to urban settings and subsequently across international borders.[34] Similar patterns are visible with women from the Philippines and eastern Europe, prompted by the rise in single parenthood in these societies and state-sponsored backing for the export of labor in the context of the global economic inequalities of the late twentieth and early twenty-first centuries.

Historians of the sex economy have also showcased the value of scrutiny of individual cities – those subject to the barter economies of military occupation such as Berlin in 1945 and those located near military forces such as Ferizaj in Kosovo, as well as the port cities where paid-for sex flourished among migrant and mobile populations. The 2017 collection by Magaly Rodriguez Garcia et al. offers long-range histories of cities such as Cairo, Amsterdam, London, and St. Petersburg.[35] In juxtaposing these port cities and cosmopolitan hubs where sex was traded by men, women, and nonbinary people, this approach offers both comparative and transnational specificity. It shows for example shared rural–urban dynamics across European and non-European settings, and the evolution across borders of moral and policy understandings of trading sex.

Historical surveys of selling sex have been alert to global dynamics but have still been relatively slow to incorporate male sex workers, whose strategies and experiences often intersect with local and transnational migration. Nicola Mai's investigation of Albanian male migrants to Greece and Italy in the post-Communist era traces the potent and tenacious ideas of honor and shame that influence male authority, family support, and sexual practices in the eastern Mediterranean. Male guardianship of family honor, he argues, made possible a dynamic, strategically employed repertoire of sexual practices that allowed Albanian male migrants within Europe to sell sex, as well as on

---

[34] Pataya Ruenkaew, "Victims of Traffic in Women, Marriage Migrants and Community Formation: A History of Migration of Thai Women to Germany," in Cho and McGetchin, *Gendered Encounters between Germany and Asia*, 253–74.

[35] The chapters in Magaly Rodríguez García, Lex Heerma van Voss, and Elise van Nederveen Meerkerk, eds., *Selling Sex in the City: A Global History of Prostitution, 1600s-2000s* (Leiden and Boston: Brill, 2017).

occasion to traffic in and profit from women who sell sex. The criminalization of male same-sex encounters alongside pornography and selling sex as "crimes against social morality" links Albania under its Communist rulers to a number of other Eastern European regimes under the orbit of the Soviet Union. But Mai argues that Albanian sexual mores can also be linked to a wider, more eclectic discourse of honor that spans Mediterranean Europe and North Africa, and which can be traced back to the Ottoman occupation of Albania and southeast Europe. Ideas of the value of active and passive sexual roles between men, for example, stem from this Ottoman legacy.[36] Indeed, the "Levantine" culture of the eastern Mediterranean has long been a fertile location for cosmopolitan sexual cultures, fueling European fantasies of "Oriental" sexual exoticism and influencing the literary, sexological, and tourist cultures of modern Europe. The broad-brush strokes and discursive focus of Edward Said's influential *Orientalism* (1978) have been fleshed out by subsequent scholarship, through accounts of Muslim and Jewish sexual discourses in the Ottoman Empire, as well as the encounters and entanglements of Ottoman and European sexual cultures.[37]

Selling sex was a strategy for those at the margins of power and wealth; however, intellectual histories of sexual discourses across European and non-European locations feature a cast of actors who were far more prominent and powerful. This is clearly illustrated in the rise of histories of reproductive policies and "family planning" as "globalizing sciences" rooted in encounters with non-European societies. Promoted globally by funders such as the International Planned Parenthood Federation, the Pathfinder Fund, and later by the United Nations, this emerging policy agenda intervened in global demographics, positioning the fertility rates of the Global South as a "Third World" problem that required curtailment.[38] This went hand in hand with the imposition of a normative nuclear family model and, as campaigners

---

[36] Nicola Mai, "Albanian Masculinities, Sex-Work and Migration: Homosexuality, AIDS and Other Moral Threats," in *National Healths: Gender, Sexuality and Health in a Cross-Cultural Context*, ed. Nana Wilson-Tagoe and Michael Worton (London: UCL Press, 2004), 45–58.

[37] Edward W. Said, *Orientalism* (Harmondsworth: Penguin, 1991); Yaron Ben-Naeh, "Moshko the Jew and His Gay Friends: Same-Sex Sexual Relations in Ottoman Jewish Society," *Journal of Early Modern History* 9, nos. 1/2 (2005): 79–108; Stephen O. Murray, "Homosexuality in the Ottoman Empire," *Historical Reflections* 33, no. 1 (2007): 101–16; Peter Drucker, "Byron and Ottoman Love: Orientalism, Europeanization and Same-Sex Sexualities in the Early Nineteenth-Century Levant," *Journal of European Studies* 42, no. 2 (2012): 140–57; and Noel Malcolm, "Forbidden Love in Istanbul: Patterns of Male–Male Sexual Relations in the Early-Modern Mediterranean World," *Past & Present*, no. 257 (2022): 1–35.

[38] Mohan Rao, *From Population Control to Reproductive Health: Malthusian Arithmetic* (New Delhi: Sage Publications, 2004); Alison Bashford, *Global Population: History, Geopolitics, and Life on Earth* (New York: Columbia University Press, 2014); and Veronika Fuechtner, Douglas E Haynes, and Ryan M Jones, eds., *A Global History of Sexual Science, 1880–1960* (Berkeley: University of California Press, 2017).

Figure 12.2 Vida Tomšič, 1961, unknown photographer.
Source: Public domain.

increasingly noted, inattention to issues of consent and safety. The pharma-
ceutical experiments and compulsory sterilization imposed on women in locations such as Mexico were essential to the development of products licensed by
European states, as well as their demographic policies.[39]

However, family planning has also emerged in recent historiography as a
discourse of anti-fascist and feminist political organizing, framed around
women's and human rights. Within Europe, this politicization of reproduction
gave rise to a variety of reproductive policy interventions that were constantly
in dialogue with global nonstate actors and hyperfocused on migrant women as
points of intervention. As Maud Bracke has shown, languages of "family" and
planning came to replace discredited ideas of race and civilization in the
debates of the 1950s onwards, across Europe and the newly labeled "Third
World." The perceived danger of overpopulation in the Global South was a
powerful rhetorical tool for shaping policies and attitudes in Europe, both in
crafting narratives of European exceptionalism and in powering debates over
who should be encouraged to reproduce. Perceptions of the "naturalness" of
the nuclear family and of stable demographic balance were deeply influenced
by the contrast drawn with non-European societies. "Family planning" is thus

[39] Dorothy E. Roberts, *Killing the Black Body: Race, Reproduction, and the Meaning of Liberty* (New York: Vintage Books, 1999).

a good example of a discourse, set of policies, and site of experience that historians have increasingly recognized as conceptually shaped by a global landscape, yet one in which Europe took a preeminent place. Indeed, for those countries located at the economic or geographic peripheries of Europe, family planning could be used as a form "modernization" that could also be understood as "Europeanization."[40]

Historians have also turned to the politics of reproduction and contraception, not only as sites of intervention in current and former colonial locations but also in relation to the growing numbers of immigrants and their descendants in Europe. Historical accounts of discourses of hypersexualized male migrants (in France, Arab and African men, particularly those performing military roles; in the United Kingdom, African Caribbean men[41]) developed alongside the positioning of migrant women as excessively fertile, undeserving of housing and other welfare benefits, and unable to embrace "modern" family planning. Nonetheless, Bracke argues, such women were also understood on occasion as vehicles for cultural change and new contraceptive practices within their communities, and thus were invested with particular reproductive agency.[42] Scholarship on the history of contraception and family planning has been able to demonstrate the entanglement of people, policies, and sponsorship that has transformed the history of European familialism and gender norms in a global landscape.

-

The impact of global historiographies on the history of feminisms has been an area of exciting growth and innovation since the 1990s.[43] Two collections, Karen Offen's *Globalizing Feminisms* and Bonnie Smith's *Global Feminisms since 1945*, helped to showcase both a more diverse European cast of historical

---

[40] Maud Anne Bracke, "Family Planning, the Pill, and Reproductive Agency in Italy, 1945–1971: From 'Conscious Procreation' to 'a New Fundamental Right'?," *European Review of History/Revue Européene d'histoire* 29, no. 1 (2022): 88–108, here p. 98.

[41] Todd Shepard, *Sex, France, and Arab Men, 1962–1979* (Chicago: University of Chicago Press, 2018); Marcus Collins, "Pride and Prejudice: West Indian Men in Mid-twentieth-century Britain," *Journal of British Studies* 40, no. 3 (2001): 391–418; and Ruth Ginio, "African Soldiers, French Women, and Colonial Fears during and after World War II," in Byfield et al., *Africa and World War II*, 324–38.

[42] Maud Anne Bracke, "Family Planning and Reproductive Agency in France: Demography, Gender, and Race (1950s-70s)," *French Historical Studies* 45, no. 4 (2022): 683–710.

[43] Early significant contributions include Leila J. Rupp, *Worlds of Women: The Making of an International Women's Movement* (Princeton: Princeton University Press, 1997); Burton, *Burdens of History*; Bonnie S. Anderson, *Joyous Greetings: The First International Women's Movement, 1830–1860* (Oxford: Oxford University Press, 2001); and Christine Bolt, *Sisterhood Questioned?: Race, Class and Internationalism in the American and British Women's Movements, c. 1880–1970s* (London: Routledge, 2004).

actors and be attentive to non-European dynamics. Offen maintains that the earliest feminist campaigns stemmed from "Atlantic Rim" or Western nations and diffused outwards.[44] However, a wider-ranging intellectual landscape that looks beyond canonical feminist thinkers of the European Enlightenment has become more prominent in recent historiography, allowing the tracking of a more diverse global landscape of theorization and resistance to inequities of gender and sex.[45] Rather than searching for origins and linear diffusion, historians have looked to "messy multiplicity" and become increasingly attentive to historical actors who sought gender justice yet ignored or actively disidentified with labels of "feminist."[46]

Recent work has seen a particular focus on the period after 1945, tracking the aftermath of global war and the turn toward gender justice through United Nations bodies such as the Commission on the Status of Women.[47] Literatures on Cold War feminisms such as Wendy Pojmann's account of the Communist Unione Donne Italiane and the Catholic Centro Italiano Femminile in Italy have done much to bring awareness of the divisive ideological backdrop to European women's organizing in the postwar period, adding breadth and comparative potential to histories of feminist activism.[48] But such histories have sometimes tended to flatten the landscape of global influences to an ideological binary and their global dimension has sometimes been little more than a backdrop. More satisfying work, also rooted in Cold War contexts, has been cognizant of the diverse inspiration offered by the Cuban and Algerian revolutions, or the specific sponsorship and shaping of women's groups by intelligence services, economic development budgets, philanthropic foundations, or religious bodies such as the Vatican and the World Council of Churches. This has helped to move beyond the insight that gender and sexuality were instrumentally deployed by Cold War powers to demonstrate

---

[44] Karen M. Offen, ed., *Globalizing Feminisms, 1789–1945* (London: Routledge, 2010), xxxiv; Bonnie G. Smith, ed., *Global Feminisms since 1945* (London: Routledge, 2000).

[45] See for example Lydia He Liu et al., *The Birth of Chinese Feminism: Essential Texts in Transnational Theory* (New York: Columbia University Press, 2013); Silvia Bermúdez and Roberta Johnson, *A New History of Iberian Feminisms* (Toronto: University of Toronto Press, 2018); and Lucy Delap, *Feminisms: A Global History* (London: Pelican Books, 2021).

[46] Nancy A. Hewitt, ed., *No Permanent Waves: Recasting Histories of U.S. Feminism* (New Brunswick: Rutgers University Press, 2010), 7; Imaobong D. Umoren, *Race Women Internationalists: Activist-Intellectuals and Global Freedom Struggles* (Oakland: University of California Press, 2018); and Jennifer Denetdale, "'To Be a Good Relative Means Being a Good Relative to Everyone': Indigenous Feminisms Is for Everyone," in *Routledge Handbook of Critical Indigenous Studies*, ed. Brendan Hokowhitu et al. (London: Routledge, 2020), 229–39.

[47] Jocelyn Olcott, *International Women's Year: The Greatest Consciousness-Raising Event in History* (New York: Oxford University Press, 2017).

[48] Wendy A. Pojmann, *Italian Women and International Cold War Politics, 1944–1968* (New York: Fordham University Press, 2013).

their liberality, powerful sponsorship, or progressiveness. Instead, historians have explored deeper entanglements and complex trajectories of reciprocal influence that do not simply point back to Moscow or Washington and instead emerged, as Celia Donert argues, as "hemmed around by national loyalties, ideological cleavages, and painful personal decisions."[49]

The work of Francisca de Haan and others on what de Haan terms "global left-feminists" has been particularly important in this regard.[50] De Haan has highlighted the ongoing influence of "Cold War paradigms" that have situated Western-backed women's groups as both globally preeminent and politically neutral. In her reading, this has distracted historians from the extensive, ideologically diverse activist networks sustained by bodies such as the Women's International Democratic Federation (WIDF).[51] Widely interpreted by North American and western European historians as a stooge body funded by Moscow to divert women into class struggle, this organization has inspired much revisionist historiography. It was founded in Paris in 1945 as an anti-fascist peace campaign that foregrounded women's and children's rights at national and international levels. Initial participants came from across the globe, though the WIDF also included prominent European feminist activists, Communist and non-Communist, and claimed the Union des Femmes Françaises as its predecessor. Its headquarters shifted in 1951 to East Berlin when its opposition to the Korean War made France an inhospitable location. Historians have continued to debate the role the organization played in European politics, but an extensive literature has also emerged on the WIDF's work across the Global South, through its affiliated national organizations and regular congresses. Yulia Gradskova has explored the tensions that arose at the center of the organization through its attempts to craft a global organization, including a lack of diversity on the WIDF's secretariat and tensions over alignment with Soviet foreign policy goals.[52] Others have used WIDF sources to trace women's organizations and feminist activism across Europe and the Global South, stressing reciprocal influence and the centrality of the anti-colonial struggle.[53]

---

[49] Celia Donert, "Women's Rights in Cold War Europe: Disentangling Feminist Histories," *Past & Present*, no. 218, supplement 8 (2013): 180–202, here pp. 181–2.

[50] Francisca de Haan, "The Global Left-Feminist 1960s: From Copenhagen to Moscow and New York," in *The Routledge Handbook of the Global Sixties: Between Protest and Nation-Building*, ed. Jian Chen et al. (Abingdon: Routledge, 2018), 230–42.

[51] Francisca de Haan, "Eugénie Cotton, Pak Chong-Ae, and Claudia Jones: Rethinking Transnational Feminism and International Politics," *Journal of Women's History* 25, no. 4 (2013): 174–89.

[52] Yulia Gradskova, "Women's International Democratic Federation, the 'Third World' and the Global Cold War from the Late-1950s to the Mid-1960s," *Women's History Review* 29, no. 2 (2020): 270–88.

[53] Katharine McGregor, "Indonesian Women, the Women's International Democratic Federation and the Struggle for 'Women's Rights,' 1946–1965," *Indonesia and the Malay World* 40, no. 117

This historiography has prompted new contributions to the history of European feminisms that foreground east, central, and southeast Europe more prominently.[54] Historians have placed feminist activists from Soviet-influenced Europe more centrally into narratives of feminist history, displacing western European organizations.[55] They have also turned to the Non-Aligned Movement to capture interactions and influences that push beyond Cold War framings. Chiara Bonfiglioli, for example, has explored the limits of WIDF affiliation through her work on Yugoslavian women's organizations.[56] Expelled from the WIDF in 1949 as Yugoslavia distanced itself from the Soviet Union, Yugoslavian women's organizations developed their own bilateral relationships with nonaligned women's bodies in the Global South, as well as with Communist women's organizations in western Europe. The flashpoints of anti-colonial and postcolonial struggles in Algeria, Cuba, Egypt, and the Congo were powerful sources of political momentum; women's political activity was oriented not only to specific concerns around gender justice but also programs of land reform, literacy, and economic development. Bonfiglioli, for example, traces the relationship Slovenian feminist Vida Tomšič sustained with Indian women's studies academic Vina Mazumdar and shows the significance of their shared commitments to women's self-reliance and economic participation in small enterprises (Figure 12.2). The UN Decade for Women (1975–85) was a particularly fertile period of global interactions on issues of women's role in economic development; expertise developed in India on female-dominated informal economic activity, for example, could be incorporated into European women's activism, a process that resonated with wider nongovernmental organization- and United Nations-sponsored interest in "Third World development" as a feminist issue.

Reflecting this interest in informal economies, historians of feminisms have turned away from canonical figures and spaces of feminist mobilization – the

---

(2012): 193–208; Katharine McGregor, "Opposing Colonialism: The Women's International Democratic Federation and Decolonisation Struggles in Vietnam and Algeria 1945–1965," *Women's History Review* 25, no. 6 (2016): 925–44; and Elisabeth Armstrong, "Before Bandung: The Anti-Imperialist Women's Movement in Asia and the Women's International Democratic Federation," *Signs: Journal of Women in Culture and Society* 41, no. 2 (2016): 305–31.

[54] Margarite Poulos, "'So That Life May Triumph': Communist Feminism and Realpolitik in Civil-War Greece," *Journal of Women's History* 29, no. 1 (2017): 63–86; and Celia Donert, "Feminism, Communism and Global Socialism: Encounters and Entanglements," in *The Cambridge History of Communism*, vol. 3, *Endgames? Late Communism in Global Perspective, 1968 to the Present*, ed. Juliane Fürst, Silvio Pons, and Mark Selden (Cambridge: Cambridge University Press, 2017), 399–421.

[55] Kristen Ghodsee, *Second World, Second Sex: Socialist Women's Activism and Global Solidarity during the Cold War* (Durham, NC: Duke University Press, 2019).

[56] Chiara Bonfiglioli, "Women's Internationalism and Yugoslav–Indian Connections: From the Non-Aligned Movement to the UN Decade for Women," *Nationalities Papers* 49, no. 3 (2021): 446–61.

cafes, libraries, bookshops, and universities of urban intellectuals – and instead examined sites of informality and migration, from beyond Europe and within its borders. Roseanna Webster's account of women's organizing for the basic goods of water and food has focused on Spain's *chabolas* – informal settlements that abounded in the era of mass rural–urban migration. Rather than a narrative of intellectual influences from established feminist movements and texts from France, Germany, and Italy that circulated in Spain from the 1970s, Webster looks to the 1960s as an earlier decade that reveals the mobilization of poor migrant women who engaged municipal authorities for *cosas básicas* such as access to water, in forceful demands couched as maternal citizenship.[57] Through the influence and sponsorship of Roman Catholic priests at the grassroots level, this historiography traces resonances between Spanish and Latin American mobilization of precarious peoples that flourished in the 1960s, aided by worker priests and Liberation Theology.[58] As Gerd-Rainer Horn has noted, the radical Catholic organizing of the Vatican II period reflected methods that were notably similar to the consciousness-raising tactics of Euro-American women's movements.[59] Quinn Slobodian has offered an additional global perspective by linking such methods to the powerful influence in France and Germany of the Chinese Cultural Revolution and its advocacy of "speaking bitterness" practices among both women and peasants.[60]

Literature on global entanglements has turned scholarly attention to specifically European networks of resistance at the intersection of sexism and racism.[61] Pamela Ohene-Nyako's account of the World Council of Churches (WCC), for example, has uncovered the European dimensions of the Women Under Racism program operated by the WCC in the 1980s and 1990s.[62] She traces the rise of political Blackness as a global ideology that had particular

---

[57] Roseanna Webster, "Women and the Fight for Urban Change in Late Francoist Spain," *Past & Present*, no. 260 (2023): 158–99. On wider global heritages of maternal feminisms see Donna J. Guy, "The Politics of Pan-American Cooperation: Maternalist Feminism and the Child Rights Movement, 1913–1960," *Gender & History* 10, no. 3 (1998): 449–69; Dina Lowy, "Love and Marriage: Ellen Key and Hiratsuka Raichō Explore Alternatives," *Women's Studies* 33, no. 4 (2004): 361–80; and James Keating, "'Woman as Wife, Mother, and Home-Maker': Equal Rights International and Australian Feminists' Interwar Advocacy for Mothers' Economic Rights," *Signs: Journal of Women in Culture and Society* 47, no. 4 (2022): 957–85.

[58] Alana Harris, *The Schism of '68 : Catholicism, Contraception and Humanae Vitae in Europe, 1945–1975* (Cham: Palgrave Macmillan, 2018).

[59] Gerd-Rainer Horn, *The Spirit of Vatican II: Western European Progressive Catholicism in the Long Sixties* (Oxford: Oxford University Press, 2015), 186.

[60] Quinn Slobodian, "Guerrilla Mothers and Distant Doubles: West German Feminists Look at China and Vietnam, 1968–1982," Studies in Contemporary History/Zeithistorische Forschungen 12 (2015): 39–65.

[61] Olivette Otele, *African Europeans: An Untold History* (London: Hurst & Company, 2020).

[62] Pamela Ohene-Nyako, "Black Women's Transnational Activism and the World Council of Churches," *Open Cultural Studies* 3, no. 1 (2019): 219–31.

force for women of color within Europe. Their encounters with African American, Afro-Brazilian, and African Caribbean churchwomen provided conceptual and activist resources which enabled resistance to European attempts to integrate economies, employment policies, and border controls in ways that exacerbated the exclusion and precarity of migrants. The free movement of Europeans enacted in the 1985 Schengen Agreement, for example, was rhetorically juxtaposed to "fortress Europe" measures that made borders increasingly hostile environments for migrants of color and ushered in aggressive forms of policing for Black European populations. These contributions to the gendered experience of Blackness have often done much to foreground women's experiences; more might be done to explore Black masculinities, as Rob Waters and Kieran Connell have recently done in their intellectual and cultural histories of Black Britain.[63] The historiography might also reflect more fully the influence not only of radical inspiration but also of voices of moderation, conservatism, and loyalty, as Zaib un Nisa Aziz has recently shown in her account of the equivocal affinities of internationalist, imperialist, and anti-colonial feminist networks of the early twentieth century.[64] Nonetheless, these contributions all highlight the validity of what Kennetta Perry and Kira Thurman have termed "Black Europe as an analytic" for historians, which unsettles what it means to be European, to be Black, and, I would add, to be a bearer of gender and sexuality.[65]

-

The process of unsettling can be easy to claim and hard to put into practice for historians in the face of archival holdings and practices that direct historical attention and imagination toward well-established channels, plots, and ruts. Michel-Rolph Trouillot reflected pessimistically in 1995 that "the history of the West is not retold in ways that bring forward the perspective of the world. Unfortunately, we are not even close to such fundamental rewriting of world history."[66] In the subsequent three decades, historians of gender and sexuality have been prominent in seeking new frameworks and methodologies for integrating "the West," Europe, and "the global." Negar Mottahedeh's recent

---

[63] Rob Waters, *Thinking Black: Britain, 1964–1985* (Oakland: University of California Press, 2019); Kieran Connell, *Black Handsworth: Race in 1980s Britain* (Oakland: University of California Press, 2019).

[64] Zaib un Nisa Aziz, "Songs of Sisterhood: Feminist Political Practice between Empire and Internationalism 1910–20," *Gender & History* 35, no. 1 (2021): 155–71.

[65] Kennetta Hammond Perry and Kira Thurman, "Black Europe: A Useful Category of Historical Analysis," *Black Perspectives, African American Intellectual History Society*, 2016, Online.

[66] Michel-Rolph Trouillot, *Silencing the Past: Power and the Production of History* (Boston: Beacon Press, 2015), 107.

account of the critical early days of the 1979 Iranian Revolution is thoughtful about how historians might find different perspectives.[67] She listens closely to the audio tapes of personal commentary recorded by the American women's liberationist Kate Millett during her visit to Iran in March 1979. Millett's attempt to rally Iranian women to her vision of feminism – understood as liberal rights and bodily autonomy – followed by her eventual deportation by the authorities of the Islamic Republic is a telling episode. Listening to Millett's taped reflections would seem likely to confirm the precedence of Anglo-American feminism and to sideline the motivations of Iranian women who participated in popular demonstrations against the shah, and against fundamentalist, patriarchal versions of Islam. Yet Mottahedeh attends instead to the contingency of the revolutionary moment by listening to the other voices on Millett's tapes: the accidentally captured dialogues in Persian between women traveling with Millett or those near her in the mass marches and occupations of the early revolution. Millett is always a step behind them in her response to the revolutionary situation, struggling to understand what Iranian women are saying and to make sense of the slogans, their strategic use of veiling, and the significance of women's acts of protest and occupation. Mottahedeh recovers debates anonymously and unwittingly captured on tape, from women who were deeply opposed to the Western-backed shah and hopeful that an Iranian revolution might meet their needs. This close listening to layers of voices is not only a reminder to incorporate promising new methodologies such as attention to auditory, sensory, sartorial, and material cultural elements in our histories of gender and sexuality. It also serves as a metaphor for how global actors and influences might insidiously be present in historical settings where the main actors seem to be already established. If historians of Europe listen again, other voices can be discerned; other trajectories, such as those relating to refugee movements, to global humanitarian interventions, and to the global dimensions of health care might become visible that displace and supplement existing narratives. As Kristen Ghodsee has argued in her study of east European and Global South women's activism, the "history written by the victors" – in her case, western European and United States-based middle- and upper-class white liberal feminists – cannot be allowed to drown out the alternatives promoted by state-sponsored, leftist, Africanist, and Indigenous activists that provide new entry points for the global to become present in European histories of gender and sexuality.[68]

---

[67] Negar Mottahedeh, *Whisper Tapes: Kate Millett in Iran* (Stanford: Stanford University Press, 2019).

[68] Ghodsee, *Second World, Second Sex*, 243.

13 Globalizing Europe's Musical Past

Kira Thurman

The Belgian singer Paul van Haver, better known as Stromae, has been a musical tour de force and whirlwind since he first broke out onto the musical scene in 2010 with his smash hit "Alors en danse," which became the number one song in several European countries. The son of a Rwandan architect and a white Belgian woman, Stromae has become a brilliant weaver of French, Caribbean, and African styles of music, and each of his subsequent albums has brought him even more public adoration. In 2013, his album *Racine carrée* topped most of the charts in western Europe, and his autobiographical song "Papoutai" tells of Stromae's search for his father, who had been killed during the 1994 Rwandan genocide. *Multitude*, his most recent album, embraces a French cabaret musical tradition reminiscent of Jacques Brel's crooner "Ne me quitte pas," while also incorporating Congolese rumba and the sounds of Cuban *son* – first made popular by musical ensembles such as the Buena Vista Social Club – with great verve and flair.

Similarly, the Parisian sisters Lisa-Kaindé Diaz and Naomi Diaz, who comprise the duo Ibeyi (Yoruba for "twins"), have been fusing together Black diasporic and French musical styles for over a decade. Using Cuban percussive instruments such as the cajón and singing in French, English, Spanish, and Yoruba, their music creates otherworldly sonic soundscapes steeped in the spiritual practice of Santería, a religion that bridges the faiths of Roman Catholic and Yoruba religious practices. Their 2015 album, *Ash*, incorporates the writings of women of color such as Mexican painter Frida Kahlo and the poet Claudia Rankine in order to examine and articulate the racism and sexism that the musicians have experienced as women of color (recalling, for example, an incident of racial profiling on the Paris Metro when Lisa Dias was sixteen years old in the song "Deathless"), all while weaving in rumba, a cappella singing, and other musical styles and traditions into their songs.

The striking fact is not that these Black European musicians have created such knockout albums to which millions of people have listened to in recent years, but rather how little we discuss them within the context of European music. If public discourses have been willing to recognize their globality, listeners and critics are often more hesitant to place them within a lineage of European music-making. What has stood in the way of understanding their musical language as belonging to both a European and a global tradition?

The purpose of this chapter is twofold: first, to examine how a narrow definition of what constituted music became the center of our historical scholarship on music in Europe, thus muting us to richer possibilities in global music history; second, to argue that in broadening both who we understand as European and what we believe to be European music, we may better recognize a greater and richer tapestry of European music's global connections. This chapter begins first by examining the history of the idea of European music in academic and public discourse before turning to newer strains of thought and methodologies that promise to undo older models of analysis.

Several factors have defined scholarship on music-making in Europe for over a century, the first being how academics understand what constitutes "European" music itself. In this regard, one of the most pressing (mis)assumptions was (and remains) that the European continent's primary musical contribution to the world has been art music.[1] Second, and relatedly, was that the musical "work" – written in Western musical notation and supposedly existing independent of the performer itself – was an object of study in its own right.[2] The third factor was that those who had composed these musical works the "best" were white European men. In *Beyond Exoticism*, Timothy D. Taylor argues that much of the nineteenth and twentieth century operated under what he calls a "classical music ideology," meaning "an ideology that has as its two foundational tenets the concepts of 'genius' and 'masterpiece,' two concepts that arose in their present form in the first half of the nineteenth century."[3]

The "classical music ideology," as Taylor defines it, became the most dominant expression of what constituted European musical advancement. What became codified over time – which scholars have historically reinforced – is a canon of musical works that emerged from a Western art music tradition.[4] Considered an objective and neutral fact instead of a factor of aesthetic difference or taste, the pieces composed by white European men dominated the concert hall – and thus were assumed to be the only pieces worth studying and teaching in academic contexts. Classical music was not only universal

---

[1] Recent scholarship often presents European history primarily through an understanding of classical music. See, for example, Matthew Riley and Anthony D., eds., Smith *Nation and Classical Music: From Handel to Copland* (Woodbridge: Boydell Press, 2016).

[2] Lawrence Kramer, *Interpreting Music* (Berkeley: University of California Press, 2010).

[3] Timothy D. Taylor, *Beyond Exoticism: Western Music and the World* (Durham, NC: Duke University Press, 2007), 3.

[4] William Weber, *The Great Transformation of Musical Taste: Concert Programming from Haydn to Brahms* (Cambridge and New York: Cambridge University Press, 2008); and Lydia Goehr, *The Imaginary Museum of Musical Works: An Essay in the Philosophy of Music* (New York: Oxford University Press, 1992).

because its composers had supposedly perfected the relationship between notes, intervals, pitches, and chords. It was universal because people believed the music closely followed and even revealed to the world the natural laws of the universe. The supposedly natural evolution of the piano sonata, of symphonic form, and of classical compositions in general was evidence of classical music's inherent worth. As Alexandra Hui has convincingly demonstrated, German scientists in the nineteenth century used Western instruments such as the violin for their sonic experiments in the fields of physics and acoustics because they operated under the assumption that classical musical instruments were as universal as the overtones Pythagoras had discovered in the creation of his tuning system.[5]

The consequences of our assumptions of who makes European art music have been severe. By centering the musical canon of art music on white European men, scholarship saw no need to examine those who fell outside this narrow definition. Not only has it meant that women have been historically excluded from European art music, even though they were often its greatest practitioners and patrons,[6] but it has also meant that for much of the twentieth century, scholarship was resistant to recognizing the globality of classical music at all. For decades, musical publics treated the musicians Bach, Beethoven, Brahms, Verdi, Wagner, and other composers as divorced from the global histories surrounding them. To conjure an image of the composer Beethoven was to imagine him in a setting that had little to do with greater global forces of race, economy, politics, and culture.

The neat bifurcation between European art music as edifying, universal, and pure, and everything else as either primitive or commercial, also greatly influenced Europe's relationship to the Global South. As David Motadel has warned, many historical narratives have reinforced a civilizing mission ideology, in which scholars write about bringing "Europe" to the world.[7] Western music – and their histories – functioned similarly, thus reinforcing the idea that European music moved out only laterally into the world. In this regard, to discuss classical music in a global context meant analyzing its impact and potentials for uplifting other supposedly "undeveloped" musical worlds. As Vanessa Agnew writes: "Apparently, European music would not only bring the benefits of the Enlightenment to those who needed it most; it would

---

[5] Alexandra Hui, *The Psychophysical Ear: Musical Experiments, Experimental Sounds, 1840–1910* (Cambridge, MA: MIT Press, 2013).

[6] Rebecca Cypess, *Women and Musical Salons in the Enlightenment* (Chicago: University of Chicago Press, 2022).

[7] Chapter 1 in this volume; and, for the case of music, the chapters in Jane Bowers and Judith Tick, eds., *Women Making Music: The Western Art Tradition, 1150–1950* (Urbana: University of Illinois Press, 1986).

also confirm, even bolster, the social, moral, and political value of serious music at a time when music's value seemed to be in question."[8]

Centuries of musical training upheld the belief that Europeans could teach the world how to compose and listen to music better. Figures such as the Parisian composer Nadia Boulanger (1887–1979) became the musical midwives of North and South American talent, for example.[9] Scholarship still frequently heralds Antonin Dvorak as the point of origin for the development of American art music, thus perpetuating the notion that only when a composer from Europe recognized what American music "was" (located in Indigenous and African American musical idioms) could anyone else hear it.[10] Academic training and scholarship also reinforced the idea that European art music was the only way to teach any student what music was. The late ethnomusicologist Bruno Nettl stated quite bluntly that "it has been clear all along" that most schools of music are "schools of Western European art music."[11] To study "music" at a conservatory of music today usually still means studying one particular kind of music. Departments continue to offer music courses such as "music theory," which Loren Kajikawa argues implies "a universal approach to musical cultivation."[12]

Approaches to music made by non-Europeans fell under the prism of "primitivism," which, while still available for academic inquiry, could only be researched through an ethnological and anthropological lens. Originating in the discipline of comparative musicology in the nineteenth century, ethnomusicology embraced folk music (loosely defined) and all music outside of Western European art music, especially the music of what they deemed to be nonliterate people.[13] Led by figures such as Erich Moritz von Hornbostel, its initial goal was to seek out "original, authentic music, uncontaminated by outside influences."[14] Searching for music hermetically sealed off from any

[8] Vanessa Agnew, "Listening to Others: Eighteenth-Century Encounters in Polynesia and Their Reception in German Musical Thought," *Eighteenth-Century Studies* 41, no. 2 (2008): 165–88.
[9] See Annegret Fauser, "Aaron Copland, Nadia Boulanger, and the Making of an 'American' Composer," *The Musical Quarterly* 89, no. 4 (2006): 524–54.
[10] Douglas Shadle's recent book, *Antonín Dvořák's New World Symphony* (New York: Oxford University Press, 2021), critiques this idea thoroughly.
[11] Bruno Nettl, *Heartland Excursions: Ethnomusicological Reflections on Schools of Music* (Urbana: University of Illinois Press, 1995), 110, cited in Loren Kajikawa, "The Possessive Investment in Classical Music: Confronting Legacies of White Supremacy in U.S. Schools and Departments of Music," *Seeing Race Again: Countering Colorblindness across the Disciplines*, ed. Kimberlé Williams Crenshaw et al. (Berkeley: University of California Press, 2019), 155–74, here p. 157.
[12] Kajikawa, "The Possessive Investment in Classical Music," 161.
[13] Carole Pegg, Philip V. Bohlman, Helen Myers, and Martin Stokes, "Ethnomusicology," in *Oxford Music Online*, 29 January 2001, Online.
[14] Anna Maria Busse Berger, *The Search for Medieval Music in Africa and Germany, 1891–1961: Scholars, Singers, Missionaries* (Chicago: University of Chicago Press, 2020), 25.

global or transnational influences became, as we will see, both a vexing concern and an impossible task.

A fundamental assumption in ethnomusicology was that the music of non-European peoples was not simply or only different but also rather primitive and more connected to ancient or medieval musical systems than to modern Western music.[15] Never held up as equal to or even better than European art music, the music of non-European peoples' value existed primarily through its perceived sense of difference, not similarity. And unfortunately, as Michael Adas points out, for even for the best-intentioned theorists in the nineteenth century, difference meant inferiority.[16] Therefore, as it developed, the field of ethnomusicology became deeply invested in producing a system of racial-cultural ordering that organized a hierarchy of sounds by dangerously connecting the biological idea of race to moral, intellectual, and cultural abilities.

To accomplish this work, ethnomusicologists turned to collecting sound recordings and samples from Asia, Africa, the Middle East, and the Indigenous Americas in the hopes of documenting primitive musical activities in their "purest" and least tainted forms.[17] Exotic, different, and inferior to European art music, the music of non-European peoples could be enticing gems of study in the same manner as a geologist unearthing a crystal of malachite. Notating their songs, melodies, and tunes in academic journals, ethnomusicologists debated the origins of these different musical cultures and how to best catalogue their musics. Not only did ethnomusicologists traipse into the desert, sail across oceans, and wander through forests and jungles in order to "discover" the music of non-European peoples but they were also instrumental in bringing "the world" to Europe through the form of world's fairs, exhibitions, and "people shows."[18] These locations became sites on the ground where

[15] See Brian Hochman, *Savage Preservation: The Ethnographic Origins of Modern Media Technology* (Minneapolis: University of Minnesota Press, 2014); Jacob W. Gruber, "Ethnographic Salvage and the Shaping of Anthropology," *American Anthropologist* 72, no. 6 (1970): 1289–99; George W. Stocking, *Victorian Anthropology* (New York: Free Press, 1987); Harry Liebersohn, *Music and the New Global Culture: From the Great Exhibitions to the Jazz Age* (Chicago: University of Chicago Press, 2019); and Kira Thurman, "Singing the Civilizing Mission in the Land of Bach, Beethoven, and Brahms: The Fisk Jubilee Singers in Nineteenth-Century Germany," special issue, *Journal of World History* 27, no. 3 (2016): 443–71.
[16] Michael Adas, *Machines as the Measure of Men: Science, Technology, and Ideologies of Western Dominance* (Ithaca, NY: Cornell University Press, 1989).
[17] Ronald Radano and Tejumola Olaniyan, eds., *Audible Empire: Music, Global Politics, Critique* (Durham, NC: Duke University Press, 2016).
[18] Eric Ames, *Carl Hagenbeck's Empire of Entertainments* (Seattle: University of Washington Press, 2008); Angela Zimmerman, *Anthropology and Antihumanism in Imperial Germany* (Chicago: University of Chicago Press, 2001); Annegret Fauser, *Musical Encounters at the 1889 Paris World's Fair* (Rochester: University of Rochester Press, 2005); Bernth Lindfors, *Early African Entertainments Abroad: From the Hottentot Venus to Africa's First Olympians*

Europeans could sonically encounter the Other – on staged, controlled, and often falsified terms.[19]

If anyone conceded that European art music was influenced by and not hermetically sealed off from the world around it, then non-European music was supposed to be the raw material to be incorporated into a more sophisticated European musical style.[20] Ironically, by the late nineteenth century, some art critics began to write that European art music was both superior to other musics and also in need of revitalization from its own modernity, which only non-European cultures could provide. A predominant question of the nineteenth century concerned how or whether different musical styles could be appropriated into a European tradition, as embodied by the rise in popularity of musical exoticism. Ralph Locke defines exoticism as "the evocation of a place, people, or social milieu that is (or is perceived or imagined to be) profoundly different from accepted local norms in its attitudes, customs, and morals."[21] Setting operas in China, Japan, Egypt, and elsewhere, white European composers turned to these far-flung locations (that they had never visited) to narrate stories of love and death. Tellingly, if composers were incorporating music by non-European musicians, it was usually Asian, Middle Eastern, or North African – not sub-Saharan African.

Regardless of locale, the problem with these forms of engaging with the non-Western world was, as Edward Said warns in his seminal text *Orientalism*, that it functioned as "a Western style for dominating, restructuring, and having authority over the Orient."[22] The relationship between Europe and the Global South was always "a relationship of power," Said writes, which made it possible for composers to imagine a world outside of their own without necessarily engaging with the people who inhabited it – on those people's terms.[23]

The "relationship of power," as Said put it, was always unstable. For to acknowledge music's ability to transform non-European peoples was to also open up the possible reality that other musics could greatly affect Europeans.

(Madison: University of Wisconsin Press, 2014); and Jane R. Goodall, *Performance and Evolution in the Age of Darwin: Out of the Natural Order* (New York: Routledge, 2002).

[19] Ames, *Carl Hagenbeck's Empire of Entertainments*, 91.

[20] Ralph P. Locke, *Musical Exoticism: Images and Reflections* (Cambridge: Cambridge University Press, 2009); Martin Clayton and Bennett Zon, eds., *Music and Orientalism in the British Empire, 1780s to 1940s: Portrayal of the East* (Aldershot and Burlington: Ashgate, 2007); Hon-Lun Yang and Michael Saffle, eds., *China and the West: Music, Representation, and Reception* (Ann Arbor: University of Michigan Press, 2017); Larry Wolff, *The Singing Turk: Ottoman Power and Operatic Emotions on the European Stage from the Siege of Vienna to the Age of Napoleon* (Stanford: Stanford University Press, 2016); and Jonathan Bellman, ed., *The Exotic in Western Music* (Boston: Northeastern University Press, 2008).

[21] Ralph P. Locke, "Exoticism," in *Oxford Music Online*, 20 January 2001, Online.

[22] Edward Said, *Orientalism* (New York: Vintage Books, 1979), 27.   [23] Ibid., 29.

As Vanessa Agnew explains, "because music has its own limited form of agency, it sometimes has the ability to surprise and disrupt our sense of ourselves and to trouble the boundaries we place on cultural difference."[24] By creating this binary that Western art music – tied to the Enlightenment – was supposed to civilize and rationalize its listener and that the music of non-Europeans was "primal" (usually located in rhythm), European musical institutions were crippled under the weight of their own anxieties and hypocrisies when confronted with musical examples that denied or defied this simple bifurcation. Often, music scholars had to deny any musical commonalities with the Global South for the sake of upholding a belief in the superiority of their own musical tradition, thus fomenting a hostile suspicion to different musical cultures. To listen to other music was to potentially make oneself vulnerable to its affect. What if white Europeans were drawn to the music of Others, almost like witchcraft, and couldn't stop themselves from swaying to its tunes?

What particularly vexed academics was the fragility of their own taxonomies. It became increasingly difficult to define just what, exactly, "pure" and untouched music from non-European peoples was. Because the invasive violence of colonialism had made it possible for academics to collect this music in the first place, it could be agony trying to figure out if the musical and cultural expressions of "primitive" non-European peoples had truly been untouched by empire. Whereas cultural mixture was to be celebrated if undertaken (in the right way) by white European composers, it was something distrustful if embraced by, say, an Indigenous Polynesian village. In this regard, academics bemoaned the loss of "authentic" non-European musical traditions. Much to their lament, Europeans could corrupt these untouched/ uncontacted tribes. Such was the case when German missionaries introduced a hymn in Samoa in 1894, only for it to be sung by Samoans on tour through Europe a few years later in 1896, now coined as an islander melody.[25] What was "authentic" anymore if everything was capable of musical and cultural mixture?

Seeking to save Indigenous musical cultures from the taint of European civilization, academics instead brushed up against the reality that perhaps Indigenous musical expressions were more complex than they could accept. The more ethnomusicologists contended with other musicking publics, the more they came up against their own limitations. Other cultures were not supposed to be able to produce complex polyphonic harmonies, for example. Yet global cultural encounters with different people constantly challenged this

---

[24] Vanessa Agnew, "Listening to Others: Eighteenth-Century Encounters in Polynesia," 170.
[25] Vanessa Agnew, "The Colonialist Beginnings of Comparative Musicology," in *Germany's Colonial Pasts*, ed. Eric Ames, Marcia Klotz, and Lora Wildenthal (Lincoln: University of Nebraska Press, 2005), 41–60, here p. 55.

refrain. Either European ethnomusicologists' writings were wrong or Indigenous musical traditions in Asia, Africa, the Middle East, and elsewhere needed to be listened to differently. Conceding that these musical styles were somehow capable of independent innovation rarely occurred – and, when mentioned, their creative capabilities were nonetheless limited by their supposed racial difference.[26]

An uneasy, ambivalent, borderline-hostile relationship to music composed by people deemed non-European and/or racialized as non-white developed across the nineteenth and twentieth centuries, perhaps best exemplified by discourses surrounding African American popular musics, notably jazz.[27] White European audiences loved this music – but also greatly feared it. African American music had of course been part of European musical culture before the 1920s. Cakewalking, Black minstrelsy, and African American spirituals had all entered popular vernacular on the European continent, and African American musicians ranging from the Fisk Jubilee Singers and Sissieretta Jones had performed in front of thousands of audiences, from royal families in the United Kingdom and Germany to social clubs in Hungary and Poland.[28] But the number of Black diasporic musicians traveling, performing, living, and settling in Europe in the 1920s and 1930s surpassed any previous generation. Flocking in droves to Paris in particular, African American musicians settled into a cultural landscape after the First World War that transformed their careers.

Some Europeans considered the presence of Black jazz musicians to be liberating. By tying Black popular performance to primitivism, European

---

[26] "If 'natural peoples' were capable of some independent musical innovation and progress, their creative abilities were nonetheless constrained by their racial type; more 'complex' musical phenomena could only be the product of correspondingly 'superior' peoples who had colonized the surrounding regions," Agnew writes. Ibid., 54.

[27] William Shack, *Harlem in Montmartre: A Paris Jazz Story between the Great Wars* (Berkeley: University of California Press, 2001); Celeste Day Moore, *Soundscapes of Liberation: African American Music in Postwar France* (Durham, NC: Duke University Press, 2021); Rashida K. Braggs, *Jazz Diasporas: Race, Music, and Migration in Post-World War II Paris* (Oakland: University of California Press, 2016); Tyler Stovall, *Paris Noir: African Americans in the City of Light* (Boston: Houghton Mifflin, 1996); Susan D. Pennybacker, *From Scottsboro to Munich: Race and Political Culture in 1930s Britain* (Princeton: Princeton University Press, 2009); George McKay, *Circular Breathing: The Cultural Politics of Jazz in Britain* (Durham, NC: Duke University Press, 2005); Marc Matera, *Black London: The Imperial Metropolis and Decolonization in the Twentieth Century* (Berkeley: University of California Press, 2015); Jonathan O. Wipplinger, *The Jazz Republic: Music, Race, and American Culture in Weimar Germany* (Ann Arbor: University of Michigan Press, 2017).

[28] See, for example, Kira Thurman, *Singing like Germans: Black Musicians in the Land of Bach, Beethoven, and Brahms* (Ithaca, NY: Cornell University Press, 2021); Kristin Moriah, "On the Record: Sissieretta Jones and Black Feminist Recording Praxes," *Performance Matters* 6, no. 2 (2020): 26–42; Daphne Brooks, *Bodies in Dissent: Spectacular Performances of Race and Freedom, 1850–1910* (Durham, NC: Duke University Press, 2006).

discourses praised Black jazz entertainers for supposedly freeing Europeans from their own civilization, which had crippled them in the wake of the First World War. "The Negroes are conquering Europe," Ivan Goll excitedly warned in 1926. "The Negro question is pressing for our entire civilization. It runs like this: do the Negroes need us? Or are we not sooner in need of them?"[29] Liberated from the strict and artificial confines of an overdeveloped and too sophisticated European cultural milieu, Europeans, these practitioners believed, were now free to dance with wild self-abandonment. Composers such as Ernst Krenek and Kurt Weill threw themselves into blending jazz with art music. Meant to "rescue" Europe by returning it to its earlier roots, jazz functioned here narrowly as a form of radical alterity upon which Europeans could flourish.

If the positive praise was damning, then racist, right-wing sentiments were even worse. The idea that Black diasporic peoples could contribute anything musically to Europe was an affront. To dance to this music was to engage in acts of degeneracy and debauchery, pure proof that Europe was sinking into decline and its youthful populations needed to be protected from such foreign elements. To that end, it was not uncommon for European politicians and statesmen to wade into music's culture wars. An Irish bishop denounced jazz in 1926.[30] A Hungarian baron founded a movement in Hungary to curtail jazz's effects on the youth.[31] Everyone from foreign ministers of Sweden to Bulgarian socialites hosting balls in the capital city of Sofia weighed in on jazz's invasive nature in European cultural life – much to the detriment of performers of color, who often faced violence or threats of violence for their musicianship.

Unfortunately, over time the public face of European music has stubbornly remained the same: white Europeans, usually men, in a classical canon. Listeners have taken great care with their compositions, whether in the form of musical exoticism or not, and some scholars still treat their works as if they were composed in a vacuum, sealed off from global developments. If there was an acknowledgment of non-European musical cultures, it had to come from ethnomusicology, from the ethnographic event, from the ethnographic field-work, from the colonial encounter with the Other.

-

[29] Ivan Goll, "The Negroes Are Conquering Europe," in *The Weimar Republic Sourcebook*, ed. Anton Kaes, Martin Jay, and Edward Dimendberg (Berkeley: University of California Press, 1994), 559–60, which was first published in 1926.
[30] "An Irish Ireland: Archbishop Denounces Jazz," *The Irish Times*, 10 August 1926, 5.
[31] "Anti-Jazz: Princess Leads New Movement in Hungary," *The Observer*, 11 April 1926, 12.

But a funny thing happened on the way to the ethnographic event. These boundaries between the supposedly white, male, European musical genre of art music and a non-European "primitive" world began to fracture. In academic discourses, scholars first began their assault on the canon in the 1980s and 1990s by critiquing the idea that European art music belongs to the purview of primarily white European men at all. Led by the "New Musicologists," their research questioned the field's obsession with musical analysis divorced from any cultural-historical contextualization and pointed out – and thereby challenged – the canon's construction.[32] Bringing feminist theory to bear on musical analysis, scholars such as Marcia Citron, Catherine Clément, and Susan McClary exposed the sexist and misogynistic underpinnings of an overwhelmingly masculine canon, whether in the form of gendered language positioning feminine subjectivity as "weak" or by illustrating the violent nature of opera that fixates on the demise of women.[33] For the New Musicologists, it was essential to undermine the elitism of the classical music tradition and flatten the hierarchies within it.[34]

Second, scholars began to question the purpose of studying music as a work-object in itself.[35] In this regard, Christopher Small's book *Musicking* broke new ground in musicology and has since become mandatory reading for cultural historians as well. It deserves even greater recognition among historians. Knocking down the Eurocentric idea that the musical "work" object – a musical score that you can physically pull up and put down – is the primary

---

[32] Joseph Kerman, *Contemplating Music: Challenges to Musicology* (Cambridge, MA: Harvard University Press, 1985); Lawrence Kramer, *Music as Cultural Practice, 1800–1900* (Berkeley: University of California Press, 1990); Olivia Bloechl, Melanie Lowe, and Jeffrey Kallberg, eds., *Rethinking Difference in Music Scholarship* (Cambridge: Cambridge University Press, 2015); Georgia Born and David Hesmondhalgh, eds., *Western Music and Its Others: Difference, Representation, and Appropriation in Music* (Berkeley: University of California Press, 2000); and Julie Brown, ed., *Western Music and Race* (Cambridge: Cambridge University Press, 2007).

[33] Marcia J. Citron, *Gender and the Musical Canon* (Cambridge: Cambridge University Press, 1993); Catherine Clément, *Opera, or the Undoing of Women* (Minneapolis: University of Minnesota Press, 1988), which was first published in 1979; Susan McClary, *Feminine Endings: Music, Gender, and Sexuality* (Minneapolis: University of Minnesota Press, 1990); Ruth A. Solie, ed., *Musicology and Difference: Gender and Sexuality in Music Scholarship* (Berkeley: University of California Press, 1993); Philip Brett, Elizabeth Wood, and Gary C. Thomas, eds., *Queering the Pitch: The New Gay and Lesbian Musicology* (New York and London: Routledge, 1994); and Suzanne G. Cusick, "Gender, Musicology, and Feminism," in *Rethinking Music*, ed. Nicholas Cook and Mark Everist (Oxford: Oxford University Press, 1999), 471–98.

[34] Ethnomusicologists and music studies scholars have of course long taken up this cause. See, for example, Philip V. Bohlman, *Focus: Music, Nationalism, and the Making of the New Europe* (New York: Routledge, 2011); and Ronald Radano and Philip V. Bohlman, eds., *Music and the Racial Imagination* (Chicago: University of Chicago Press, 2000).

[35] See Joseph Kerman's famous essay, "How We Got into Analysis, and How to Get out," *Critical Inquiry* 7, no. 2 (1980): 311–31.

way to think about music, Small proposes instead that we consider who is involved in the act of music-making. The question, for Small, is not: "What is the nature or meaning of this work of music?" To ask so "leaves us trapped in the assumptions of the modern Western concert tradition."[36] Rather, the more important question to ask is: "What does it mean when this performance (of this work) takes place at this time, in this place, with these participants?"[37] Small's pertinent questions opened up space in academic scholarship for a more expansive understanding of how to study music and, more importantly, its makers.

What if we were to take Small's definition of musicking as the basis on which we are to understand global musical exchange? In other words: What if instead of focusing on the musical "work" – which, Small argues, doesn't exist independently of the performer anyway – we were to focus on the people *doing* the work? What if we move beyond the pages of the score to instead uncover, detect, and interrogate the names of those involved in producing, disseminating, listening to, and evaluating a musical event?[38]

The advantages to switching our focus are many. By dismantling European art music as an object at the center of our analysis, we no longer privilege or create a hierarchy of music-making that ignores so many participants. Moreover, doing so encourages us to see the richness of European engagements with global events but in a way that takes seriously the agency of musicians beyond white European men. Instead of becoming trapped in a cycle that reduces intercultural contact to a process whereby either Europe influences the world or the world influences Europe, it would behoove scholars to consider how people are co-constituting musical styles and worlds. In her article on the Japanese opera singer Miura Tamaki, musicologist and American studies scholar Mari Yoshihara proposes exactly that same methodological scrutiny. She writes that recognizing how multiple agents can participate in the production of musical discourses "enables us to see that cultural hegemony operates in ways much more complex than a one-directional flow of power from the West to the rest."[39] Resisting the "West and the rest" framework is imperative to creating new histories that involve European music-making.[40]

---

[36] Christopher Small, *Musicking: The Meanings of Performing and Listening* (Hanover: University Press of New England, 1998), 10.

[37] Ibid., 10.

[38] Keith Negus and Hyunjoon Shin, "Eurasian Entanglements: Notes towards a Planetary Perspective of Popular Music Histories," *Popular Music* 40, no. 1 (2021): 158–64.

[39] Mari Yoshihara, "The Flight of the Japanese Butterfly: Orientalism, Nationalism, and Performances of Japanese Womanhood," *American Quarterly* 56, no. 4 (2004): 975–1001, here p. 998.

[40] Stuart Hall, "The West and the Rest: Discourse and Power," in *Essential Essays*, vol. 2, *Identity and Diaspora*, ed. David Morley (Durham, NC: Duke University Press, 2018), 141–84, which was first published in 1992.

The examples of European engagement with global musical forces abound – if and when we know how to look for it.[41]

Let us return to Small's central question: "What does it mean when this performance (of this work) takes place at this time, in this place, with these participants?"[42] Each of Small's clauses suggests a revisiting of fundamental aspects of musical performances that can be reworked. Let us divide them up accordingly.

"At this time." Avoiding teleological narratives of progress, we can be sensitive to historically contingent factors that determine a musical act in a global world. European art music was never divorced from global elements, and indeed was often called upon to celebrate them, whether in the form of Bach's *Coffee Cantata* or Verdi's opera *Aida*, which heralded the opening of the Suez Canal. Music-making was also imbricated in the project of empire. Some recent scholarship has begun to investigate how figures such as the composer Handel participated in the transatlantic slave trade.[43] Others are noting how much Western art music became a tool of empire, whether through a civilizing mission ideology or as a means to instill cultural values across the Global South, during and after the era of decolonization.[44] The building of opera houses in North Africa, southeast Asia, and Latin America, and the coronation of church organs in Lagos, Nigeria or Accra, Ghana have become important historical moments that allow historians to rewrite histories of European music-making in a way that takes into better account the wider range of agents involved in music's construction.[45] By placing European music-making in a global time frame, newer stories and personalities abound that are ripe for investigation.

"In this place." Opera houses, philharmonic halls, music clubs, and dance halls have all functioned as spaces of global musical encounter that bring

---

[41] A new wave of scholarship in musicology writing global histories of music are proving this point. See Olivia Bloechl, Hedy Law (Convenor), Olivia Bloechl, Jessica Bissett Perea, Alexandria Carrico, Parkorn Wangpaiboonkit, Pablo Palomino, and Daniel F. Castro Pantoja, "Forum: Centering Discomfort in Global Music History," in *Journal of Musicology* 40, no. 3 (1 July 2023): 249–307; Gavin Lee and Christopher Miller, "Introduction to the Special Issue on Global Musical Modernisms" in *Twentieth-Century Music* 20 no. 3 (2023): 274–91.

[42] Small, *Musicking*, 10.

[43] David Hunter, "Handel Manuscripts and the Profits of Slavery: The 'Granville' Collection at the British Library and the First Performing Score of *Messiah* Reconsidered," *Notes* 76, no. 1 (2019): 27–37; and Ellen T. Harris, "Critical Exchanges: Handel and Slave-Trading Companies," *Music and Letters* 103, no. 3 (2022): 541–8, are examples.

[44] Caroline Ritter, *Imperial Encore: The Cultural Project of the Late British Empire* (Oakland: University of California Press, 2021); and Jann Pasler, "The Utility of Musical Instruments in the Racial and Colonial Agendas of Late Nineteenth-Century France," *Journal of the Royal Musical Association* 129, no. 1 (2004): 24–76.

[45] Parkorn Wangpaiboonkit, "Voice, Race, and Imperial Ethnology in Colonial Siam: *Madama Butterfly* at the Court of Chulalongkorn," *The Opera Quarterly* 36, nos. 3/4 (2020): 123–51.

together different interlocutors to participate in a cultural moment. For example, in her book on Hamburg's raucous rock and roll scene, Julia Sneeringer examines the role of underground music halls where young teenagers encountered the Beatles and Rolling Stones to illustrate how one particular place can build a musical culture. Sneeringer writes: "A social history of early rock'n'roll in Hamburg offers an alternative German history from the perspective of a place built on self-expression and bodily liberation – impulses from the margins that became culturally central as the Sixties progressed."[46] Studying one square mile of St. Pauli's famous entertainment district – a port city with long ties to colonialism and a greater world of merchants and markets – Sneeringer successfully demonstrates how different people came and went through it. In St. Pauli, Dutch "Indo-rock" bands made of Indonesian and Moluccan migrants played music "laced with Hawaiian and Krontjong musical elements" along with African American groups and others.[47]

Patron-endorsed spaces have long continuous lives, becoming institutions unto themselves. The electronic music that people danced to in sweaty clubs represented a key nexus of musical and cultural activity of intense collaboration between actors from within and outside of Europe. The birth of disco, for example, brought together musicians from around the Americas, Europe, and elsewhere onto shared dance floors in cities such as Ibiza, Detroit, and Berlin. In the city of Berlin, the club Berghain became a symbol of post-1989 collapse and rebirth. As one "Techno tourist" in Berlin reflected: "Berlin was like an island, it collected many people who thought differently and had different ideas about how things could work. Open-minded people. In German we use the word *querdenker* – mavericks."[48] In the club, on the dance floor, patrons embraced new beats, melodies, and rhythms and forged their own communities. "Although Germany has been framed in the historiography of electronic dance music as fertile ground for electronics-driven popular genres," Luis Manuel-Garcia writes, "this cultural fertility has arisen out of contact with 'foreign' influences such as African American dance music, Italo-Disco, and pan-European synthpop."[49] Emerging out of intercultural contact, the sounds emanating from disco floors that came to dominate radios around the world

---

[46] Julia Sneeringer, *A Social History of Early Rock 'n' Roll in Germany: Hamburg from Burlesque to the Beatles, 1956–1969* (London: Bloomsbury Academic, 2018), 2.
[47] Ibid., 52.
[48] Matthew Collin, *Rave On: Global Adventures in Electronic Dance Music* (London: Serpent's Tail, 2018), 52.
[49] Luis-Manuel Garcia, "'With Every Inconceivable Finesse, Excess, and Good Music': Sex, Affect, and Techno at Snax Club in Berlin," in *Dreams of Germany: Musical Imaginaries from the Concert Hall to the Dance Floor*, ed. Neil Gregor and Thomas Irvine (New York: Berghahn Books, 2019), 73–96, here p. 74.

illustrate the importance of dance clubs as sites of aesthetic inspiration, transformation, and even revolution.

Similarly, musical spaces have functioned as vital sites of musical and cultural collaboration across diasporas. A vibrant transatlantic and transnational network brought together from musicians across the British Empire to London, Manchester, and other cities to perform calypso and jazz in clubs in the 1920s and 1930s, perhaps best embodied in the formidable institution known as the Florence Mills Club, which invited people of African descent to share dance floors and musical moments. Lionel Yard described it as "a calypso club with bamboo decorations, creole food, and the haunting melody of American jazz and blues."[50] In the post-1945 era, Black communities in Great Britain later encountered Jamaican reggae in spaces unique to them: their own neighborhoods. Because the BBC refused to play reggae on radio stations throughout the 1970s, Black musicians traveled in vans blasting the music out of stereo systems to neighborhoods of West Indians and their descendants. In this manner, reggae not only thrived but found new homes and new modes of expression from up-and-coming British musicians and songwriters.

"With these participants." In addition to considering space, we can sidestep the usual figures that public discourse holds up as imperative to histories of music-making by asking ourselves instead the question: *who else* musicks and why? Scholars have pointed out everything from European missionaries to East Africa participating in church services to pirates singing shanty tunes on boats in the Polynesian islands. For the purposes of this chapter, I focus on Europeans of color, especially in the wake of decolonization, who have been at the forefront of creating new musical worlds and pushing musical boundaries for decades. Here, we find not only untold stories but also new practices of music-making that resist our current definitions of European music.

The immense, transformative nature of decolonization undergirds our histories of European popular and musical cultures, even if it has yet to be established at the center of many music histories. As Fatima El-Tayeb points out, "in public narratives colonialism is remembered as having taken place outside of Europe (if it is remembered at all)." Locating colonial histories anywhere but in Europe, many narratives of empire thus often isolate white European citizens from colonialism as an everyday experience.[51] But, as Edward Said writes: "Imperialism did not end, did not suddenly become 'past' once decolonization had set in motion the dismantling of the classical

---

[50] Matera, *Black London*, 146.
[51] Historians have pushed back against this line of thought for decades. See, for example, Catherine Hall and Sonya O. Rose, eds., *At Home with the Empire: Metropolitan Culture and the Imperial World* (Cambridge: Cambridge University Press, 2006); and the chapters in Frederick Cooper and Ann Laura Stoler, eds., *Tensions of Empire: Colonial Cultures in a Bourgeois World* (Berkeley: University of California Press, 2006).

empires."[52] Decolonization not only meant the liberation of the Global South from European empires but, equally as important, an even greater surge of communities from Africa, Asia, the Caribbean, and the Middle East to the former metropole. "Decolonization," Elizabeth Buettner writes, "was never merely a chronologically and politically contained 'transfer of power' from rule by Europeans to independence as new Asian, African, and Caribbean nations after 1945."[53] Rather, decolonization was and remains a "dialogue with the colonial past," Arjun Appadurai argues.[54]

More importantly, decolonization sped up even faster the redefinition of just who was a European as well. As even more communities of color built their lives and passed on their cultural and musical experiences to later generations in places ranging from London to Moscow, they transformed the metropole into younger and more diverse spaces.[55] European musicians of color, from Sade, the R&B group Milli Vanilli, and Charli XCX, to KT Tunstall, Eagle-Eye Cherry, the dance-pop group Army of Lovers, and Belgian-Vietnamese singer Quynh Anh, are and have been "as European as those worrying about them," Fatima El-Tayeb quips.[56]

The explosion of music-making and cultural hybridity that has taken place in the wake of decolonization has been astonishing. Vibrant, genre-bending, and boundary-pushing musical styles have taken over our sonic landscapes since the post-1945 era, offering up to millions of listeners music that is both global and European. What these different musical styles and traditions illustrate, Fatima El-Tayeb argues, is "a process long in the making, namely the emergence of multicultural minority communities in continental European urban centers characterized by the ambiguous and precarious living conditions of its inhabitants."[57] In other words, the music histories of Europeans of color since 1945 are fascinating, fresh histories of cultural and musical development, often sparked and/or inspired by global cultural contact.

Because decolonization brought even more people from the colonies to the metropole, the music they brought with them altered Europe's musical landscape and fostered the creation and cultivation of entirely new musical styles, languages, and ideas. For example, Cabo Verdeans, under some form of Portuguese rule since the fifteenth century, dispersed throughout Europe in

[52] Edward Said, *Culture and Imperialism* (New York: Vintage, 1994), 278.
[53] Elizabeth Buettner, *Europe after Empire: Decolonization, Society, and Culture* (Cambridge: Cambridge University Press, 2016), 4; see also Paul Gilroy, *Postcolonial Melancholia* (New York: Columbia University Press, 2004).
[54] Arjun Appadurai, *Modernity at Large: Cultural Dimensions of Globalization* (Minneapolis: University of Minnesota Press, 1996), 89.
[55] Fatima El-Tayeb, *European Others: Queering Ethnicity in Postnational Europe* (Minneapolis: University of Minnesota Press, 2011), xii.
[56] Ibid., xii.   [57] Ibid., 13.

the wake of war and decolonization in the 1970s. Residing in greater numbers outside of Cape Verde than in the archipelago and island country, their presence in Europe changed the popular charts, turning the singer Val Xalino into a popular musical icon in Sweden, for example. Similarly, Surinamese jazz musicians such as Ronald Snijders became integral to the Dutch jazz scene, bridging Surinamese *kaseko* with atonal jazz musical practices. Decolonization has also produced the genre of batida (Portuguese for "my beat" or "my crew's beats"), which brought music from the former Portuguese colony of Angola to the metropole of Lisbon, creating a new electronic dance music practice using Afrobeat and Angolan drumming in the underground club scene. In France, the popular dance style of French Zouk in the 1970s and 1980s combined Caribbean dance styles such as merengue and salsa with disco in the 1970s. The all-female Guadeloupe-based musical group Zouk Machine became a blockbuster hit in France in the 1980s and 1990s with songs such as "Maldon." Similarly, the band Kassav's song "Zouk-la sé sel médikaman nou ni" also became a global hit.[58]

The unmistakable traces of reggae in the music of British acts such as Culture Club or Sting and The Police have less to do with Jamaican reggae than with the birth of roots reggae that emerged out of West Indian diasporic communities in United Kingdom.[59] Blasted from the stereo systems of cars through West Indian neighborhoods in British cities such as Birmingham, Liverpool, and Leeds, Jamaican reggae found an audience in younger generations of West Indian Britons, who in turn created their own reggae music that expressed their experiences of being Black in the United Kingdom.[60] Their music was at once popular, global, and hyperlocal. For example, the musical group Steel Pulse, formed in Birmingham, became the first non-Jamaican act to win a Grammy for Best Reggae Album. Aswad, a London-based musical group whose moniker is Arabic for "black," turned out popular numbers such as "Don't Turn Around," which the Swedish pop group Ace of Base later used

---

[58] See Jocelyne Guilbault, *Zouk: World Music in the West Indies* (Chicago: University of Chicago Press, 1993); and Paul Cohen, "Zouk Is the Only Medicine We Need: Kassav and the Cultural Politics of Music in the French Caribbean," *French Historical Studies* 45, no. 2 (2022): 319–53.

[59] See Peter Hughes Jachimiak, "'Curious Roots & Crafts': Record Shops and Record Labels amid the British Reggae Diaspora," in *Narratives from beyond the UK Reggae Bassline: The System Is Sound*, ed. William "Lez" Henry and Matthew Worley (Cham: Palgrave Macmillan, 2021), 209–32; Jon Stratton, *When Music Migrates: Crossing British and European Racial Faultlines, 1945–2010* (Burlington,: Ashgate, 2014); Paul Oliver, ed., *Black Music in Britain: Essays on the Afro-Asian Contribution to Popular Music* (Milton Keynes: Open University Press, 1990). For recent scholarship illustrating the legacies of decolonization on musical development, see Keith Negus and Adrian Sledmere, "Postcolonial Paths of Pop: A Suburban Psychogeography of George Michael and Wham!" *Popular Music* 41, no. 2 (2022): 131–51

[60] Kennetta Hammond Perry, *London Is the Place for Me: Black Britons, Citizenship, and the Politics of Race* (New York: Oxford University Press, 2015); Rob Waters, *Thinking Black: Britain, 1964–1985* (Oakland: University of California Press, 2018).

as a cover for their own popular hit. Both musical acts comprised British-born descendants of Jamaicans.

Not only did Black British reggae crash across global radio waves; its cultural and political power transformed British social worlds. After the white British guitarist Eric Clapton declared his support for Enoch Powell, whose racist "Rivers of Blood" speech decried Great Britain's growing and thriving Black communities, musicians formed the eponymous "Rock Against Racism" event in 1976. In a letter to the popular British magazine *NME*, Red Saunders railed:

> When I read about Eric Clapton's Birmingham concert when he urged support for Enoch Powell, I nearly puked. What's going on, Eric? You've got a touch of brain damage. So you're going to stand for MP and you think we're being colonised by black people. Come on ... Own up. Half your music is black. You're rock music's biggest colonist. You're a good musician but where would you be without the blues and R&B?[61]

Bringing together audiences and political activists across the genres of punk, reggae, and rock, "Rock Against Racism" illustrated the potential power of Black European music-making to challenge worldviews and fight the tide of racist and xenophobic ideologies.

As cultural historians begin to write histories of the 1980s – the Thatcher era, the fall of communism, etc. – it has become imperative to consider another postcolonial musical output that was routinely on the forefront of criticizing European states: hip hop.[62] It's not simply or only that major musicians have come out of Europe through the genre of hip hop, such as MC Solaar or M.I.A. European hip hop has also produced entirely new globally influenced musical genres, such as British grime or Asian underground. Turning to Afrobeat, bhangra, jazz fusion, or other musical styles, European hip hop has developed musical languages and forms that are uniquely their own.[63] Perhaps no greater example of that exists than that of British grime, which took Afrobeat and Caribbean dancehall music and created a genre of electronic music instantly recognizable for its low bassline and spitfire vocals.

---

[61] David Widgery, *Beating Time: Riot 'n' Race 'n' Rock 'n' Roll* (London: Chatto and Windus, 1986), 40; see also Ashley Dawson, "'Love Music, Hate Racism': The Cultural Policies of the Rock against Racism Campaigns, 1976–81," *Postmodern Culture* 16, no. 1 (2005), Online; and Paul Gilroy, *There Ain't No Black in the Union Jack: The Cultural Politics of Race and Nation* (Chicago: University of Chicago Press, 1987).

[62] See, for example, Felicia McCarren, *French Moves: The Cultural Politics of Le Hip Hop* (Oxford: Oxford University Press, 2013); Maria Stehle, *Ghetto Voices in Contemporary German Culture: Textscapes, Filmscapes, Soundscapes* (Rochester: Camden House, 2012); Justin Williams, *Brithop: The Politics of UK Rap in the New Century* (New York: Oxford University Press, 2021); and Adriana Helbig, *Hip Hop Ukraine: Music, Race, and African Migration* (Bloomington: Indiana University Press, 2014); J. Griffith Rollefson, *Flip the Script: European Hip Hop and the Politics of Postcoloniality* (Chicago: University of Chicago Press, 2017).

[63] Anjali Gera Roy, "Black Beats with a Punjabi Twist," *Popular Music* 32, no. 2 (2013): 241–57.

Hip hop in Europe has historically had myriad functions – musical, cultural, social, and political. First, it emerged as a powerful form of critiquing states, empires, and nations. For example, the Hustlers HC, a Sikh hip hop group from West London, rapped directly about postimperial politics on their song "Big Trouble in Little Asia."[64] Rapping in the style of New York-based hip hop group Public Enemy, Hustlers HC incorporated reggae beats, jazz fusion, and hip hop. In their song "Big Trouble in Little Asia," rappers Paul Arora and Mandeep Walia state: "You close your ears to the stories that they tell / of India in days gone by / the civilization that caused such frustration / that it had to be captured and controlled / made to fit the mould / a jewel in an empire made of gold / now it's raped and left out in the cold." Similarly, as the former East and West Germany reorganized into a new federal republic, hip hop groups such as Advanced Chemistry became a dominant force in articulating how people of color were being left out of Germany's new national imagination.[65]

But perhaps just as importantly, hip hop has functioned as a form of identity-making, allowing Europeans of color to create a "language that defines them as Europeans," to use Fatima El-Tayeb's phrase.[66] Or, to put it differently, European hip hop artists have employed "the African American musical protest strategies of hip hop, both to differentiate themselves from and relate themselves to their respective majority societies," Griff Rollefson writes.[67] Rejecting narratives of assimilation and integration that place the burden on minorities to "prove" themselves worthy of European citizenship, hip hop musicians have historically expressed their marginalization in ways that fostered opportunities for local community building.[68] Here, the flexibility of hip hop as a musical genre created by and *for* racial minorities has yielded invaluable fruit since the 1970s and 1980s. Not only did Europeans of color musically reject calls for them to "integrate" into a violent social landscape but they also used hip hop to position themselves as Europeans – on their own terms. Identifying with but not as African Americans, they rapped in their own native languages of Italian, French, German, Dutch, Hungarian, Ukrainian, and other tongues to build their own musical and cultural worlds.[69]

–

---

[64] Colin Larkin, "Hustlers HC," *The Encyclopedia of Popular Music* (Oxford: Oxford University Press, 2006).

[65] Sonya Donaldson, "After the Berlin Wall: Hip-Hop and the Politics of German Reunification," *African and Black Diaspora* 8, no. 2 (2015): 190–201.

[66] El Tayeb, *Queering Ethnicity*, xli.

[67] J. Griffith Rollefson, *Flip the Script: European Hip Hop and the Politics of Postcoloniality* (Chicago: University of Chicago Press, 2017), 2.

[68] Ibid., 4–5.   [69] El Tayeb, *Queering Ethnicity*, 30.

The more one considers how musical languages become hybridized, how they evolve, how they remain constantly in flux, the more it becomes imperative to recognize the musicians responsible for doing this important cultural work. Always in contact with and inspired by the world around them, their music-making activities were sparkling catalysts of connection and rebirth. Because European cultures have constantly changed and evolved over time, their musical worlds were never sealed off from global developments. Rather, the transnational actors involved in creating new musical communities, languages, and sounds continually brought different aesthetic and cultural values to their performances.

To put it differently, by moving away from a canon of European art music that has relegated anything outside of high art music written primarily by white European men at the center, historians can better attend to the kinds of transnational and global music-making activities that theorists have long pointed out have defined our modern world – including in Europe. Shifting our focus makes it possible to better see what Françoise Lionnet and Shu-mei Shih describe as "a space of exchange and participation wherever processes of hybridization occur and where it is still possible for cultures to be produced and performed without necessary mediation by the center."[70] In so doing, the world-changing, genre-defying musical activities of other actors become more apparent – and vital – members of our histories.

As I write this chapter, Beyoncé's album *Renaissance* is blowing up the charts, breaking records, and winning awards. An homage to her gay uncle Johnny who passed away, Beyoncé's album celebrates queer musical cultures through sonic references to the disco era, New Orleans bounce, and 1990s club culture in addition to celebrating the sounds of Afrobeat and other forms of global Black diasporic music-making. And it is worth considering not only how globally influenced it is but also how many Europeans – especially Europeans of color – were involved in the making of this blockbuster album. Some of the figures behind its production include A. G. Cook, a British producer with Israeli parents, the Nigerian British producer P2J, and GuiltyBeatz, a Ghanian DJ born in Italy. Other songs feature Black Americans who are, like many others, participants in a longer transatlantic history of Black musicians traveling to Europe. DJ Honey Dijon, a trans Black American woman based in both New York and Berlin, remixed the first single to be released from Beyoncé's album, *Break My Soul*.

Beyoncé's final track "Summer Renaissance" might be the most encompassing of European music history's global traces. Sampling from "I Feel

---

[70] Françoise Lionnet and Shu-mei Shih, "Introduction: Thinking through the Minor, Transnationally," in *Minor Transnationalism*, ed. Françoise Lionnet and Shu-mei Shih (Durham, NC: Duke University Press, 2005), 1–23, here p. 5.

Love," co-written by Italian composer Giorgio Moroder and English composer Pete Bellotte and sung by the legendary African American singer Donna Summer (who started her career in Germany), Beyoncé's celebration of love, sex, hedonism, and pleasure is steeped in a global disco era that the European continent helped to nourish. In Cold War-era Berlin, Munich, London, Paris, Ibiza, and elsewhere, disco thrummed in heady clubs, its dancers, DJs, and practitioners writhing in spaces of contact created just for them. Here, in these moments, people from around the world came together to dance to enticing beats, encounter each other, and free themselves from the confines of national borders, cultures, and expectations. Harkening back to those decades, Beyoncé's "Summer Renaissance" – produced by Leven Kali, a Black musician who grew up in the Netherlands and in the United States – is a testament to Europe's musical global past and present. And by considering European music-making in a global frame, the lives and stories of Leven Kali and others can finally become the melodies and tunes that we hear.

14   Global Histories of European Art

Caroline van Eck

Global art histories predate the emergence of art history as an academic discipline. The first chair of art history was established at the University of Berlin in 1810 and held by the art historian, archaeologist, and neoclassical theorist Alois Hirt. Its intellectual program was largely inspired by Johann Joachim Winckelmann's *Geschichte der Kunst des Altertums*, first published in 1764.[1] The first attempt at a global history of an art, however, had already been published in 1686: the *Traité des Statues*, written by François Lemée, a lawyer who produced a worldwide historical survey of the religious use of sculpture, based on travelogues, antiquarian writings, and Greco-Roman sources. Lemée wrote this book to defend Louis XIV against accusations of presumption and incitement to idolatry that arose after the inauguration of his statue on the Place des Victoires in Paris. This showed the king crowned by victory, trampling statues of the defeated nations of the Germans, Dutch, Spanish, and Turks, with the dedication "divo immortali," and endowed with a ritual of perpetual adoration that came dangerously close to the adoration of statues of God, Christ, Mary, or the saints. Lemée's book was the first of a series of histories of religious statues of global ambitions. This culminated in Antoine-Chrysostome Quatremère de Quincy's study of the statue of Zeus in Olympia, published in 1815. Here he produced a narrative of sculpture's emancipation as a fine art from its religious servitude in the Egypt of the pharaohs.[2] Starting in the seventeenth century, collections were also formed which would provide the laboratory for subsequent attempts at global art histories: the Musaeum Kircherianum in Rome, founded by the Jesuit polymath Athanasius Kirchner; and the Museo Borgiano, founded by Cardinal Stefano Borgia in Velletri, who filled the museum with the religious statuary,

---

[1] On the history of art history as a discipline, see most recently Christopher S. Wood, *A History of Art History* (Princeton: Princeton University Press, 2019); on Hirt and the Berlin Chair, see Michael Podro, *The Critical Historians of Art* (New Haven and London: Yale University Press, 1982), 1–27.

[2] On Lemée and Quatremère, see Caroline van Eck, *François Lemée et la statue de Louis XIV: Les origines des théories ethnologiques du fétichisme* (Paris: Centre Allemand d'histoire de l'art/ Maison des Sciences de l'Homme, 2013).

images, and cult objects brought back to Rome by Catholic missionaries as part of the Vatican's commitment to document all the religions of the world.[3] Vivant Denon, the first director of the Musée Napoléon, subsequently Musée du Louvre, collected artworks from all over the known world, and left an unpublished manuscript at his death setting out to write a world history of art.[4] These eighteenth-century ethnographic collections are the ancestors, together with the Kunst- and Wunderkammer of German princes, of the great anthropological museums founded in the nineteenth century. But there is a big difference. These early modern or eighteenth-century collections were driven by interests in comparative religion, princely magnificence, and Enlightenment ideals. The major nineteenth-century institutions were all the product of colonial empires. The Pitt-Rivers Museum in Oxford (founded in 1884), the Museum of Natural History in New York (1869), or the Musée d'Ethnographie du Trocadéro in Paris (1878) all owed their collections to a very large degree to colonial expeditions. The trajectory of some of these institutions, and the changes in their nomenclature, reflect their troubled history and the challenges they pose today. Thus the Musée d'Ethnographie was refounded as the Musée de l'Homme in 1937 and in 2006 moved to the Quai Branly in its latest incarnation as a Musée des Arts Premiers. The ethnographical collections in Berlin, probably the largest in the world, embody this trajectory even more clearly. They go back to the Kunst- and Wunderkammer of the prince-electors of Brandenburg, and were inherited by the Hohenzollern Prussian kings. They were opened to the public in 1829 as the Ethnographische Sammlung. After the Second World War they were housed in the Berlin suburb of Dahlem and renamed as an Ethnological Museum; and after a long period of closure they are now on display at the Humboldt Forum in 2020, where a great effort is made to show the provenance of each of the constituting collections.[5]

---

[3] Georgius de Sepibus, ed., *The Celebrated Museum of the Roman College of the Society of Jesus: A Facsimile of the 1678 Amsterdam Edition of Giorgio de Sepi's Description of Athanasius Kircher's Museum* "Musæum Celeberrimum Collegii Romani Societatis Jesu" (Philadelphia: Saint Joseph's University Press, 2015); Paula Findlen, *Athanasius Kircher: The Last Man Who Knew Everything* (New York: Routledge 2004); and Marco Nocca, *Le quattro voci del mondo: arte, culture e saperi nella collezione di Stefano Borgia 1731–1804* (Naples: Electa, 2001).

[4] Dominique Vivant-Denon and Amaury Pineu Duval, *Monuments des arts du dessin chez les peuples tant anciens que modernes* (Paris: Brunet Denon, 1829).

[5] The bibliography on these developments is vast. See for instance Joseph Alsop, *The Rare Art Traditions: The History of Art Collecting and Its Linked Phenomena Wherever These Have Appeared* (New York: Harper & Row, 1982); Tony Bennett, *The Birth of the Museum: History, Theory, Politics* (London and New York: Routledge, 1995); Samuel Quiccheberg, *The First Treatise on Museums: Samuel Quiccheberg's Inscriptiones, 1565*, trans. Mark A. Meadow and Bruce Robertson (Los Angeles: Getty Research Centre, 2013); James J. Sheehan, *Museums in the German Art World: From the End of the Old Regime to the Rise of Modernism* (Oxford: Oxford University Press, 2000); Tim Barringer and Tom Flynn, eds., *Colonialism and the*

Lemée's *Traité des statues* was still firmly anchored in a Catholic and absolutist agenda; its survey of statuary across the world served as a defense against Protestant accusations of idolatry. In a similar vein, Bernard Picart and Jean Frédéric Bernard's *Cérémonies et coutumes religieuses de tous les peuples du monde* (1723–37) set out to document world religion to demonstrate the superiority of Christianity, but actually served as a major source for Enlightenment critiques of that claim, and provided a vast visual compendium of what we would now call the material culture of religion (Figure 14.1).[6]

Throughout the early modern period, European countries engaged with art from other parts of the world. The trade empires of Portugal, the Dutch Republic, Britain, and France imported artifacts from India, China, Japan, and the Americas, which contributed to fashions for Chinese, Japanese, or Indian art, but they also brought European art to their colonies and trade partners. In China, for instance, the landscape art and engravings of cities and townscapes brought by Jesuit missionaries led to significant stylistic changes in Chinese landscape painting; but conversely the arrival of Chinese porcelain or Japanese lacquer in Europe led to transformations of interior design and collecting crazes, as recorded in the still lifes of Willem Kalff.[7]

Object: Empire, Material Culture and the Museum (London: Routledge, 1998); Donald Preziosi and Claire Farago, eds., *Grasping the World: The Idea of the Museum* (Aldershot: Ashgate, 2004) is a very useful sourcebook. On the Paris museums, see Sally Price, *Paris Primitive: Jacques Chirac's Museum on the Quai Branly* (Chicago: Chicago University Press, 2007); and Nélia Dias, *Le Musée d'Ethnographie du Trocadéro (1878–1908): anthropologie et muséologie en France* (Paris: Editions du CNRS, 1991); on Pitt-Rivers see William Ryan Chapman, "Arranging Ethnology: A. H. L. F. Pitt Rivers and the Typological Tradition," in *Objects and Others: Essays on Museums and Material Culture*, ed. George W. Stocking, Jr. (Madison: University of Wisconsin Press, 1985), 15–48; on the Berlin museum, see Sigrid Westphal-Hellbusch, "Hundert Jahre Museum für Völkerkunde Berlin: Zur Geschichte des Museums," special issue, *Baessler-Archiv: Beiträge zur Völkerkunde* 21 (1973): 1–99.

[6] Lynn Hunt, *The Book that Changed Europe: Picart and Bernard's "Religious Ceremonies of the World"* (Cambridge, MA: Harvard University Press, 2010).

[7] On artistic exchanges between China and Europe see Lianming Wang, "Europerie und Macht: Akteure und Publika der transkulturellen Bilderbauten aus der Regierungszeit des Kaisers Qianlong," in *Wechselblicke: Zwischen China und Europa 1669–1907*, ed. Matthias Weiß, Eva-Maria Troelenberg, and Joachim Brand (Berlin: Michael Imhof, 2017), 56–77; Petra ten-Doesschate Chu and Ning Ding, eds., *Qing Encounters: Artistic Exchanges between China and the West* (Los Angeles: Getty Research Institute, 2015), 95–110; Greg M. Thomas, "Yuanming/ Yuan-Versailles: Intercultural Interactions between Chinese and European Palace Cultures," *Art History* 32, no. 1 (2009): 115–43; on the Jesuit encounter with China see also John Parker, *Windows into China: The Jesuits and Their Books, 1580–1730* (Boston: Trustees of the Public Library of the City of Boston, 1978); for case studies of the trajectories of Chinese objects to Europe and their appreciation see the special issue of the *Rijksmuseum Bulletin* 63, no. 4 (2015).

Figure 14.1 "Diverses pagodes et pénitences des faquirs," printed in Bernard Picart's *Histoire des religions et des moeurs de tous les peoples du monde*, Paris, 1726.
Source: Public domain.

It is against this background of religious and political controversy, Enlightenment quests for the origins of human culture, expanding trade empires, and colonialism that the first essays in world histories of art must be considered. Architectural history played a pioneering role here. Johann Bernhard Fischer von Erlach's inclusion of Turkish, Syrian, Arabian, Persian, Siamese, Chinese, and Indian monuments in his *Entwurff einer historischen Architectur* (1721) is generally considered as the first global history of architecture, but it is in fact a *livresque* projection of biblical and ancient history onto architecture, visualized through the adaptation of images in travelogues and the tradition of the Seven Wonders of the Ancient World. Next, the French architects and historians Julien-David Leroy and Jean-Nicolas-Louis Durand laid the foundation for a visual, comparative analysis of building types and structures across the world, which would continue to be a major model for architectural history to the present day, as is attested by the handbooks by Banister Fletcher, *A History of Architecture on the Comparative*

Method (1898), still much used, or Jarzombek, Prakash, and Ching, *A Global History of Architecture* (2010).[8] Until the recent wave of global histories of architecture, however, these panoramas were largely structured around European construction types such as the vault and a very European – that is classical – view of architecture, imposing for instance the Western distinction between surface ornament and deep structure, or the five orders of architecture on the building styles of China or Japan.[9]

If we leave architectural history aside and turn to the visual and decorative arts, we can broadly distinguish three varieties of world art histories written in Europe, which succeed in chronological order but do not entirely replace each other: those driven by religious concerns briefly mentioned earlier; global concept-based projects inspired by nineteenth-century developments in psychology, anthropology, or the life sciences; and globalization studies. At present we see a renewal of global art history conceived as a history of the mobility of objects, creating transcultural practices across parts of the world connected by the rise of global commercial empires. The trade routes between China and the Dutch, British, and French empires, for instead, led not only to the craze for all things Chinese in the West but also to what one might call "Occidenterie" in China.[10] In this chapter, I first discuss these varieties and their development, and then turn to French eighteenth-century art, in particular the rococo, which at present has become one of the most thriving fields for the globalization of the discipline.

-

The development of a globalizing historiography of art is intimately connected to the arrival of objects from all over the world in Europe. In antiquity, successive waves of political and trade connectivity, from the Bronze Age, through the Hellenistic to the Roman imperial period, led to the migration of materials, techniques, and artistic styles across the Mediterranean basin. Thus Egyptian forms and crafts traveled to the kingdoms of the Middle East.[11] During the Hellenistic period, Alexandria became the marketplace for goods

[8] Sir Banister Fletcher, *A History of Architecture on the Comparative Method* (London: B. T. Batsford, 1896), which was most recently republished as *Sir Banister Fletcher's Global History of Architecture, ed. Murray Fraser*, 2 vols. (London: Bloomsbury, 2019); and Francis D. K. Ching, Mark Jarzombek, and Vikramaditya Prakash, *A Global History of Architecture* (London: John Wiley, 2010).

[9] The chapters in Matteo Burioni, ed., *Weltgeschichten der Architektur: Ursprünge, Narrative, Bilder 1700–2016* (Passau: Dietmar Klinger Verlag, 2016).

[10] Nebahat Avcioğlu and Finbarr Barry Flood, "Introduction," special issue, *Ars Orientalis*, 39 (2010): 7–38.

[11] Marian H. Feldman, *Diplomacy by Design: Luxury Arts and an "International Style" in the Ancient Near East, 1400–1200 BCE* (Chicago: University of Chicago Press, 2006).

to arrive from all over the known world and a hub for artistic and scientific innovation. From Alexandria, Egyptian and Greek styles migrated to imperial Rome, where stylistic elements from all the parts of the empire were incorporated and the first attempts were made to think about artistic development in terms of regions, for instance in Quintilian's classification of both rhetoric and sculpture as Attic, Rhodian, or Asian.[12] Such connectivity was accelerated in the early modern period, with the opening up of trade routes to the Americas and Asia. As mentioned, colonial trade and conquest and the missionary collecting of religious artifacts, led to the first essays in world art history and the creation of displays and visual compendia in the seventeenth and eighteenth centuries.[13]

The Great Exhibition of 1851 was in many respects the culmination of these successive waves of global connectivity, but it added two major new elements: It was the first time an exhibition was organized showing art and artifacts from all over the world, whose selection was determined in conversation with participating countries, not imposed by a colonizing European power; and its display was based on organizing principles that reflected emerging concepts of a global history of human material culture. The guiding spirit behind this second innovation was the German architect and theorist Gottfried Semper. Inspired by what he saw at the Great Exhibition, he developed what may be called the first concept-based history of world material culture. Inspired by the bamboo hut from the Caraibes, he posited four "primitive" crafts – weaving, ceramics, masonry, and carpentry – as the basic elements from which all artifacts are made. The origin of architecture was the creation of space by means of using textiles to demarcate an interior from an exterior. Material culture then developed by means of the migration or *Stoffwechslung* of crafts and techniques from one material or art form to another, and from the ephemeral to the monumental. Textiles, for instance, originating in ancient Egypt, migrated to the Middle East, where it was first used to demarcate space and next represented in another medium, that of terracotta tiles used to create solid walls; in the subsequent phase the ephemeral tapestries used in Roman triumphs were represented in marble triumphal arches.[14] Although subsequent

---

[12] Quintilian, *Institutio Oratoria* II.xiii, ed. Tobias Reinhardt and Michael Winterbottom (Oxford: Oxford University Press, 2006), 9–11, which was first published in the year 92. On style in Graeco-Roman sculpture the fundamental recent study is Tonio Hölscher's *The Language of Images in Roman Art* (Cambridge: Cambridge University Press, 2004); see also Miguel John Versluys, *Visual Style and Constructing Identity in the Hellenistic World: Nemrud Dağ and Commagene under Antiochos I* (Cambridge and New York: Cambridge University Press, 2016).

[13] Nebahat Avcioğlu and Anne Lafont, eds., *1740, Un Abrégé du Monde: Savoirs et collections autour de Dezallier d'Argenville* (Lyon: Fage, 2012), for instance.

[14] Caroline van Eck, "Masking, Dressing, Tattooing and Cannibalism: From Architectural History to the Anthropology of Art," in *Architectural History and Globalized Knowledge: Gottfried*

historians, chief among them Alois Riegl, refuted many of Semper's conjectures, particularly about the primacy of textiles, the conceptual richness, intellectual scope, and wealth of archaeological and anthropological data of Semper's main work *Der Stil* (1860–3) remain at the center of current thought about human material culture. Even though ethnographic knowledge has expanded immeasurably since the 1850s and 1860s, and the conceptual armature is very different, Philippe Descola's recent structuralist theories of human image making as embodying four different ontologies are a late descendant of Semper in their shared ambition to provide a systematic or structuralist conceptual scaffolding to study global material culture.[15]

Semper's work was an important factor in the development of the so-called Vienna School around 1900. Its most influential representative, Alois Riegl, was a keeper of tapestries in the imperial Habsburg collections, and here we see again how the arrival of hitherto unknown artifacts forced art historians to think about art in a context beyond Europe. Starting from Semper's method of tracing the transformation of motifs and the representation of techniques in different media, he developed a method of formal analysis of ornamental patterns, in which the notion of *Kunstwollen* was introduced to explain the dynamics of such transformations. At the same time the Berlin art historian Karl Woermann published the first modern world art history, from the prehistory to the nineteenth century: *Die Kunst aller Zeiten und Völker* was published in six volumes between 1900 and 1911 (Figure 14.2). This was equally inspired by Semperian formal analysis and ethnographic knowledge. Sadly, the rise of Nazi ideology put an end to this early stage of German world art history.

Slightly later the Swiss art historian Heinrich Wölfflin moved away from the famously obscure concept of Riegl's *Kunstwollen* to draw on the experimental psychology of perception developed by Wilhelm Wundt to develop what he called his five art-historical fundamental principles or *kunsthistorische Grundbegriffe*. These were actually five pairs of oppositions (pictorial–linear, flatness–depth, optic–haptic, plurality–unity, and clarity–lack of clarity) that would allow the historian to define the characteristics of a particular painter or period's style and analyze its development. The *Kunsthistorische Grundbegriffe: Das Problem der Stilentwicklung in der neueren Kunst*, first published in 1915, although exclusively concerned with Italian, Northern Renaissance, and Baroque art, has become the one truly global art-historical

---

Semper in London, ed. Michael Gnehm and Sonja Hildebrand (Mendrisio: Mendrisio Academy Press/gta Verlag, 2022), 159–79.

[15] Philippe Descola, *Les Formes du Visible: une anthropologie de la figuration* (Paris: Seuil, 2021); and Philippe Descola, *La Fabrique des Images: visions du monde et formes de la représentation* (Paris: Somogy-Musée du quai Branly, 2010).

a Blütenrand eines Bildes der Höhle 14 bei Ming-Öi. Nach Grünwedel. — b Tierfries aus der „Halle mit dem Tierfries" bei Kirisch. Nach Grünwedel. — c Landschaftsgemälde in der „Hippokampenhöhle" zu Kyzyl. Nach Grünwedel. — d Landschaftsornament aus der Höhle 15 zu Ming-Öi. Nach Grünwedel. — e Beschnitzte Holzbank vom Niyailuß. Nach Stein. — f Geschnitzte Holzstücke aus der Lopwüste. Nach Stein.

Figure 14.2 Page from Karl Woermann, *Die Kunst aller Zeiten und Völker*, vol. 2 (*Die Kunst der Naturvölker und der übrigen nichtchristlichen Kulturvölker, einschliesslich der Kunst der Islam*), Leipzig, 1915. *Source*: Universitätsbibliothek Heidelberg.

method, very widely used in the Americas and China from the 1920s onwards to analyze art from these parts of the world.[16]

A different variety of concept-based, formal global art history was developed at Yale by George Kubler, a student of the French formalist Henri Focillon and a specialist in the art and architecture of ancient America and pre-Columbian art, in his short essay *The Shape of Time*: *Remarks on the History of Things* (1962). Kubler rejected the formalism of Wölfflin and the use of biological metaphor to define stylistic development, and in fact style altogether as the main analytical tool. He also dismissed the focus on meaning of art-historical iconography because it was too narrowly tied up to the classical and Christian traditions of the West to be used as a viable instrument for the arts of other parts of the world. Instead, in an essay that would prefigure many much more recent developments in archaeology and anthropology, he proposed to look at series and sequences of objects and object types and the laws that determine their invention, adaptation, or duplication over time. Like his teacher, Henri Focillon, whose essay *La vie des formes* he translated into English, Kubler was interested in the problem that exercised the founders of the Annales school of history: how to relate the perspectives of *longue durée* and *courte durée*, the slow evolvement of the environment with the short time span over which events occur. The designs of artifacts for Kubler are solutions to problems, and the task of the historian becomes to identify these problems, how they evolve, and the artifactual response to them. As with Semper, this concept-based outline of a global history of human culture did not generate much research that engaged directly and critically with Kubler's conjectures, but his book has attracted much attention recently as a methodological model, not least because of his replacement of artifacts, let alone art, by "things" as the main focus of his inquiry, which anticipated the wave of "things" theories that arrived on the scene in the 1980s and 1990s.[17] They both moved the focus of their inquiries from the creative innovations of individual artists of genius to classes of artifacts, series, and sequences and the migration of motifs. In doing so, Kubler and Focillon deconstructed Europe's central position in art historiography to date, which from Vasari's *Lives of the Artists* onwards had considered such individual inventions as the chief motors of artistic development, as well as the foundation of claims for Europe's artistic excellence.

--

---

[16] The chapters in Evonne Levy and Tristan Weddigen, eds., *The Global Reception of Heinrich Wölfflin's Principles of Art History* (New Haven and London: Yale University Press, 2020).

[17] On recent receptions of Focillon and Kubler see for instance the chapters in Christian Brand and Alice Thomine, eds., *La vie des formes: Henri Focillon et les arts* (Ghent: Snoeck 2014); and Michael F. Zimmermann, ed., *Vision in Motion: Streams of Sensation and Configurations of Time* (Zurich: Diaphanes, 2016).

The designs for global studies of art mentioned until now all started from a particular conception of human material culture: as originating in four original crafts, for instance in the case of Semper; or by singling out one particular feature of artifacts, such as formal patterns. But they had less to say about actual historical development. For a theory of the history of art, or rather image making, we have to turn to the work of Aby Warburg. Born into a family of German Jewish bankers and by training a specialist in Italian Renaissance iconography, he devoted his life to understanding the historical process of the *longue durée* he identified as the problem of the afterlife of antiquity: how to understand the resurgence, throughout European art history, of the same forms, gestures, and shapes, in particular drapery, to express intense emotion, even in cultural contexts that had little direct knowledge of Greco-Roman art. To understand this *Nachleben der Antike* or afterlife of antiquity and the recurrent use of what he called *Pathosformeln* or pathos formulas, he initially, in the 1880s and 1890s, drew on Darwin's late work on the expression of emotions and the studies of the Italian anthropologist Tito Vignoli to find a basis in animal psychology and human anthropology for these recurrent uses of similar forms to express emotions. During his stay with the Pueblo Indians in New Mexico and the Hopi Indians in Arizona from 1895 to 1896, he witnessed the snake rituals performed by these societies, and the similarities with entertainments performed at the Medici court in the 1580s made him completely rethink the geographical scope and scientific foundations for his theory of the resurgence of ancient forms. He then argued that there are what we would now call anthropological constants in practices of human image making, which serve to deal with the phobic fear instilled by the natural world in the earliest human societies. By representing sequences such as draught, thunder and lightning, rain, and a good harvest in ritual, Warburg argued, so-called primitive societies act out causal sequences they hope to set in motion. Dance rituals such as those of the Pueblo Indians are what he called "getanzte Causalität," a causality that is represented in dance and thus allows for the acting out of fears and hopes. To this anthropology of image making he added a theory of human memory or *Mnemosyne*: Following Darwinist theories of the replication of phylogeny by ontogeny, he argued that humans all have some access to the memory of mankind, which acts as a storehouse filled with very old ways of representing intense emotions such as fear, despair, anger, or grief. To demonstrate these continuities, Warburg created in the last years of his life the *Mnemosyne Atlas*, panels on which he showed the migration of images through time and space by means of collages drawn from his vast collection of photos.[18]

---

[18] The literature on Warburg is immense. The best short introduction to his work is in the volume of selected writings edited by Martin Treml, Sigrid Weigel, and Petra Ladwig, see Aby Warburg, *Werke in einem Band* (Berlin: Suhrkamp, 2010). This volume now includes the most

Warburg did not live to see the forced emigration to London of the Kultur wissenschaftliche Bibliothek he founded in Hamburg; but recently, after having faded into obscurity, his work has moved again into the center of art-historical research, and the Warburg Institute now hosts a research program called *Bilderfahrzeuge*, which continues his investigations into these long-term migrations of images and artifacts across the world.

-

Since the 1980s a different variety of world art history has evolved. It originated in Germany, the United Kingdom, and the Netherlands and considers contemporary art in a global perspective.[19] It has a substantial pedigree in modernism, which was presented as an international style, most famously in the exhibition Modern Architecture: International Exhibition, curated by Philip Johnson at the Museum of Modern Art (MoMA) in 1932. Another important feature that this variety of world art history shares with modernism is its global spread and concern with globalization. In fact, it could be argued that it is a variety of globalization studies concerned with the political, economic, and social aspects of contemporary art and design across the world. The University of East Anglia and Leiden University were among the first departments to offer programs in world art history, inspired not only by the presence of significant collections of world art and of departments of Asian and African studies but also by the economic pressures of the 1980s on humanities departments. In both departments, John Onians was the leading figure. He published an *Atlas of World Art* in 2004; in 2008 his Leiden colleagues Kitty Zijlmans and Wilfred van Damme published *World Art Studies: Exploring Concepts and Approaches*, to date one of the most inclusive surveys of this rapidly expanding field. This new field is interdisciplinary and is quite close to the German discipline of *Bildwissenschaft*, which has an outlook that is not primarily historical, nor concerned with fine art exclusively, but instead develops a systematic, multidisciplinary study of image making and reception. As defined by Zijlmans, this New World art history has three main parts: to study the earliest human image making; intercultural

---

complete version of Warburg's travels to the Pueblo Indians. The website of the Warburg Institute in London hosts a virtual display of the *Mnemosyne* panels.

[19] Kitty Zijlmans and Wilfried van Damme, eds., *World Art Studies: Exploring Concepts and Approaches* (Amsterdam: Valiz, 2008); Hans Belting and Andrea Buddensieg, eds., *The Global Art World: Audiences, Markets, and Museums* (Ostfildern: Hatje Cantz, 2009); James Elkins, ed., *Is Art History Global?* (London: Routledge, 2007); James Elkins, Zhivka Valiavicharska, and Alice Kim, eds., *Art and Globalization* (University Park: Pennsylvania State University Press, 2010); and Klaus Volkenandt, ed., *Kunstgeschichte und Weltgegenwartskunst: Konzepte, Methoden, Perspektiven* (Berlin: Reimer, 2004).

comparisons of art across the world in its cultural contexts; and interculturali zations, that is, to trace the influences of one artistic culture on another or their cross-fertilization. In recent years, for instance, the traffic of artifacts from Japan, India, and China to Europe from the 1600s onwards, and the arrival in the opposite direction of European objects in Asia, have inspired to innovative studies of the dynamics of such cross-fertilization. The arrival in China of Western perspectival landscape engravings, for instance, brought to Beijing by French Jesuits, led to major stylistic and technical changes in Chinese land-scape painting. In its early stages, this recent kind of world art history tried to develop a neuroaesthetics of art. After promising beginnings in the study of the physical aspects of image viewing, this project now seems to have lost traction, possibly because of the great methodological difficulties of mapping what goes on in the brain specifically when a person looks at a representation.[20]

At the same time, art history departments in Britain and the United States radically revised their curriculum and hiring policies under the influence of advocates for a more inclusive teaching offer and research agenda. Thus the traditional canon, which consisted mainly of dead white male artists from Europe and to a lesser degree the United States, was replaced in most depart-ments by programs that included the arts of Asia and Africa, Islamic art, and a revised canon of artists. For the early modern period, one of the most profound changes caused by such rethinking has taken place in the field of Mediterranean art history. Deborah Howard and Hans Beltings's work on the artistic, religious, and trade relations between Venice or Florence and the Byzantine and Ottoman empires has completely transformed traditional per-ceptions of these cities. The traditional view of Venice as a Western republic, with an artistic tradition rooted in the Roman Empire and attuned entirely from the Quattrocento to developments in the rest of Italy, has been replaced by a view of the city as a connectivity hub between the Middle East and Asia on the one hand and Europe on the other, with a visual culture that was a unique synthesis of many local traditions and practices.[21] In his book on Florence and Baghdad, Belting has reconstructed how linear perspective, hitherto seen as the

---

[20] John Onians, "Neuroarthistory as World Art History: Why Do Humans Make Art and Why Do They Make It Differently in Different Times and Places?," in *Crossing Cultures: Conflict, Migrations and Convergence: Proceedings of the 32nd Conference of the International Congress in the History of Art*, ed. Jaynie Anderson (Carlton: Miegunyah Press, 2009), 78–81; see also the critique of neuroarthistory and other neurosciences of culture in Fernando Vidal and Fernando Ortega, "On the Neurodisciplines of Culture," in *The Palgrave Handbook of Biology and Society*, ed. Maurizio Meloni et al. (New York: Palgrave Macmillan, 2018), 371–90.

[21] Deborah Howard, *Venice and the East: The Impact of the Islamic East on Venetian Architecture, 1100–1500* (New Haven: Yale University Press, 2008); and Catherine Hess, *The Arts of Fire: Islamic Influences on Glass and Ceramics of the Italian Renaissance* (Los Angeles: J. Paul Getty Museum, 2004).

archetypal Western artistic invention, was in fact the result of parallel investigations into optics in western Europe and the Arabian world, but it was rooted in very different cultural conceptions of human vision and what in the West was called naturalism.[22]

Decolonizing the curriculum and writing of world art histories are ongoing processes but they operate at different speeds. The transformation of teaching and research programs is a matter of a few decades, but the research needed to produce world art histories that integrate European art into a global history, show its global entanglements, and offer perspectives that are not, or not exclusively, Eurocentric will take much longer. This state of affairs is shown by many world art histories produced recently. They are often visual compendia or atlases, or offer overviews of developments across the world in one particular period; usually they depart from Western notions of the fine arts and Western concepts of aesthetics, and they rarely take into account for instance the rich Chinese tradition of art historiography.

This all too brief overview of existing varieties of world art histories thus shows not only some of its conceptual underpinnings but also that many remain very conjectural or deeply rooted in Western developments such as modernism. To see what a history of the global entanglements of European art could look like, I now turn to recent work on French art circa 1750, and in particular the emerging field of global Rococo, one of the most innovative aspects of art history at present.

-

At the height of its powers in the 1750s, France's Atlantic empire was the largest and most lucrative empire in the world. Like the Dutch empire, it was driven by commercial interests, not by missionary zeal or the urge to create a political empire like the Romans. The *culture de l'exotique* developed in the long eighteenth century was shaped by a combination of commercial and scientific (in particular geographical) developments and politics. Images played a major role in its first stage, from the 1650s to the 1730s; the second stage, which would continue into Napoleon's empire, was more defined by transcultural material practices. The vast quantities of goods shipped to the Netherlands and France by their respective West and East India Companies played a major role in this. Amsterdam in particular became the entrepôt, the storage and European sales hub for exotic goods. The trade expeditions of the Dutch to Africa and Asia also produced travel accounts, which gave rise to a new scientific discipline which flourished from 1675 to the 1730s: that of exotic, visual geography addressed to

---

[22] Hans Belting, *Florenz und Bagdad: eine westöstliche Geschichte des Blicks* (Munich: C. H. Beck, 2008).

a visual European spectator. The *Galérie agréable du monde*, published in 1729 in Leiden in French, is the culmination of this genre. Published in thirty-six volumes, and lavishly illustrated by Romeyn de Hooghe and others, it is one of the most beautiful books ever published and offered a synthesis of exotic geography (Figure 14.3). The arrival of goods from Asia was recorded in the sumptuous still lifes of Kalff and others, but one could argue that this exotic culture was in its early stages largely a *livresque* culture, based on the images in travelogues such as Johan Nieuhof's *Description of China*, Olfert Dapper's *Description of Asia* of 1681, and the *Ambassades mémorables de la Compagnie des Indes Orientales des Provinces Unies, vers les Empereurs du Japon* by Arnoldus Montanus (Figure 14.4).[23]

The wide dissemination of these books across Europe, in various editions and translations, contributed not only to diverse varieties of exoticism, ranging from the adoption of Chinese textiles and dress to Japanese tea ceremonies or the inclusion of Asian building types such as the pagoda in picturesque garden design, but also to changes in categories of aesthetic appreciation. Instead of the classical aesthetic of rational harmony, symmetry, and decorum, a new sensibility emerged that valued features of artifacts that are easy to experience but difficult to define, such as porcelain's sheen or lacquerwork's power to dazzle and suggest unfathomable depths of color.[24]

Starting in the 1720s, when Paris became the hub of the trade in Asian luxury goods and precious materials from Africa and the Caribbean, various transcultural practices emerged that were no longer based on images but on the presence of artifacts in this new, globalized objectscape.[25] The new aesthetic and such practices came together in the creation of the most costly objects created in Paris from the 1720s onwards: monochrome Chinese porcelain vases, deep blue or red, mounted in gilt bronze rocaille ornament. These artifacts were created by the so-called *marchands-merciers*, purveyors of luxury goods for the richest collectors among the aristocracy and royal family. Two of these are now in the Frick Collection in New York (Figure 14.5). These are Chinese jars, dated on the basis of their exceptional deep-blue monochrome glazing as early eighteenth century. Each was cut in France at the shoulder to create a lidded jar. The designer of the mounts is unknown, but the date of the tax stamp suggests they must have been made before 1749, possibly 1743. The art critic and collector

[23] Cf. Benjamin Schmidt, *Inventing Exoticism: Geography, Globalism and Europe's Early Modern World* (University Park: Pennsylvania University Press, 2015), 83–163.

[24] Anna Grasskamp, "EurAsian Layers: Netherlandish Surfaces and Early Modern Chinese Artefacts," *The Rijksmuseum Bulletin* 63, no. 4 (2015): 362–99; and Jonathan Hay, *Sensuous Surfaces: The Decorative Object in Early Modern China* (Honolulu: University of Hawai'i Press, 2010).

[25] Martin Pitts and Miguel John Versluys, "Objectscapes: A Manifesto for Investigating the Impacts of Object Flows on Societies," *Antiquity* 95, no. 380 (2021): 367–81.

Figure 14.3 Engraving from *La Galérie agréable du monde*, vol. 3 (*La Cour du Grand Tatar*), Leiden, 1729.
Source: Royal Collection Trust.

Charles-François Julliot noted that the refined glazes elicited a unique aesthetic response, *le tact flou*, defined as a "certain sensation that connoisseurs experience at the sight of these porcelains."[26] Their creation may have been inspired by Jesuit accounts of how the Chinese mended broken porcelain by drilling holes in it and connecting parts by very thin copper wire. In France they may also have been cut and mounted to camouflage damage. The practice of mounting vases and jars is itself a transcultural phenomenon with an old pedigree. It is documented in China and the Ottoman Empire, and the earliest case known in Europe is that of a Turkish jar mounted in Hungary around 1300 CE. The French kings constantly mounted and remounted the artifacts in the royal treasury which came from the Roman, Byzantine, and Ottoman empires, but the eighteenth-century specimens stand out by the extreme lavishness of both the artifacts and their mounts.

---

[26] Kristel Smentek, *Rococo Exotic: French Mounted Porcelains and the Allure of the East* (New York: Frick Collection, 2007), 15.

Figure 14.4 Engraving of the Palace of the Japanese emperor in Kyoto by
Jacob van Meurs, printed in Arnoldus Montanus, *Ambassades mémorables de
la Compagnie des Indes Orientales des Provinces Unies, vers les Empereurs
du Japon*, Amsterdam, 1680.
Source: Public domain.

At first sight, these mounted jars all thematize the porous frontier between
art and nature. Porcelain, it was long believed, was made from ground
shells; shells were praised for their porcelain-like sheen. Hence the frequency
of marine and shell elements in mounts may refer to these associations,
strengthened by the popularity of Chinese and Japanese shell-shaped porcelain
that was mounted as well. At second sight, these objects also embody a
different questioning of borders: those between East and West. They embody
not only the supreme craftsmanship of Chinese potters but also the interest in
transcultural practices that characterize French eighteenth-century cultures of
exoticism, and thus go beyond the tradition of appropriating prestigious
objects from the past by adding handles, lids, or legs that is so frequent in
the French Royal Treasury. As Kristel Smentek has recently argued, the use
of rococo mounts cannot be reduced to a gesture of material appropriation.

Figure 14.5 Chinese porcelain jar with French gilt bronze mount, jar ca. 1720, mount ca. 1740.
Source: Frick Collection, New York.

The mounts also serve to mitigate the disorientation posed by these large, blank, monochrome spaces of color, to appreciate the vases, and to activate them by setting up a complex dialectic between the costly familiarity of the rococo mount and the uniqueness of these monochrome jars: One has to imagine how they would dazzle the viewer when placed in front of a mirror, as was the custom, and lit by the flickering light of candles.[27]

-

In this chapter I have sketched the development of global art histories written in Europe from the first, religiously motivated varieties, through highly theoretical nineteenth-century projects for world histories of human material culture and twentieth-century globalization studies, to recent work on cultures of exoticism and global rococo in France circa 1750. As I hope to have shown, this is not a simple tale of Europeans writing about the arts of other parts of the world to show the superiority of European art or to demonstrate its triumphant dissemination among the nations. When motivated by religious or Enlightenment ideas, we can detect a narrative of gradual evolution from the idolatry of paganism to the light of Christian revelation; but as we have seen, these attempts often backfired and in fact contributed to what we would now call cultural relativism. Linear perspective is another case of the complex interrelations between European art and that of other parts of the world. Chinese landscape painters, as we saw, eagerly took over this technique of visual representation but immediately adapted it to their own style of landscape painting. These processes of exportation and exchange intensified in the eighteenth century, when the major European colonial and trade empires reached global expansion. This century thus presents a fascinating interval between Renaissance and nineteenth-century varieties of empire.[28] It offers a series of complex involvements with what was called the exotic at the time that go beyond easy classifications such as appropriation or the exportation of European styles. To understand these transcultural practices and entanglements, traditional art history had little to offer, because of its emphasis on stylistic and iconographical analysis, focus on the work of individual artists of genius as the agents of change, and theoretical foundation in classical art theory. Instead, recent work on global rococo in France shows a highly

[27] Ibid.; and Kristel Smentek, "Other Antiquities: Ancients, Moderns and the Challenge of China in Eighteenth-Century France," in *Eighteenth-Century Art Worlds Global and Local Geographies of Art*, ed. Michael Youan and Stacey Sloboda (New York: Bloomsbury, 2019), 153–79, for the wider context of such practices in the awareness that China's culture predated the Biblical flood. I am much indebted to Dr. Smentek for some insights from her forthcoming book *Objects of Encounter: China in Eighteenth-Century France*.
[28] Avcioğlu and Flood, "Introduction," 7.

innovative integration of work done in anthropology and archaeology – on connectivity, objectscapes, and materiality – with the close visual analysis proper to art history to analyze in detail what goes on in the transcultural artifacts discussed here. Thus the historiography of global art history is a tale not only of the gradual extension of the geographical scope of the discipline but also of conceptual and methodological transformation.

15   Globalizing European Military History

Michelle Moyd

European military historians often work from the unacknowledged assumption that their subfield is inherently "white" history.[1] To change this, scholars and readers must interrogate the underlying racisms that continue to treat Europe as a "white mythic space," decoupling "military history" from its understood, if not always explicit, meaning: European and North American military history.[2] Western militaries continue to wage war against peoples and places that military thinkers, strategists, and leaders deem outside of modernity, outside of humanity, and thus legitimate targets of war-making. Despite thick layers of international law designed to regulate the conduct of warfare, those who are most likely to experience violence by European and North American militaries rarely see the benefits from these institutions and agreements.[3] All of these wars contain the relevant markers of imperial warfare, even if they are not named as such.

The knowledge that informs how Western powers go to war today rests on racist and civilizationist assumptions reminiscent of those that underpinned Western imperial armies' actions in the long nineteenth century.[4] These patterns from the nineteenth century continued into the Second World War and the Cold War. And even beyond the major twentieth-century wars that have occupied historians' attention, military logics and practices shape an array of everyday experiences around the world. The notion of "fortress

---

[1] As Manuela Boatcă puts it, "the label of 'Europe' always includes both Western Europe and its white populations, but Eastern Europe needs to be named in full in order to be included in the overarching term. Black Europe, for a long time unthinkable in most social science, still needs to be argued, defended, and explained." Manuela Boatcă, "Thinking Europe Otherwise: Lessons from the Caribbean," *Current Sociology* 69, no. 3 (2021): 389–414, here p. 390.

[2] Stefan Aguirre Quiroga, "Race, *Battlefield* I and the White Mythic Space of the First World War," *Alicante Journal of English Studies* 31 (2018): 187–93.

[3] See, for example, Philippe Sands, *The Last Colony: A Tale of Exile, Justice and Britain's Colonial Legacy* (London: Weidenfield and Nicholson, 2023) on the Chagossians, deported by the British from the Chagos islands between 1965 and 1973 to make way for a US military complex.

[4] Patrick Porter, *Military Orientalism: Eastern War through Western Eyes* (New York: Columbia University Press, 2009).

Europe," for example, delineates a fictional white Europe that guards against the perceived encroachment by immigrants whose race, religion, economic status, or a combination thereof renders them undesirable. This fiction is policed by the European Border and Coast Guard agency (Frontex), backed by anti-immigration policies and actions that derive from military sensibilities and the pursuit of "security" over care for immigrants, many of whom come from Africa, Asia, and Latin America.[5] People are dying because of it.[6] The de facto southward push of EU borders into places such as Morocco, Tunisia, and Sudan, and the effects of these politics on refugee populations or those at risk of becoming refugees, underscore the urgency of a global turn in European military history.

A global lens on European military history exposes the racist foundations upon which European empires have gone to war around the world over centuries. When the First World War began in August 1914, for example, past experiences of warfare shaped military leaders' perceptions of its potential costs, especially regarding the scale of the lives that would be lost.[7] The vast available technological reservoirs that came to define warfighting in Europe from 1914 to 1918 coexisted with backward-looking, romanticized, imperial remembrances of warfare.[8] This disjuncture between nostalgia, martial masculine desire, and racist disdain for the imagined simplicity of imperial wars abroad on the one hand, and the scale of violence in Europe that began in August 1914 on the other, exemplifies the importance of globalizing European military history.[9] As John Whiteclay Chambers II wrote: "The ruthlessness of

---

[5] The capsizing of the fishing boat *Adriana* off the coast of Greece in June 2023, which was carrying migrants from Libya to Italy, drew attention once again to the thousands of deaths occurring each year in the Mediterranean as migrants attempt to cross in search of better lives. An estimated 600 people died in the shipwreck. Activist rescue group Seebrücke International tweeted just after the disaster: "This shipwreck is neither an accident nor an unavoidable tragedy, but a direct consequence of deliberate political decisions aimed at further sealing off Fortress Europe instead of creating safe passages." *Twitter Seebruecke_Intl*, Online. See also Jori Pascal Kalkman, "Frontex: A Literature Review," *International Migration* 59, no. 1 (2020): 165–81; and Nick Vaughan-Williams, "Borderwork beyond Inside/Outside? Frontex, the Citizen-Detective and the War on Terror," *Space and Polity* 12, no. 1 (2008): 63–79.

[6] The Missing Migrants Project reports that as of 9 June 2023, 19,563 migrants have died or disappeared in the Mediterranean since 2016. They report that 1,655,535 have attempted the crossing in the same time frame, *Missing Migrants*, Online.

[7] Herbert Kitchener, Winston Churchill, Charles Mangin, Hubert Lyautey, and Joseph Gallieni all had significant experiences of colonial warfare before they took on leadership roles in the First World War.

[8] John Ellis, *The Social History of the Machine Gun* (Baltimore: Johns Hopkins Press, 1975); and John Whiteclay Chambers, "The American Debate over Modern War, 1871–1914," in *Anticipating Total War: The German and American Experiences, 1871–1914*, ed. Manfred F. Boemeke, Roger Chickering, and Stig Förster (Cambridge: Cambridge University Press, 1999), 274–9.

[9] Emmanuel Kreike, *Scorched Earth: Environmental Warfare as a Crime against Humanity and Nature* (Princeton: Princeton University Press, 2021), 6–7, 14–17.

colonial warfare, with its lack of restraints, would return to haunt Europe in the slaughter of World War I."[10] It would return again in the Second World War, a point that Aimé Césaire scathingly addressed in *Discourse on Colonialism*, published in 1955. Césaire's oft-cited perspective on the links between European colonial violence and the atrocities of the Second World War also described the ongoing modes of violence that Europeans were using against colonized peoples around the world. European counterinsurgencies against armed anti-colonial movements in Kenya, Algeria, and Indochina occurred against the backdrop of the Cold War and the nuclear age. In the 1960s, France conducted nuclear tests in Algeria and Polynesia, poisoning those who lived and breathed in these spaces.[11] After the global turn, these layered histories of colonialism, militarism, and environmental catastrophe deserve sustained intellectual engagement within European military historiography, because they emanated from European imperialism.

What is meant by "Europe" when it comes to military history? Despite the fast-growing literature on Europe's global entanglements and incursions, the word typically references a bounded, sealed space racialized as white. The boundaries around this racialized space have been porous in certain times and places, fortress-like in others.[12] On both the practical and discursive levels, "Europe" has sometimes encompassed the spaces its great powers colonized, but with specific racialized limits on who qualified as "Europeans" within those spaces. In military terms, imperial armies built in colonized spaces were composed mainly of Indigenous troops, led by white officers and non-commissioned officers (NCOs) from Europe, trained in styles of warfighting that emerged in earlier European wars, using weapons mainly produced in the West. Indigenous peoples provided the labor – often coerced – that colonial armies needed to prosecute war. For example, colonial armies in the East African campaign of the First World War employed hundreds of thousands of African porters – men, women, and youth – who carried out most of the logistical work they required while on the march and in battle.[13] This mode of

---

[10] Chambers, "The American Debate over Modern War, 1871–1914," 247.
[11] Bengt Danielsson, "Poisoned Pacific: The Legacy of French Nuclear Testing," *Bulletin of Atomic Scientists* 46, no. 2 (1990): 22–31; John-Marc Regnault, "France's Search for Nuclear Test Sites, 1957–1963," *The Journal of Military History* 67, no. 4 (2003): 1223–48; and Thomas Fraise and Austin R. Cooper, "France Struggled to Relinquish Algeria as a Nuclear Test Site, Archives Reveal," *The Conversation*, 3 August 2022, Online.
[12] Morrow, *The Great War*, 10, 12; and Vaughan-Williams, "Borderwork beyond Inside/Outside?"
[13] Mahon Murphy, "Carrier Corps," in *1914–1918 Online: International Encyclopedia of the First World War*, Online; Edward Paice, *Tip and Run: The Untold Tragedy of the Great War in Africa* (London: Phoenix, 2007), 280–90; Melvin Page, *The Chiwaya War: Malawians and the First World War* (Boulder: Westview, 2000); Tammy M. Proctor, *Civilians in a World at War* (New York: NYU Press, 2010), 62–3, 142–4.

logistical transport and military support had roots in East African long-distance caravans and expeditions.[14] Colonial armies' ways of war were as much African as they were European.[15]

Yet the histories of these armies and the wars they waged are marginal within European (or Western) military historiography.[16] Colonial warfare features peripherally in European military history, although it is a vibrant subgenre of imperial history.[17] Even very recent historiography, which could incorporate insights from the body of work on imperial warfare, not to mention African, Asian, and Latin American historiographies, continues this trend.[18] For example, the notion that "Europe" lived through a century of peace before it was interrupted by the Great War is a popular assumption that unravels as soon as empire enters the frame.[19] By framing European wars in African

---

[14] Andreas Greiner, *Human Porterage and Colonial State Formation in German East Africa, 1880s-1914: Tensions of Transport* (Cham: Palgrave Macmillan, 2022); and Stephen Rockel, *Carriers of Culture: Labor on the Road in Nineteenth-Century East Africa* (Portsmouth: Heinemann, 2006).

[15] Michelle R. Moyd, "Imagining African Warfare: War Games and Military Cultures in German East Africa," in *Warfare and Culture in World History*, ed. Wayne E. Lee (New York: NYU Press, 2020), 212–39; see also Michelle R. Moyd, *Violent Intermediaries: African Soldiers, Conquest, and Everyday Colonialism in German East Africa* (Athens, OH: Ohio University Press, 2014).

[16] With some exceptions; see Benjamin Claude Brower, *A Desert Named Peace: The Violence of France's Empire in the Algerian Sahara, 1844–1902* (New York: Columbia University Press, 2009); Robert Gerwarth and Erez Manela, eds., *Empires at War, 1911–1923* (Oxford: Oxford University Press, 2014); Isabel V. Hull, *Absolute Destruction: Military Culture and the Practices of War in Imperial Germany* (Ithaca, NY: Cornell University Press, 2006); Wayne E. Lee, *Waging War: Conflict, Culture, and Innovation in World History* (Oxford: Oxford University Press, 2016); Tammy M. Proctor, *Civilians in a World at War, 1914–1918* (New York: NYU Press, 2010); Morrow, *The Great War*; Jennifer E. Sessions, *By Sword and Plow: France and the Conquest of Algeria* (Ithaca, NY: Cornell University Press, 2011); Lawrence Sondhaus, *World War One: The Global Revolution* (Cambridge: Cambridge University Press, 2021); William Kelleher Storey, *The First World War: A Concise Global History* (Lanham: Rowman and Littlefield, 2021); and Bertrand Taithe, *The Killer Trail: A Colonial Scandal in the Heart of Africa* (Oxford: Oxford University Press, 2009)

[17] Tanja Bührer, Christian Stachelbeck, and Dierk Walter, eds. *Imperialkriege von 1500 bis heute: Strukturen, Akteure, Lernprozesse* (Paderborn: Ferdinand Schöningh, 2011); Dierk Walter, *Colonial Violence: European Empires and the Use of Force* (Oxford: Oxford University Press, 2017); J. A. de Moor and H. L. Wesseling, eds., *Imperialism and War: Essays on Colonial Wars in Asia and Africa* (Leiden: Brill, 1989); and H. L. Wesseling, *Imperialism and Colonialism: Essays on the History of European Expansion* (Westport: Greenwood Press, 1997).

[18] Richard Overy, *Blood and Ruins: The Last Imperial War, 1931–45* (New York: Viking, 2022); and Peter H. Wilson, *Blood and Iron: A Military History of the German-Speaking Peoples since 1500* (Cambridge, MA: Harvard University Press, 2023).

[19] Jürgen Osterhammel, *The Transformation of the World: A Global History of the Nineteenth Century* (Princeton: Princeton University Press, 2014), 512. Henk Wesseling also explicitly separated war in "Europe" from war in "the imperial hinterlands," ignoring wars on Europe's peripheries, and arguing that "Europe experienced a period of prolonged peace between 1871 and 1914"; and Henk Wesseling, "Imperialism and the Roots of the Great War," *Daedelus* 134, no. 2 (2005): 100–7, here p. 100.

spaces as "punitive expeditions" or "small wars," military officials and historians alike suggest a qualitative difference between such wars and the "real"
wars fought among presumed equals. To assert that Europe had a century of
peace between 1815 and 1914, historians must exclude the Greek Revolution,
Crimean War, South African War, Russo-Japanese War, Balkan Wars, and
countless colonial wars fought in Africa and elsewhere.[20] In making such
arguments, historians leave aside the many wars fought outside of Europe,
which often used armies assembled from Indigenous recruits who were then
led by European officers and NCOs. Yet until the German wars of unification
returned war to central Europe, colonial warfare was in fact the dominant
recurring mode of European warfare after Napoleon's defeat. Imperial
Germany, for example, fought many colonial wars in Africa and East Asia
between the 1880s and 1914. French imperial wars were fought even earlier in
the nineteenth century. Europeans were, in fact, constantly at war in the
nineteenth century and earlier.[21]

Why then does European military history so rarely include these histories?
In its current form, military history seems to exist largely to perpetuate ideas
about Europe's global dominance, an "extension of imperialism that seeks to
control the narrative of heroism and the meaning of war itself."[22] The racisms
and nationalisms embedded in the narration of Europe's military past prevent it
from fully making the global turn.[23] Historiographies dabble around the edges
but rarely challenge the foundations.[24] The study of war and militarization
without the global turn enables the continued avoidance of questions that
inherently challenge the nationalist, patriotic, and frequently racist and
misogynist foundations that have long shaped the field. Given the ways that
historians also influence the creation and revision of museums and memorials,
they must do more to stop perpetuating these omissions.

These foundations extend to ostensibly global historiographies. In his 1,000-
page book *The Transformation of the World*, historian Jürgen Osterhammel
ends a section on Europe's imperial wars with this endnote: "We have to skip
the precolonial military history of these continents." Osterhammel's decision
to limit his global history by "skipping" all precolonial military history that
preceded Europe's imperial wars is a choice, and a powerful reminder of how

---

[20] Jonas Kreienbaum, "Colonial Policy, Colonial Conflicts and War before 1914," in *1914–1918 Online: International Encyclopedia of the First World War*, Online; Lara Kriegel, *The Crimean War and Its Afterlife: Making Modern Britain* (Cambridge: Cambridge University Press, 2022; and Mark Mazower, *The Greek Revolution: 1821 and the Making of Modern Europe* (London: Allen Lane, 2021).

[21] Linda Colley, *The Gun, the Ship, and the Pen: Warfare, Constitutions, and the Making of the Modern World* (New York: Liveright, 2021).

[22] Tammy Proctor, personal communication, May 2023.   [23] Morrow, *The Great War*, 10.

[24] One notable exception is Lee, *Waging War*.

little the global turn has done to shift the parameters of European military history. This refusal to engage African, Asian, Latin American, and Indigenous military histories demonstrates the parameters of "the global": It is defined by where and when Europeans left their continent, armed to the teeth, to travel great distances with goals of extraction, enslavement, and evangelization. Warfare was the bloody engine that propelled European expansion.[25]

Using the military formations and tools at hand – their "precolonial" military heritage – peoples all over the world took up arms against Europeans, resisting their incursions, aggressions, "improvements," and the violent extractive economies they built. Histories of anti-colonial resistance are often treated as "episodic, even exceptional," yet they are as much a part of European military history as any other wars.[26] During the First World War, Africans seized the opportunity to reclaim space and sovereignty from colonizers through revolution and rebellion.[27] European colonizers defeated most of these insurgencies, continuing their exploitative politics and economics even in the midst of an all-consuming global war. By excising "counternarratives of protest, resistance and revolution" from histories of European warfare, national and imperial wars are valorized as the means by which to maintain the status quo and to ensure the continuation of global structures of violence that kill, immiserate, and subjugate millions of people.[28] Seeing the colonized and their forms of resistance within the same frame of "military history" should also be part of globalizing European military history. Situating European military history more firmly in the global unsettles assumed knowledge about European military dominance and takes seriously armed struggles against empire within the same field of study.[29]

-

These histories of a Europe bounded by whiteness, mostly without "war" from 1815 to 1914, rely on definitions of war that largely exclude violence happening overseas or in areas perceived as being on Europe's margins. The rich variety of sources that enable the narration of different kinds of histories

---

[25] Jennifer E. Sessions, "'Unfortunate Necessities': Violence and Civilization in the Conquest of Algeria," in *France and Its Spaces of War: Experience, Memory, Image*, ed. Patricia M. E. Lorcin and Daniel Brewer (Basingstoke: Palgrave Macmillan, 2009), 29–44, here p. 29.

[26] Priyamvada Gopal, *Insurgent Empire: Anticolonial Resistance and British Dissent* (London: Verso, 2019), 12.

[27] Michelle R. Moyd, "Resistance and Rebellions (Africa)," in *1914–1918 Online: International Encyclopedia of the First World War*, Online.

[28] Antoinette M. Burton, *The Trouble with Empire: Challenges to Modern British Imperialism* (New York: Oxford University Press), 2.

[29] Vincent Brown, *Tacky's Revolt: The Story of an Atlantic Slave War* (Cambridge, MA: Harvard University Press, 2020); and Linda M. Heywood, *Njinga of Angola: Africa's Warrior Queen* (Cambridge, MA: Harvard University Press).

are underused, and when they are used, it is mostly in colonial or imperial histories, not European ones. To again take an example from the First World War, those who lived, fought, and worked in Belgium and France seem to have encountered African and Asian troops and workers regularly, as photography and art from the war years attest.[30] Why haven't historians made better use of these abundant materials?

Reading the sources multidirectionally, and using them more fully, allows for recovery of global military histories that better represent the past. Ample evidence to do this work exists. In addition to the voluminous official materials documenting Europe's wars overseas, numerous military memoirs also exist. Most scholars who study European military history can read these materials because they were written in European languages and, often enough, they are stored in European archives. Photography and other kinds of graphic sources also await further study. These materials can and should disrupt the temporal and spatial lines that separate European military histories from other kinds of military histories, when in fact they should be intertwined. Joseph Clarke and John Horne make this point by drawing attention to "the experience of ordinary men uprooted from their ordinary lives who went to the borders of Europe and beyond, and who, in doing so, crossed the limits of what they considered to be 'civilization'."[31] They wrote accounts about their own experiences, which contribute to the large source base for remaking European military history. In another vein, Linda Colley has argued that after the 1750s, written constitutions "proliferated exponentially and in connected waves across multiple frontiers" because of "a growth in the geographical range, frequency, intensity and demands of warfare and cross-border violence."[32] Much of this violence was fueled by imperial competition and the wars generated by it.[33] At the same time, the scale of this violence and European expansion "caused some outside the West who were at risk and exposed to its force to experiment with their own defensive and distinctive constitutions", as Linda Colley put it.[34] Not only did military men play central roles in shaping what Europeans knew about the rest of the world through their writing, art, photography, maps, and the objects they often stole from

---

[30] Dominiek Dendooven, *Asia in Flanders Fields: Indians and Chinese on the Western Front, 1914–1920* (Barnsley: Pen and Sword Military, 2022); Richard S. Fogarty, *Race and War in France: Colonial Subjects in the French Army, 1914–1918* (Baltimore: Johns Hopkins University Press, 2008).

[31] Joseph Clarke and John Horne, "Introduction: Peripheral Visions – Militarized Cultural Encounters in the Long Nineteenth Century," in *Militarized Cultural Encounters in the Long Nineteenth Century: Making War, Mapping Europe*, ed. Joseph Clarke and John Horne (Cham: Palgrave Macmillan 2018), 1–21, here p. 2; and Colley, *The Gun, the Ship, and the Pen*.

[32] Colley, *The Gund, the Ship, and the Pen*, 3 and 5.   [33] Ibid., 8.   [34] Ibid., 10.

Indigenous peoples, but they often influenced the production of constitutional documents that became a hallmark of political modernity.[35]

Periodization and spatial demarcations present methodological problems as well. The dominance of "modern" history in the historical field can obscure the longer histories of European imperial wars and the "ravages of empire" that sustained them over the centuries.[36] These histories also span wider terrains, crossing oceans and connecting continents beginning from at least the late fifteenth century and continuing to the present.[37] These too can help reconfigure a European military historiography into one that is more responsive to the global turn.[38] The reliance on the military history of nation-states also contributes to the problem. As Andrew Jarboe and Richard Fogarty put it: "Any metropolitan sense of the 'nation' in 1914 was thoroughly entwined with ideas of the empire, for the simple reason that nations, if we might borrow Mrinalini Sinha's term, were themselves 'imperial social formations.'"[39]

Many useful global military histories involving European powers come from the long nineteenth century – a productive temporal scale for thinking about what transpired in Europe's relationships with the rest of the world, especially between 1870 and 1920. Some of the best-studied examples in African history include the Anglo-Zulu wars, the wars against the Mahdist army in Sudan, and Adwa in Ethiopia. In Southeast and South Asia, Indochina and India's Northwest Frontier have also received significant scholarly attention. These military histories received contemporary coverage back in Europe, fueling the imaginations of European youth, especially, from the 1870s on. Yet such wars had also occurred in the first half of the nineteenth century and earlier. As Fergus Robson shows, revolutionary and Napoleonic French troops learned to value "the need for vigorous force in dealing with 'uncivilized' populations who rejected French domination." They demonstrated continuities in French military thought, as well as their civilizationist resolve in 1845, when "Colonel Pélissier's troops killed hundreds by setting fires at the entrances to a cave complex [Dahra] in Algeria."[40] In 1896–7, British forces

---

[35] Ibid., 1 and 34–55.

[36] Tsitsi Dangarembga, *Black and Female: Essays* (Minneapolis: Graywolf Press, 2022), 23.

[37] Ibid., 23   [38] Brown, *Tacky's Revolt.*

[39] Andrew Tait Jarboe and Richard S. Fogarty, "Introduction: An Imperial Turn in First World War Studies," in *Empires in World War I: Shifting Frontiers and Imperial Dynamics in a Global Conflict*, ed. Andrew Tait Jarboe and Richard S. Fogarty (London: I. B. Tauris, 2014), 1–20, here p. 6.

[40] Fergus Robson, "French Soldiers and the Revolutionary Origins of the Colonial Mind," in Clarke and Horne, *Militarized Cultural Encounters in the Long Nineteenth Century*, 25–47, here p. 28; see also Tom Menger, "Concealing Colonial Comparability: British Exceptionalism, Imperial Violence, and the Dynamiting of Cave Refuges in Southern Africa, 1879–1897," *The Journal of Imperial and Commonwealth History* 50, no. 5 (2022): 860–89.

used dynamite to blow up cave refuges in Mashonaland, as Tom Menger's recent research has shown.

European-led colonial armies continued to use similar methods against African peoples in the twentieth century. One of the best-known examples is fascist Italy's use of chemical weapons in 1935–6 against Ethiopians.[41] In 1939, Italian troops again used mustard gas in their counterinsurgency against Ethiopian combatants and noncombatants who had retreated to Ametsegna Washa, a large cave. This Italian atrocity, which flouted international law against the use of chemical weapons, killed some 800 resistance fighters.[42] British torture and internment of Kenyans during the Land and Freedom Army's armed struggle against colonialism in the 1950s is well documented, as are the many abuses carried out by the French against Algerians during their liberation struggle. Britain's counterinsurgency in Malaya similarly exemplified the horrors of war fought in the twilight of formal empire. The continuities in their ways of war, and the continuing effects of their violence on peoples all over the world, illustrate the importance of understanding European imperial military histories and legacies in relation to the histories of the peoples who challenged them and their descendants.[43]

-

Without the global, European military history sustains whiteness and its gaze. But looking *with* the global, cultivating a global gaze, European military history unfurls in different directions. Analyzing visual evidence from within European military history helps with this work of cultivating a global gaze. The visual archive is one of the least appreciated and most underused source bases that European military historians could channel into a global turn. Visual methods widen the kinds of sources that can be used, rooting historical analysis in visual evidence that has the potential to shape how readers think about European histories of conflict and militarization.[44]

[41] Susan Grayzel, *The Age of the Gas Mask: How British Civilians Faced the Terrors of Total War* (New York: Cambridge University Press), 82–7; and Stephen J. Rockel, "Collateral Damage: A Comparative History," in *Inventing Collateral Damage: Civilian Casualties, War, and Empire*, ed. Stephen Rockel and Rick Halpern (Toronto: Between the Lines, 2009), 1–93, here pp. 42–4.

[42] Frederic Wehrey, "In the Cave of the Rebel," *New York Review of Books*, 21 June 2023. The site is sometimes also called the "cave of Zeret"; see also Alfredo González-Ruibal, Yonatan Sahle, and Xurxo Ayán Vila, "A Social Archaeology of Colonial War in Ethiopia," *World Archaeology* 43, no. 1 (2011): 40–65.

[43] Tom Menger, "A Conversation with Tom Menger about Colonial Warfare: 'There Were Great Similarities between the Empires'," *Global Dis:Connect Blog*, 3 July 2023, Online.

[44] Morgot Kahleyss, "Muslimische Kriegsgefangene in Deutschland im Ersten Weltkrieg: Ansichten und Absichten," in *Fremdeinsätze: Afrikaner und Asiaten in europäischen*

Figure 15.1 *Épisode de le bataille de Charleroi*, 1918, Paris, unknown artist.
Source: Bibliothèque nationale de France.

A colorful print of the Battle of Charleroi, which took place in Belgium from
21 to 23 August 1914, provides a useful example (Figure 15.1).[45] The battle
represented in *Épisode de le bataille de Charleroi* resulted in "massive French
losses."[46] Notably, the image depicts African troops in close combat against
white German soldiers, one of whom lies dying or dead, slightly off the
image's center. The African soldiers are identifiable by their skin color as well
as their uniforms. Some wear vibrant "zouave" uniforms, some wear khaki
accented by their red fezzes.[47] Both contrast with the German soldiers' gray
uniforms and spiked helmets. The German use of horses also stands out.

Kriegen, 1914–1945, ed. Gerhard Höpp and Brigitte Reinwald (Berlin: Verlag des Arabische
Buch, 2000), 79–117.
[45] The Battle of Charleroi was part of the Battle of the Frontiers. Erwin Le Gall, "Charleroi, Battle
of," in *1914–1918 Online: International Encyclopedia of the First World War*, Online.
According to Le Gall, the "Battle of Charleroi" was not "a single battle" but "a streak of
contiguous fights that occurred a few kilometers to the east of the city of Charleroi."
[46] Le Gall, "Charleroi," 1. Image can be found at *Gallica*, Online.
[47] On the history of Zouave uniforms in North Africa, see Thomas S. Abler, *Hinterland Warriors
and Military Dress: European Empires and Exotic Uniforms* (Oxford: Berg, 1999), 99–103.

This image does not look at all like typical representations of the First World War. There are no trenches or mud. There are no machine-guns or artillery pieces, though the German use of both kinds of weapons in this battle caused mass casualties for the French.[48] Instead, the image shows close combat, bayonets, and horses. The one death depicted shows pastel-toned blood flowing from the German officer's head wound, but the image does not otherwise attempt to convey the gruesomeness of battle. When I have shown this image in classes, students express surprise at the clear depiction of African troops fighting in Europe this early in the war. The depiction of soldiers wearing such colorful, elaborate uniforms is, understandably, jarring, when previous images they've seen of the First World War were likely in shades of gray. The image is out of time and out of place from popular understandings of the war's prosecution.

A visual genealogy of imperial warfare connects nineteenth-century images with the 1914 Battle of Charleroi image.[49] *Épisode* recalls images of nineteenth- and early twentieth-century colonial battlefields, the sites of imperial wars fought outside of Europe. These artful, sanitized scenes project martial heroism, valor, and courage and are not primarily concerned with the suffering, pain, or terror of combat. As Michelle Gordon argues in her work on British atrocity images from the Battle of Omdurman, however, "greater engagement with images of violence from the British Empire is . . . an important antidote to popular representations of the Empire."[50] Photographic images of African combatants killed by colonial armies in the countless wars fought in the nineteenth and early twentieth centuries circulated widely, both in the press and in private collections. They coexisted with the romance of images such as *Épisode*.[51]

If globalizing military history mattered to more historians of European militaries and warfare, images such as *Épisode* would provide compelling entry points for asking new questions about old narratives and representations.[52] Such images expose a continuing problem in European military

---

[48] Le Gall, "Charleroi," 2.   [49] Tait Jarboe and Fogarty, "Introduction," 6.

[50] Michelle Gordon, "Viewing Violence in the British Empire: Images of Atrocity from the Battle of Omdurman, 1898," *Journal of Perpetrator Research* 2, no. 2 (2019): 65–100, here p. 66.

[51] Daniel Foliard, *The Violence of Colonial Photography* (Manchester: Manchester University Press, 2020), 98–102; Paul Fox, "Kodaking a Just War: Photography, Architecture and the Language of Damage in the Egyptian Sudan, 1884–1898," in Clarke and Horne, *Militarized Cultural Encounters in the Long Nineteenth Century*, 97–124. Gordon, "Viewing Violence in the British Empire," 65–100; Kim A. Wagner, "Savage Warfare: Violence and the Rule of Colonial Difference in Early British Counterinsurgency," *History Workshop Journal* 85, (2018): 217–37.

[52] Clarke and Horne call for paying "particular attention to iconography" because "the encounters that concern us were constructed by image as well as prose." Clarke and Horne, "Introduction," 3.

historiographies: Histories of its wars and militarization processes took place within and alongside its histories of imperial expansion and violent subjugation of peoples around the world. Yet in downplaying these histories, European military historians also downplay essential parts of European history.[53] Colonial wars were fought against Indigenous armies around the world because of European imperial expansion and aggression. But to read about these wars, scholars would have to venture outside of European military historiography, to an adjacent subgenre, the history of European imperial warfare, or to histories of other parts of the world.[54]

How can *Épisode de le bataille de Charleroi* serve as a kind of portal into global military history? Imperial warfare before 1914 mattered a great deal to Europeans. These wars were represented in the press, literature, art, and advertising as sites of heroism and sacrifice, sacred blood spilled in distant lands for the good of empire. In the relatively few examples of European-led colonial armies succumbing to battlefield defeat in Africa and elsewhere, defeat became the basis for revenge, when colonial armies returned with better plans, more troops, and deadlier weaponry to punish those who had defeated them previously. Perhaps an image such as *Épisode de le bataille de Charleroi* stirred some of these reassuring colonial memories.[55] At the same time, as Raffael Scheck has shown, French and German soldiers perceived African soldiers in the Second World War, including those depicted in *Épisode de le bataille de Charleroi*, as brutes prone to committing battlefield atrocities.[56] The combination of "respect and horror" that shaped how the French viewed North African troops fighting in Belgium and France in 1914 can only be fully

---

[53] There are of course exceptions, including (but not limited to) Tanja Buehrer, Dominiek Dendooven, Rick Fogarty, Heather Jones, Christian Koller, Jonas Kreinbaum, Susanne Kuss, Wayne Lee, Ulrike Lindner, Tom Menger, John Morrow, Michael Neiberg, Tammy Proctor, Mahon Murphy, and Dierk Walter. Earlier scholarship by Wesseling, Klein, Chickering, Förster, and others also recast European military histories within imperial, transnational, transimperial, and global frames.

[54] Dierk Walter, *Colonial Violence*; Bührer, Stachelbeck, and Walter, eds., *Imperialkriege*. African military history is a thriving and dynamic field that approaches colonial violence from African vantage points. See *The Journal of African Military History* and publications in the Ohio University Press series. For excellent writing about Africa and the Second World War, see Judith A. Byfield et al., eds., *Africa and World War II* (New York: Cambridge University Press, 2015). The Australian journal *War and Society* has also included scholarly work on European wars fought around the world.

[55] Similar grayscale images were published in *The Illustrated War News* in September 1914. See, for example, "Coloured Troops Who are Fighting for France against the German Hordes: The Famous Turcos, Natives of Algeria and Tunisia, Who are Doing Magnificent Work in the Field – A Bayonet Charge," *The Illustrated War News*, 2 September 1914, 30–1, Online.

[56] Raffael Scheck, "'They Are Just Savages': German Massacres of Black Soldiers from the French Army in 1940," *The Journal of Modern History* 77, no. 2 (2005): 325–44; see also John Horne and Alan Kramer, *German Atrocities 1914: A History of Denial* (New Haven: Yale University Press, 2001), 17–53, 362–3, 402, 405–7; and Michael Howard, *The Franco-Prussian War* (London: Routledge: 2021 [1961]), 256–62.

understood within a global frame that shows how their deployment was both a French operational imperative *and* a racist discursive mobilization that fixed African soldiers in place as brutes.[57] A global perspective brings more interpretive power to *Episode* and other similar images, revealing French nostalgia and hope that referenced knowledge of imperial warfare. In visual culture at least, representations of colonial warfare reassured Europeans that their empires were sites of mastery and dominance, dressed up in khaki and military regalia. Visual evidence of European warfare could be used much more productively by European military historians, but it would require military historians to find value in other kinds of histories, including cultural and labor histories, to aid in more fully interpreting operational histories.[58]

-

"[T]ying the world together, in both past and present," writes Michelle Lynn Kahn, "is one of the historian's paramount tasks."[59] Yet the persistent divides between military historians who study Europe and North America and military historians who study Africa, for example, impede grasping the devastating effects of Europe's centuries of wars overseas. Historians of Africa often end up researching and writing aspects of European military history because (1) they understand how European racisms have influenced historiography and (2) they understand the making of colonial armies, which informs their understandings of colonial warfare, colonialism, and European racisms and quests for authority, power, and extractive wealth more generally.[60] But reciprocal effort on the part of European military historians is less common: Meaningful engagement with the war-making and militarizing processes of peoples who challenged European colonial armies' incursions in Africa and elsewhere remains frustratingly superficial.[61] Historians' lack of training in African history becomes an excuse for representing African histories of warfare with

[57] Eugene Rogan, "No Stake in Victory: North African Soldiers of the Great War," *Studies in Ethnicity and Nationalism* 14, no. 2 (2014): 322–33, here p. 327

[58] Wayne Lee's body of work has consistently probed this intersection, see Wayne E. Lee, "Conquer, Extract, and Perhaps Govern: Organic Economies, Logistics, and Violence in the Pre-industrial World," in *A Global History of Early Modern Violence*, ed. Erica Charters, Marie Houllemare, and Peter H. Wilson, (Manchester: Manchester University Press, 2020), 235–60.

[59] Michelle Lynn Kahn, "Rethinking Central Europe as a Migration Space: From the Ottoman Empire through the Cold War and the Refugee Crisis," *Central European History* 55, no. 1 (2022): 118–37, here p. 136; see also Boatcă, "Thinking Europe Otherwise," 390–1.

[60] Richard Reid, "Revisiting Primitive War: Perceptions of Violence and Race in History," *War and Society* 26, no. 2 (2007): 1–25.

[61] Anne-Isabelle Richard and Larissa Schulte Nordholt, "'There Is Still a Certain Rejection of African History in the West.' An Interview with Catherine Coquery-Vidrovitch," *Itinerario* 46, no. 1 (2022): 1–13, here pp. 9–10; and see Wayne Lee, *Waging War*, for an exception.

inadequate depth or texture.[62] This is what allows Osterhammel to simply footnote the decision to exclude other continents' military histories from his analysis. To be sure, this is a known structural problem of the disciplines and subdisciplines that often interferes with thinking and writing across subfields. As Sven Beckert and Dominic Sachsenmeier put it in a recent overview of the field: "The power to interpret the world has been and continues to be distributed in radically uneven ways."[63]

If European military historians want to explain European military pasts after the global turn, they must challenge this "radically uneven" distribution of interpretive power. In other words, more purposeful engagement with the global would situate the military histories within global histories of racism, slavery, and other forms of unfree labor, capitalist extraction, and imperial violence across different registers.[64] Active incorporation of European wars fought outside of Europe or on its margins reveals them as important, if often unspoken, structural drivers of military, political, economic, and intellectual change within Europe.[65] The Rif War (1921–6), in which Spain, later joined by France, launched a counterinsurgency against the Rif Republic in Morocco, destroyed Moroccan communities and lands through aerial bombings, land operations, and the use of poison gas in 1924.[66] Later, in the 1930s, Francisco Franco's fascist "campaign to 'cleanse Spain' resembled that in Morocco: intelligence-gathering through torture, summary executions, forced labour, rape, and the sadistic killing of military prisoners."[67] This connection shows the importance of considering warfare in the colonies within the same frame as wars fought in Europe. Anti-slavery and anti-colonial rebellions also shaped European military formations, tactics, strategies, and technologies in earlier periods. As Vincent Brown argues in his study of Tacky's Revolt of 1760–1, "[t]ransatlantic warfare highlighted ... how geographical space reflected

---

[62] Compare to Kahn, "Rethinking Central Europe as a Migration Space," 120.

[63] Sven Beckert and Dominic Sachsenmeier, "Introduction," in *Global History, Globally*, ed. Beckert and Sachsenmeier (London: Bloomsbury Academic, 2018), 1–18, here p. 8.

[64] Matthew Evenden, "Aluminum, Commodity Chains, and the Environmental History of the Second World War," *Environmental History*, 16, no. 1 (2011): 69–93.

[65] Colley, *The Gun, the Ship, and the Pen*; Ferdinand Mount, "Collect Your Divvies," review of Anne Murphy, *Virtuous Bankers: A Day in the Life of the Eighteenth-Century Bank of England* in *London Review of Books*, 15 June 2023, 23–6.

[66] Martin Thomas, *Empires of Intelligence: Security Services and Colonial Disorder after 1914* (Berkeley: University of California Press, 2008), 145–57; Pascal Daudin, "The Rif War: A Forgotten War?" *International Review of the Red Cross* 105, no. 923 (2023): 914–46; and Frederic Wehrey, "The Many Repercussions of the Rif Rebellion," *New York Review of Books*, 18 December 2021.

[67] Alan Kramer, "From Great War to Fascist Warfare," in *Fascist Warfare, 1922–1945: Aggression, Occupation, Annihilation*, ed. Miguel Alonso, Alan Kramer, and Javier Rodrigo (Cham: Springer International Publishing, 2019), 25–50, here p. 32.

Figure 15.2 "Turcos, wounded at Charleroi, in Paris," 1914,
unknown photographer.
Source: Library of Congress.

complicated lines of political contention across a vast theater of events."[68]
Colonial and imperial histories of warfare disrupt self-contained European
military histories in myriad ways.

What would it mean for military historians who study Europe to respond to
the global turn? Returning to the Charleroi image discussed in the previous
section, viewers might ask what happened to the many North African soldiers
(*tirailleurs algériens*, often referred to as "Turcos") who were wounded in the
battle? Photography from 1914 shows "Turcos, wounded at Charleroi, in
Paris" wearing their uniforms, walking with a French officer (Figure 15.2).[69]
They must have been transported from the front to a hospital, and they must
have encountered Belgian and French medical personnel, many of whom were
white women.[70] Using a global lens on the fighting at Charleroi, and

---

[68] Brown, *Tacky's Revolt*, 28.
[69] "Turcos, Wounded at Charleroi, in Paris," *Library of Congress*, 1914, Online.
[70] Dominiek Dendooven, "Living Apart Together: Belgian Civilians and Non-white Troops and
Workers in Wartime Flanders," in Das, *Race, Empire, and First World War Writing*, 143–74,
Santanu Das, Race, Empire, and First World War Writing (Cambridge: Cambridge University
Press, 2011).

connecting it to the photo of wounded North African soldiers in Paris, makes it possible to ask different questions about the military and cultural history of the war, about race, gender, and disability, and about what Europeans understood about the soldiers who came from distant places to fight for France.[71]

Making the global turn means crossing temporal and spatial lines, tacking back and forth, zigzagging across, and zooming in and out to consider the many ways that European military history shaped global history. By following African, East Asian, Southeast Asian, South Asian, African American, Caribbean, Indigenous, and Latin American soldiers and workers to European and other theaters of the First World War, for example, historians have shown how the global war affected them and how they affected the war.[72] Their memoirs and other forms of remembered histories deserve inclusion in European military histories of the war.[73] By following European officers, NCOs, explorers, and scientists to occupied colonized spaces, historians can show how their whiteness shaped operations, campaigns, and the violence inherent in them, as well as the contours of their military comradeship with African troops, which was essential to operational success, and simultaneously rooted in racist paternalism.

In my own work, I have traced the lives of African soldiers who fought for the Germans in East Africa until 1918, hoping to find their radical postwar potentials, but usually finding quite conservative realities.[74] Yet the African colonial soldier haunted other distant histories long after their sudden demise as an army. The Nazis employed military auxiliaries from the Baltics, who they often referred to as "askari," in war zones far from the word's Arabic and Kiswahili origins.[75] Later, in South Africa, "askari" was used to refer to men who betrayed the African National Congress to work with the South African police state.[76] In both of these examples of traveling language, the label "askari" resonated in new contexts because the term's essence – militarized men from colonized, occupied spaces who aligned themselves with the occupiers in service of racist and genocidal ideologies – echoed across time and space despite the relative brevity of German colonialism in Africa. Life

---

[71] Fogarty, *Race and War in France*, 212–13; Lunn, *Memoirs of the Maelstrom*, 172.

[72] Lunn, *Memoirs of the Maelstrom*; Royal A. Christian, *Porter, Steward, Citizen: An African American's Memoir of World War I*, ed. Pellom McDaniels III (New York: Oxford University Press, 2017).

[73] Christian Koller, "Representing Otherness: African, Indian and European Soldiers' Letters and Memoirs," in Das, *Race, Empire and First World War Writing*, 127–42.

[74] Michelle R. Moyd, "Radical Potentials, Conservative Realities: African Veterans of the German Colonial Army in Post-World War I Tanganyika," *First World War Studies* 10, no. 1 (2019): 88–107.

[75] Michelle R. Moyd, "Askari," in *1914–1918 Online: International Encyclopedia of the First World War*, Online.

[76] Jacob Dlamini, *Askari: A Story of Collaboration and Betrayal in the Anti-Apartheid Struggle* (Oxford: Oxford University Press, 2015).

histories of African and African diaspora soldiers who made lives for themselves in Europe after the world wars also complicate European military histories by highlighting the inequalities and injustices that shaped their lives, and sometimes caused their deaths.[77]

Colonial military histories haunted European officers in similar ways. French fierceness in fighting the Germans at Charleroi in August 1914 evoked for German troops the specter of the *franc-tireur*, which then became for them a "justification for the massacres of civilians that took place in [Belgian] villages such as Tamine or Dinant."[78] These echoes of francs-tireurs from the Franco-Prussian War of 1870–1 affected German martial memory decades later in both the First and Second World Wars.[79] Their anxieties about the *franc-tireur* resembled those of colonial officials and officers in Africa who heard rumors of rebellion and who confronted modes of African irregular warfare. Military histories from German East Africa have shown that African fighters, whom German officers frequently described as unthinking, unruly mobs, knew far more about how to wage war against colonial armies than German officers gave them credit for.[80] Reflecting in 1918 on what had happened at Charleroi four years earlier, a British officer compared the German execution of the Schlieffen Plan in August 1914 to "the horn tactics by which the Zulus conquered all the native races of South-East Africa."[81] Even in 1918, after four years of innovation and bloodshed on European battlefields, the British officer reached back to the Anglo-Zulu wars for what he considered an apt comparison to narrate German actions in August 1914. Historians should know as much about these histories as they do about those that perpetuate dominant modes of understanding European military history that are limited to wars fought in "Europe."

The history of the British Empire's violence in what became Nigeria and elsewhere shows how imperial armies systematically destroyed people's communities, including through the theft of sacred and valuable objects as well as human remains. The reverberations of British military crimes in Kenya during its counterinsurgency against the Land and Freedom Army and the thousands

---

[77] Marianne Bechhaus-Gerst, *Treu bis in den Tod: Von Deutsch-Ostafrika nach Sachsenhausen: Eine Lebensgeschichte* (Berlin: Ch. Links Verlag, 2007).

[78] Le Gall, "Charleroi," 2.

[79] Raffael Scheck, *Hitler's African Victims: The German Army Massacres of Black French Soldiers in 1940* (Cambridge: Cambridge University Press, 2006), 85–8; and Horne and Kramer, *German Atrocities*; Le Gall, "Charleroi."

[80] Examples are given in the chapters in Bethwell A. Ogot, ed., *War and Society: Ten Studies* (London: F. Cass, 1972); see also David Pizzo, "'To Devour the Land of Mkwawa': Colonial Violence and the German–Hehe War in East Africa c. 1884–1914" (PhD diss., Chapel Hill University, 2008).

[81] Major T. E. Compton, "The Battle of Charleroi," *Royal United Services Institution Journal* 63, no. 449 (1918): 9–27, here p. 12.

of Kenyans who were tortured, interned, and killed during the Emergency finally brought these crimes to British publics in the form of veterans' claims against the British state, resulting in the opening of formerly hidden archives and monetary restitution to some of the survivors. Historians have written extensively about these examples but not necessarily as military histories. This needs to change. Recent scholarly work on restitution and reparations related to cases such as the Emergency in Kenya are in fact doing a form of military history.[82] Other European empires have similar histories that demand continued analysis of how operational histories are intertwined with histories of extraction, theft, and genocide. The continued separation between postcolonial and imperial histories and military histories tends to reinforce the ease with which scholars write about these wars without reference to the racialization of, and racism against, peoples who stood in the way of European imperial priorities, militarization processes, and warfare.

-

One of the outcomes of globalizing European military history will be an honest accounting for racism as a shaper of imperial military actions, recruitment strategies, and labor mobilizations.[83] Writing from her perspective as a Zimbabwean woman whose life was shaped by her experiences of British colonialism, acclaimed novelist Tsitsi Dangarembga encapsulates it this way: "The first wound for all of us who are classified as 'black' is empire."[84] For example, consider the range of ways that African and African American soldiers featured in French military thought as valuable, brave combatants but simultaneously as caricatures.[85] During the First World War, they were held up as bulwarks against German aggression, even as French commanders knew their deployment would humiliate Germans who were unable to countenance a military occupation by African troops.

The continuing power of racist thought and practice manifested in myriad ways, easily crossing the supposed temporal boundaries between war and postwar. "Racial discourses," writes Christian Geulen, "survived the World War of 1914–1918 almost unharmed."[86] For example, France used North

---

[82] Caroline Elkins, *Imperial Reckoning: The Untold Story of Britain's Gulag in Kenya* (New York: Henry Holt, 2005); for a study of British military violence in Nigeria and the looting of sacred objects, see Daniel Hicks, *The Brutish Museums: The Benin Bronzes, Colonial Violence and Cultural Restitution* (London: Pluto Press, 2020).

[83] Tait Jarboe and Fogarty, "Introduction," 7.   [84] Dangarembga, *Black and Female*, 19.

[85] Fogarty, *Race and War in France*, 133–4.

[86] Christian Geulen, "The Common Ground of Conflict: Racial Visions of World Order 1880–1940," in *Competing Visions of World Order: Global Moments and Movements, 1880–1930s*, ed. Sebastian Conrad and Dominic Sachsenmaier (New York: Palgrave Macmillan, 2007), 69–96, here p. 69.

African troops in their occupation of the German Rhineland. Germans responded with a virulent propaganda campaign that used profoundly racist imagery to portray Black occupiers as apelike rapists who preyed upon white German women.[87] In this public discourse, there was no room for distinction between rape and the possibility of consensual sex.[88] Some German women became pregnant and bore mixed-race children. Later, these young adults were sterilized, becoming some of the earliest victims of Nazi eugenics programs.

The effects of racism in peoples' everyday lives in the aftermath of war manifested alongside the racist design and implementation of the new international order that was enshrined in the Versailles Treaty and the founding of the League of Nations. It referenced the prewar imperial order and simultaneously engendered a new one, established by the victors, who set about redistributing the territories that had been under German rule. The British insistence on including in the Versailles Treaty a demand that Germany return the stolen severed head of Hehe leader Mkwawa recalled the extreme, though unexceptional, violence carried out by the German colonial army in the 1890s.[89] The League of Nations, which was supposed to secure global peace, seemed incapable and unwilling to ensure minimum standards of care for peoples still living under colonial rule. For example, Belgian failures to properly manage food supplies and logistics in Rwanda resulted in famine in 1928–30, which killed 35,000–40,000 people and impoverished many others.[90] "A whole social world died with them," writes Susan Pedersen.[91] This was the extended aftermath of war for many Africans, whose continuing status as colonial subjects under mandate authority made them vulnerable to continued abuse and neglect from the colonizing powers.

Yet Western racisms also galvanized new political formations among Black folks around the world, who saw new opportunities to organize themselves against sustained and deadly racist abuses.[92] As Chad Williams's work illustrates, African American soldiers' experiences in France in 1918–19 threw into sharp

---

[87] Julia Roos, "Nationalism, Racism and Propaganda in Early Weimar Germany: Contradictions in the Campaign against the 'Black Horror on the Rhine'," *German History* 30, no. 1 (2012): 45–74.

[88] Khary Oronde Polk, *Contagions of Empire: Scientific Racism, Sexuality, and Black Military Workers Abroad, 1898–1948* (Chapel Hill: University of North Carolina Press, 2020).

[89] Jeremiah Garsha, "The Head of Chief Mkwawa and the Transnational History of Colonial Violence, 1898–2019" (PhD diss., Cambridge University, 2019).

[90] Susan Pedersen, *The Guardians: The League of Nations and the Crisis of Empire* (New York: Oxford University Press, 2015), 247. Two other famines in the region ("Rumanura" 1916–18 and "Gakwege" 1925–26) preceded the "Rwakayihura" famine of 1928–30.

[91] Pedersen, *The Guardians*, 247.

[92] Dangarembga, *Black and Female*, 20, citing Toni Morrison; Richard Smith, "'Heaven Grant You Strength to Fight the Battle for Your Race': Nationalism, Pan-Africanism and the First World War in Jamaican Memory," in *Race, Empire, and First World War Writing*, ed. Das, 265–82.

relief the horrors of racist terror against Black people in the United States, including the thousands of veterans who had fought on the western front. While visiting African American troops in France in late 1918 and early 1919, W. E. B. Du Bois observed that the French military seemingly treated the *tirailleurs sénégalais* better than the US Army treated African American troops. French commanders had also recognized African American soldiers' battlefield accomplishments with the Croix de Guerre, while US commanders had maintained white supremacy on French soil, refusing to treat Black soldiers with anything but contempt. Du Bois briefly imagined France as a space of new possibilities for Black troops, a model heralding a future in which full citizenship for African Americans was realizable.[93] He later recognized the limits of this perception of France.[94] Still, as Williams explains: "Although their experiences varied widely, as did the particular aspects of their lives, servicemen of African descent shared a common internalized and imposed identity as veterans, a status that was at once highly personal and deeply political."[95] Black soldiers returning from war "contest[ed] the legitimacy of empire in ways both subtle and dramatic."[96] "Mobilization," for Williams, refers both to the military mobilization of men, as well as political mobilization toward freedom dreams. In this way, the First World War and its aftermath was an incubator for Black internationalism and global anti-colonial organizing, which occurred unevenly and in various ways but which were all rooted in the war's meanings for Black veterans and the wider understanding many of them had regarding the continual violence of empire, beyond the violence of Europe's many wars fought to preserve it.[97]

"Empire might be hard to make out from the mainland, but from the sites of colonial rule themselves, it's impossible to miss," writes Daniel Immerwahr.[98] Focusing on imperial warfare in its many forms, which seem similarly "hard to make out from the mainland," historians can show how anti-colonial actions and colonial counterinsurgencies are wars that must be studied as such, and not merely as sideshows, "small wars," or asymmetrical wars, all of which center Western sensibilities about what constituted real war. Ignoring how these wars irrevocably changed peoples' lives around the world perpetuates the violence into the present for these peoples' descendants.

[93] Chad Williams, *The Wounded World: W. E. B. Du Bois and the First World War* (New York: Farrar, Straus and Giroux, 2023), 130–43.
[94] Williams, *The Wounded World*, 141.
[95] Chad Williams, "A Mobilized Diaspora: The First World War and Black Soldiers as New Negroes," in *Escape from New York: The New Negro Renaissance beyond Harlem*, ed. Davarian L. Baldwin and Minkah Makalani (Minneapolis: University of Minnesota Press, 2013), 247–70, here p. 249.
[96] Williams, "A Mobilized Diaspora," 257.
[97] See also Polk, *Contagions of Empire*, 140–60, 208–12.
[98] Daniel Immerwahr, *How to Hide an Empire: A History of the Greater United States* (New York: Farrar, Straus and Giroux, 2019), 15.

European military history and historiography have perpetuated imperial systems and strategies, silencing those who opposed them and downplaying the histories of racist abuse embedded within them. "[T]oday," writes Dangarembga, "those subjugated by empire speak. This speaking exposes imperial systems and strategies whose purpose has long been to hide the effects of race in the world."[99] Those who write European military history are obligated to choose differently if they want to remain relevant in a world characterized by forms of imperialist violence and militarization processes that continue the abusive, extractive projects that Europe undertook beginning in the fifteenth century. They can no longer "relegat[e] to the backburner" the themes of "racism, slavery, and colonialism."[100] Similarly, European military historians' reluctance to engage the histories of subjugated peoples' recurring use of force against European imperialist projects serves the ongoing project of whiteness and white supremacy. It is, to put it bluntly, a refusal to recognize armed resistance as a common path to embodying and realizing "freedom dreams" and "yearning for deliverance" that are as consequential as the canonical representations of military history as a centuries-long parade of great men, great battles, and great sacrifice in the name of empire.[101]

---

[99] Dangarembga, *Black and Female*, 20.

[100] Michel-Rolph Trouillot, *Silencing the Past: Power and the Production of History* (Boston: Beacon Press, 1995), 98.

[101] Robin D. G. Kelley, *Freedom Dreams: The Black Radical Imagination* (Boston: Beacon Press, 2002); Michael A. Gomez, *Reversing Sail: A History of the African Diaspora* (Cambridge: Cambridge University Press, 2005), 109. See also Anne Donlon, "Thyra Edwards's Spanish Civil War Scrapbook: Black Women's Internationalist Writing," in *To Turn the World over: Black Women and Internationalism*, ed. Keisha Blain and Tiffany Gill (Urbana: University of Illinois Press, 2019), 103–22. The histories of African and African diaspora soldiers who fought in France and elsewhere in the two world wars also merit more purposeful inclusion within European military history. See Stephen Bourne, *Black Poppies: Britain's Black Community and the Great War* (Stroud: The History Press, 2014); Ray Costello, *Black Tommies: British Soldiers of African Descent in the First World War* (Liverpool: Liverpool University Press, 2015); Fogarty, *Race and War in France*; Adriane Lentz-Smith, *Freedom Struggles: African Americans and World War I* (Cambridge, MA: Harvard University Press, 2009); and Erica R. Edwards, *The Other Side of Terror: Black Women and the Culture of US Empire* (New York: NYU Press). On the complexities of African veterans of colonial wars and their navigation of postwar political, economic, and social life see Lunn, *Memoirs of the Maelstrom*; Mann, *Native Sons*, 63–145; and Zimmerman, *Militarizing Marriage*.

16   Deglobalizing the Global History of Europe

Stephen W. Sawyer

Standing on the shores of continental Europe today, one might believe that the winds of history blow tirelessly out to sea. Indeed, few historical narratives have been as centrifugal as the global. Even the most provincial historian hears the call to pull up anchor and push beyond the crashing waves toward distant horizons. So deep does this theme run that the basic assumption of a structural and ever-creeping global integration would seem increasingly baked into how we choose, periodize, and investigate all historical subjects. In the flash of an eye, once noble monographic subjects have become pitifully parochial, trips to archives are counted in continents instead of towns and series, and we have gone from carefully hiding to drowning in deep regret of our linguistic inadequacy. Neither air travel nor the internet was necessary to feed the long-distance ties of colorful characters of the past; familial networks spread fortune and misfortune across oceans; remote towns turned out to have hemispheric hinterlands. Histories of Europe have stumbled upon global interconnectedness earlier than expected, in surprising places, and through unlikely objects, and in so doing have emboldened us to state the obvious: Modern European history has always been global.

There is much truth here. Writing European history after the global turn would be more than ill-served by a reactionary skepticism, misplaced isolationism, belligerent nationalism, or an about-face reversal against the massive scientific gains achieved by grasping the full depth and reach of global connections. But questions remain. And deep interrogations have only amplified as we see, before our very eyes, a shift in the structures, technologies, and modes of the globalization inherited from the post-Cold War world that fueled our most recent round of global history.[1] Among the most important of these questions are considerations of the crosswinds and contradictory dynamics of the global past and present. Indeed, as two leading global historians, Stefanie Gänger and Jürgen Osterhammel, have highlighted, one of the most troubling dimensions of global history over the past three decades has been a tacit

---

[1] Paul B. Cheney, "The French Revolution's Global Turn and Capitalism's Spatial Fixes," *Journal of Social History* 52, no. 3 (2019): 575–83.

assumption "of increasing globalization, a continuous consolidation of the world's economic as well as ecological, cultural, and social contexts."[2] One might reasonably respond that the problem is not so much our tacit assumption that there has been a generalized movement toward global integration over the last 300 years, uncovered through complex histories that analyze processes, actors, and objects from a global lens. By most measures, and certainly the plethora of histories cited in this volume, the implicit hypothesis of underlying globalization since at least the eighteenth century seems incontestable. Rather, the challenge would seem to lie elsewhere. What if globalization has never been simply a subterranean structural force that historians are only now recognizing but was also a phenomenon grasped by actors in the past?

David Motadel's call in Chapter 1 to reflect back on the "global turn" has further implications from a historical and historiographical point of view: It also pushes us to recognize that past apprehensions of the global itself have changed over time. Indeed, as we reflect on the global histories of the last three to four decades, which have done so much to improve our understanding of modern Europe and its place in world history, we must also recognize that they have been part of just one, more recent and quite specific, mode of global awareness in an already long history of European global historical and scientific consciousness. Though the term "globalization" itself may not have existed as such in previous periods, there was nonetheless a "global understanding" among historical actors.[3] Moreover, earlier mindfulness of global forces in turn contributed to shaping globalization itself. In other words, it is not so much a question of contesting whether or not global integration has steadily taken place and should be the subject of our global histories as the fact that these processes have been observed by historical actors who have in turn responded to their perceptions of global forces. European history after our most recent "global turn" must then also take seriously previous modes of global awareness and how globalization itself has been shaped by this knowledge.

There are many lessons to be drawn from accounting for the agentive reactions to earlier perceptions of globalization. Among them is the (at first) contradictory observation that a continuity and even deepening in global interconnectedness did not systematically imply more open borders, increased interdependency, or growing cultural fluidity. Disintegrating and downscaling

---

[2] Stefanie Gänger and Jürgen Osterhammel, "Denkpause Für Globalgeschichte," *Merkur* 74, no. 855 (2020): 79–86.

[3] "The absence of the label 'global history' until very recently hardly signifies that the question was not posed." See Guillaume Carnino and Jérôme Lamy, interview with Liliane Hilaire-Pérez, "L'histoire des techniques a longtemps été la discipline la plus simplificatrice," *Zilsel* 5, no. 1 (2019): 229–67, here p. 259.

modes of social organization were invented and reinvigorated in response to perceived global forces. There were conscious attempts to channel the fruits and accumulations of global processes based on an awareness of their potentially enriching *and* destabilizing impact. These attempts to take control of globalization did not stop it but they did give it a specific shape in particular moments. This history must also be written.

As a point of departure for such histories, we may observe that historically one of the most important technologies designed to direct and shape globalization toward specific ends in Europe was the imperial nation-state. Coming to grips with how actors conceived – and reconceived – the relationship between such scales as the nation, Europe, empire, and the world in the past remains an essential task for historians of Europe after our most recent global turn. For historical actors have consistently reinvested or refused modes of social coordination based on their own conceptions of how and for whom global integration should be ordered. It is therefore particularly problematic – but also very telling – that in our most recent round of global histories some subglobal categories have been given pride of place while others, and specifically the nation, have consistently appeared to be anti-global, or at the very least in tension with structural processes of globalization. And yet, the nation, nationalism, and empire in the first half of the nineteenth century in Europe may also be understood as a formidable technology for redirecting, reorienting, and reprioritizing the forces of globalization in order to *serve* specific European interests.

The first half of the nineteenth century in France offers a particularly interesting window onto this problem. Even if the final result of the nineteenth century was greater global integration, the path was hardly linear. The Napoleonic Wars, a growing nationalism across the European continent, protectionism, the birth of the social sciences, new modes of imperial power, and a reinvention of democratic practices all shifted in profound ways how localities and nations understood their relationships to the global pressures inherited from the eighteenth century. While France remained nested in European and global networks, in many cases, individuals and groups resisted various modes of what they perceived as threats wrought by the global connectivity of the previous century. One may even uncover new forms of retrenchment toward increased localism, nationalism, and imperial ambition in the service of the nation, through which actors sought to reshape, reorient, and rehierarchize processes of global integration – as well as the terms used to understand it. In the end, what emerged was a profoundly different conception of *how* France should be global.

As a point of departure, there seems little doubt that the latter half of the eighteenth century witnessed a steady and impressive – both in scale and depth – acceleration in hemispheric, oceanic, and even global economic integration.[4] From the expansion of global commodity markets,[5] threats to sovereignty,[6] new modes of war,[7] cross-border cultural practices,[8] and a "global underground"[9] that undermined the legitimacy of the state itself under Louis XVI,[10] to the internationalization of the banking sector,[11] the rise of international trade,[12] and the massive expansion of bills of exchange, "the causes, internal dynamics, and consequences of the French Revolution all grew out of France's increasing participation in the processes of globalization."[13] While historians have expressed some doubts about apprehending this period from a global perspective,[14] the overwhelming accumulation of evidence suggests that at the very least the age of Atlantic Revolutions,[15] and the collapse of the French monarchy, marked a high point in a "primitive," "proto," "early," or "first" globalization.[16]

---

[4] Rafael Dobado-González, Alfredo García-Hiernaux, and David E. Guerrero, "The Integration of Grain Markets in the Eighteenth Century: Early Rise of Globalization in the West," *The Journal of Economic History* 72, no. 3 (2012): 671–707.

[5] See for example the many papers presented at "Opening Markets: Trade and Commerce in the Age of Enlightenment," Fourteenth International Congress for Eighteenth-Century Studies, International Society for Eighteenth-Century Studies, Erasmus University, Rotterdam, 26–31 July 2015.

[6] Roger Deacon, "Despotic Enlightenment: Rethinking Globalization after Foucault," *Confronting Globalization: Humanity, Justice and the Renewal of Politics*, ed. Patrick Hayden, Jacqui True, and Chamsey el-Ojeili (London: Palgrave Macmillan, 2005), 34–49.

[7] Richard Whatmore, "The End of Enlightenment and the First Globalisation," in *E-International Relations*, 16 July 2020, Online.

[8] Gilles Havard, "Le rire des jésuites: Une archéologie du mimétisme dans la rencontre franco-amérindienne (XVIIe–XVIIIe siècle)," *Annales HSS* 62, no. 3 (2007): 539–73.

[9] Michael Kwass, *Contraband: Louis Mandrin and the Making of a Global Underground* (Cambridge, MA: Harvard University Press, 2014).

[10] Paul B. Cheney, *Revolutionary Commerce: Globalization and the French Monarchy* (Cambridge, MA: Harvard University Press, 2010).

[11] Jan De Vries, "The Limits of Globalization in the Early Modern World," *Economic History Review* 63, no. 3 (2010): 710–33.

[12] Istvan Hont, *Jealousy of Trade: International Competition and the Nation-State in Historical Perspective* (Cambridge, MA: Harvard University Press, 2006).

[13] Suzanne Desan, Lynn Hunt, and William Max Nelson, "Introduction," in *The French Revolution in Global Perspective*, ed. Suzanne Desan, Lynn Hunt, and William Max Nelson (Ithaca, NY: Cornell University Press, 2013), 4.

[14] David Bell, "Questioning the Global Turn: The Case of the French Revolution," *French Historical Studies* 37, no. 1 (2014): 1–24; and Jeremy Adelman, "What Is Global History Now?" *Aeon*, 2 March 2017, Online; and, in response, Richard Drayton and David Motadel, "The Futures of Global History," *Journal of Global History* 13, no. 1 (2018): 1–21.

[15] R. R. Palmer, *The Age of Democratic Revolution: A Political History of Europe and America, 1760–1800*, 2 vols. (Princeton: Princeton University Press, 2014 [1959–64]); and Jacques Godechot, *Les Révolutions (1770–1799)* (Paris: Presses universitaires de France, 1986 [1963]).

[16] Bailey Stone, *Reinterpreting the French Revolution: A Global-Historical Perspective* (Cambridge: Cambridge University Press, 2002); and Matthias Middell, "The French Revolution in the Global World of the Eighteenth Century," in *The Routledge Companion to the French Revolution in World History*, ed. Alan Forrest and Matthias Middell (London: Routledge, 2015).

As Gänger and Osterhammel point out, the story of the legacy of this first globalization into the nineteenth century has overwhelmingly focused on continuity.[17] No doubt, the global connections that continued and even accelerated across the nineteenth century drew upon processes of the eighteenth century.[18] There is little doubt that the modes of eighteenth-century globalized commerce, for example, remained pertinent and greatly expanded in the nineteenth century, just as they were coupled with new technologies and modes of integrative global empire. Nonetheless, it is important not to confuse continuities in structural social and economic processes with continuities in perception of the benefits, challenges, and even potential pitfalls of this globalization. From this perspective it is significant that while historical works have accurately emphasized continuities in global integration between the eighteenth and nineteenth centuries, those focusing on continuousness have tended to locate the major processes of this further global integration in the second half of the nineteenth century.[19] The first half of the nineteenth century has certainly not been ignored. But what has received far less attention is how actors of the period immediately following the French revolution interpreted and reacted to the global integration they too considered at least partially responsible for the Revolution and the world it created.

Nineteenth-century global history has had its foils. And if there is one framework that has been most commonly signaled as the global's bungling but persistent rival, it is the nation. National histories have straightjacketed our methodologies within the strict confines of abstract borders, limited the very kinds of questions historians and social scientists may ask, and tacitly subjected the entire discipline to a mode of historical inquiry that prevents large portions of the human experience from finding a narrative.[20] Much has indeed

---

[17] Gänger and Osterhammel, "Denkpause für Globalgeschichte"; Annie Jourdan, "Napoleon and Europe: The Legacy of the French Revolution," in *The Routledge Companion to the French Revolution in World History*, ed. by Alan Forrest and Matthias Middell (London, 2016: Routledge), 207–24; and Alexander Mikaberidze, *The Napoleonic Wars: A Global History* (Oxford: Oxford University Press, 2020).

[18] For just one example, see Emma Rothschild, *An Infinite History: The Story of a Family in France over Three Centuries* (Princeton: Princeton University Press, 2021); see also the chapters in Pierre Singaravélou and Sylvain Venayre, eds., *Histoire du Monde au XIXe siècle* (Paris: Fayard, 2017), which propose a vision of the nineteenth century as so many "segments of time to which we accord an internal coherence," 9.

[19] "Contrary to popular belief, the most impressive episode of international economic integration which the world has seen to date was not the second half of the twentieth century, but the years between 1870 and the Great War": Kevin H. O'Rourke, "Europe and the Causes of Globalization, 1790 to 2000," in *Europe and Globalization*, ed. Henryk Kierzkowski (New York: Palgrave, 2002), 64–86, here p. 65; and Michael Geyer and Charles Bright, "Global Violence and Nationalizing Wars in Eurasia and America: The Geopolitics of War in the Mid-nineteenth Century," *Comparative Studies in Society and History* 38, no. 4 (1996): 619–57, here pp. 638–48.

[20] The contributions in Speranta Dumitru, ed., "Les sciences sociales sont-elles nationalistes?" special issue, *Raisons politiques* 54, no. 2 (2014):

been lost in the fetishization of the nation as the structural foundation of a "modern" history.[21] And yet such consistent targeting of the nation as *the* anachronistic and irredentist foe is in many ways surprising when one considers the extent to which other scales, including discrete objects, individuals, cities, continents, hemispheres, or empires have not only been considered compatible with global histories but even, in some cases, the best ways to pursue it. Such consistent targeting of the nation would seem historically unwarranted: nations and nationalism, especially in Europe, took shape and, in some cases, reached an initial zenith at precisely the moment that new forms of globalization were taking shape. Indeed, some early theorists of globalization, though they didn't necessarily call it that, were setting their sights on a renewed and even triumphant nationalism against old modes of world organization and in favor of new ones. After all, early socialist ideas culminating in Karl Marx's blanket condemnation of industrial capitalism were pronounced on the backdrop of a triumphant, almost impenetrable, bourgeois nationalism. Global capitalism was stuffing the coffers of nation-states and naturalizing the very borders it was surpassing.

Marx was of course right. Fewer than two decades after Napoleon attempted perhaps the first great "decoupling" as he tried to consolidate the continental economy through the blockade against Britain, France was artificially drawing borders around its national economy at the same time that it expanded its European and global influence through empire. This comes as little surprise: As imperial, transborder, and even global as they may have been, Napoleon's economic ambitions always harbored a reprioritization of the place of France on the continent and in the world. The economic nationalism and protectionism that followed in the first half of the nineteenth century thrived on these experiments even as they consciously sought to feed and feed upon the *expansion* of a global economy. Just a few short years later, Friedrich List, a German émigré, traveled to the United States to study infrastructural development before heading to France to work alongside Adolphe Thiers to formulate early plans for the same there. Such globetrotting certainly contributed to a new globalization of economic policy and expertise, but it did so in the service of a new economic nationalism. Eighteenth-century economic doctrines, List argued, "had only ever seen humanity and individuals, not nations."[22]

---

[21] Andreas Wimmer and Nina Glick Schiller, "Methodological Nationalism, the Social Sciences, and the Study of Migration: An Essay in Historical Epistemology," *International Migration Review* 37, no. 3 (2003): 576–610.

[22] Friedrich List, *Système national d'économie politique* (Paris: Capelle, 1851), 2, which was first published in 1841.

Thiers's commitment to tariffs, national consolidation of the economy, and France-first commercial policies were legion and deeply influential.[23] While he remained deeply committed to France's imperial expansion across the Mediterranean and beyond, he also cultivated a veritable obsession with what we would call today "onshoring." French dependence on foreign production was, he insisted, the product of dangerous and ill-informed economic doctrines of the previous century. His was a mania to prevent French dependence on other nations' production. "It is a question of national interest," Thiers declared of French industrial capacity, invoking "interests as diverse as national production, all interests that the government must heed, that it must reconcile if it can, but that it must protect from the incursions of others."[24] This national political economy was expressly designed to undermine the misguided forms of economic liberalization and international integration that had contributed to what he called the laissez-faire excesses of the French Revolution: "This is the fine argument of the '*Laissez faire*' and the '*Laissez passer*' ... which has never done the world any good."[25]

This new global political economy in which the nation came first was also shored up by a direct attack on the scientific assumptions that underpinned earlier modes of global integration. The social science that emerged in the nineteenth century did not predate globalism but was in fact a rejection of the kind of abstract global universalism that had animated scientific inquiry in the previous century – giving rise to a methodological nationalism with which social scientists still struggle today.[26] In the field of historical production dominated in France by figures such as Jules Michelet, François Guizot, and

---

[23] David Todd, *L'identité économique de la France, libre-échange et protectionnisme, 1814–1851* (Paris: Grasset, 2008); and Stephen W. Sawyer, *Adolphe Thiers: La contingence et le pouvoir* (Paris: Armand Colin, 2018).

[24] Adolphe Thiers, "Discours sur la loi des douanes prononcé le 15 avril 1836," in *Discours parlementaires de M. Thiers, première partie (1830–1836)*, vol. 3, no. 58, ed. Antoine Calmon (Paris: Calmann Lévy, 1879), 269–93, here p. 273.

[25] Adolphe Thiers, *Discours sur le régime commercial en France, prononcés à l'Assemblée nationale les 27 et 28 juin 1851* (Paris: Paulin, Lheureux & cie, 1851), 23; *Speech of M. Thiers on the Commercial Policy of France and in Opposition to the Introduction of Free-Trade into France, Delivered in the National Assembly of France on the 27th June, 1851* (London: J. Ollivier, 1852), 14.

[26] See for example the review article by Martin Gierl, "L'historicisation globale du monde des Lumières: De la médiatisation de l'historiographie au 18e siècle à sa numérisation aujourd'hui," *Dix-huitième siècle* 46, no. 1 (2014): 203–18, here p. 207. Discussing J. G. A. Pocock's study of Edward Gibbon's *History of the Decline and Fall of the Roman Empire* (1776–1788), Gierl describes how, "alongside Gibbon's Rome as a metaphor of culture and power, Pocock deploys the political and ideological space of the contemporary global understanding of history and culture. The eighteenth century's historicization of consciousness via the inscription of local historicity into a global history of the world and of culture is discernible in Gibbon and his reception of pre-Enlightenment and extra-European worlds, and it can be documented through local studies, partial studies, and analyses of different types of sources."

Edgar Quinet, the *roman national* provided a means of at once lifting France above regional identities and reprioritizing its place in a more integrated world. "France ... possessed annals, but no history at all," was Michelet's damning assessment of his Enlightenment forebears.[27] His *Introduction à l'histoire universelle* thus observed, in words that sound particularly familiar to us, that his contemporary world was "caught up in a hurricane, which moves so quickly that even the most surefooted experience a vertigo that weighs upon every chest." As a result, his universal history, he insisted, "leaped off from far and high; explaining the history of France provides no small share of the history of the world." This was true to such an extent that "this small book could also be called *Introduction a l'histoire de France*; for it is in France that it concludes."[28]

No matter what their historical understanding actually owed to the eighteenth century, Michelet and his nineteenth-century progenies tirelessly asserted that it was time for a new history of the world in which the French nation was the privileged scale of historical knowledge. A global France recognized the achievements of globalization past but privileged the nation as the new vehicle for global integration. Michelet's fusional relationship with France was not a denial of universality and world history so much as a refusal of the specific form it had taken in Enlightenment histories, from Adam Ferguson's essay on civil society to Jean-Jacques Rousseau's account of the origins of inequality.[29] He sought to reorient universal history, to rehierarchize the scales through which such universality could be attained. For Michelet, like many of his contemporaries, universal history needed to be *re*written, France first.

And Michelet was certainly not alone. Of course, global conceptions of history and processes of globalization existed before such appellations were assigned by social scientists. But it is precisely for this reason that the birth of the social sciences marks such an important moment in the contradictory processes of world-making. Their emergence in France was rooted in a critique of the "abstract" and "metaphysical" assumptions that figures such as Auguste Comte argued were at the core of Enlightenment philosophy. Comte scoffed at those foolish generations whose transcendent perspective

---

[27] Jules Michelet, "Preface de 1869," in *Histoire de France* (Sainte-Marguerite-sur-Mer: Éditions des Équateurs, 2013 [1869]), 7.

[28] Michelet, *Introduction à l'histoire universelle* (Paris: Hachette, 1831), 1.

[29] Adam Ferguson, *An Essay on the History of Civil Society*, ed. Fania Oz-Salzberger (Cambridge: Cambridge University Press, 1996), which was first published in 1767; and Jean-Jacques Rousseau, *Discours sur l'origine et les fondements de l'inégalité parmi les hommes* (Amsterdam: Marc Michel Rey, 1755). See also the European Research Project ENGLOBE, "Enlightenment and Global History" (Potsdam University, 2009–13), which argues that the Enlightenment "was the first moment in history when questions and problems arising out of globalization processes became an issue," Online.

prevented any concrete or precise grasp of the "the social" as such. The "society" Comte studied so scientifically was decidedly French. Methodological nationalism was not a sui generis invention, ignorant of eighteenth-century Europe's pretentions to embody a universal humanity; it was to the contrary specifically geared to challenge such borderless conniving. The lessons and models it provided to the world stemmed from its intentional grounding in a national context. As Comte argued in the fourth volume of his *Philosophie positive*, the excesses of the French Revolution had been precisely the result of "the philosophical elaboration of this doctrine, which can be seen everywhere uniformly dominated by the strange metaphysical notion of a so-called state of nature, the primordial and invariable type of any social state."[30] A similar movement can be seen in literary texts. Even as global references could be found throughout the fictions of the famed *docteur es sciences sociales* Honoré de Balzac, he also self-consciously presented his oeuvre as the inheritor of naturalists such as the Comte de Buffon, Étienne Geoffroy Saint-Hilaire, and Georges Cuvier. One of the more unexpected effects of this shift from the *espèces zoologiques* (zoological species) of his predecessors to his own *espèces sociales* (social species) of the *Comédie humaine* was a nationalization of the very scientific categories he claimed to be inheriting: "If some scientists do not admit yet that Animality is transferred into Humanity by an immense current of life," Balzac argued, "the grocer certainly becomes a peer of France."[31] In this slippage from the universality of the animal world to the social profile of a member of France's upper house, Balzac effectively nationalized a scientific project that had once been transversal.

As Balzac suggested, the challenge was also political. Having lit the lamp of revolution and given voice to an undivided universalism, by the second decade of the nineteenth century the continent that had been briefly dominated and unified under one of the great inheritors of 1789 was once again splintered. On the heels of Napoleon's First Empire, in 1815 the Treaty of Vienna established a hybrid system in which a divided Europe reasserted itself along with a restored monarchy in France. The dreams of a new, unified Europe collapsed as quickly as they had become a reality.[32] The disintegration of this first project of European integration had real consequences. The "statification" of French society was also a process of nationalizing set against the backdrop of forces of globalization that had been so influential in

---

[30] Auguste Comte, *Cours de philosophie positive*, vol. 4, *La philosophie sociale et les conclusions générales* (Paris: Bachelier, 1839), 4:72.

[31] Honoré de Balzac, "Avant-propos de la *Comédie Humaine*," in *La comédie humaine*, vol. 1 (Paris: Gallimard, 1976), 7–20, here p. 9, which as an edition was first published in 1942.

[32] Thierry Lentz, "Napoléon est le précurseur de la construction européenne," in *Napoléon* (Paris: Le Cavalier Bleu, 2001), 23–7.

the previous century.[33] This statification was not neutral but was shaped by the rival ideologies that animated the successive regimes of the first half of the nineteenth century in France. For all of their focus on individual rights and their skepticism of certain forms of state intervention, liberals backed the colonial expansion that radically reshaped the contours of global trade. It is now widely recognized that in spite of – or indeed because of – his commitment to individual liberty in France, Alexis de Tocqueville supported imperial expansion into Algeria to strengthen the nation and reinforce France's position in Europe and the world.[34] The author who wrote of "democracy that fills the world" in the original manuscript of *Democracy in America* also extolled the positive consequences of an aggressive imperialism,[35] arguing that it was only by engaging in heinous forms of imperial war that France would be able to consolidate its national pride and grandeur. Nineteenth-century liberalism proved to be particularly amenable to global systems founded on an uneven distribution of political and economic rights. Statification, imperialism, and globalization were all part of the same movement.

But even as these liberal ideals endured they confronted other political themes born in the French revolution, most notably the notion of popular sovereignty. The fact that this was never scaled up to the world as a whole but took root in "nations" deeply impacted how globalization would be experienced and pursued. Certainly, the idea of constructing a *demos* on the scale of a state as large as France was already daunting. Even as democracy took root internationally across the middle decades of the nineteenth century, the idea that a meaningful mode of democratic organization could exist on a continental scale, much less a global one, struck many as absurd. The "self" in self-government was decidedly national. As a result, the uneasy equilibrium between sovereignty and globalization that existed under the monarchy in the second half of the eighteenth century was hardly stabilized in the post-revolutionary period. Indeed, the construction of a popular sovereignty became an inexhaustible source for feeding ideas about national character, a passion for equality within French borders, and a "practical" spirit within a rapidly globalizing context.

---

[33] On the process of social statification see in particular, Emmanuel Fureix and François Jarrige, *La modernité désenchantée : Relire l'histoire du XIXe siècle français* (Paris: La Découverte, 2017).

[34] See the texts collected in Alexis de Tocqueville, *Tocqueville's Writings on Slavery and Empire*, ed. Jennifer Pitts (Baltimore: Johns Hopkins University Press, 2001).

[35] Alexis de Tocqueville, *Democracy in America*, ed. Eduardo Nolla, (Indianapolis: Liberty Fund, 2012), note 1025, which was first published in 1840. This English version is based on the manuscript held at Yale University; the phrase is strangely absent from the standard French edition of Alexis de Tocqueville, *De la démocratie en Amérique* (Paris: Gallimard/La Pléiade, 1992), 1128–29, note 1139.

Republicanism was no doubt one of the paths through which popular sovereignty and an insurgent nationalism were joined most tightly with growing global pressures; indeed, such national affirmation in the face of international forces became a marker of the French Republic. The paradox was that this new investment in Republicanism was shared by other European and Atlantic states even as they denied the same opportunities of political engagement on their colonial peripheries. From this perspective, French republicanism in the first half of the nineteenth century was also a force in dis-integrating, redirecting, and readjusting the processes of global integration that had structured the previous century. The revolts that spread across Europe in the 1830s and 1840s ironically contributed to these processes. While not nationalist in our contemporary sense, dyed-in-the-wool republicans such as Alexandre Ledru-Rollin, Louis Blanc, and François-Vincent Raspail were fighting for a more just France, the devolution of power to the French people, the interests of French workers, *and* a more just humanity. The push for electoral reform, the expansion of suffrage, the new correspondence committees, and calls for social regulation throughout the first half of the nineteenth century incrementally reinforced the weight of the national administration. While it was hoped that the French embrace of democratic socialism would inspire other nations, to exist at all it required, at some level, a reinvestment in *French* solidarity which had been sorely missing under the monarchies of Europe's *ancien régime*.

The era of the First Empire and the decades that followed witnessed what might be called a deglobalizing globalization; that is, a moment when global integration certainly did not stop but when the scales of belonging and those structuring global process were perceived as contrary influences and acted upon to create strong headwinds. These forces profoundly transformed global connections and reforged them at least partially around new national concerns. Teasing out the opposing and even regressive movements that hindered, shaped, and shifted processes of globalization is particularly important if we are to grasp the events of the first half of the nineteenth century and the global history of Europe more broadly. The outline here suggests just some of the ways that conceptions of the global in European history could be shaped by changing priorities, hierarchies, and prejudices. After the global turn, writing such European histories will require a profoundly reflexive approach to how the scales on which we conceive our political, social, and global interactions have been historically constructed. What we have come to see as global history – uncovering global connections and revealing hidden international and world networks – cannot be projected onto a becalmed ocean. The contrary winds that buffet the global historian's craft blow onshore as often as they drive us toward distant horizons.

Afterword: Global Histories of Modern Europe

Richard J. Evans

For many decades, the history of modern Europe was told in textbook surveys as a self-contained subject, particularly when it was dominated by political, diplomatic, and military historians. Through most of the twentieth century, issues of war and peace understandably dominated the subject, along with the rise of modern nation-states and the course of diplomatic relations between them. Economic and social history was treated as something outside this political mainstream, but it too was largely contained within the bounds of the European nation-state. The wider world generally appeared, if at all, only in separate chapters devoted to "empire," and here too historians treated the topic as an extension of European history, echoing Otto von Bismarck's famous statement on colonial issues: "My map of Africa lies in Europe. Here is Russia and here is France, and we are in the middle; that is my map of Africa."[1] The great international conferences (notably Berlin in 1884) were analyzed purely in terms of relations between European powers.[2]

As Richard Drayton rightly remarks in Chapter 6, what is new about the global turn is its insistence that "European and extra-European have . . . existed in a dynamic relationship of reciprocal influence" through much of history – a point also made by David Motadel, among others.[3] European interactions with the rest of the world were a two-way process. To take just a few examples, the end of the Spanish and Portuguese empires in South and Central America in the 1820s had a huge influence on political processes within Europe, leading to upheavals in Spain and Portugal and infusing liberal and revolutionary

---

[1] Otto von Bismarck to Eugen Wolf, 5 December 1888, in Otto von Bismarck, *Die gesammelten Werke* (Berlin: Stollberg, 1924–35), 8:646.

[2] For a fairly random but typical example of good, reliable textbook surveys, see Tim Blanning, *The Pursuit of Glory: Europe 1648–1815* (London: Allen Lane, 2007) (only brief mentions); Robert Gildea, *Barricades and Borders: Europe 1815–1914* (Oxford: Oxford University Press, 1987) (one short chapter out of fifteen); Jonathan Sperber, *Europe, 1850–1914: Progress, Participation, and Apprehension* (London: Routledge, 2009) (brief sections, including one entitled "Eurocentric Diplomacy"); and Derek W. Urwin, *Western Europe since 1945: A Political History* (London: Longman, 1968) (one short chapter out of twenty-two).

[3] Chapter 6 in this volume.

movements in Europe more generally with new energy and determination.[4] The legitimist French monarchy might not have been overthrown in 1830 but for events in Algeria.[5] The unification of Italy owed an enormous amount to the military and political experience acquired by the radical nationalist leader Giuseppe Garibaldi during his time fighting in South America.

Indeed, migration has played a huge role in blurring the boundaries between Europe and the rest of the globe. The emigration of some sixty million Europeans to other parts of the world in the nineteenth century was a process of enormous importance: In the case of Italy, around 40 percent of those who emigrated between 1897 and 1906 returned, a figure that rose to 66 percent in 1913.[6] But of course many of them returned several times, so that there was very much a two-way traffic between Europe and the Americas or other destinations of European emigrants. Many sent back money to their families at home, and their financial contribution was vital to impoverished families in areas such as Sicily or Calabria. Ideas, experiences, and social mores were not merely exported from Europe to Australasia or the Americas, they were also reimported in an altered form that would in turn shape society and culture in Europe itself. Already by the late nineteenth century, American industry was exerting an enormous influence on European society, as American consumer goods and products began to transform everyday life. By the end of the 1920s an economic crash on Wall Street could plunge Europe into a depression so deep that it had a transformative effect on political life, most notably in Germany, where Hitler would not have come to power without it.

In the nineteenth century, the rhetoric of anti-slavery campaigns in the Americas was adapted to play a central role in the propaganda of emancipatory movements in Europe, such as the labor and feminist movements. The supposed contrast to which Sven Beckert alludes in Chapter 3, between free wage labor in Europe and forms of unfree labor in other parts of the world, was far more blurred than has sometimes been assumed.[7] Serfdom endured in large parts of Europe until the 1860s, and in a few places later even than that, while sharecropping rendered labor effectively unfree across southern Europe into the twentieth century. Many poor people who left for the Americas to work as indentured laborers came from such backgrounds and would not have noticed much difference in their new situation. Still, even sharecroppers had some rights, unlike plantation slaves: The reduction of human beings to chattels in slave-owning societies provided powerful linguistic ammunition to feminists

---

[4] Matthew Brown and Gabriel Paquette, eds., *Connections after Colonialism: Europe and Latin America in the 1820s* (Tuscaloosa: University of Alabama Press, 2012).

[5] Richard J. Evans, *The Pursuit of Power: Europe 1815–1914* (London: Allen Lane, 2016), 15–20 and 63–5; and Munro Price, *The Perilous Crown: France between Revolutions, 1814–1848* (London: Macmillan, 2007).

[6] Evans, *The Pursuit of Power*, 351.   [7] Chapter 3 in this volume.

in Europe, who identified strongly with enslaved people across the Atlantic and their lack of legal autonomy.[8]

The nineteenth century in Europe was a period of relative peace, certainly compared to the eras that preceded and followed it. This was partly due to the fact that the European states, terrified by the breakdown of the international order between 1789 and 1815, were determined to resolve their differences through negotiation in the congresses and conferences of the "Concert of Europe," a loose system of cooperation that failed only in the 1850s and 1860s as Bismarck, Cavour, and Napoleon III embarked on a series of wars that resulted in the unification of Germany and Italy. Even these were limited in their aims, their duration, and their extent, however. In the eighteenth and again the twentieth centuries, European conflicts played out on the global stage, but in the nineteenth century the British command of the oceans, following the defeat of the French in Canada and India, ensured that conflicts outside Europe did not lead to wars within it. Where rivalries, particularly in Africa, threatened to disrupt the European consensus, they were quickly settled by international agreement.

The Concert of Europe finally broke down at the beginning of the twentieth century, for reasons that cannot be understood unless that breakdown is placed in the broader context of the age of European imperialism, with satiated colonial powers turning against each other and ideologies spawned by the imperial experience, notably racism and Social Darwinism, fueling antagonisms within Europe itself. The First World War, after all, unlike all other armed conflicts based in Europe since 1815, was a war not between nation-states so much as between empires, extending across the globe. On the western front at least it turned into a war of attrition largely because of two of the less admirable inventions to have come to Europe from America: barbed wire and the machine-gun. The peace settlement in 1918–19 was shaped in a crucial way by the United States, whose subsequent withdrawal into isolationism did not alter the basic global dominance it was now positioned to exert, as the onset of the Depression in 1929 so clearly showed.

Europe and the rest of the world existed in a symbiotic relationship in myriad ways, and not only in the twentieth century; the continent's boundaries – political, intellectual, cultural, social, economic, and intellectual – were porous and hard to define, but this makes writing European history more interesting than if we merely assumed its identity was unproblematic or

---

[8] Price, *The Perilous Crown*, 85–113; Jerome Blum, *The End of the Old Order in Rural Europe* (Princeton: Princeton University Press, 1978); David I. Kertzer, *Family Life in Central Italy, 1880–1910: Sharecropping, Wage Labor, and Coresidence* (New Brunswick: Rutgers University Press, 1984), for a regional study of sharecropping, a system of exploitation common in the American South, colonial Africa, and the Indian subcontinent as well as southern Europe; see also Jonathan J. Liebowitz, "Tenants, Sharecroppers, and the French Agricultural Depression of the Late Nineteenth Century," *Journal of Interdisciplinary History* 19, no. 3 (1989): 429–45.

self-contained.[9] In Chapter 5, Abigail Green draws attention to the ways in which religious belief and institutions transcended the bounds of Europe. The continent's religious minorities, above all Muslims and Jews, "belong to religious worlds that have historically transcended both Europe and its nation-states," she argues, and of course this was particularly the case with the Ottoman Empire, which controlled most of the Balkans until immediately before the outbreak of the First World War.[10] In areas such as Bosnia, Ottoman rule had led to mass conversion to Islam, and, as Green rightly remarks, Albanian Muslims were central to the Ottoman administration – one example would be Tepedelenli Ali Pasha, "the Lion of Ioannina," a retired Albanian brigand whose brutal and corrupt rule over a large part of northern Greece helped spark the movement for Greek independence in the 1820s.[11]

Stretching across the Balkans, the Middle East, and North Africa, the Ottoman Empire blurred the boundaries between Europe and Asia, and the growth of movements for independence in its European territories, beginning with Greece and spreading across the region in the course of the nineteenth century, was in part a self-assertion of European identity, based on Christianity. In this sense at least, Green is right to suggest that Europe was synonymous with Christianity, but long before the nineteenth century this had ceased to be the case in a more general sense: The term "Europe" came into general use in the fifteenth and sixteenth centuries as a secular replacement for "Christendom," resulting from the division of Christianity first into Orthodox and Catholic, and then into Catholic and Protestant. Above all, perhaps, the spread of Christianity across the world by Jesuit and later other missionaries, rendered otiose the employment of "Europe" and "Christendom" as synonyms. Europeans had been able for centuries to ignore the Coptic Church in Africa, but they could not ignore the existence of growing numbers of Christians scattered across the globe owing their allegiance to churches based in Europe. In the nineteenth century, too, the Russian conquest of Central Asia and Siberia, with its concomitant if only partially successful export of Orthodox Christianity, further undermined any equation of Europe with the Christian religion. In this sense, it is entirely correct to claim that "Europe" was essentially constituted by global conjunctures, though, one has to add, not exclusively so.[12]

---

[9] As Peter Burke remarked, "Europe is not so much a place as an idea": Burke, "Did Europe Exist before 1700?" *History of European Ideas* 1 (1980): 21–9, here p. 21. Note, however, the caveat of Robert Bartlett, *The Making of Europe: Conquest, Colonization and Cultural Change, 950–1350* (London: Allen Lane, 1993), 1 and 209, that "Europe is both a region and an idea": "By saying Europe is a construct we are not saying that it is a purely metaphorical creation."

[10] Chapter 5 in this volume.   [11] Evans, *The Pursuit of Power*, 53–5.

[12] Richard J. Evans, "What Is European History? Reflections of a Cosmopolitan Islander," *European History Quarterly* 40 (2010): 593–605.

Yet such global conjunctures are often downplayed in histories of modern Europe. Eric Hobsbawm's famous volumes *The Age of Revolution, The Age of Capital*, and *The Age of Empire* do a great deal to integrate European and global history, as the title of the third volume suggests.[13] Of course, these books were not conceived as histories of the world in their respective periods; rather, they were studies of the impact of the "dual revolution" – British industrialization and French political ideologies – on the rest of the world. For Hobsbawm that influence was not always one way: Note for example his thesis that British industrialization would not have occurred but for the creation of markets in India for cotton grown in America on the backs of slaves transported from Africa, one of many linkages encapsulated in the title of his economic history of modern Britain, *Industry and Empire*.[14] At the same time, however, there is no escaping these books' essential Eurocentrism, as, seen in the round, they document and analyze Europe's spreading influence on other parts of the globe. This is particularly obvious in the final volume in Hobsbawm's great *Age of . . .* series, *The Age of Extremes*, whose designation of the years from the end of the Second World War to the economic downturn of the 1970s as a "golden age" ignored the disasters that befell China, Korea, Vietnam, and other parts of Asia during this period, as Perry Anderson pointed out in a perceptive review.[15] Other general surveys of modern European history, even the best and most comprehensive ones, seldom raise their gaze above Europe's own horizons, unless it is in order to describe and analyze the age of imperialism and the "scramble for Africa."[16]

There is no doubting the fact that the "global turn" in historical scholarship has brought major benefits for the study of European history. A good example is the recent book by the Oxford historian Paul Betts, *Ruin and Renewal: Civilising Europe after the Second World War*.[17] All surveys of European history after the end of the Second World War include a chapter or section on decolonization – for instance Ian Kershaw's magisterial *Roller-Coaster: Europe,*

---

[13] Richard J. Evans, *Eric Hobsbawm: A Life in History* (Oxford: Oxford University Press, 2019), 397–404, 474–9, and 535–44; Eric J. Hobsbawm, *The Age of Revolution: Europe 1798–1848* (London: Weidenfeld and Nicholson, 1962); Eric J. Hobsbawm, *The Age of Capital: 1848–1875* (London: Weidenfeld and Nicholson, 1975); and Eric J. Hobsbawm, *The Age of Empire: 1875–1914* (London: Weidenfeld and Nicholson, 1987).

[14] Eric J. Hobsbawm, *Industry and Empire: From 1750 to the Present Day* (London: Weidenfeld and Nicholson, 1968), 432–8.

[15] Eric J. Hobsbawm, *The Age of Extremes: The Short Twentieth Century, 1914–1991* (London: Michael Joseph, 1994); Perry Anderson, "Confronting Defeat," *London Review of Books* 24, no. 20 (17 October 2002): 10–17.

[16] See for example the excellent textbooks by John Merriman, *A History of Modern Europe from the Renaissance to the Present* (New York: W. W. Norton & Co., 1996); and Robert Gildea, *Barricades and Borders: Europe, 1800–1914* (Oxford: Oxford University Press, 1987).

[17] Paul Betts, *Ruin and Renewal: Civilising Europe after the Second World War* (London: Profile Books, 2020).

1950–2017 or Martin Conway's *Western Europe's Democratic Age, 1945–1968.*[18] Betts points out, however, that what immediately preceded decolonization was just as important: The reconstitution of European overseas empires after 1945 was, he argues persuasively, an integral part of the reconstruction of European civilization overall. Central to this effort was the claim that the colonial empires were justified because they extended the benefits of European civilization to parts of the world that were still uncivilized in many ways. Europe was shaped not merely by the shedding of most of its overseas colonies in the postwar era but also by the massive and ultimately futile attempt to reconstitute them. It continues in many ways to be marked by this experience today, not least in the case of Great Britain, where a key element in the ideology behind Brexit has been nostalgia for Britain's imperial past and a belief that it can somehow be resurrected by turning away from Europe toward a future defined by "global Britain" and the "Anglosphere."[19]

How far will the "global turn" go? Will it result in the permanent transformation of the field? Motadel describes the "global turn" as a long-term development; those who still "feel uneasy about attempts to open up the continent's history" he portrays as old-fashioned, resisting the globalizing imperatives now sweeping across the profession, so that, because of this obduracy, global history appears to remain controversial.[20] But the global history textbook he cites as having run into criticism in nationalist circles, the *Histoire mondiale de la France*, was published in 2017, no doubt after several years of preparation.[21] While it might well have been conceived on the crest of the globalizing wave, the finished volume arrived into a very different context. Rather than a lingering effect of the outdated genre of national histories, as Motadel suggests, Robert Tombs's massive book *The English and Their History*, published in 2014, is part of a new wave of national, indeed nationalist, histories (it is not irrelevant to note here that Tombs has been one of the leading intellectual proponents of Brexit).[22]

The reaction against globalization, itself of course a global phenomenon, that followed the economic crash of 2008 has created a new political context for historical scholarship, prompting the hollowing out of the political center in one country after another. It has stimulated the rise of a new nationalism,

---

[18] Ian Kershaw, *Roller-Coaster: Europe, 1950–2017* (London: Penguin, 2018); Martin Conway, *Western Europe's Democratic Age: 1945–1968* (Princeton: Princeton University Press, 2020).

[19] Robert Tombs, *This Sovereign Isle: Britain in and out of Europe* (London: Allen Lane, 2021), 160–2.

[20] Chapter 1 in this volume.

[21] Patrick Boucheron, ed., *Histoire mondiale de la France* (Paris: Éd. du Seuil, 2017); and "*Histoire mondiale de la France*: le livre qui exaspère Finkielkraut, Zemmour et Cie," *Le Nouvel Observateur*, 1 February 2017.

[22] Robert Tombs, *The English and Their History* (London: Allen Lane, 2014).

fueled by a resentful hostility to immigration, that in many cases spills over into xenophobia and racial hatred. The reaction to the *Histoire mondiale de la France* is not a hangover from a previous era in which national history held sway but the product of this new culture in which populist parties such as the Rassemblement National or the Alternative für Deutschland articulate an aggressive form of nationalism built on a narrow and exclusively positive concept of national history.[23]

The political turn from globalism to nationalism is already having an effect on teaching, writing, and research in the historical profession. In the United Kingdom, successive governments have sought to encourage schools to teach a patriotic version of British, or in fact mainly English, history as a means of cementing national identity and transmitting it to immigrants and their children. It was under the Labour Party governments of Tony Blair and Gordon Brown (1997–2010) that school history curricula and examinations were revised to include a greater proportion of English history. As Conservative secretary of state for education from 2010 to 2014, Michael Gove tried to make schools teach nothing but English history, and though he was eventually forced to withdraw his proposals by the combined efforts of the British Academy, the Royal Historical Society, and the Historical Association, political pressure on historians to focus more on English history, narrowly conceived, is not going to go away.[24] A huge chasm has opened up between the political world and the academic world, between nationalist conceptions of history and globalized ones. This is almost inevitably resulting in funding cuts for history teaching and research at universities and increased government interference in what is being taught in schools.

Historical scholarship, however, has its own, internally driven dynamic of evolution and change, responding not just to the general political and cultural environment in which it is written but also to intellectual influences and developments that exert their own particular impact. At one time or another, we have been told that social history is the only way to understand the past, including past politics; that we have to embrace quantification or psychoanalysis; that we must focus on language, since everything is expressed through it and so determined by it; that culture, including political culture, is the key to grasping the real causes of events such as the French Revolution; that

---

[23] Julian Göpffarth, "How Alternative für Deutschland Is Trying to Resurrect German Nationalism," *New Statesman*, 28 September 2017; Michael Bröning, "The Rise of Populism in Europe: Can the Center Hold?" *Foreign Affairs*, 3 June 2016.

[24] Richard J. Evans, "The Wonderfulness of Us (the Tory Interpretation of History)," *London Review of Books* 33, no. 6 (17 March 2011): 9–12; Richard J. Evans, "The Folly of Putting Little England at the Heart of History," *Financial Times*, 8 February 2013, 11; and Richard J. Evans, "The Rote Sets In: Michael Gove's New History Curriculum," *New Statesman*, 15–21 March 2012, 60–1.

counterfactual speculation provides the best means of explaining real events in the past; or even that we cannot really know anything about history because all texts, including historical documents, are given meaning solely by the reader and never by the writer. Each time there is a new development, its advocates proclaim that it will utterly transform historical studies and nothing will ever be the same again. Over time, such grandiose claims generally become more modest, and the new perspective becomes more of an addition to existing ones than a substitution for them.[25] Whatever happens, however, it is certain that writing European history will no longer be possible without a global perspective, and that surely is to the good.

[25]   Richard J. Evans, *In Defense of History* (London: Granta Books, 1997), 13–27 and 173–81.

Index

www.ingramcontent.com/pod-product-compliance
Ingram Content Group UK Ltd.
Pitfield, Milton Keynes, MK11 3LW, UK
UKHW021012050325
455880UK00011B/34